Her Majesty's Dog

2

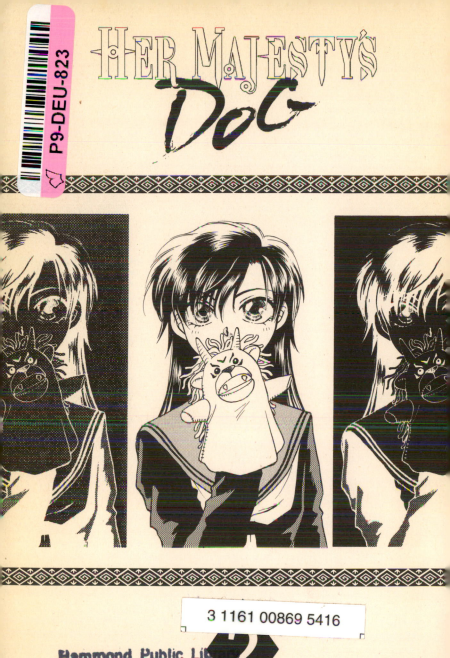

Translation – Akira Tsubasa
Lettering & Design – Jake Forbes
Production Assistant – Mallory Reaves
Editor – Jake Forbes

A Go! Comi manga

Published by Go! Media Entertainment, LLC

Jo-ousama no Inu Volume 2
© MICK TAKEUCHI 2002
Originally published in Japan in 2002 by Akita Publishing Co., Ltd., Tokyo.
English translation rights arranged with Akita Publishing Co., Ltd.
through TOHAN CORPORATION, Tokyo.

Visit us online at www.gocomi.com
e-mail: info@gocomi.com

ISBN 0-9768957-7-3

First printed in January 2006

2 3 4 5 6 7 8 9

Manufactured in the United States of America.

STORY AND ART BY
MICK TAKEUCHI

VOLUME 2

go!comi

10.99
g

Concerning Honorifics

At Go! Comi, we do our best to ensure that our translations read seamlessly in English while respecting the original Japanese language and culture. To this end, the original honorifics (the suffixes found at the end of characters' names) remain intact. In Japan, where politeness and formality are more integrated into every aspect of the language, honorifics give a better understanding of character relationships. They can be used to indicate both respect and affection. Whether a person addresses someone by first name or last name also indicates how close their relationship is.

Here are some of the honorifics you might encounter in this book:

-san: This is the most common and neutral of honorifics. The polite way to address someone you're not on close terms with is to use "-san." It's kind of like Mr. or Ms., except you can use "-san" with first names as easily as family names.

-chan: Used for friendly familiarity, mostly applied towards young women and girls.

-kun: Like "-chan," it's an informal suffix for friends and classmates, only "-kun" is usually associated with boys. It can also be used in a professional environment by someone addressing a subordinate.

-sama: Indicates a great deal of respect or admiration.

Sempai: In school, "sempai" is used to refer to an upperclassman or club leader. It can also be used in the workplace by a new employee to address a mentor or staff member with seniority.

Sensei: Teachers, doctors, writers or any master of a trade are referred to as "sensei." When addressing a manga creator, the polite thing to do is attach "-sensei" to the manga-ka's name (as in Takeuchi-sensei).

[blank]: Not using an honorific when addressing someone indicates that the speaker has permission to speak intimately with the other person. This relationship is usually reserved for close friends and family.

♥ Sweet life as a dog ♥

CONTENTS

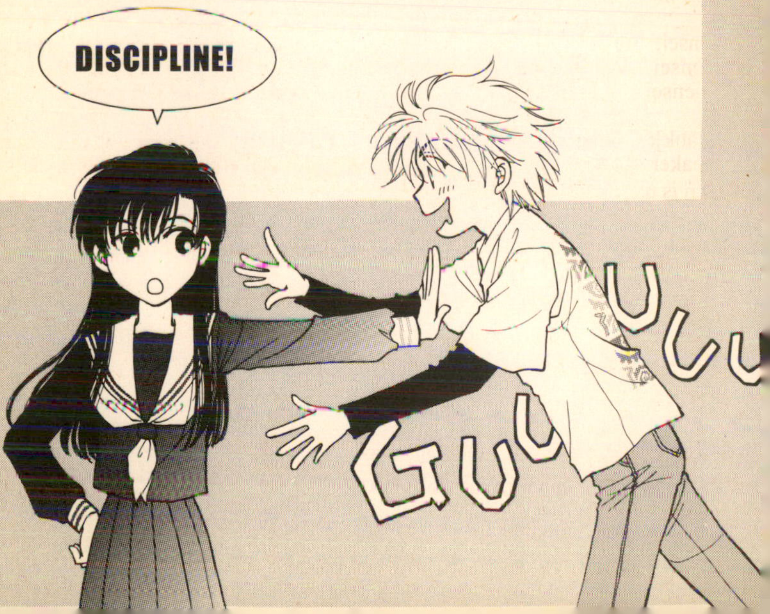

DISCIPLINE!
GUUUUUU

CAST OF CHARACTERS

AMANE KAMORI

There's much more to this high school first year girl than meets the eye. Amane comes from a rural village where magic and superstition are still a way of life. She is a "Manatsukai," a medium who can control anyone or anything using "kotodama," or word magic. The most powerful of her kind, Amane was both revered and feared at home. In order to escape the oppressive ways of her clan, Amane moves to Tokyo with her guardian, Hyoue, and tries to live a normal life as a student. Adjusting to city life isn't easy for Amane, and neither is keeping her powers a secret. But for a chance of living a normal life, it's worth the risk!

HYOUE INUGAMI

Hyoue is a Koma-Oni, a guardian demon whose sole purpose in life is to protect his master. Currently, Hyoue is serving Amane (but his feelings for her are more than those of a servant for a master!). Usually he looks like an ordinary teenager, but when the situation calls for it, Hyoue can transform into a fiery demon-dog. By pressing lips with Amane he can feed on her life force—her kiss literally brings out the demon in him!

TAKAKO NISHINA

Amane's first and best friend. Amane once saved Takako's life, but afterward blocked her friend's memories using kotodama. Level-headed Takako helps to keep the socially inept Amane out of trouble.

HAYATO HIRAKA

Amane's counsin and fellow user of "Mana," he's currently teaching Classical Japanese at Amane's school. Hiraka came to Tokyo at the behest of the village elders in order to watch over Amane. His koma-oni, Tsubute, takes the form of a shadowy demon bird.

DOGFIGHT 6
ドッグファイト シックス

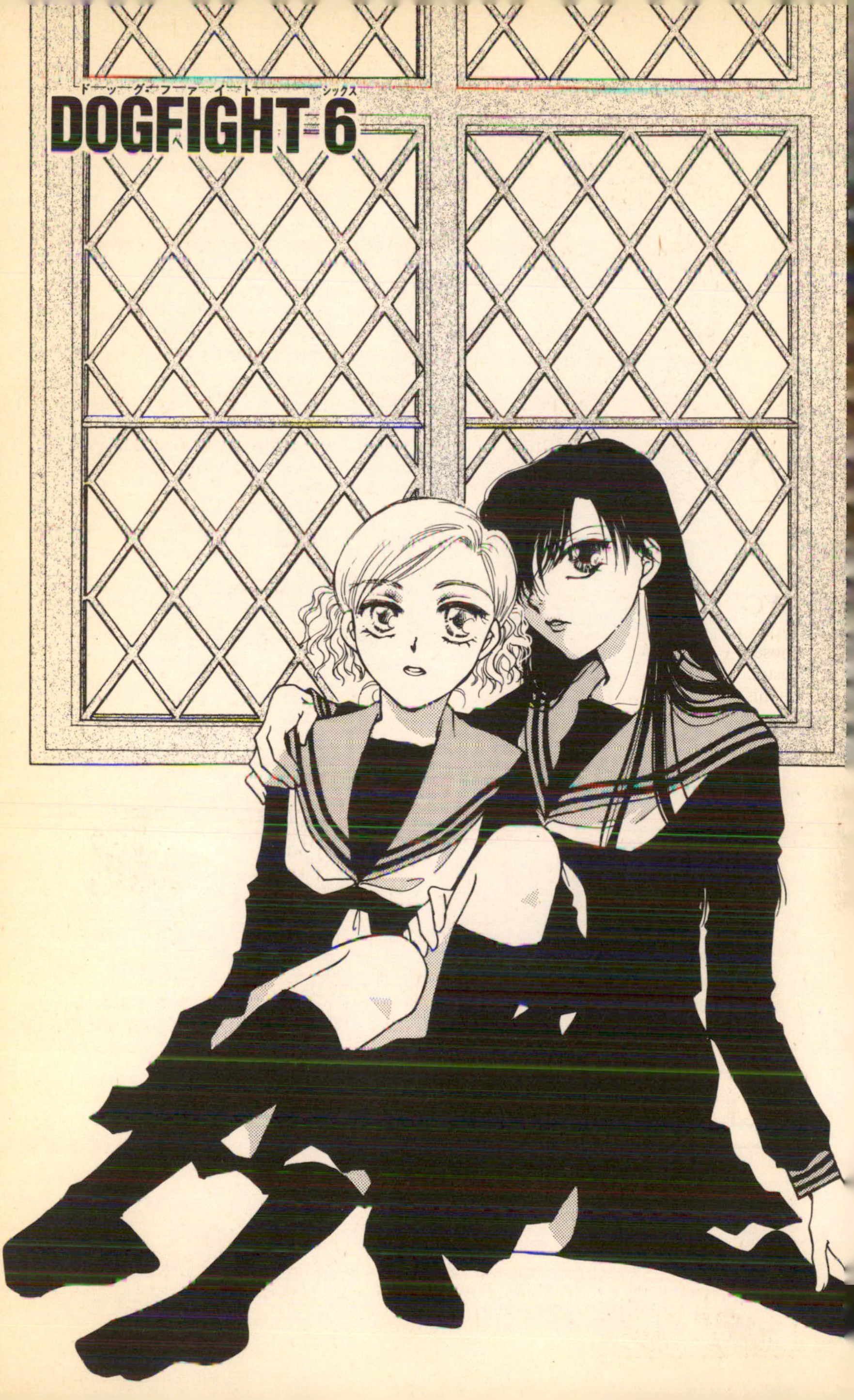

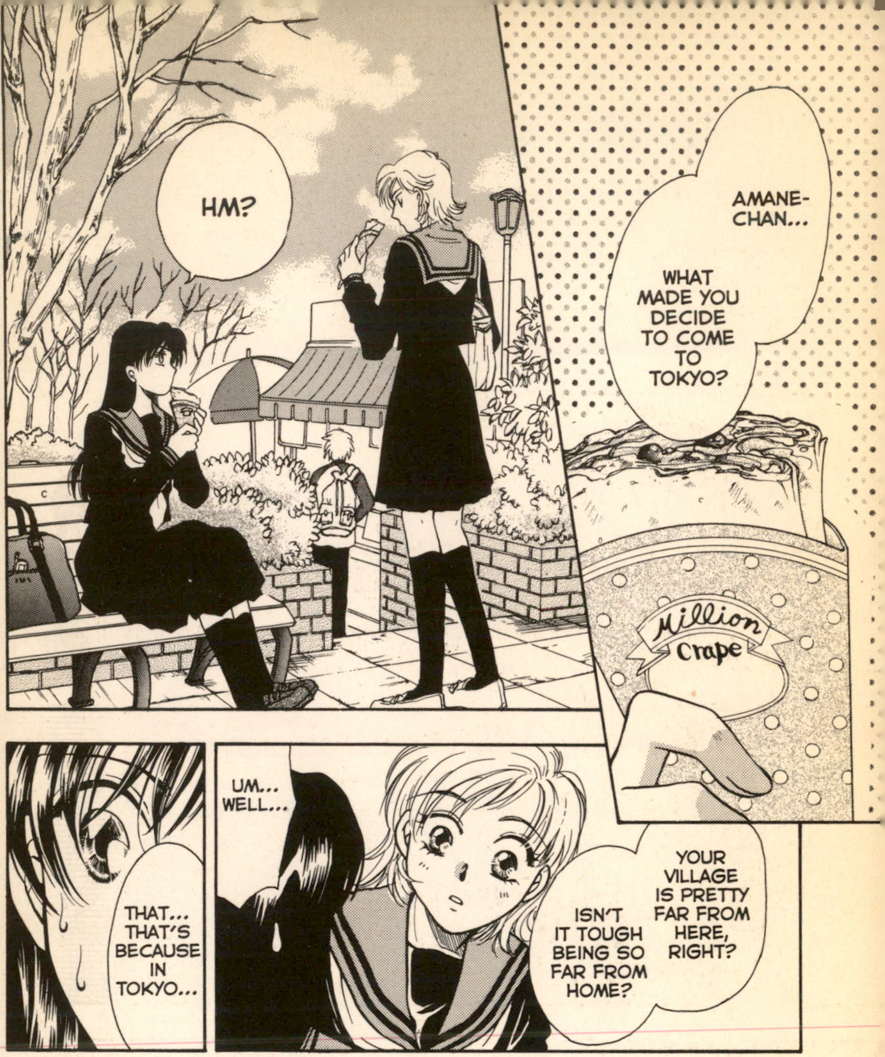
AMANE-CHAN...
WHAT MADE YOU DECIDE TO COME TO TOKYO?
Million Crape
HM?
YOUR VILLAGE IS PRETTY FAR FROM HERE, RIGHT?
ISN'T IT TOUGH BEING SO FAR FROM HOME?
UM... WELL...
THAT... THAT'S BECAUSE IN TOKYO...

KONNICHIWA! ♡ THIS IS MICK TAKEUCHI. ♡

THANKS TO EVERYONE'S SUPPORT, THERE'S NOW A VOLUME 2! EVER SINCE THE FIRST VOLUME OF HER MAJESTY'S DOG WAS PUBLISHED, I'VE RECEIVED MANY FAN LETTERS AND, MUCH TO MY SURPRISE, THE RESPONSES WERE OVERWHELMINGLY POSITIVE. THAT MADE ME FEEL QUITE HAPPY BUT AT THE SAME TIME, QUITE HUMBLE. I WAS DELIGHTED TO KNOW THAT SO MANY PEOPLE CARE!

IT'S THAT KIND OF FEEDBACK THAT MADE ME WHO I AM TODAY. I REALLY APPRECIATE YOUR SUPPORT! I APOLOGIZE FOR NOT BEING ABLE TO WRITE BACK TO YOU VERY OFTEN... AT LEAST I'LL TRY TO WRITE YOU NEW YEAR'S CARDS OR SUMMER GREETING CARDS SO PLEASE CONTINUE TO SHOW ME YOUR SUPPORT.

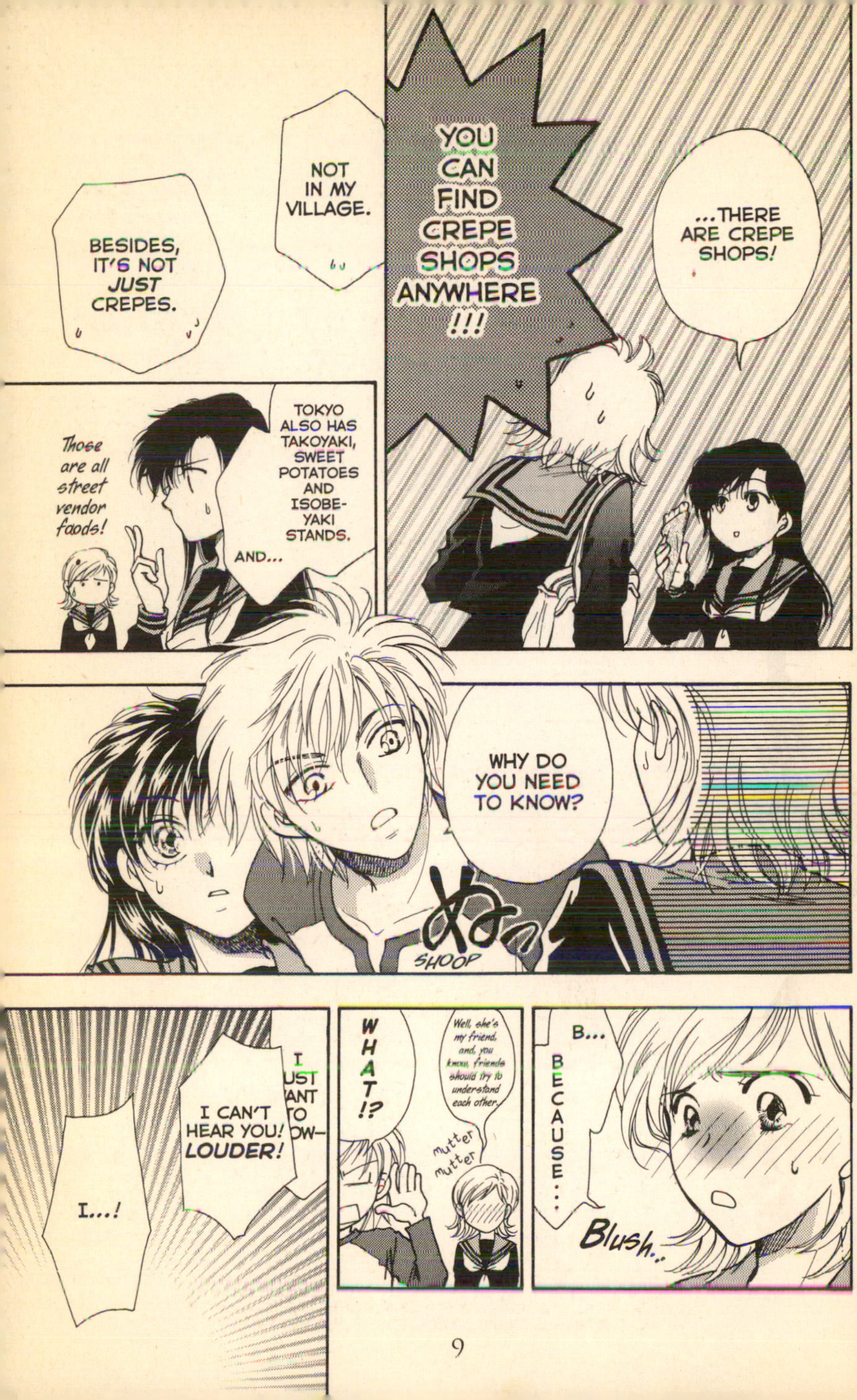
...THERE ARE CREPE SHOPS!
YOU CAN FIND CREPE SHOPS ANYWHERE!!!
NOT IN MY VILLAGE.
BESIDES, IT'S NOT *JUST* CREPES.
TOKYO ALSO HAS TAKOYAKI, SWEET POTATOES AND ISOBE-YAKI STANDS.
AND...
Those are all street vendor foods!
WHY DO YOU NEED TO KNOW?
SHOOP
B...
BECAUSE...
Blush..
WHAT!?
Well, she's my friend, and, you know, friends should try to understand each other.
mutter mutter
I UST ANT TO OW—
I CAN'T HEAR YOU! **LOUDER!**
I...!

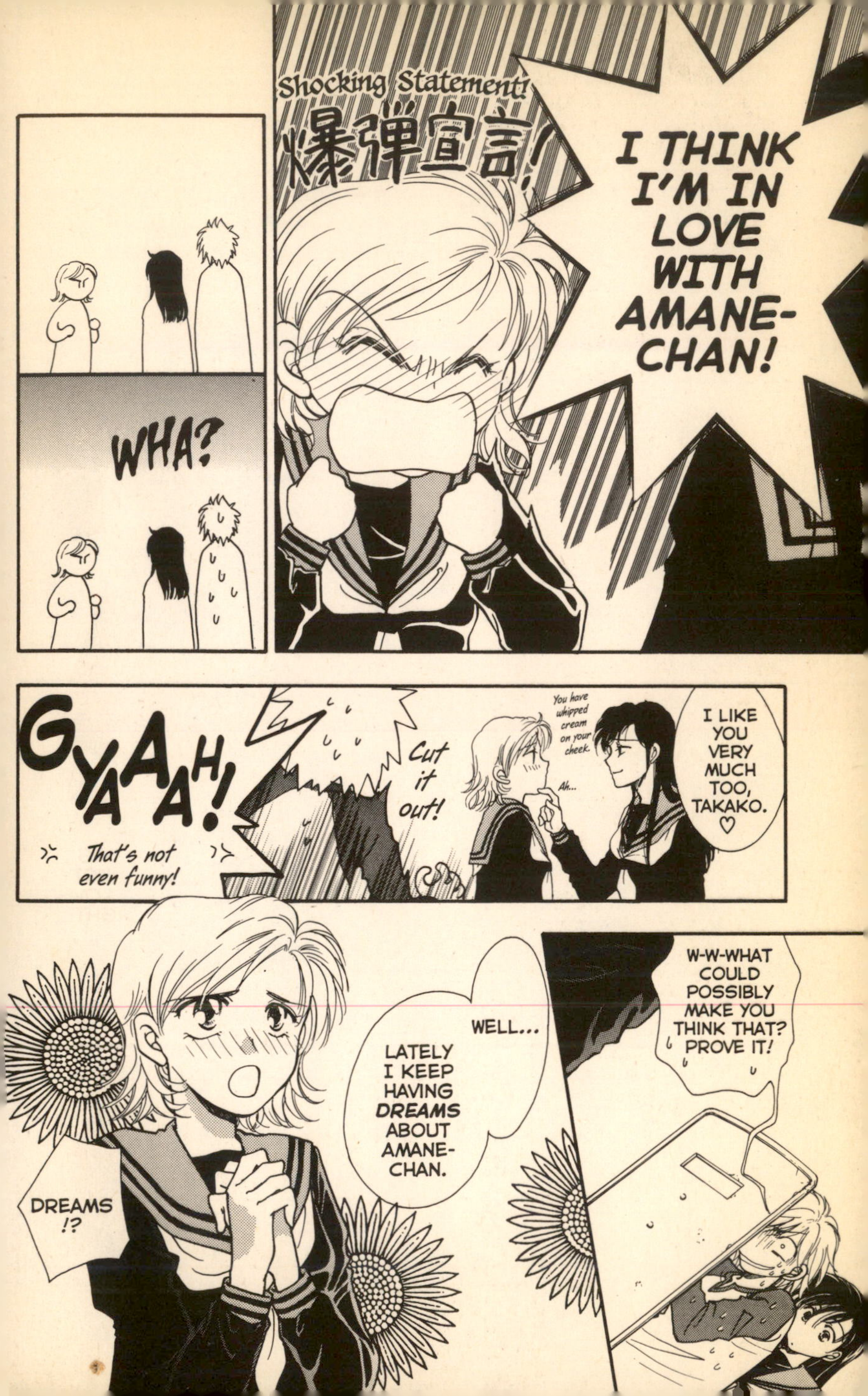

Shocking Statement!
爆弾宣言!
I THINK I'M IN LOVE WITH AMANE-CHAN!
WHA?
I LIKE YOU VERY MUCH TOO, TAKAKO. ♡
You have whipped cream on your cheek.
Ah...
Cut it out!
GYAAAH!
That's not even funny!
W-W-WHAT COULD POSSIBLY MAKE YOU THINK THAT? PROVE IT!
WELL...
LATELY I KEEP HAVING DREAMS ABOUT AMANE-CHAN.
DREAMS!?

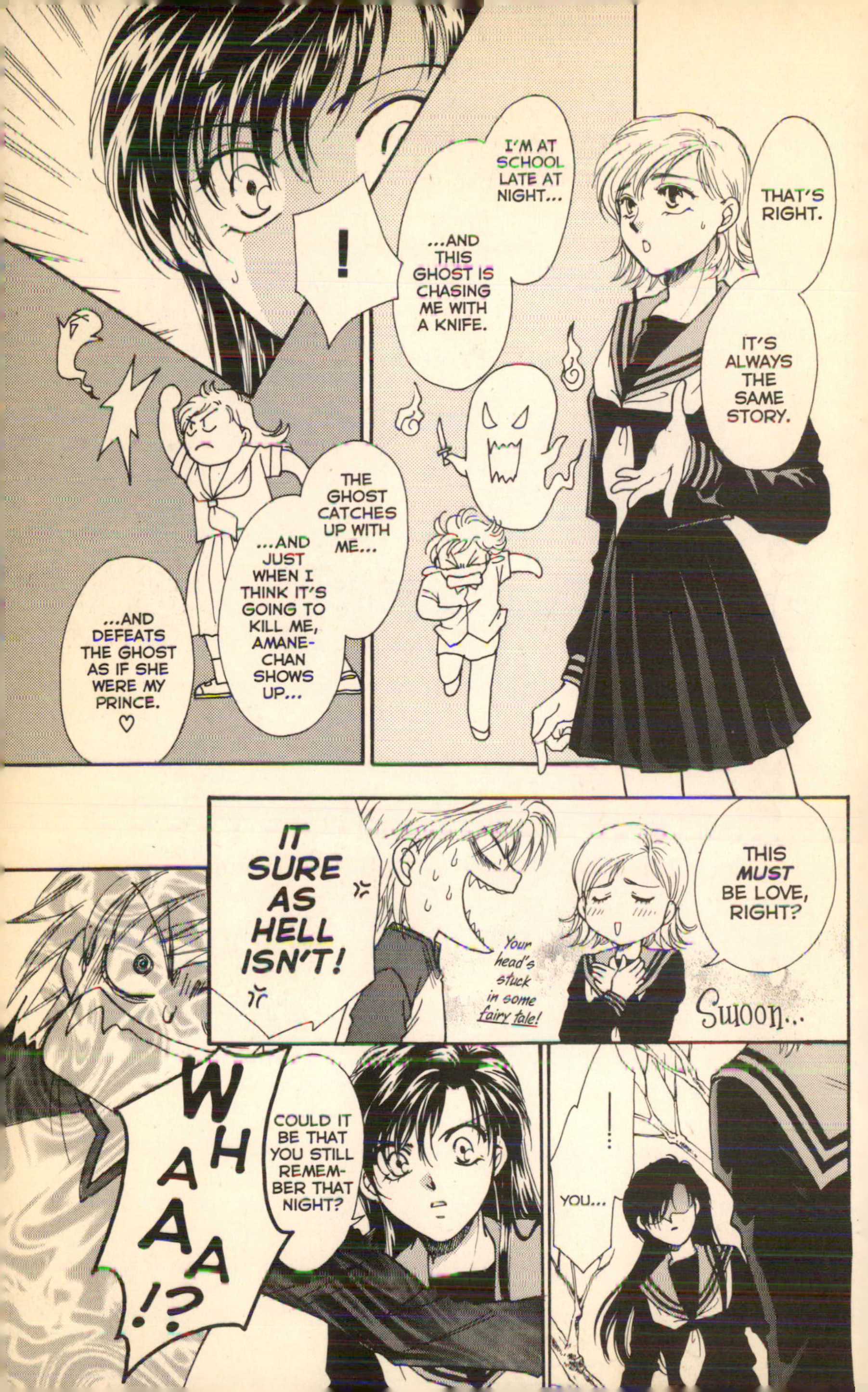
THAT'S RIGHT.
IT'S ALWAYS THE SAME STORY.
I'M AT SCHOOL LATE AT NIGHT...
...AND THIS GHOST IS CHASING ME WITH A KNIFE.
THE GHOST CATCHES UP WITH ME...
!
...AND JUST WHEN I THINK IT'S GOING TO KILL ME, AMANE-CHAN SHOWS UP...
...AND DEFEATS THE GHOST AS IF SHE WERE MY PRINCE. ♡
THIS MUST BE LOVE, RIGHT?
Swoon...
IT SURE AS HELL ISN'T!
Your head's stuck in some fairy tale!
...!
YOU...
COULD IT BE THAT YOU STILL REMEMBER THAT NIGHT?
WHAAAA!?

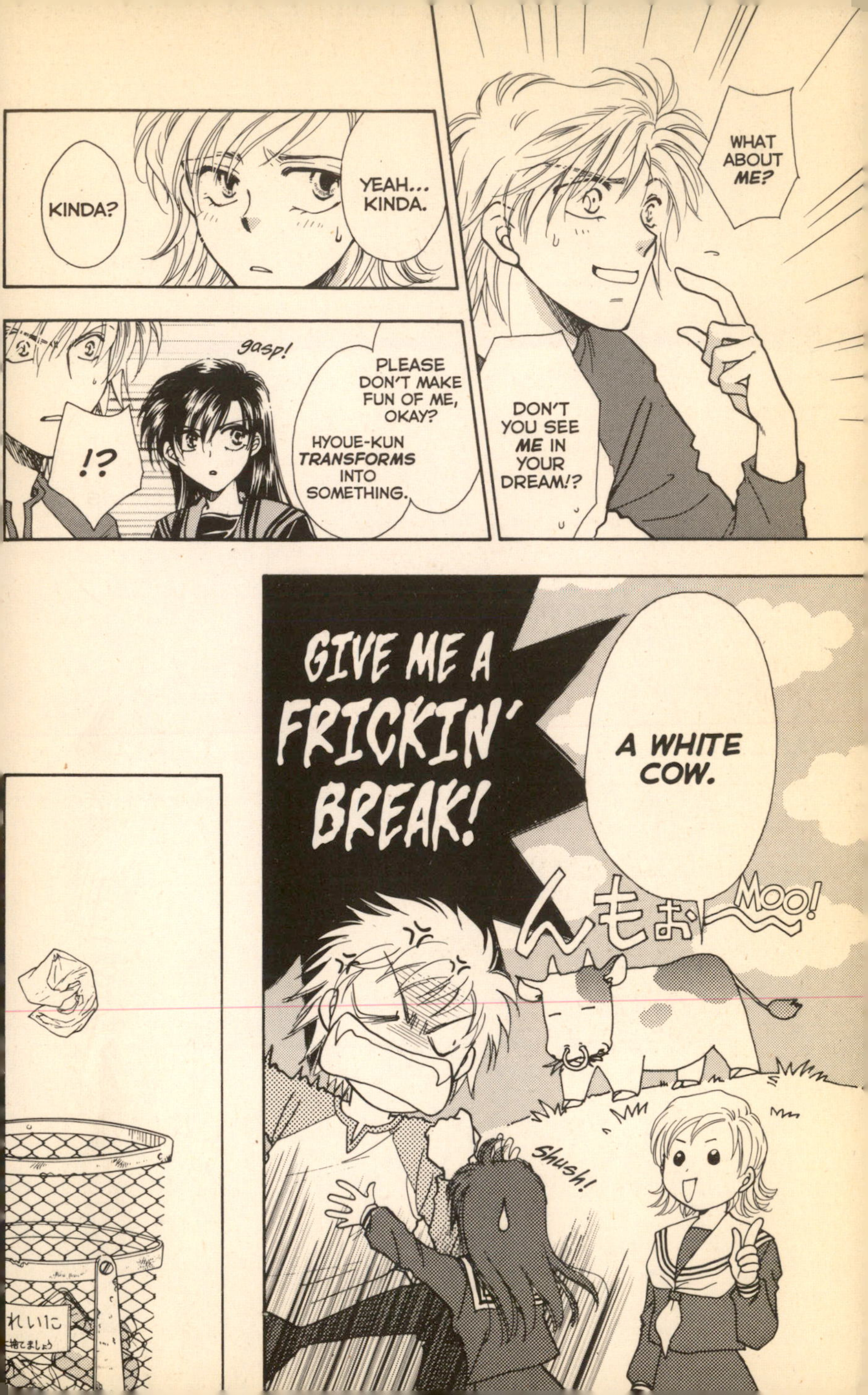
WHAT ABOUT *ME?*
DON'T YOU SEE *ME* IN YOUR DREAM!?
YEAH... KINDA.
KINDA?
PLEASE DON'T MAKE FUN OF ME, OKAY?
HYOUE-KUN *TRANSFORMS* INTO SOMETHING.
gasp!
!?
A WHITE COW.
んもぉ～
MOO!
GIVE ME A FRICKIN' BREAK!
Shush!
れいに

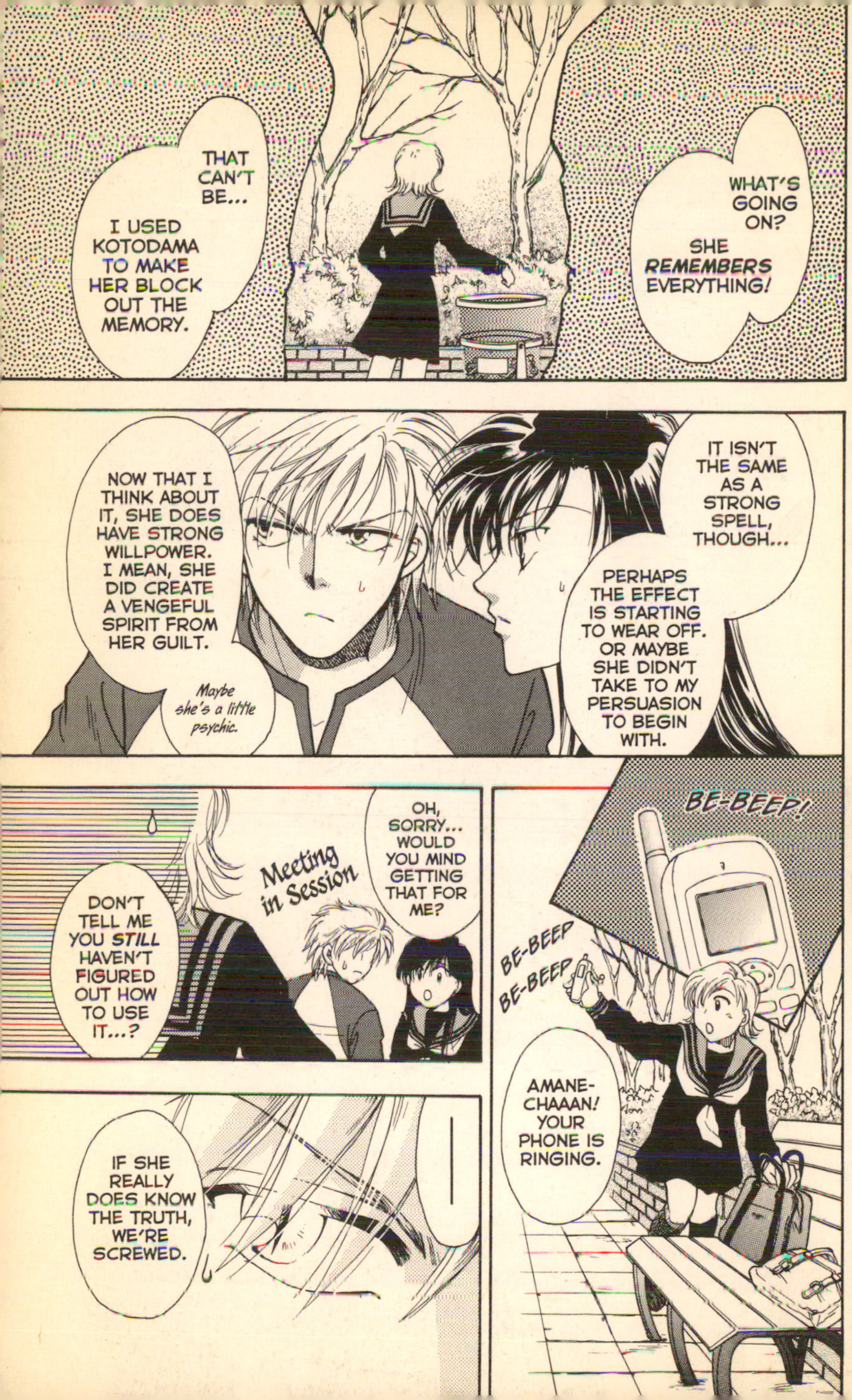
WHAT'S GOING ON?
SHE *REMEMBERS* EVERYTHING!
THAT CAN'T BE...
I USED KOTODAMA TO MAKE HER BLOCK OUT THE MEMORY.
IT ISN'T THE SAME AS A STRONG SPELL, THOUGH...
PERHAPS THE EFFECT IS STARTING TO WEAR OFF. OR MAYBE SHE DIDN'T TAKE TO MY PERSUASION TO BEGIN WITH.
NOW THAT I THINK ABOUT IT, SHE DOES HAVE STRONG WILLPOWER. I MEAN, SHE DID CREATE A VENGEFUL SPIRIT FROM HER GUILT.
Maybe she's a little psychic.
BE-BEEP!
BE-BEEP
BE-BEEP
AMANE-CHAAAN! YOUR PHONE IS RINGING.
OH, SORRY... WOULD YOU MIND GETTING THAT FOR ME?
Meeting in Session
DON'T TELL ME YOU *STILL* HAVEN'T FIGURED OUT HOW TO USE IT...?
IF SHE REALLY DOES KNOW THE TRUTH, WE'RE SCREWED.

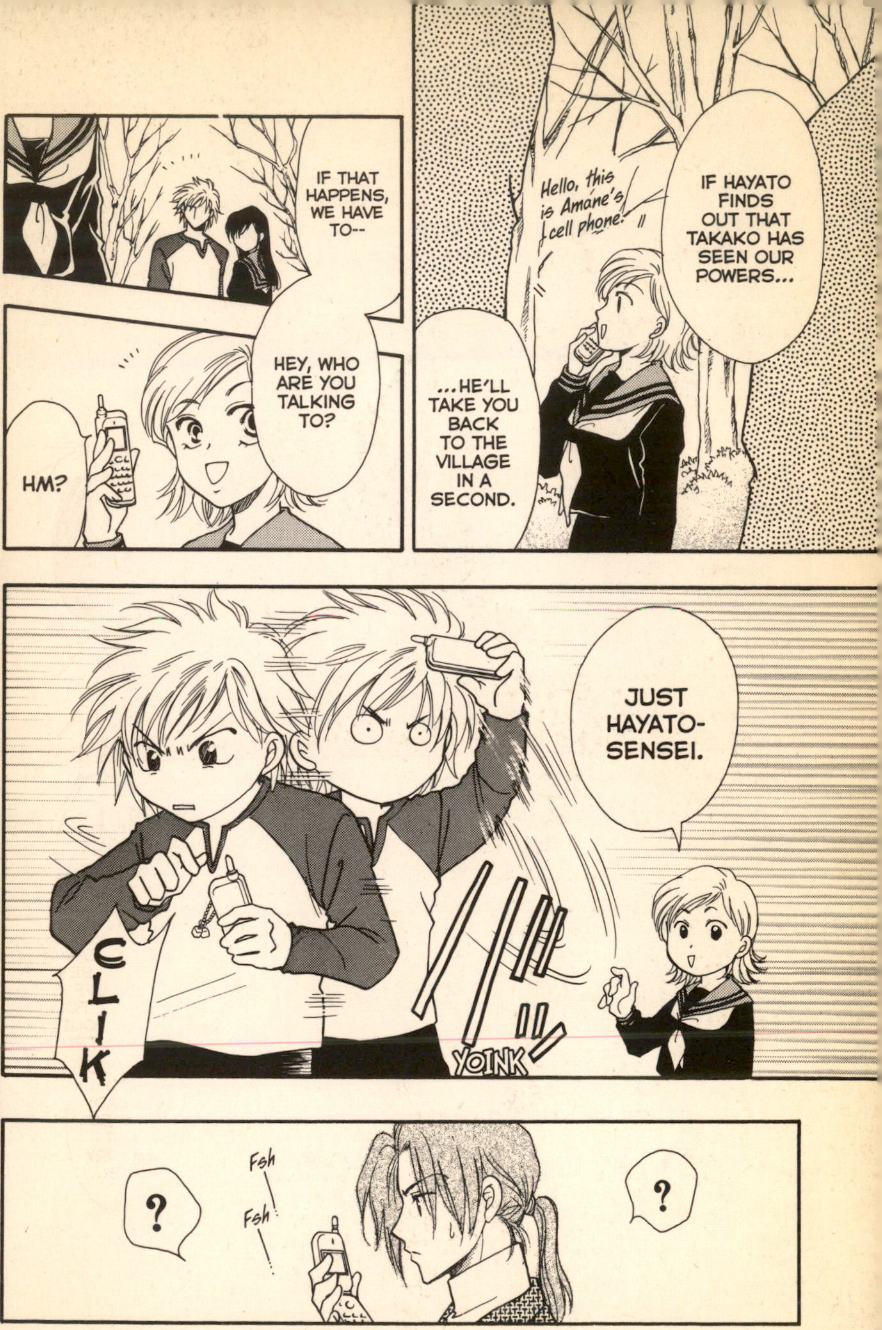
IF HAYATO FINDS OUT THAT TAKAKO HAS SEEN OUR POWERS...
Hello, this is Amane's cell phone.
...HE'LL TAKE YOU BACK TO THE VILLAGE IN A SECOND.
IF THAT HAPPENS, WE HAVE TO--
HEY, WHO ARE YOU TALKING TO?
HM?
JUST HAYATO-SENSEI.
YOINK
CLIK
?
Fsh
Fsh
?

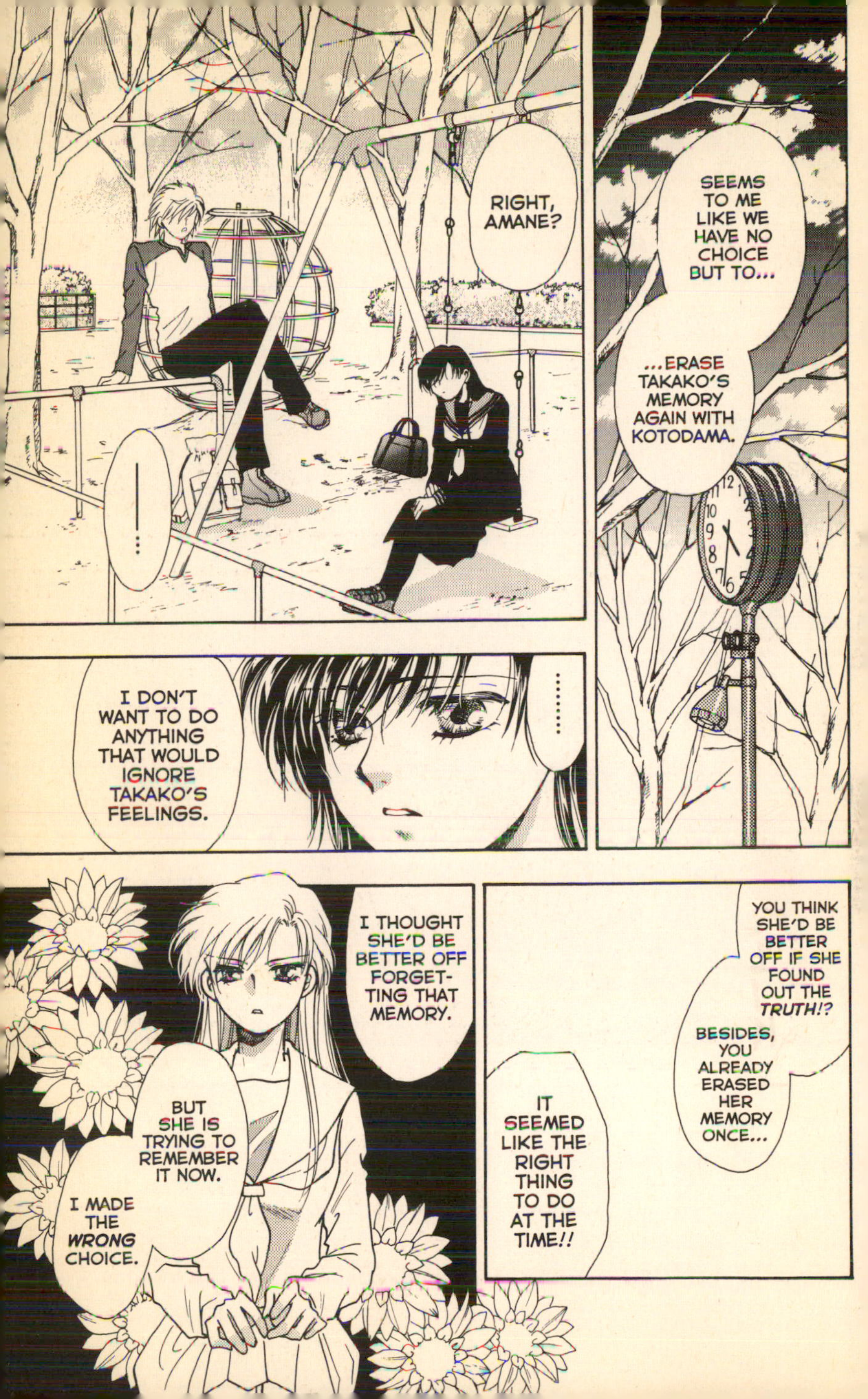

SEEMS TO ME LIKE WE HAVE NO CHOICE BUT TO...
...ERASE TAKAKO'S MEMORY AGAIN WITH KOTODAMA.
RIGHT, AMANE?
—...
......
I DON'T WANT TO DO ANYTHING THAT WOULD IGNORE TAKAKO'S FEELINGS.
YOU THINK SHE'D BE BETTER OFF IF SHE FOUND OUT THE *TRUTH!?*
BESIDES, YOU ALREADY ERASED HER MEMORY ONCE...
IT SEEMED LIKE THE RIGHT THING TO DO AT THE TIME!!
I THOUGHT SHE'D BE BETTER OFF FORGET-TING THAT MEMORY.
BUT SHE IS TRYING TO REMEMBER IT NOW.
I MADE THE *WRONG* CHOICE.

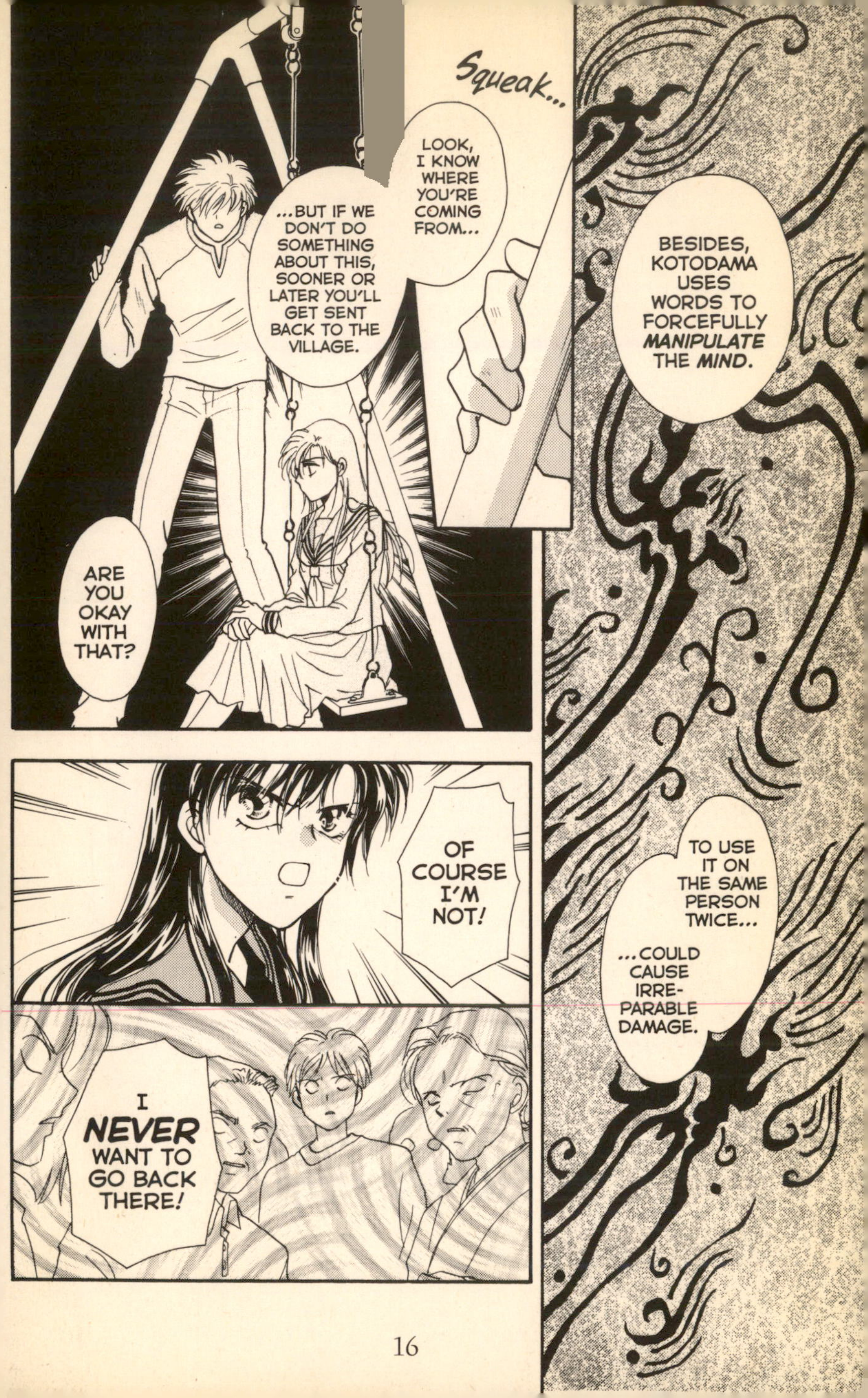
BESIDES, KOTODAMA USES WORDS TO FORCEFULLY *MANIPULATE* THE *MIND*.
TO USE IT ON THE SAME PERSON TWICE...
...COULD CAUSE IRRE-PARABLE DAMAGE.
Squeak...
LOOK, I KNOW WHERE YOU'RE COMING FROM...
...BUT IF WE DON'T DO SOMETHING ABOUT THIS, SOONER OR LATER YOU'LL GET SENT BACK TO THE VILLAGE.
ARE YOU OKAY WITH THAT?
OF COURSE I'M NOT!
I *NEVER* WANT TO GO BACK THERE!

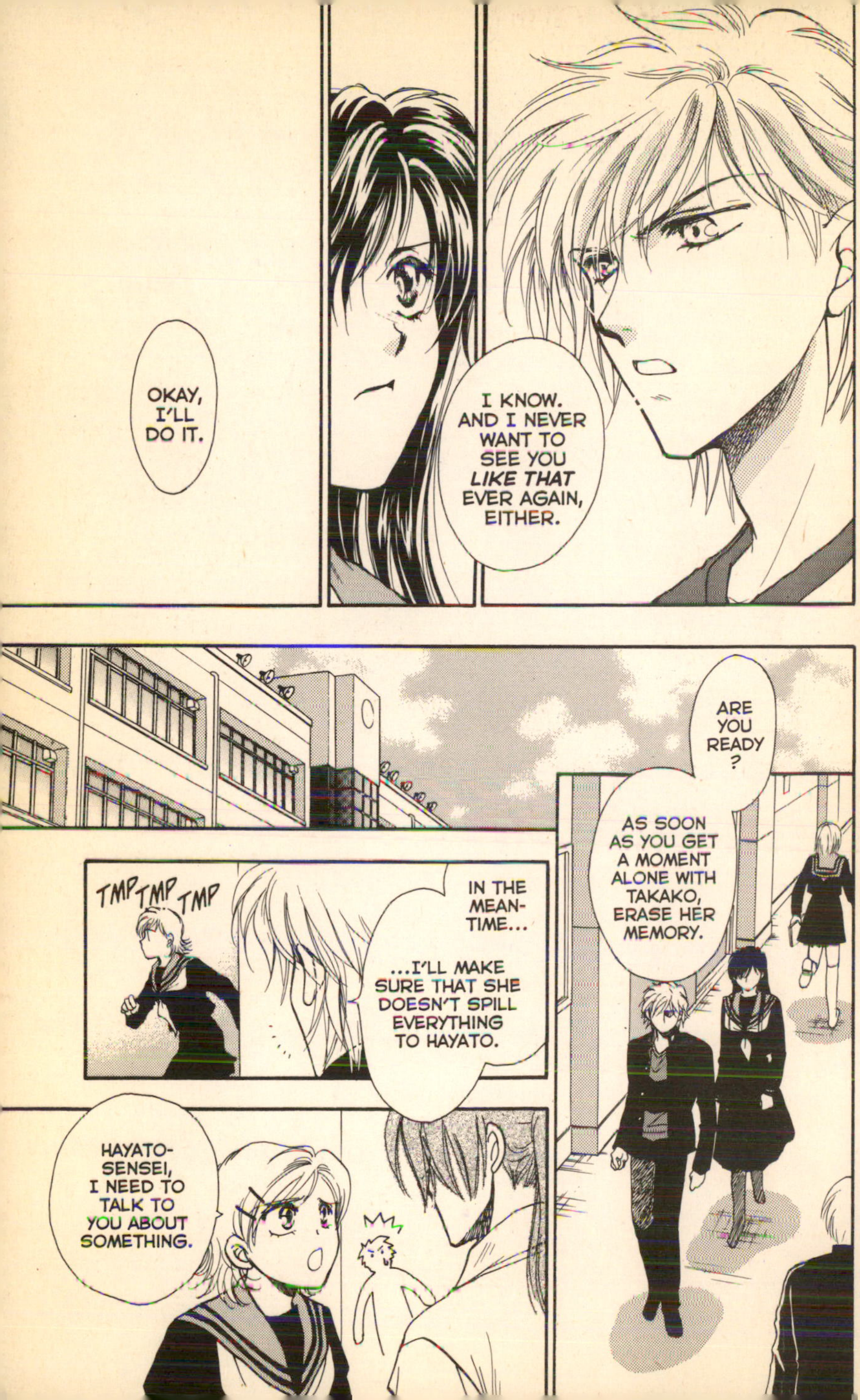
I KNOW. AND I NEVER WANT TO SEE YOU *LIKE THAT* EVER AGAIN, EITHER.
OKAY, I'LL DO IT.
ARE YOU READY?
AS SOON AS YOU GET A MOMENT ALONE WITH TAKAKO, ERASE HER MEMORY.
IN THE MEAN-TIME...
...I'LL MAKE SURE THAT SHE DOESN'T SPILL EVERYTHING TO HAYATO.
TMP TMP TMP
HAYATO-SENSEI, I NEED TO TALK TO YOU ABOUT SOMETHING.

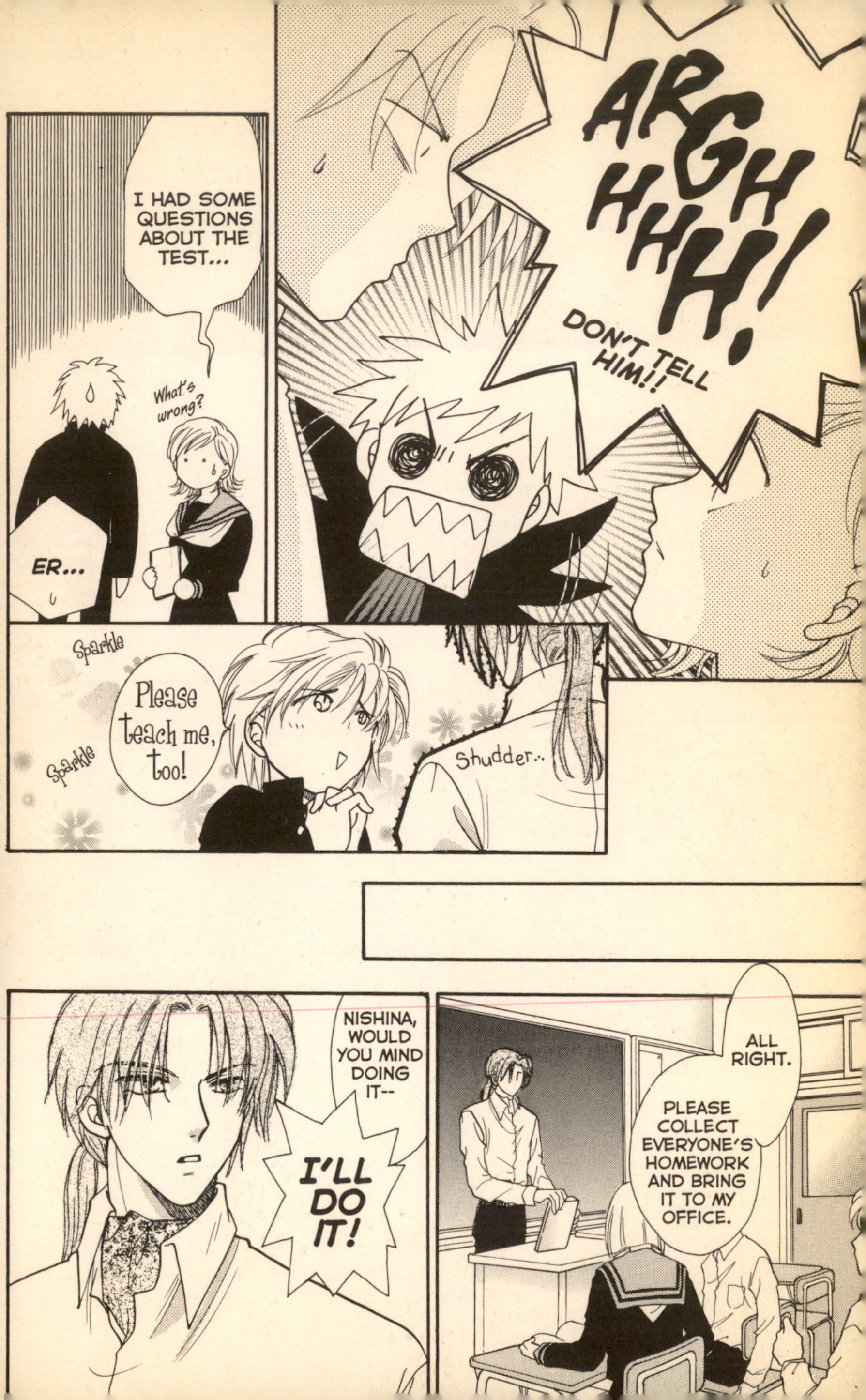
ARGHHHH!
DON'T TELL HIM!!
I HAD SOME QUESTIONS ABOUT THE TEST...
What's wrong?
ER...
Shudder...
Please teach me, too!
Sparkle
Sparkle
ALL RIGHT.
PLEASE COLLECT EVERYONE'S HOMEWORK AND BRING IT TO MY OFFICE.
NISHINA, WOULD YOU MIND DOING IT--
I'LL DO IT!

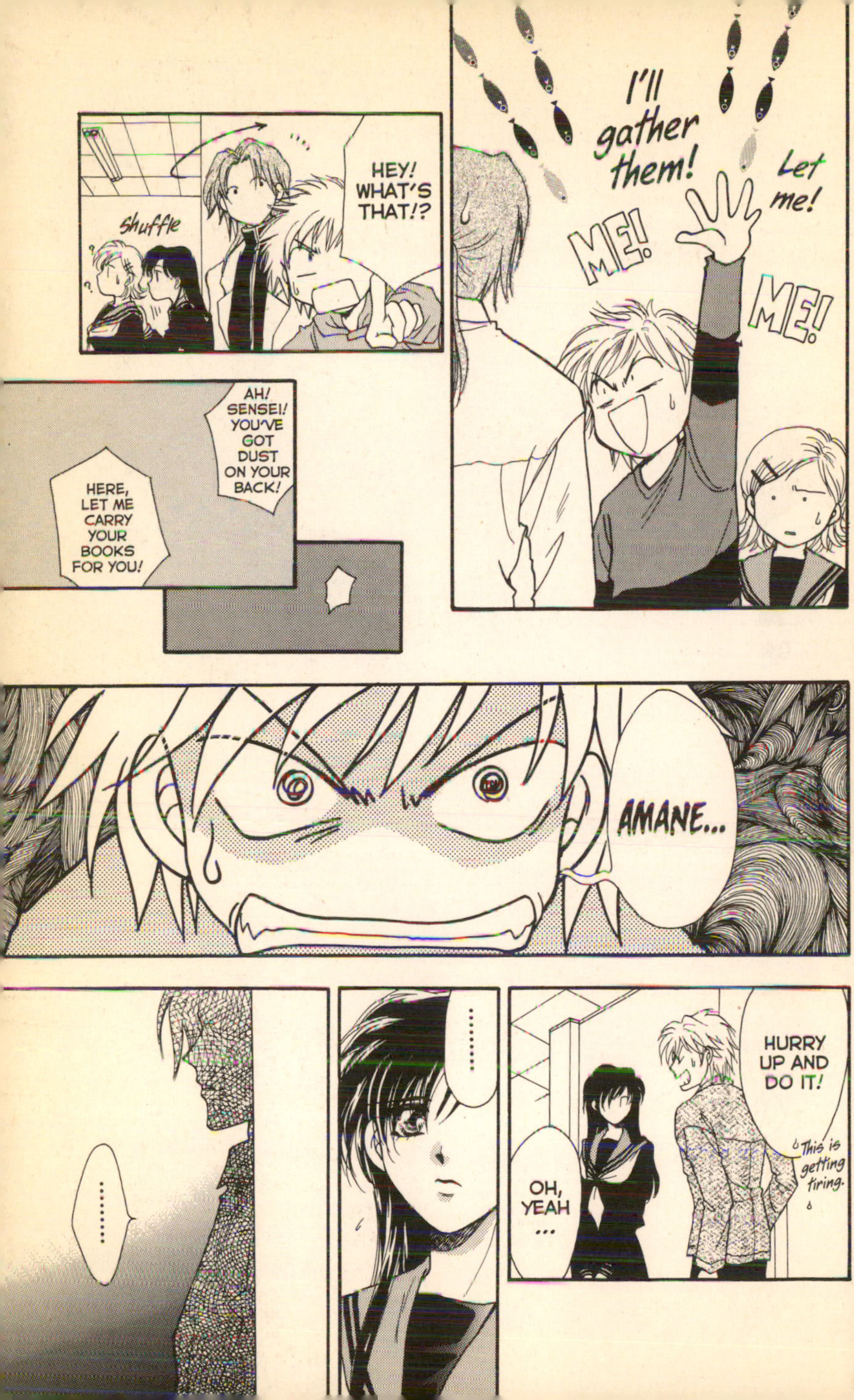
Let me!
I'll gather them!
ME!
ME!
HEY! WHAT'S THAT!?
shuffle
AH! SENSEI! YOU'VE GOT DUST ON YOUR BACK!
HERE, LET ME CARRY YOUR BOOKS FOR YOU!
AMANE...
HURRY UP AND DO IT!
This is getting tiring.
OH, YEAH ...
....
....

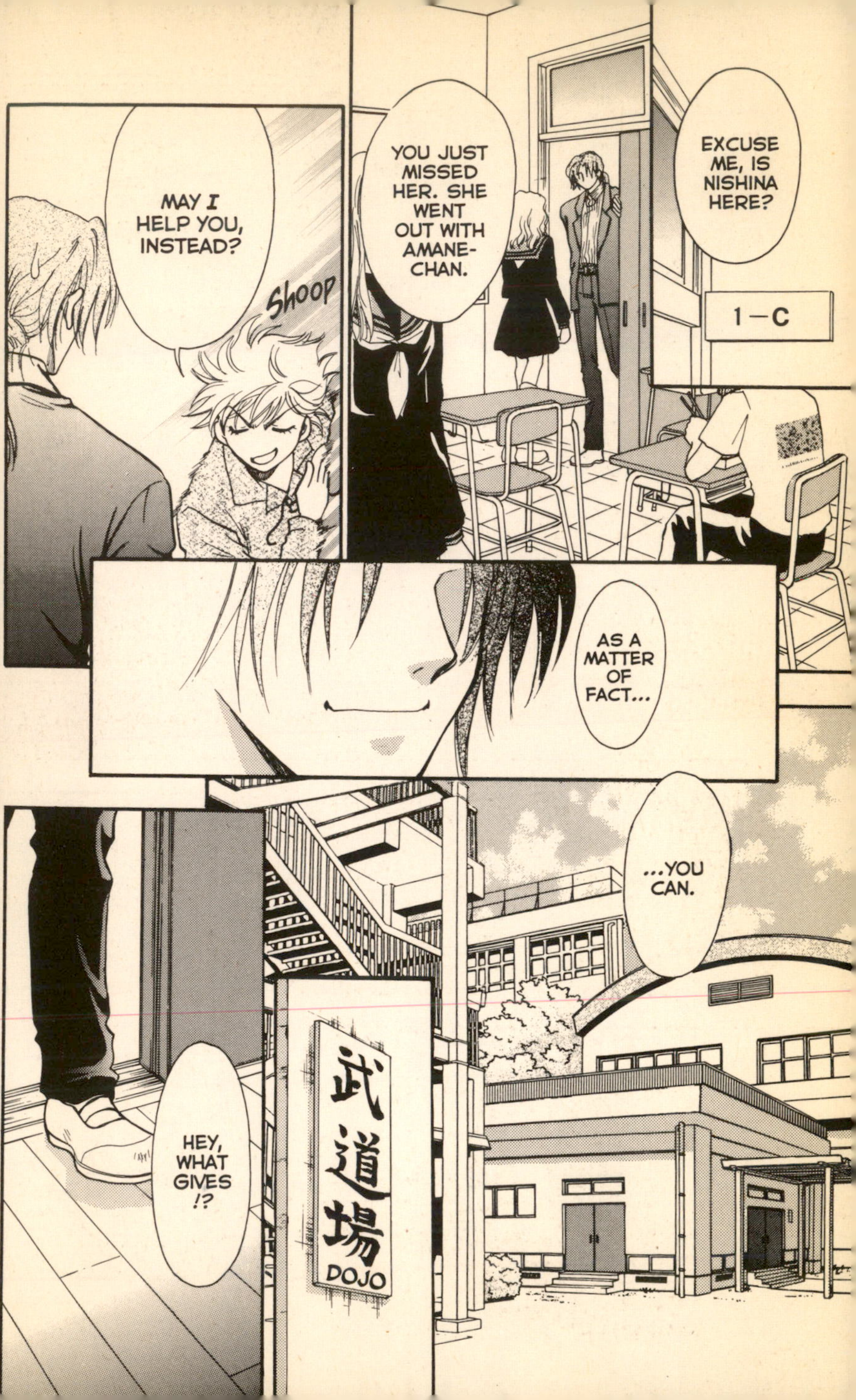
EXCUSE ME, IS NISHINA HERE?
1—C
YOU JUST MISSED HER. SHE WENT OUT WITH AMANE-CHAN.
MAY I HELP YOU, INSTEAD?
Shoop
AS A MATTER OF FACT...
...YOU CAN.
武道場
DOJO
HEY, WHAT GIVES!?

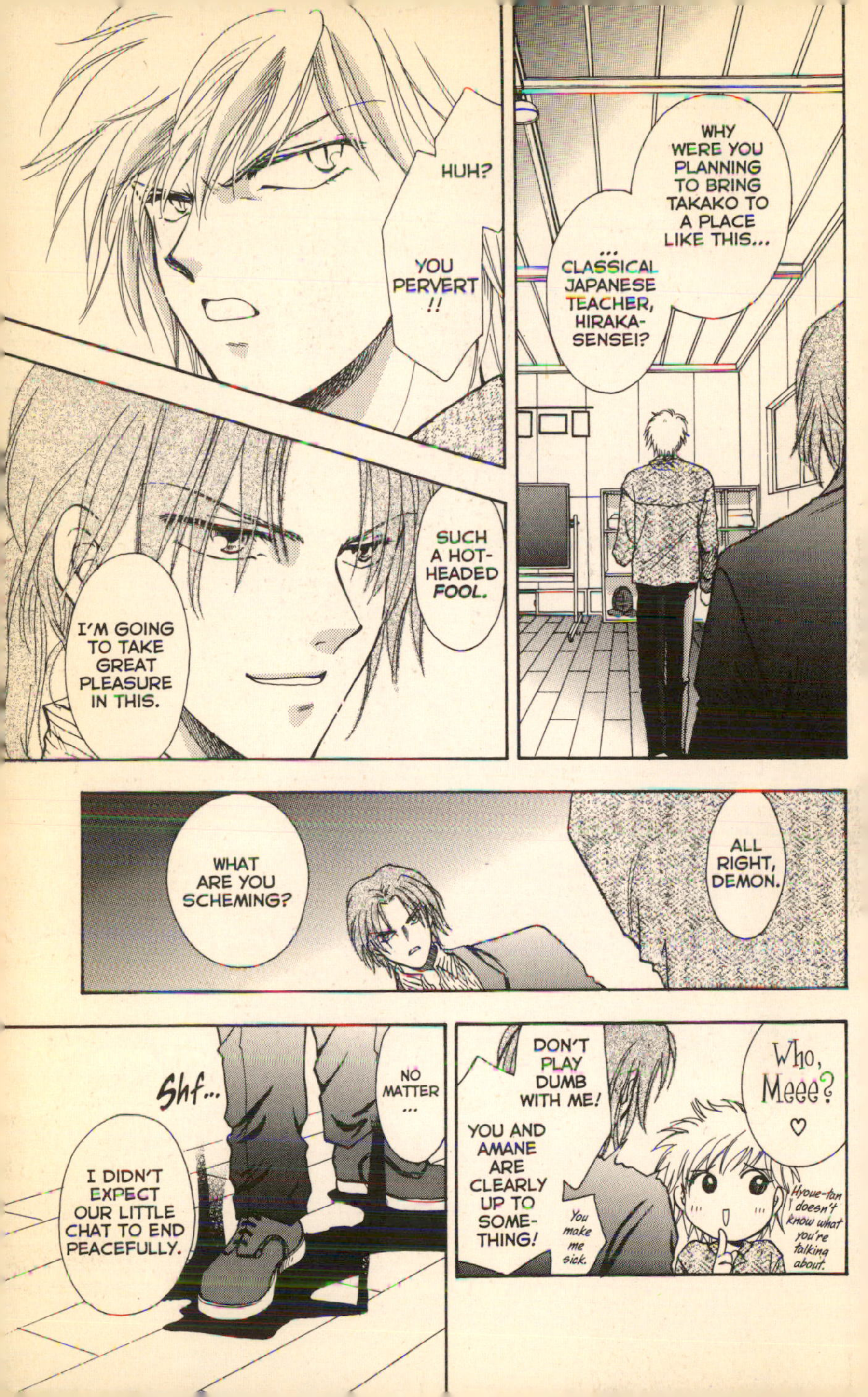
WHY WERE YOU PLANNING TO BRING TAKAKO TO A PLACE LIKE THIS...
...CLASSICAL JAPANESE TEACHER, HIRAKA-SENSEI?
HUH?
YOU PERVERT!!
SUCH A HOT-HEADED FOOL.
I'M GOING TO TAKE GREAT PLEASURE IN THIS.
ALL RIGHT, DEMON.
WHAT ARE YOU SCHEMING?
Who, Meee? ♡
DON'T PLAY DUMB WITH ME!
YOU AND AMANE ARE CLEARLY UP TO SOMETHING!
Hyoue-tan doesn't know what you're talking about.
You make me sick.
NO MATTER...
Shf...
I DIDN'T EXPECT OUR LITTLE CHAT TO END PEACEFULLY.

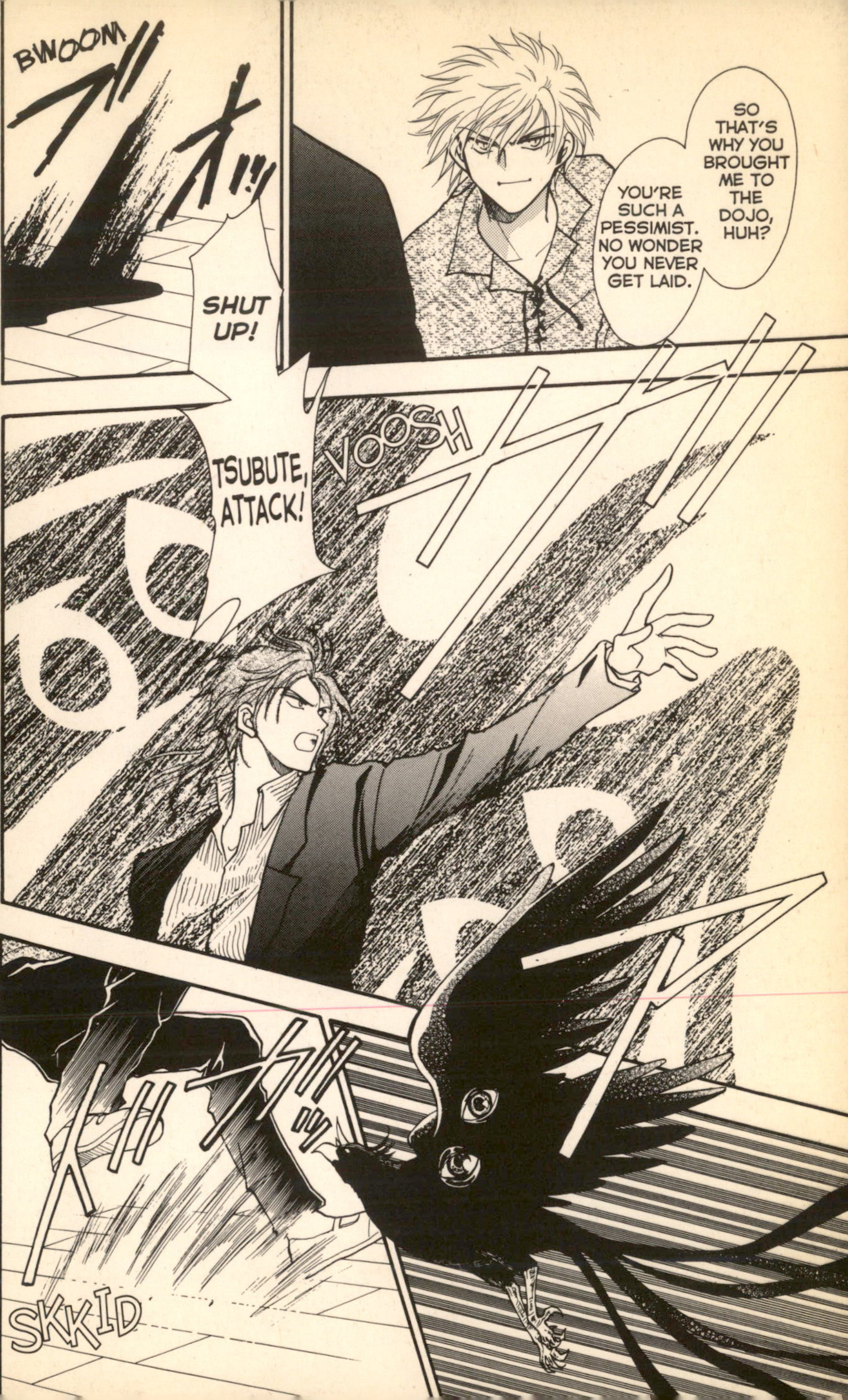
SO THAT'S WHY YOU BROUGHT ME TO THE DOJO, HUH?
YOU'RE SUCH A PESSIMIST. NO WONDER YOU NEVER GET LAID.
BWOOM
SHUT UP!
VOOSH
TSUBUTE, ATTACK!
SKKID

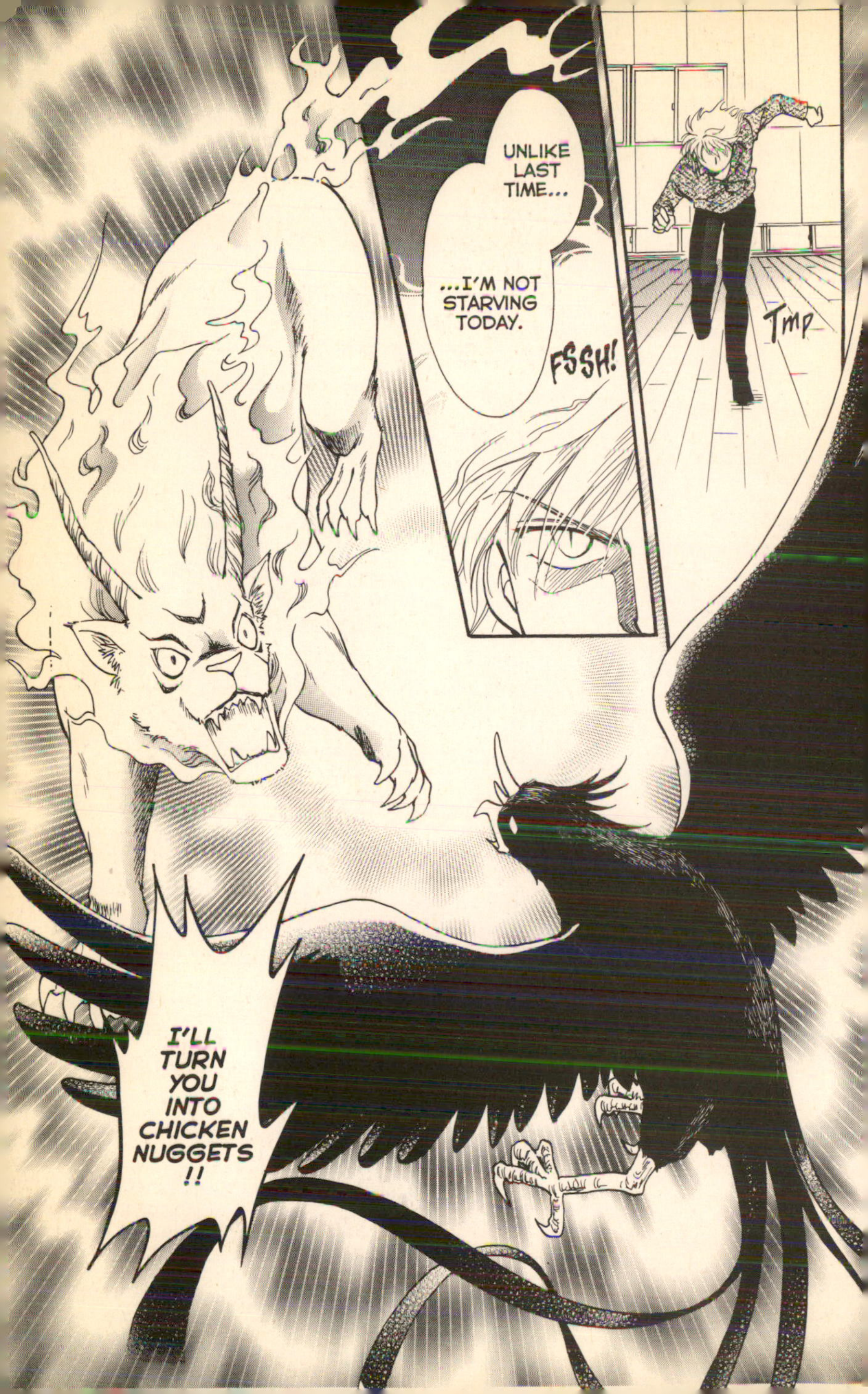
Tmp
UNLIKE LAST TIME... ...I'M NOT STARVING TODAY.
FSSH!
I'LL TURN YOU INTO CHICKEN NUGGETS !!

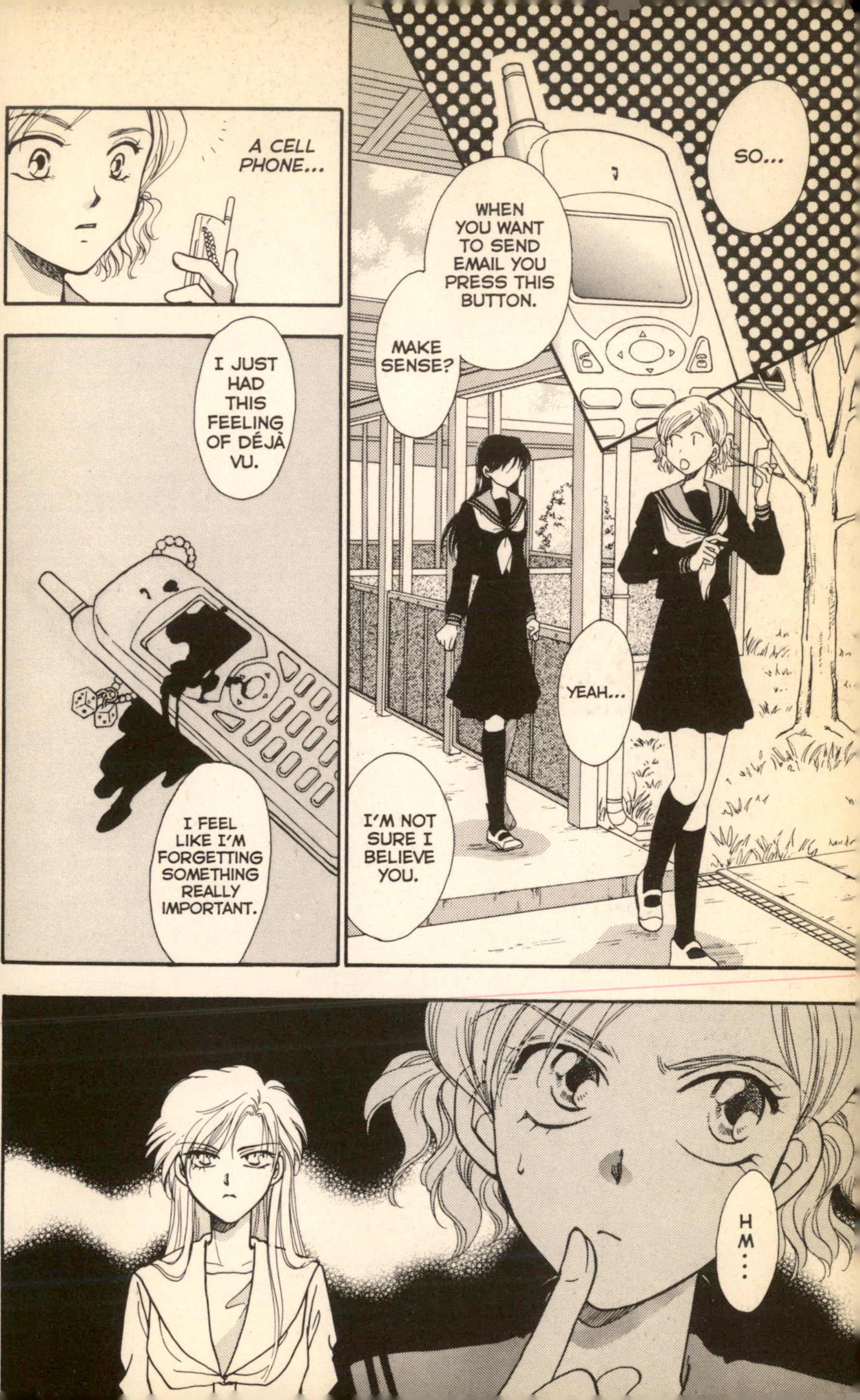
SO...
WHEN YOU WANT TO SEND EMAIL YOU PRESS THIS BUTTON.
MAKE SENSE?
YEAH...
I'M NOT SURE I BELIEVE YOU.
A CELL PHONE...
I JUST HAD THIS FEELING OF DÉJÀ VU.
I FEEL LIKE I'M FORGETTING SOMETHING REALLY IMPORTANT.
HM...

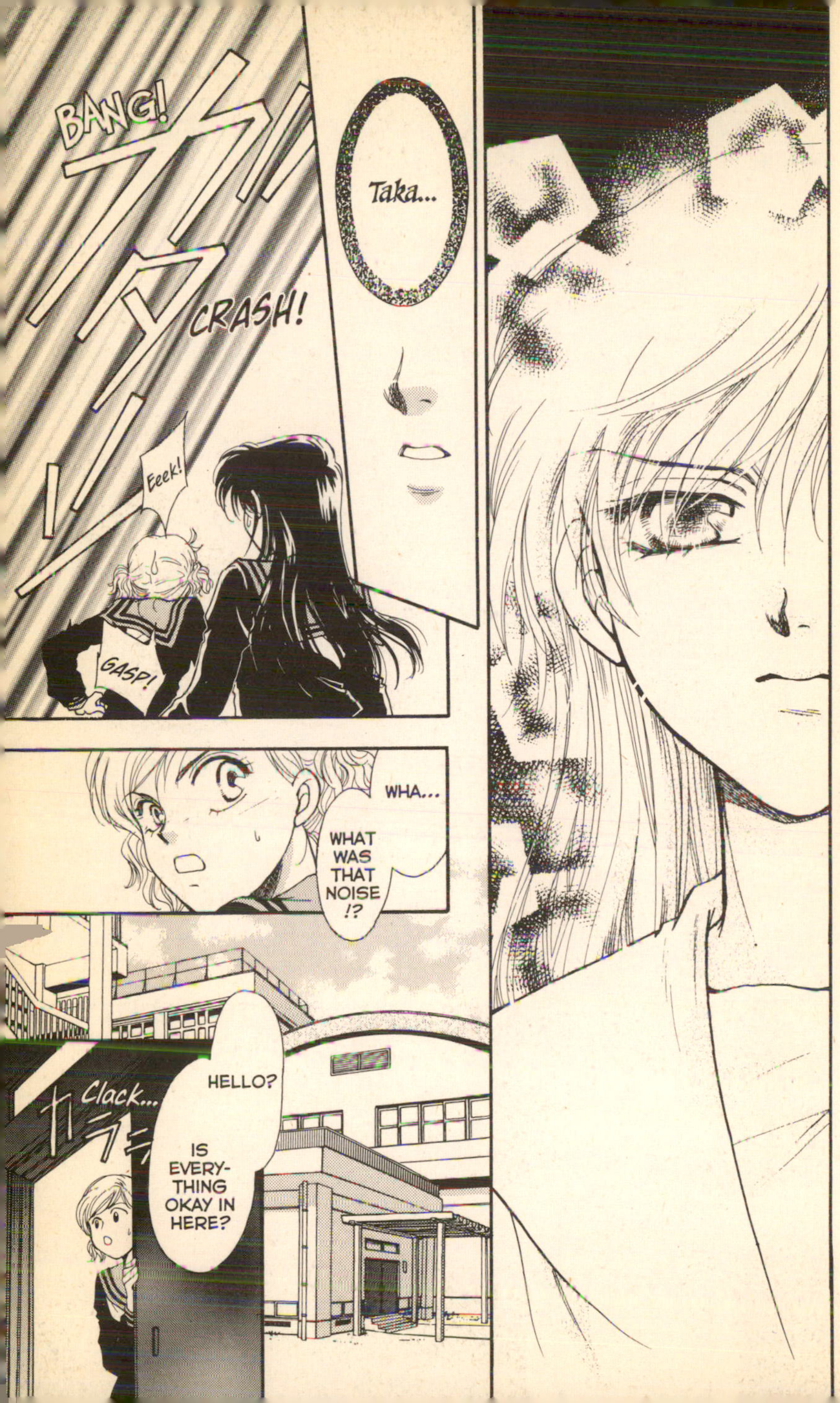

Taka...
BANG!
CRASH!
Eeek!
GASP!
WHA...
WHAT WAS THAT NOISE !?
Clack...
HELLO?
IS EVERY-THING OKAY IN HERE?

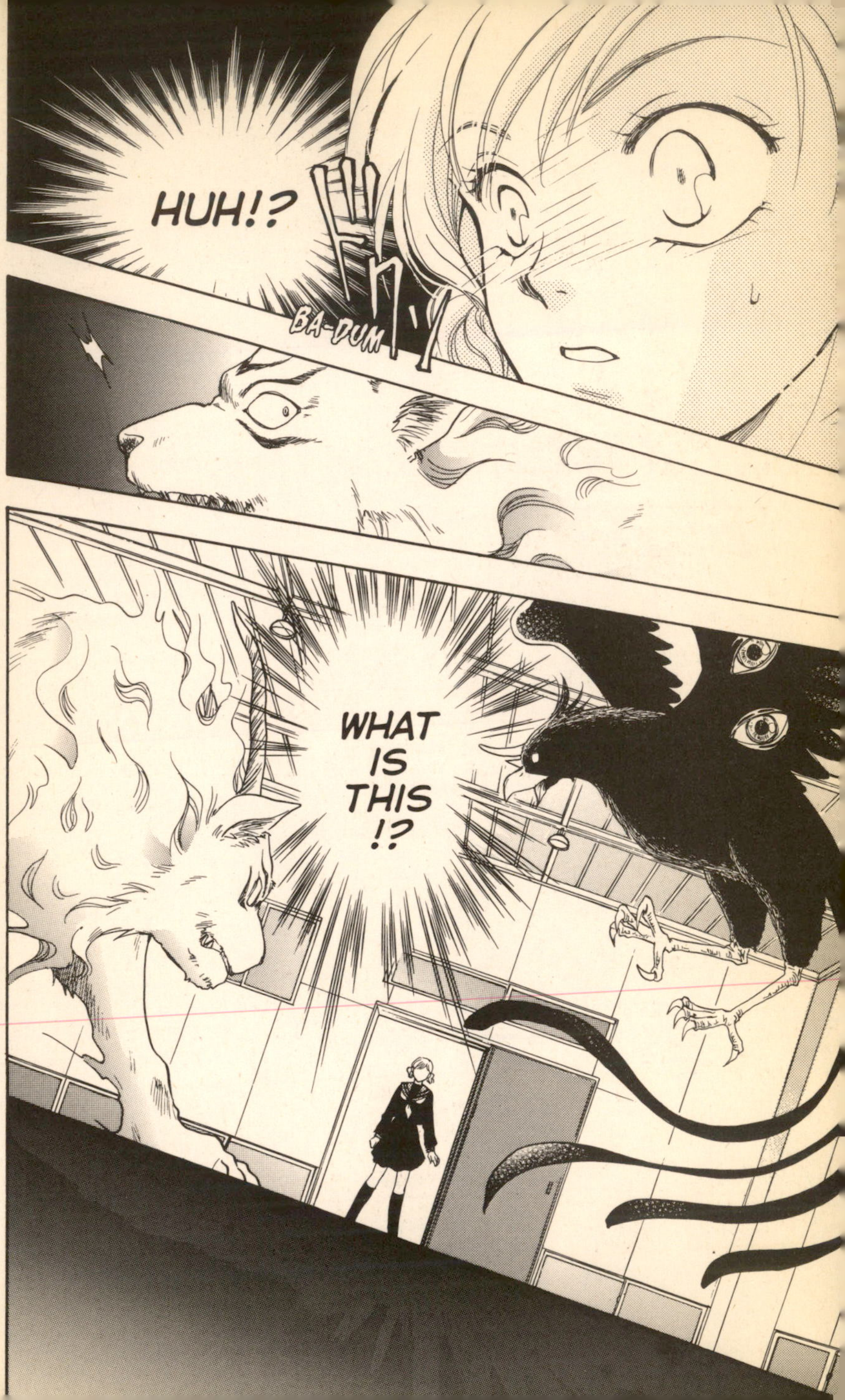
HUH!?
BA-DUM
WHAT IS THIS !?

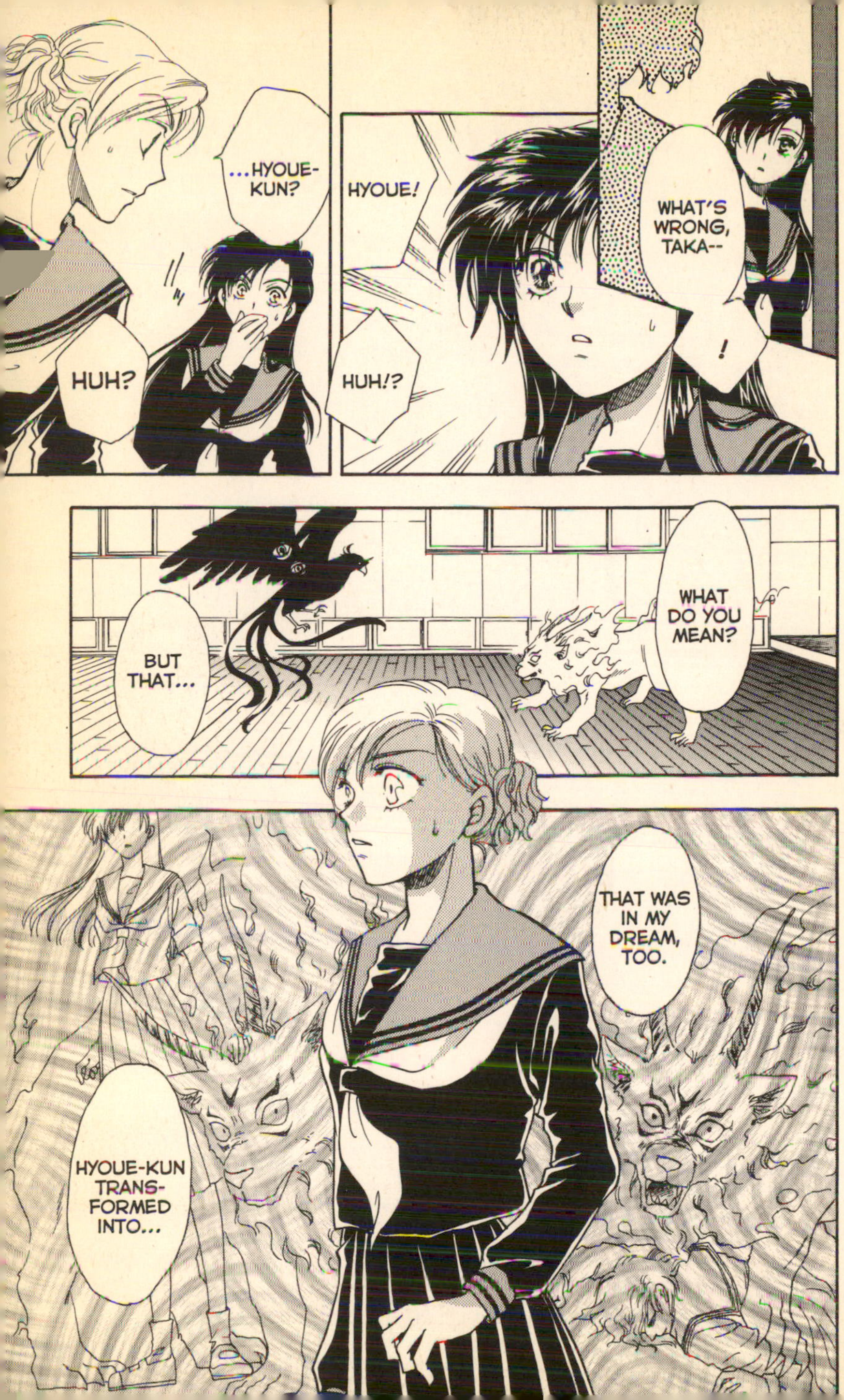
WHAT'S WRONG, TAKA--
!
HYOUE!
HUH!?
...HYOUE-KUN?
HUH?
WHAT DO YOU MEAN?
BUT THAT...
THAT WAS IN MY DREAM, TOO.
HYOUE-KUN TRANSFORMED INTO...

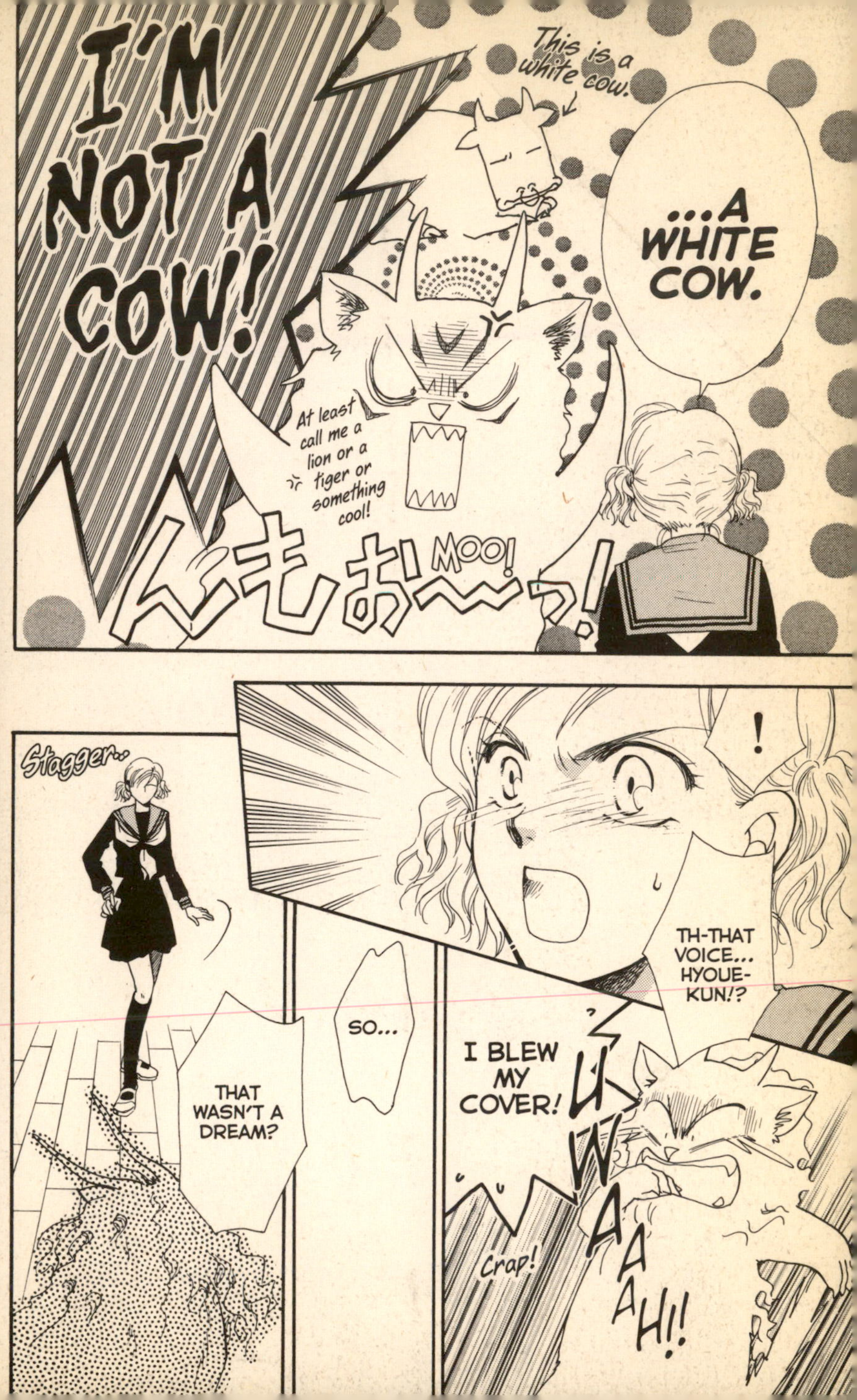

...A WHITE COW.
This is a white cow.
I'M NOT A COW!
At least call me a lion or a tiger or something cool!
んもお〜っ!
MOO!
!
TH-THAT VOICE... HYOUE-KUN!?
UWAAAH!!
I BLEW MY COVER!
Crap!
SO...
Stagger..
THAT WASN'T A DREAM?

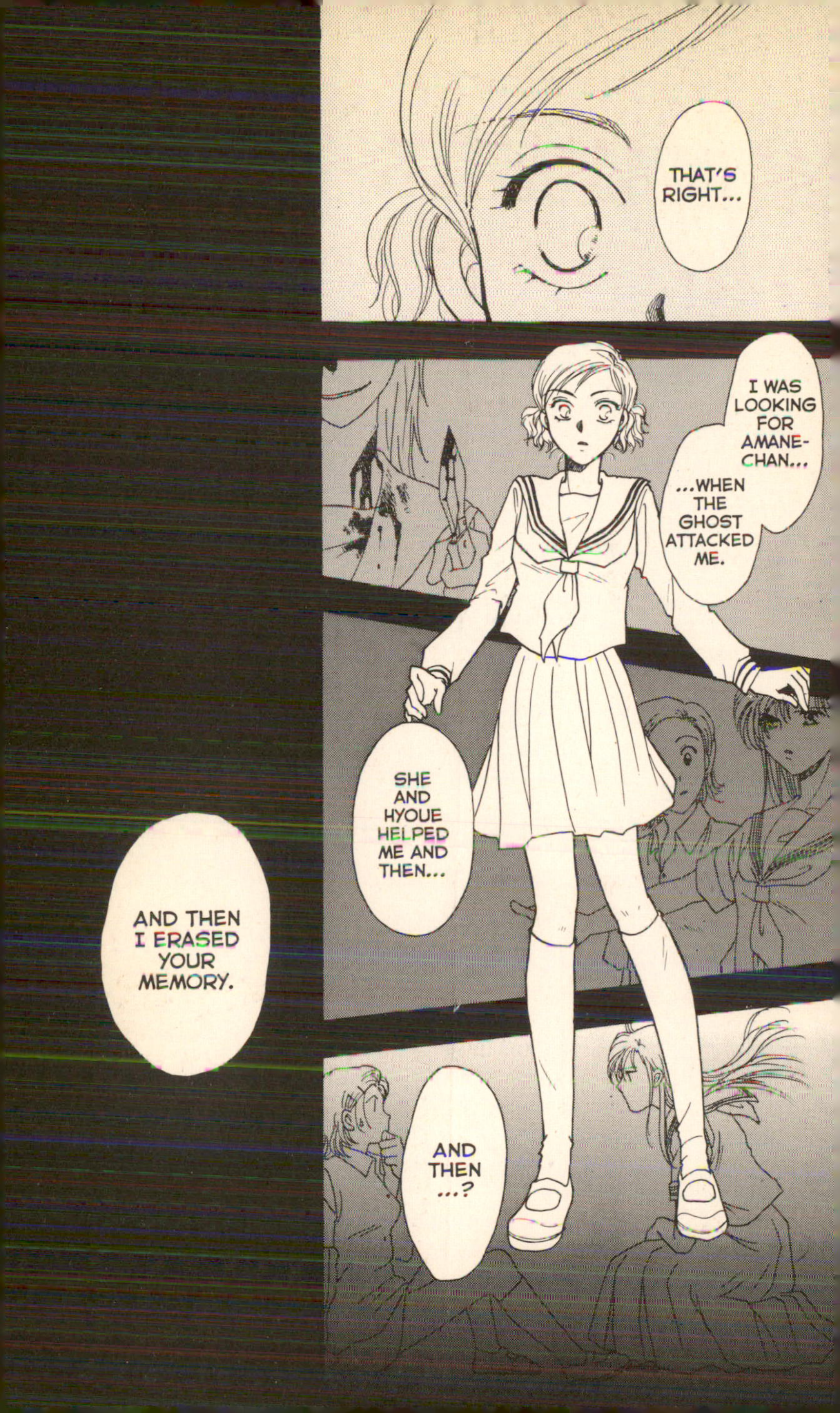
THAT'S RIGHT...
I WAS LOOKING FOR AMANE-CHAN...
...WHEN THE GHOST ATTACKED ME.
SHE AND HYOUE HELPED ME AND THEN...
AND THEN ...?
AND THEN I ERASED YOUR MEMORY.

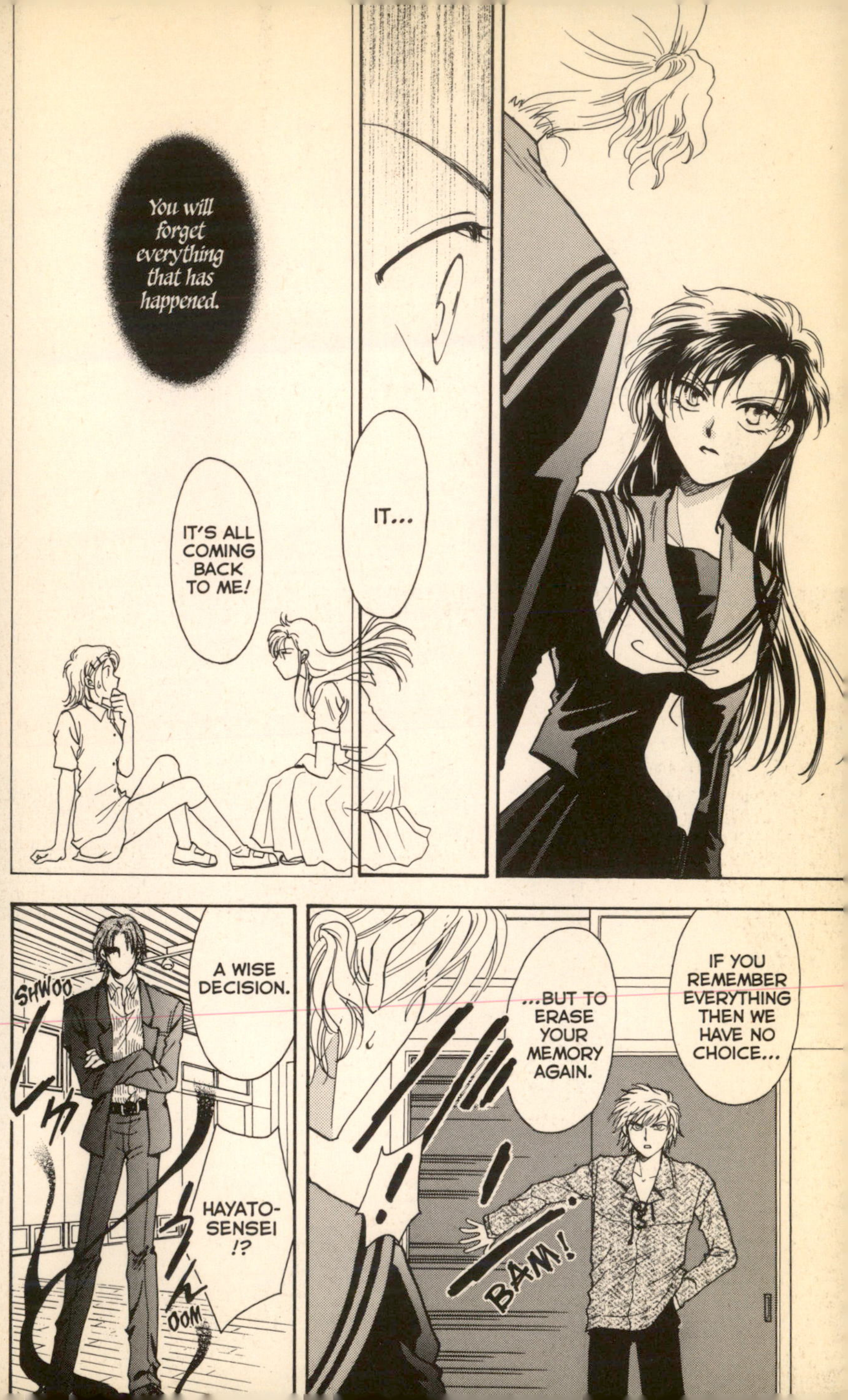
IT...
You will forget everything that has happened.
IT'S ALL COMING BACK TO ME!
IF YOU REMEMBER EVERYTHING THEN WE HAVE NO CHOICE...
...BUT TO ERASE YOUR MEMORY AGAIN.
BAM!
A WISE DECISION.
SHWOO
HAYATO-SENSEI !?
OOM

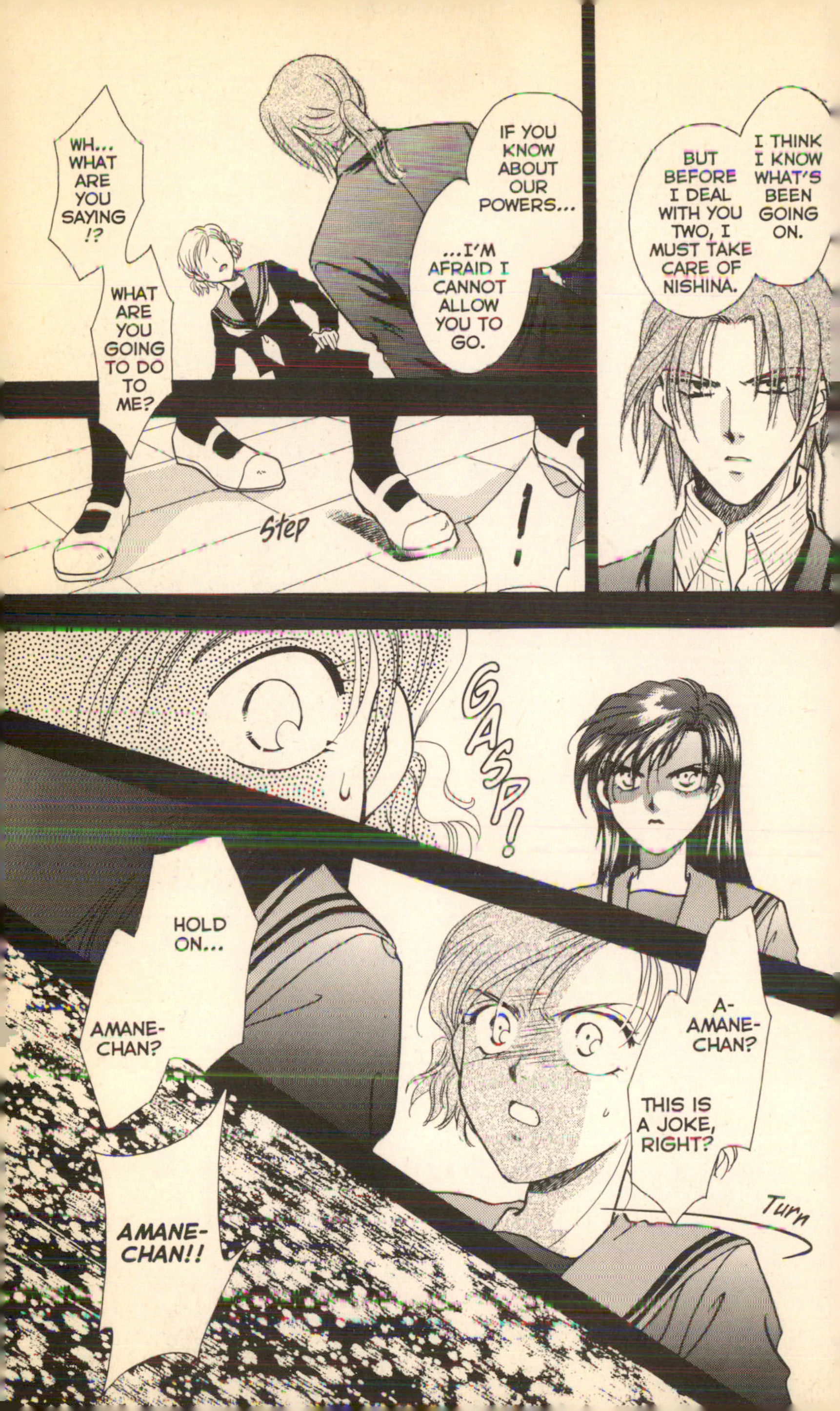
I THINK I KNOW WHAT'S BEEN GOING ON.
BUT BEFORE I DEAL WITH YOU TWO, I MUST TAKE CARE OF NISHINA.
IF YOU KNOW ABOUT OUR POWERS...
...I'M AFRAID I CANNOT ALLOW YOU TO GO.
WH... WHAT ARE YOU SAYING!?
WHAT ARE YOU GOING TO DO TO ME?
!
Step
GASP!
A- AMANE-CHAN?
THIS IS A JOKE, RIGHT?
Turn
HOLD ON...
AMANE-CHAN?
AMANE-CHAN!!

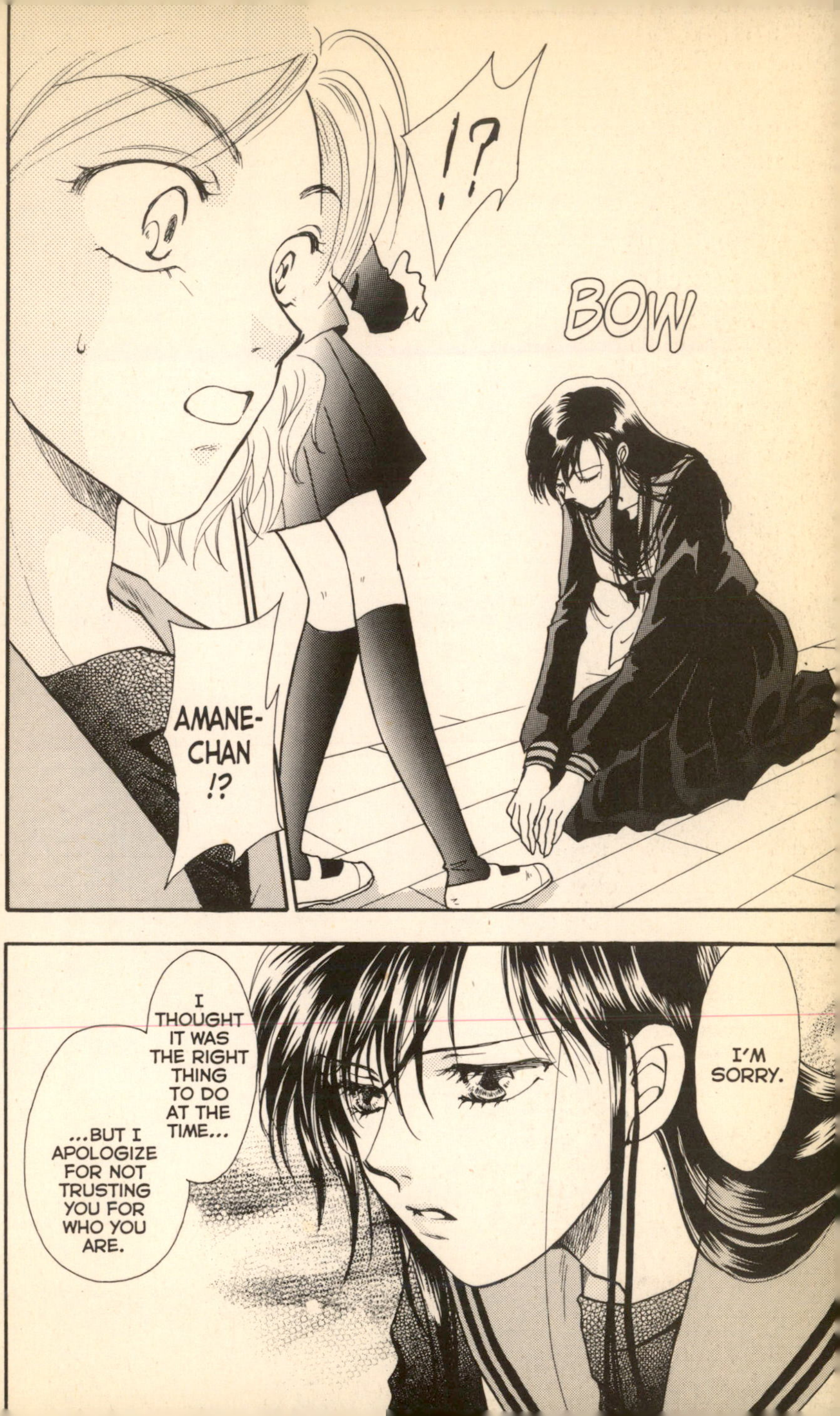
!?
BOW
AMANE-CHAN !?
I'M SORRY.
I THOUGHT IT WAS THE RIGHT THING TO DO AT THE TIME...
...BUT I APOLOGIZE FOR NOT TRUSTING YOU FOR WHO YOU ARE.

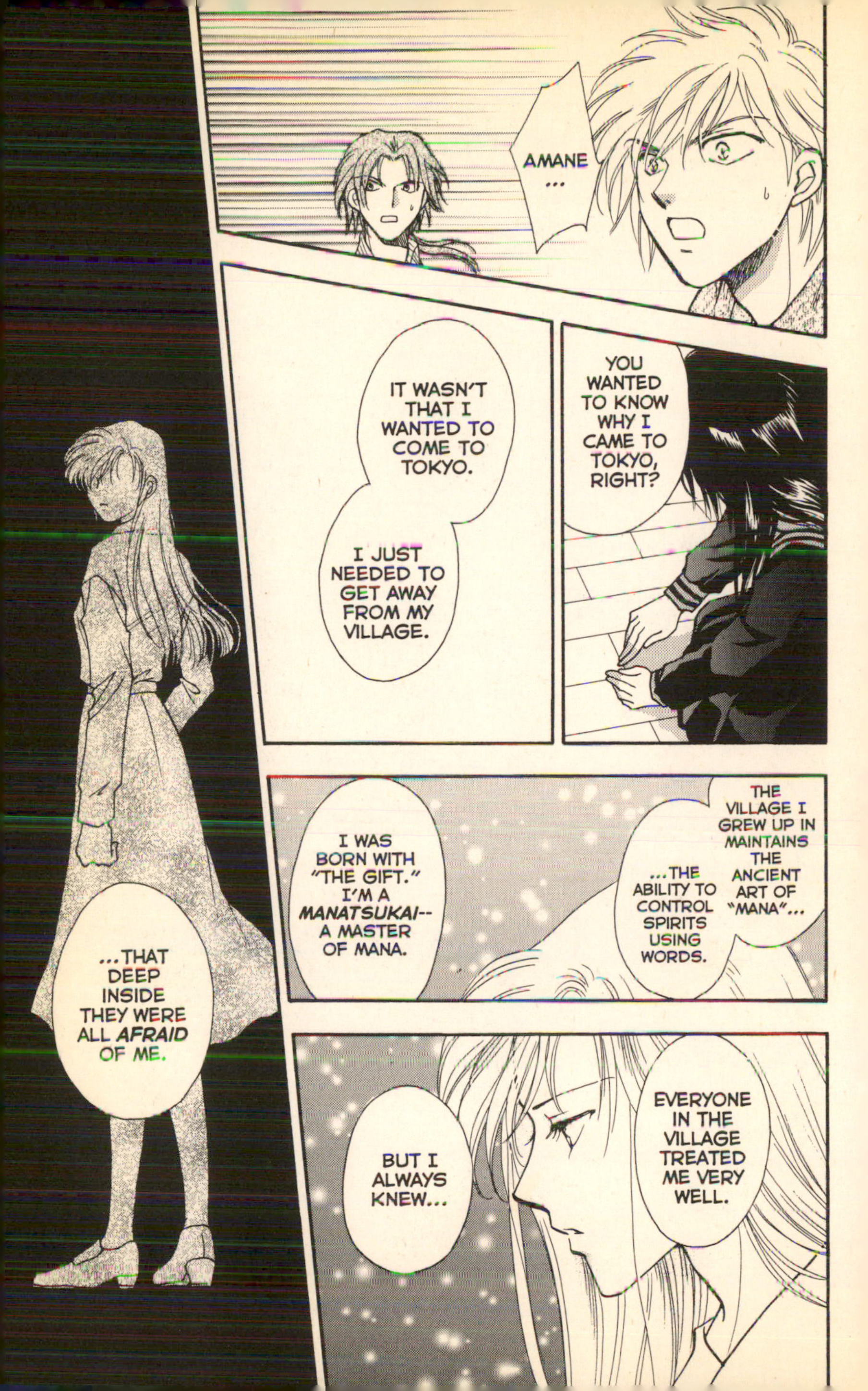
AMANE ...
YOU WANTED TO KNOW WHY I CAME TO TOKYO, RIGHT?
IT WASN'T THAT I WANTED TO COME TO TOKYO.
I JUST NEEDED TO GET AWAY FROM MY VILLAGE.
THE VILLAGE I GREW UP IN MAINTAINS THE ANCIENT ART OF "MANA"...
...THE ABILITY TO CONTROL SPIRITS USING WORDS.
I WAS BORN WITH "THE GIFT." I'M A *MANATSUKAI*-- A MASTER OF MANA.
EVERYONE IN THE VILLAGE TREATED ME VERY WELL.
BUT I ALWAYS KNEW...
...THAT DEEP INSIDE THEY WERE ALL *AFRAID* OF ME.

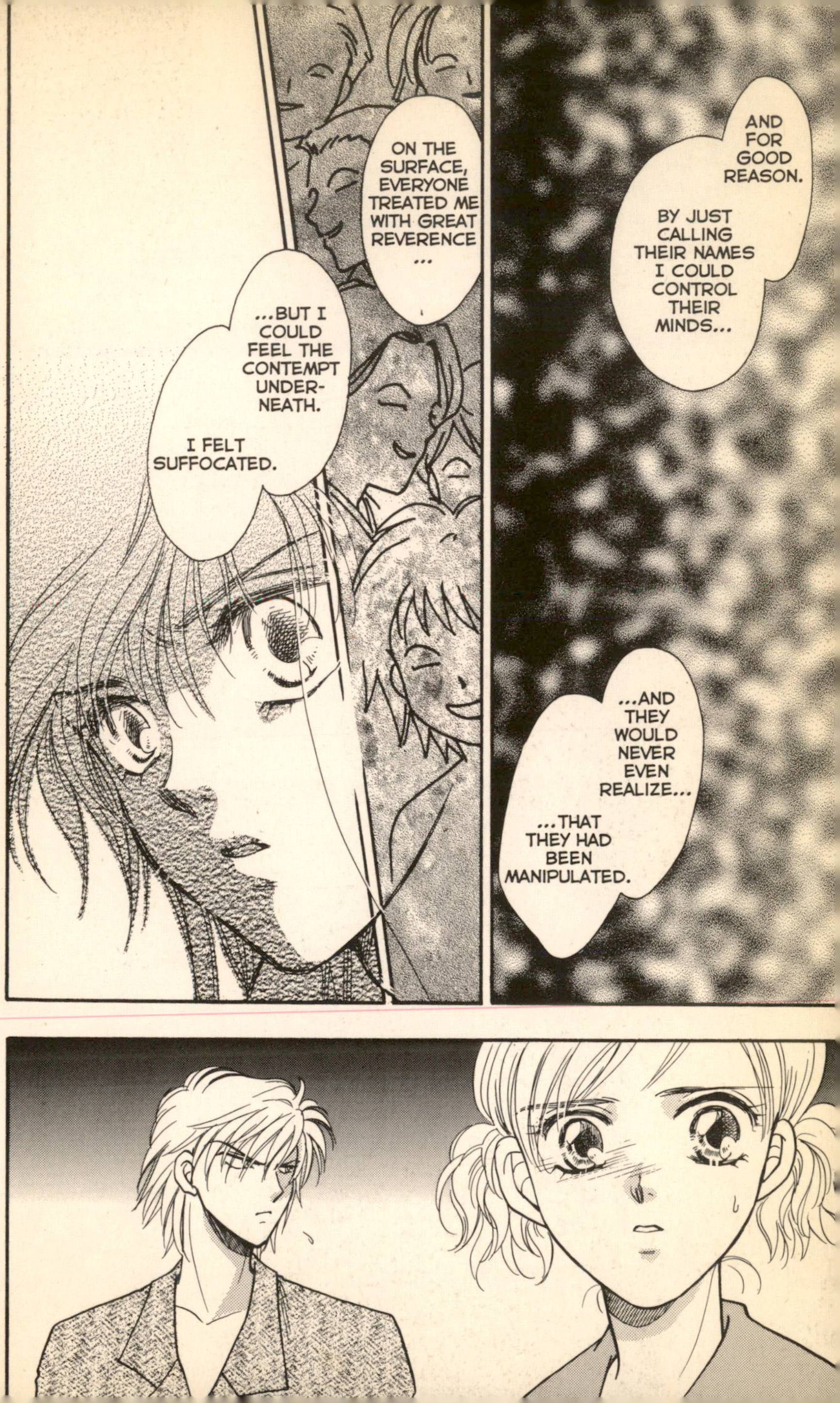
AND FOR GOOD REASON.
BY JUST CALLING THEIR NAMES I COULD CONTROL THEIR MINDS...
...AND THEY WOULD NEVER EVEN REALIZE...
...THAT THEY HAD BEEN MANIPULATED.
ON THE SURFACE, EVERYONE TREATED ME WITH GREAT REVERENCE...
...BUT I COULD FEEL THE CONTEMPT UNDER-NEATH.
I FELT SUFFOCATED.

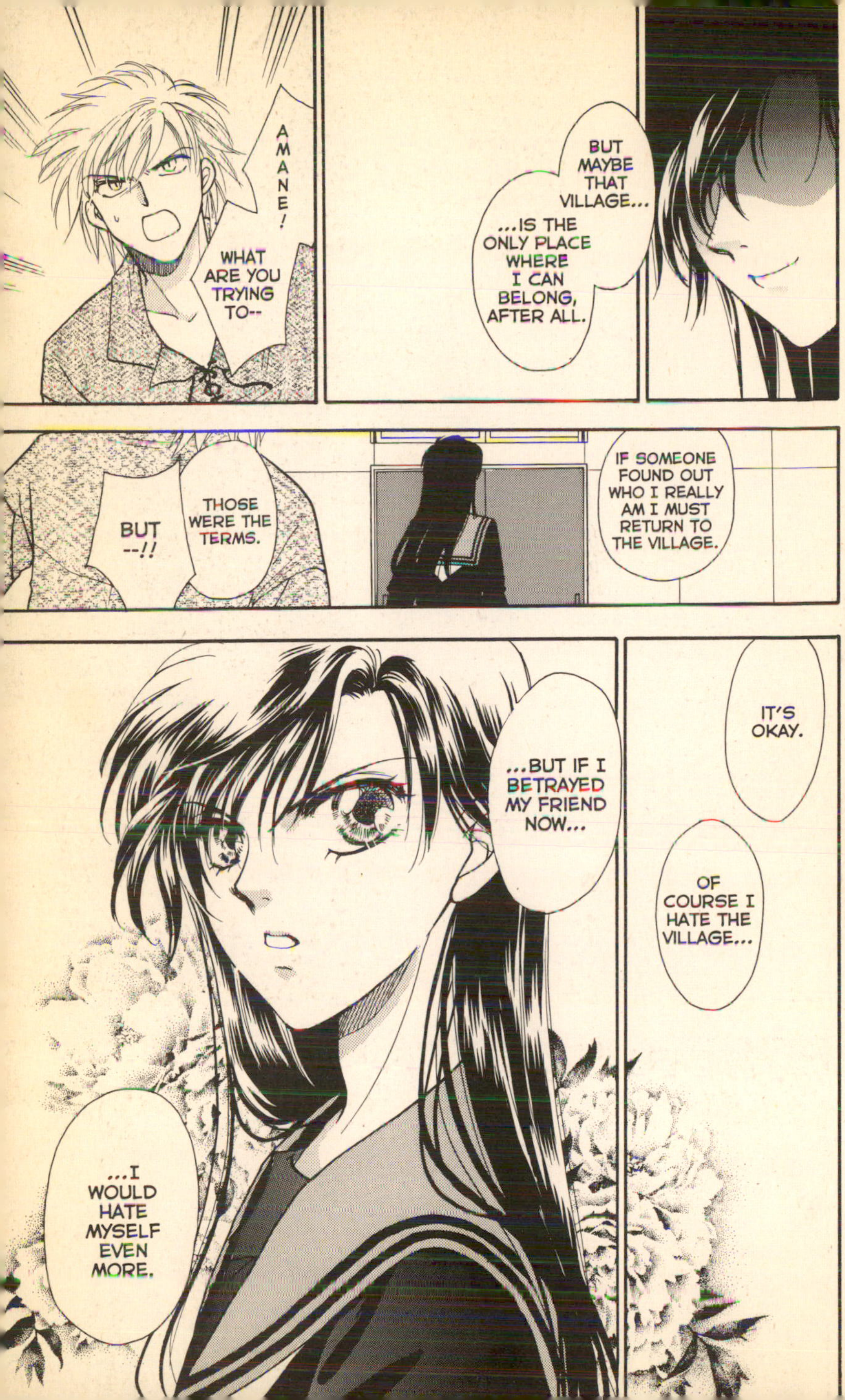
BUT MAYBE THAT VILLAGE...
...IS THE ONLY PLACE WHERE I CAN BELONG, AFTER ALL.
AMANE!
WHAT ARE YOU TRYING TO--
IF SOMEONE FOUND OUT WHO I REALLY AM I MUST RETURN TO THE VILLAGE.
THOSE WERE THE TERMS.
BUT --!!
IT'S OKAY.
OF COURSE I HATE THE VILLAGE...
...BUT IF I BETRAYED MY FRIEND NOW...
...I WOULD HATE MYSELF EVEN MORE.

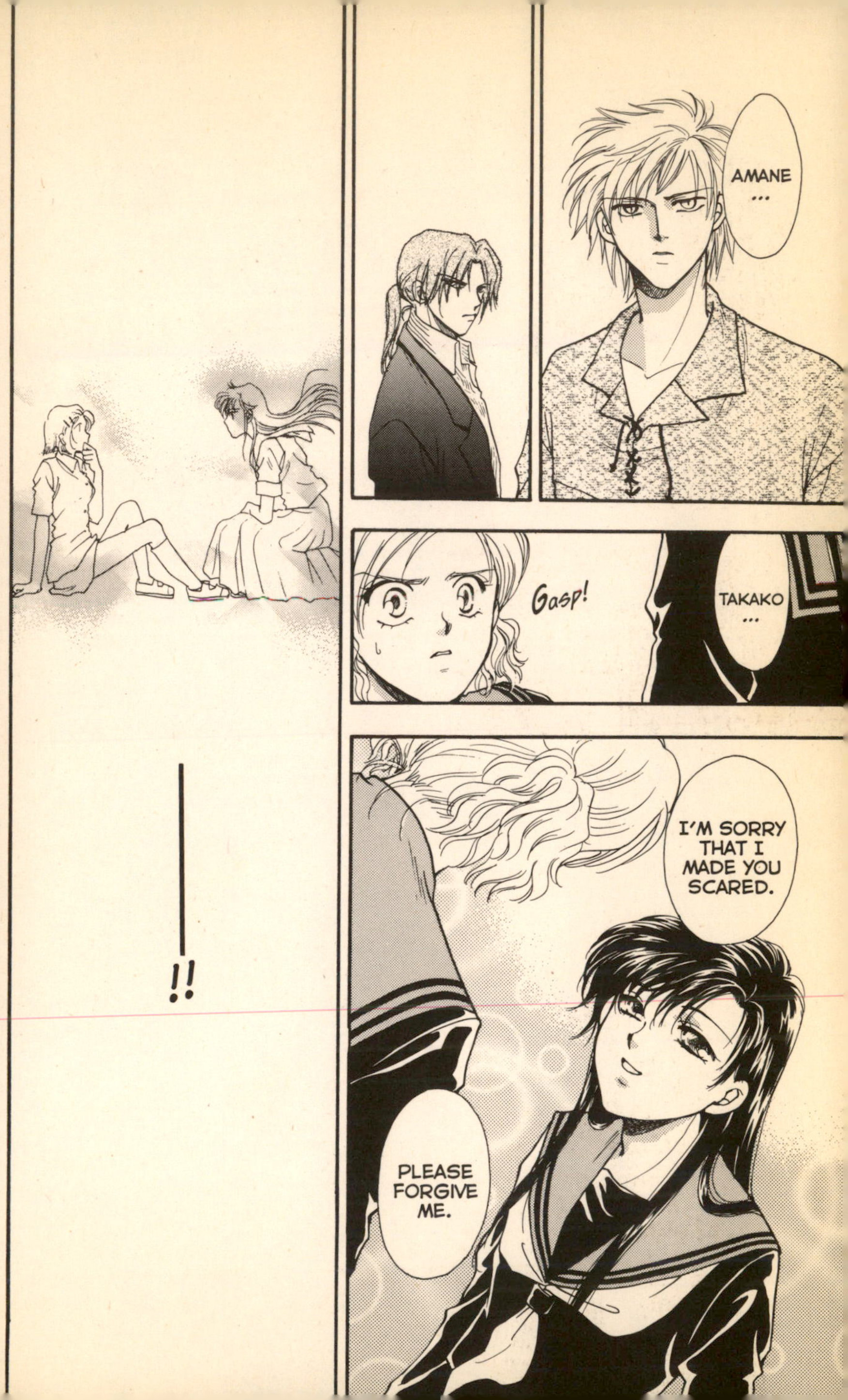
AMANE ...
TAKAKO ...
Gasp!
I'M SORRY THAT I MADE YOU SCARED.
PLEASE FORGIVE ME.
—!!

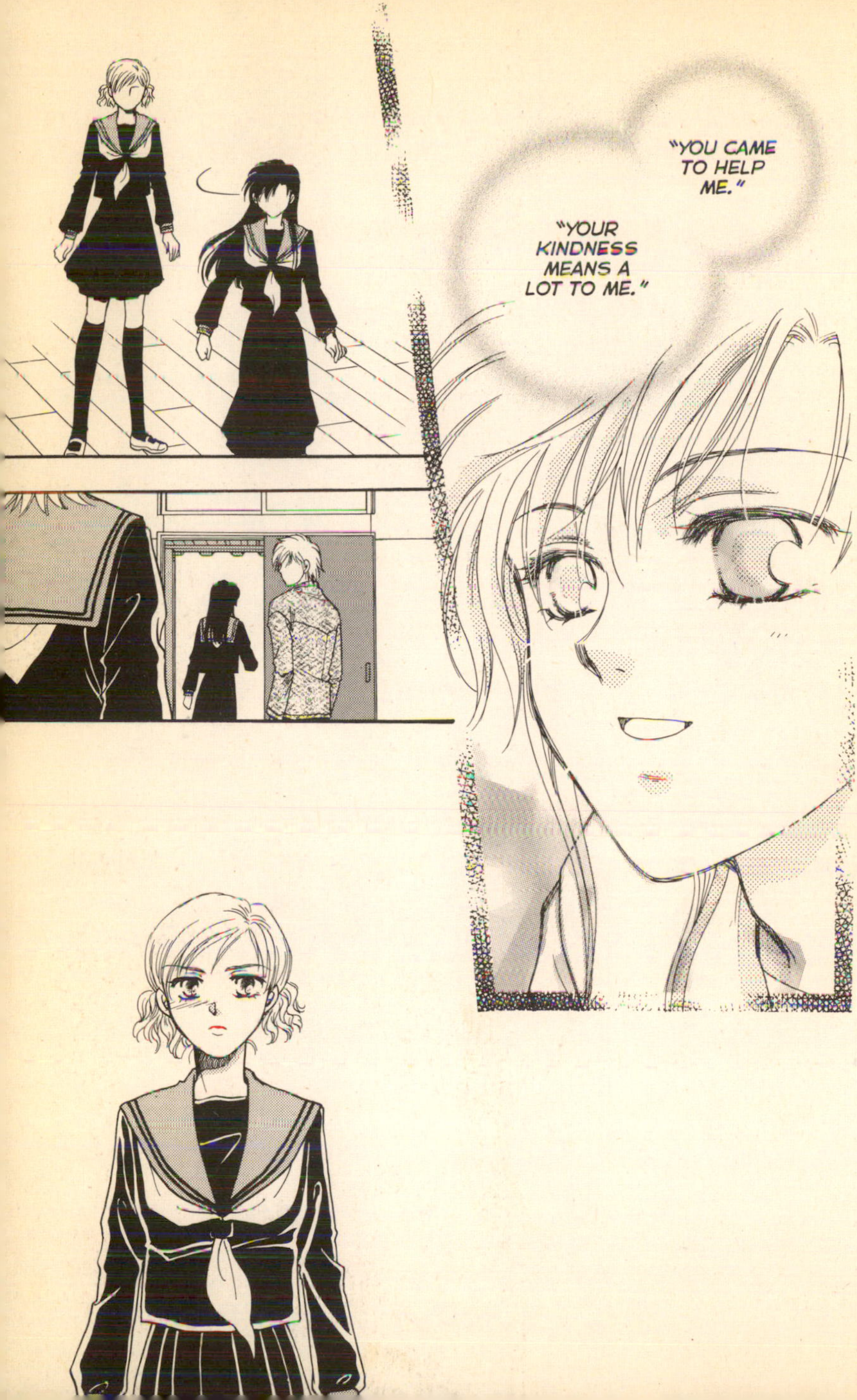
"YOU CAME TO HELP ME."
"YOUR KINDNESS MEANS A LOT TO ME."

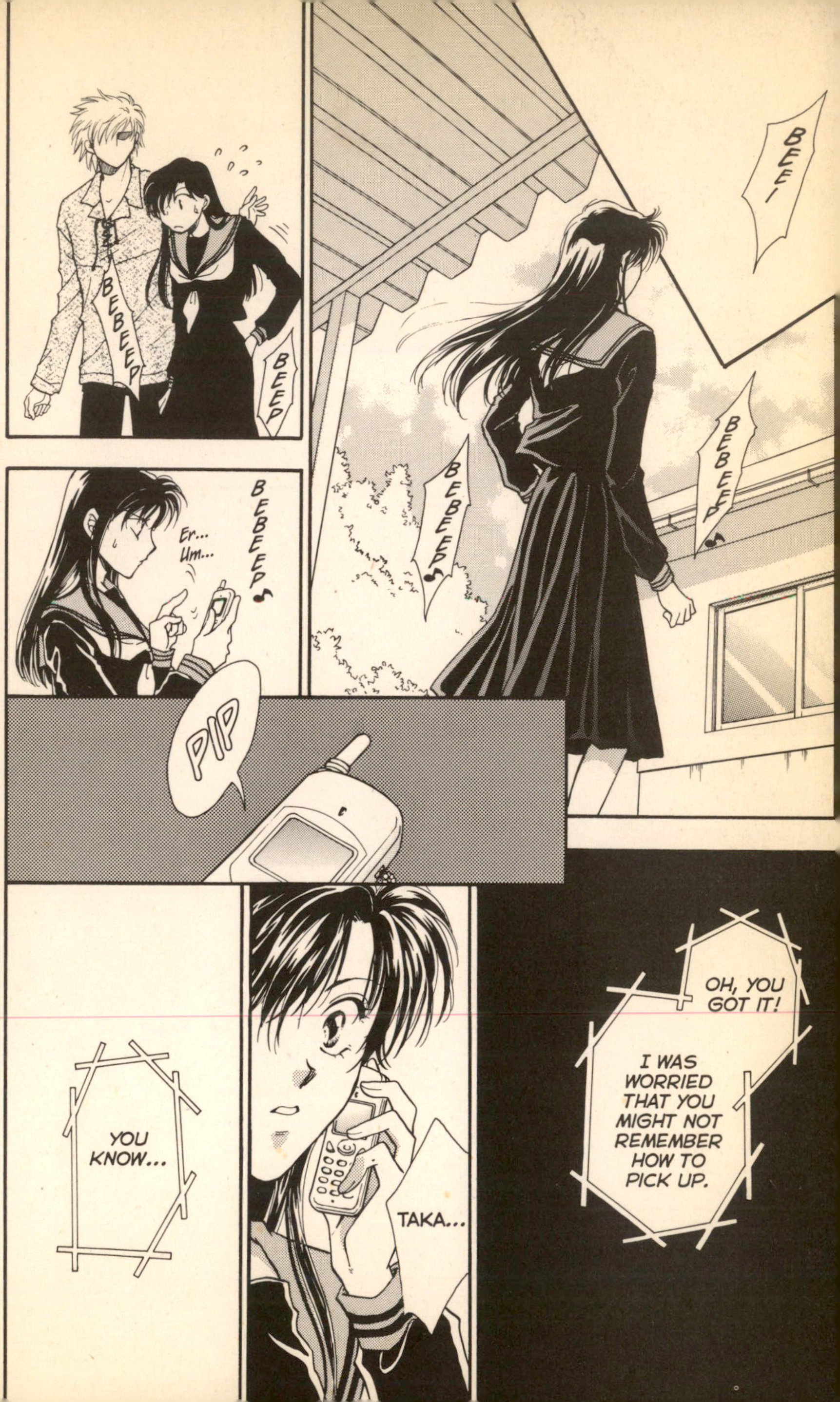
BEEE
BEBEEP
BEBEEP
BEEP
BEBEEP
BEBEEP
Er... Um...
PIP
OH, YOU GOT IT!
I WAS WORRIED THAT YOU MIGHT NOT REMEMBER HOW TO PICK UP.
TAKA...
YOU KNOW...

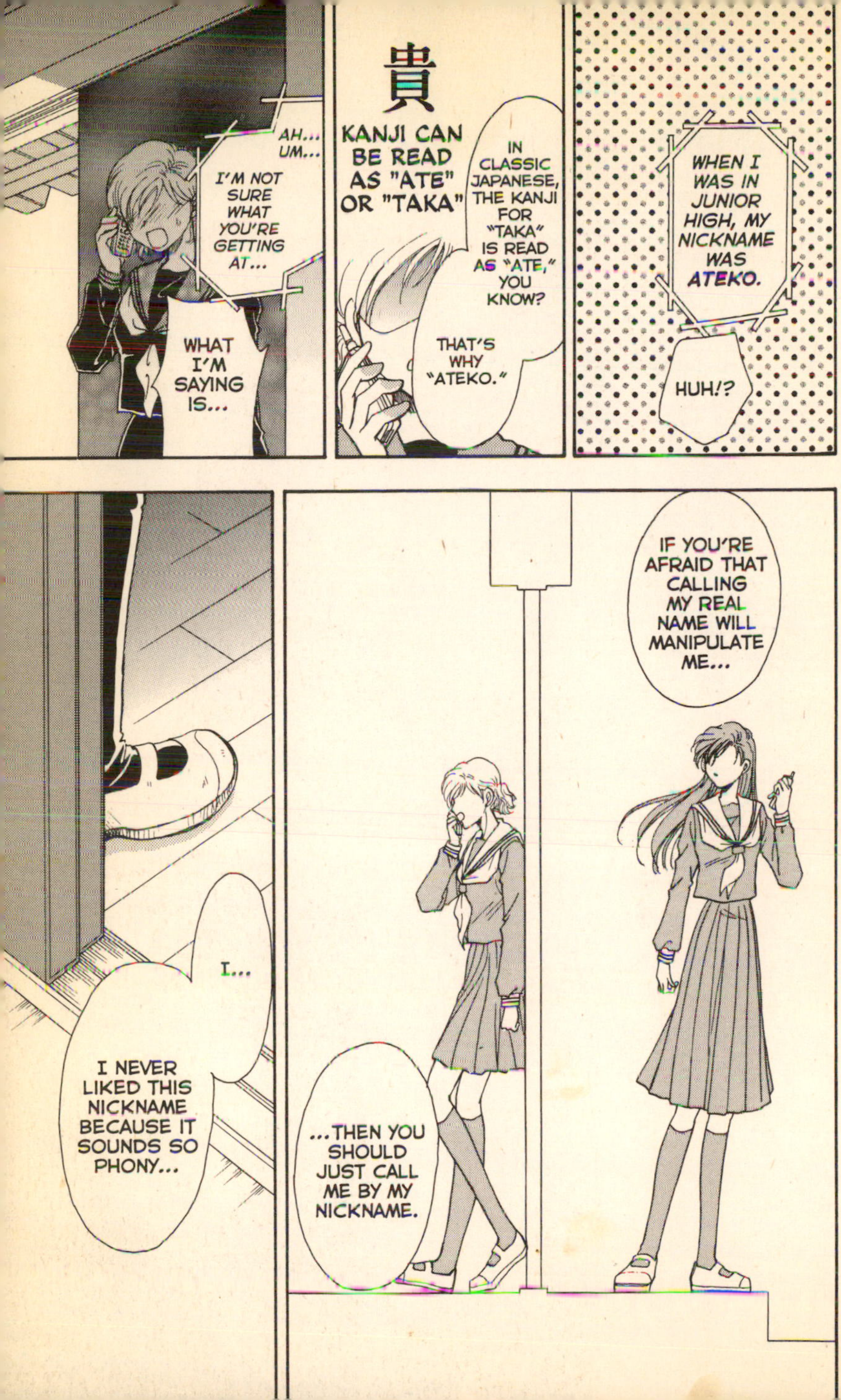
WHEN I WAS IN JUNIOR HIGH, MY NICKNAME WAS ATEKO.
HUH!?
貴
KANJI CAN BE READ AS "ATE" OR "TAKA"
IN CLASSIC JAPANESE, THE KANJI FOR "TAKA" IS READ AS "ATE," YOU KNOW?
THAT'S WHY "ATEKO."
AH... UM...
I'M NOT SURE WHAT YOU'RE GETTING AT...
WHAT I'M SAYING IS...
IF YOU'RE AFRAID THAT CALLING MY REAL NAME WILL MANIPULATE ME...
...THEN YOU SHOULD JUST CALL ME BY MY NICKNAME.
I...
I NEVER LIKED THIS NICKNAME BECAUSE IT SOUNDS SO PHONY...

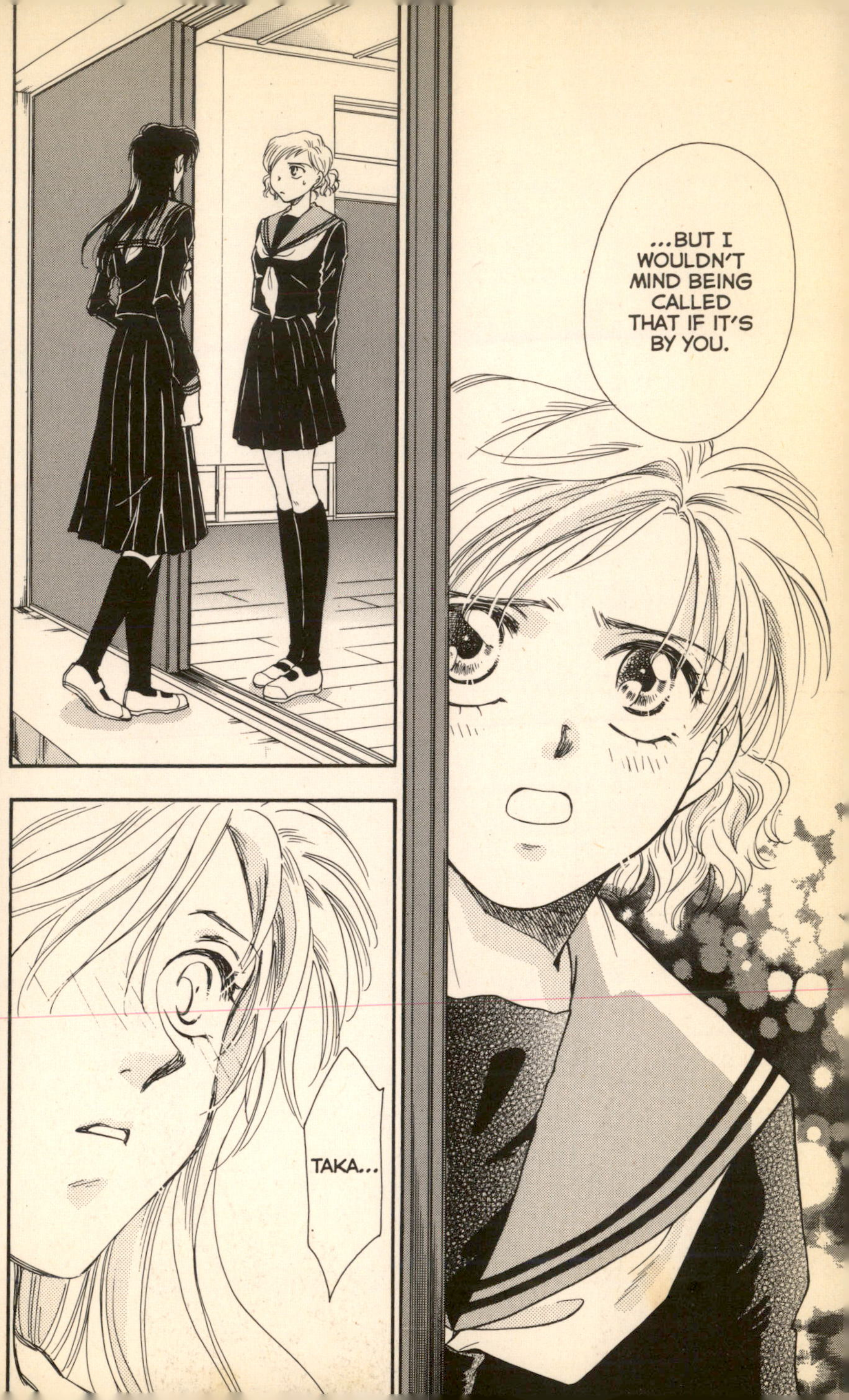
...BUT I WOULDN'T MIND BEING CALLED THAT IF IT'S BY YOU.
TAKA...

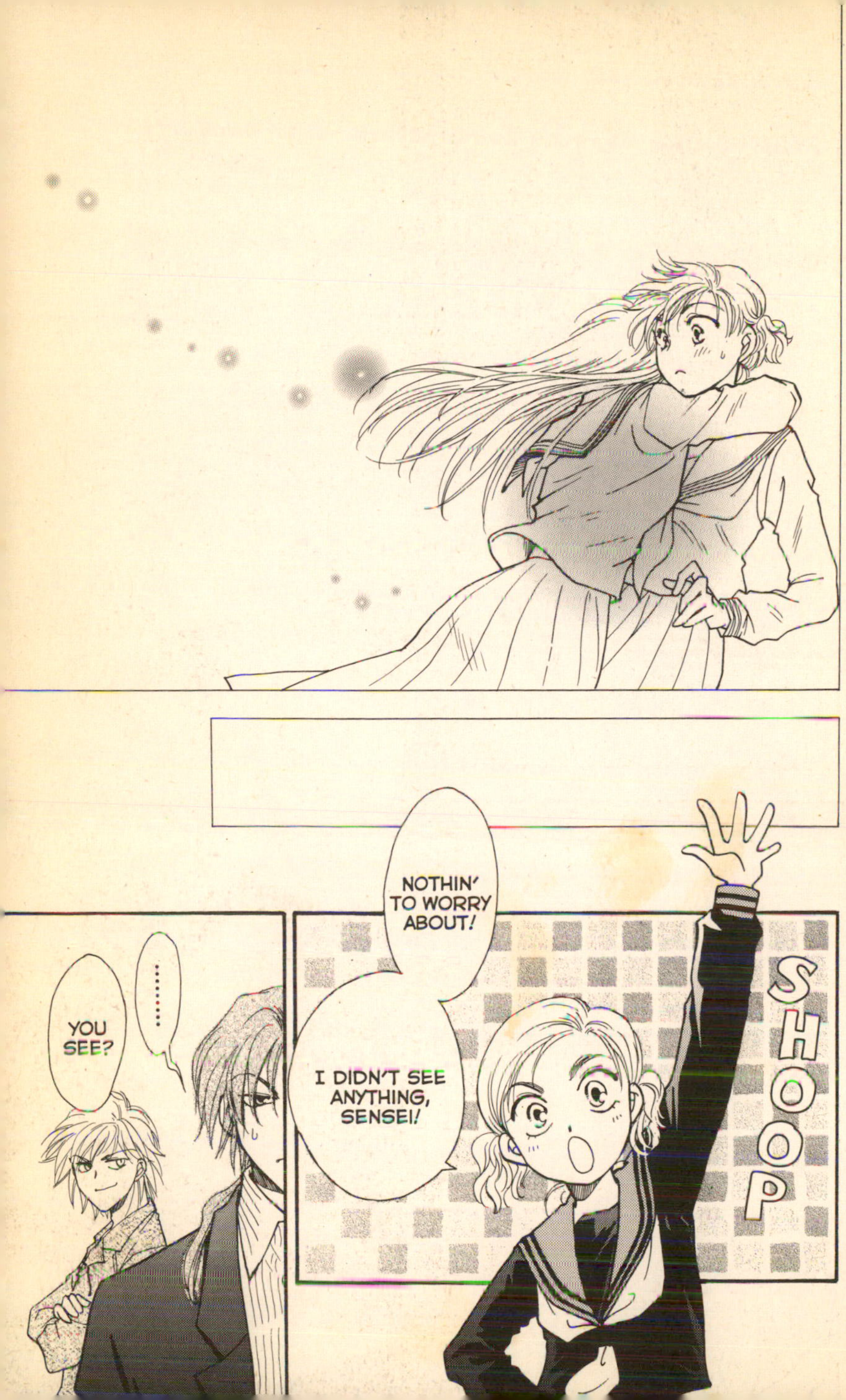
NOTHIN' TO WORRY ABOUT!
I DIDN'T SEE ANYTHING, SENSEI!
SHOOP
......
YOU SEE?

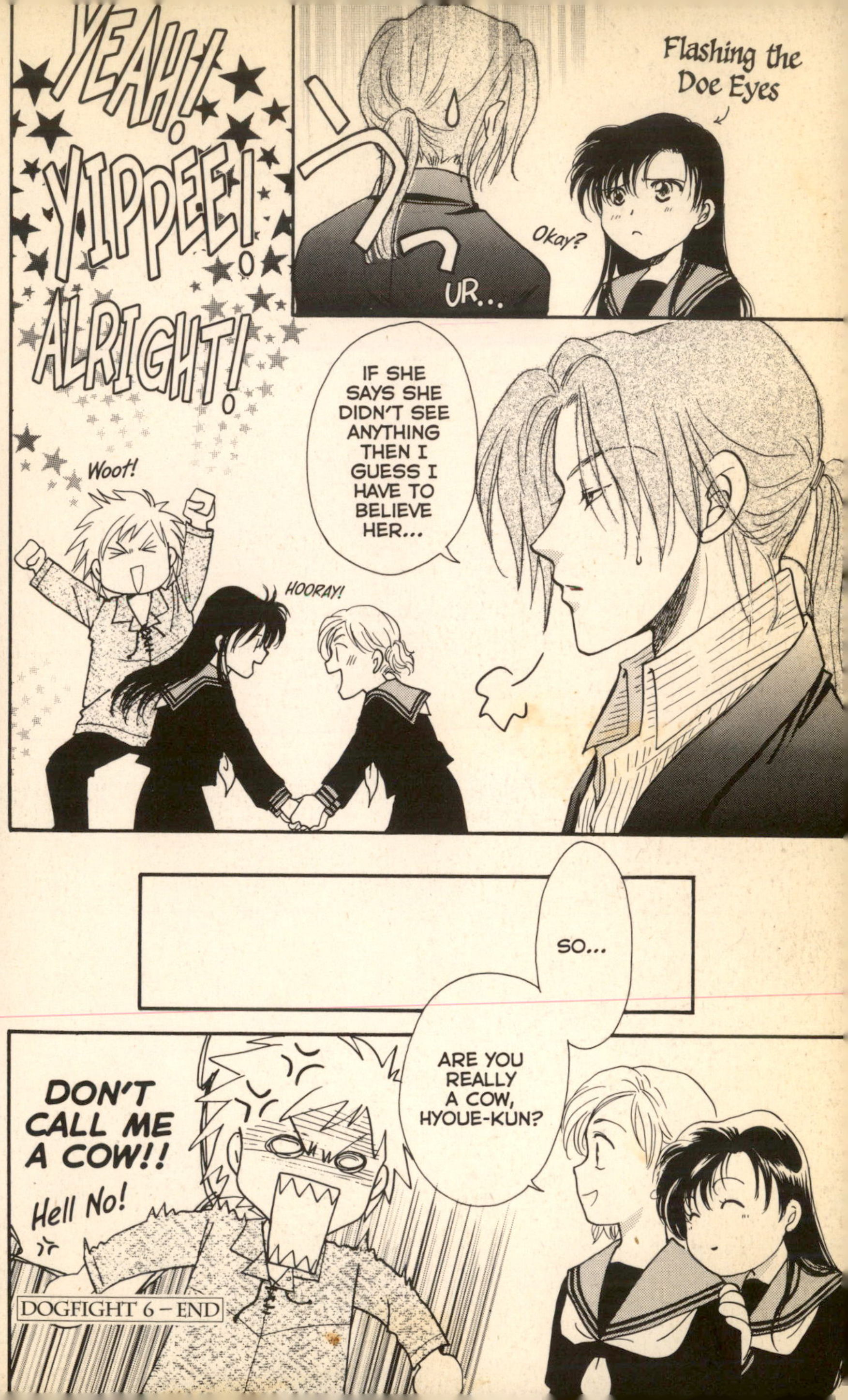
Flashing the Doe Eyes
Okay?
UR...
IF SHE SAYS SHE DIDN'T SEE ANYTHING THEN I GUESS I HAVE TO BELIEVE HER...
YEAH!
YIPPEE!
ALRIGHT!
HOORAY!
Woot!
SO...
ARE YOU REALLY A COW, HYOUE-KUN?
DON'T CALL ME A COW!!
Hell No!
DOGFIGHT 6 – END

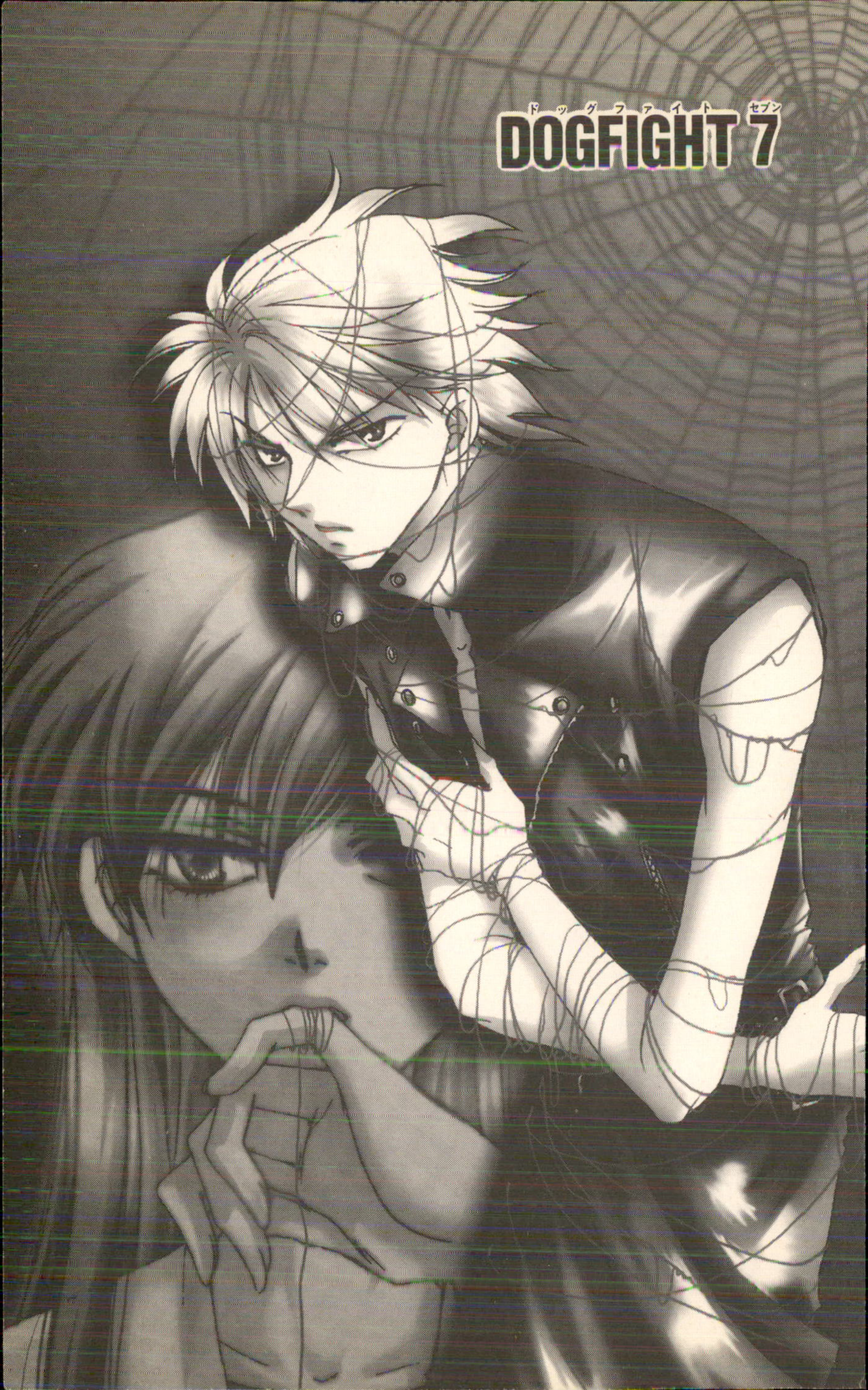
ドッグファイト セブン
DOGFIGHT 7

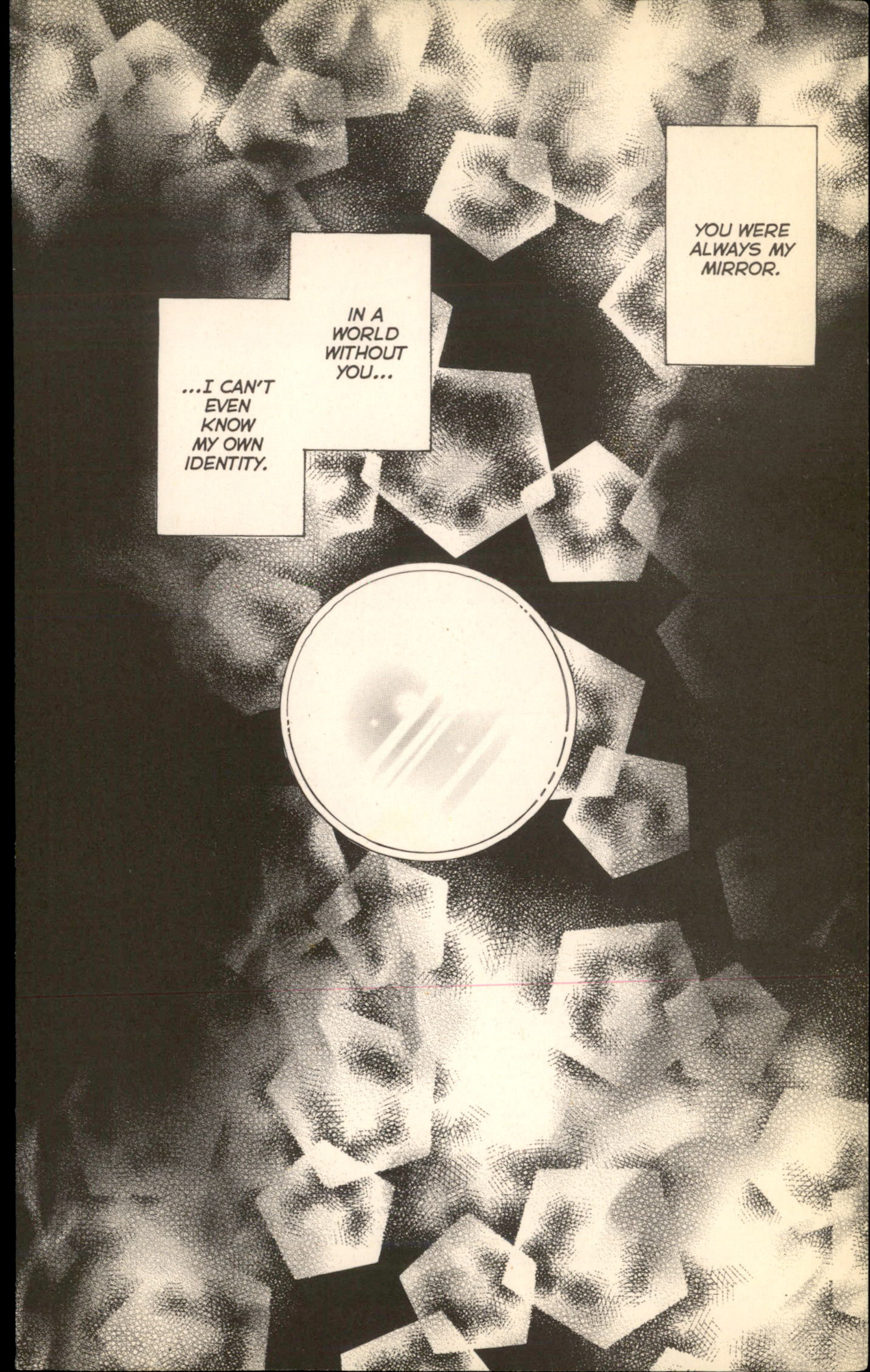
YOU WERE ALWAYS MY MIRROR.
IN A WORLD WITHOUT YOU...
...I CAN'T EVEN KNOW MY OWN IDENTITY.

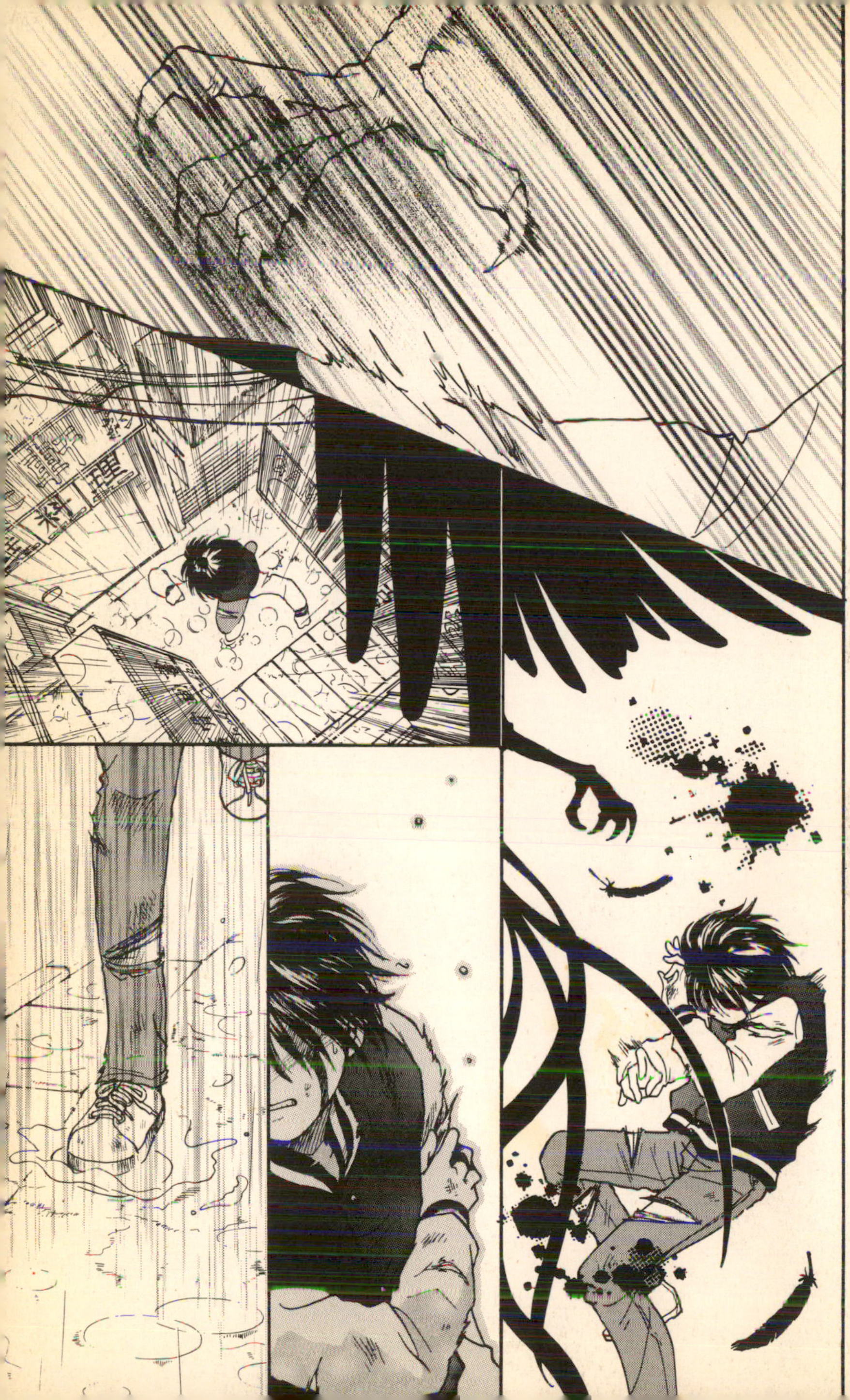

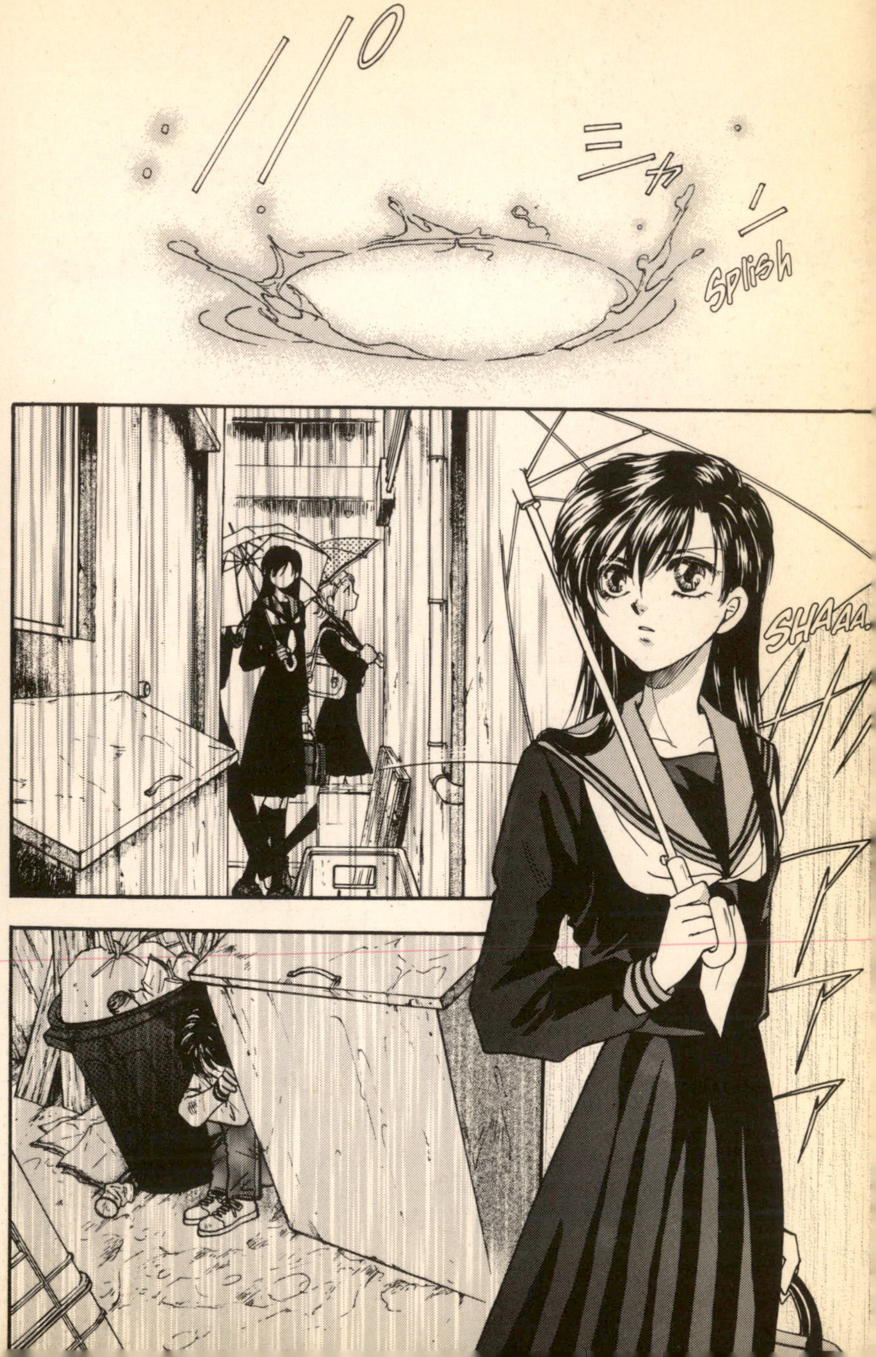
Splish
SHAAA...

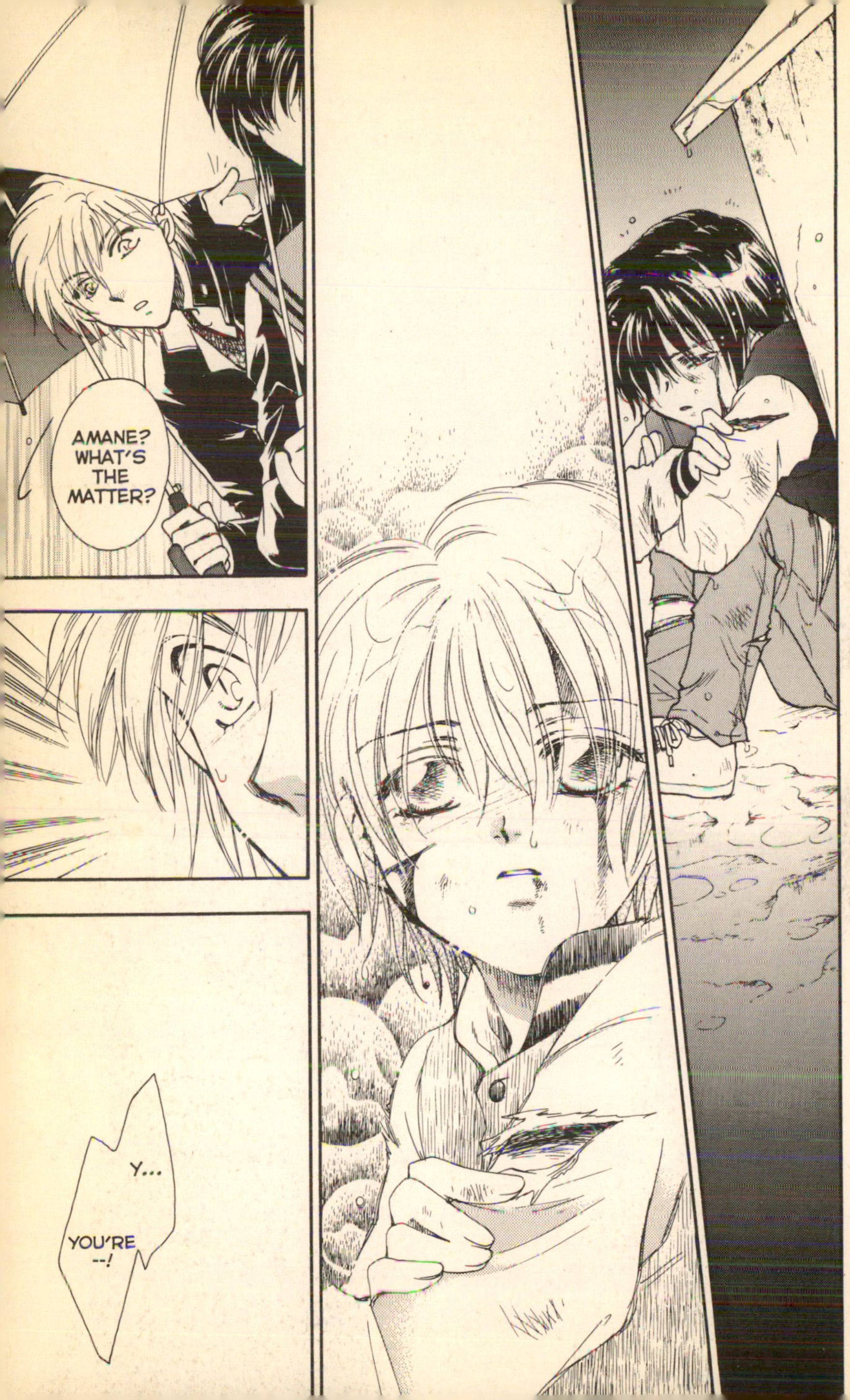
AMANE? WHAT'S THE MATTER?
Y...
YOU'RE --!

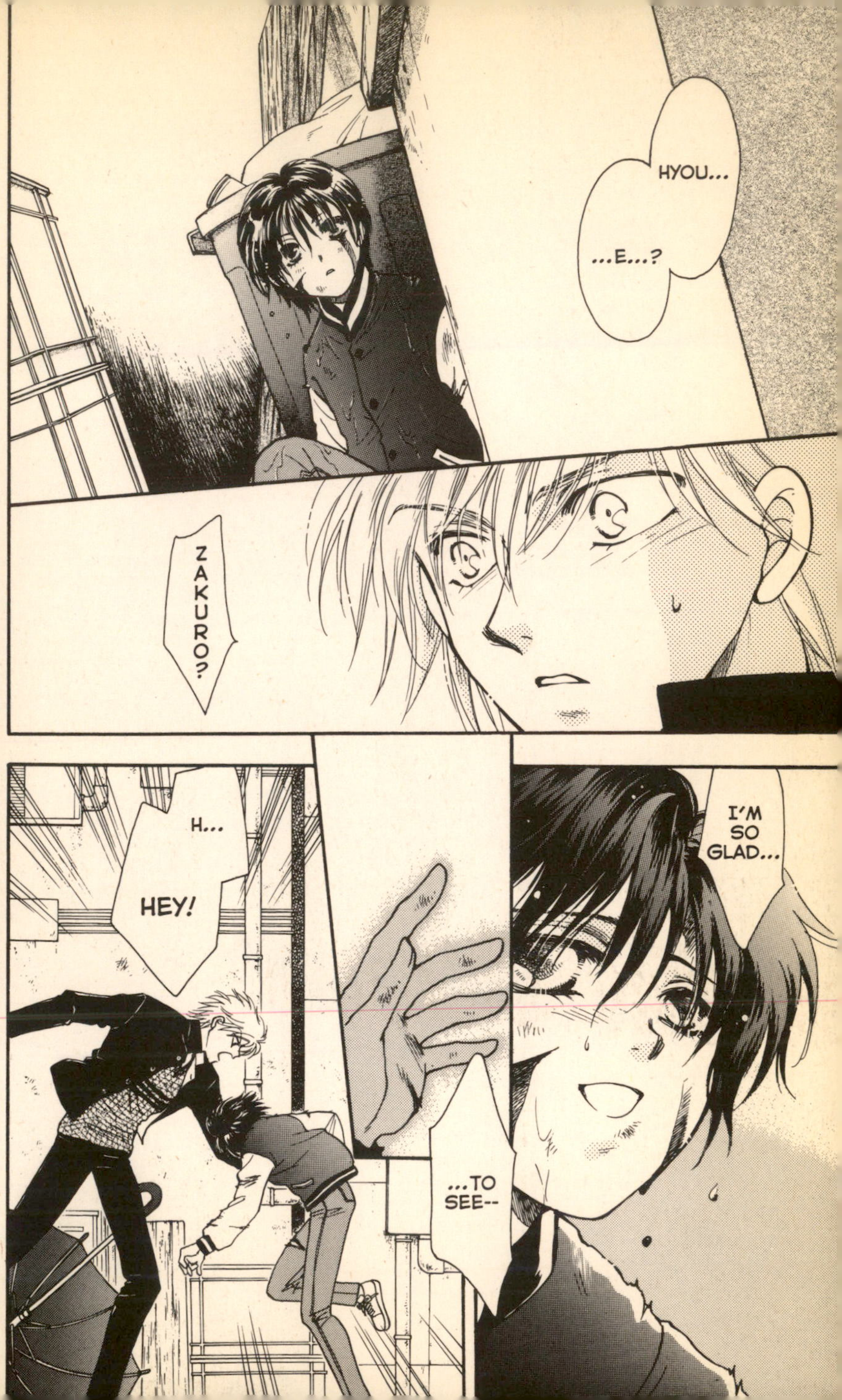
HYOU...
...E...?
ZAKURO?
I'M SO GLAD...
...TO SEE--
H...
HEY!

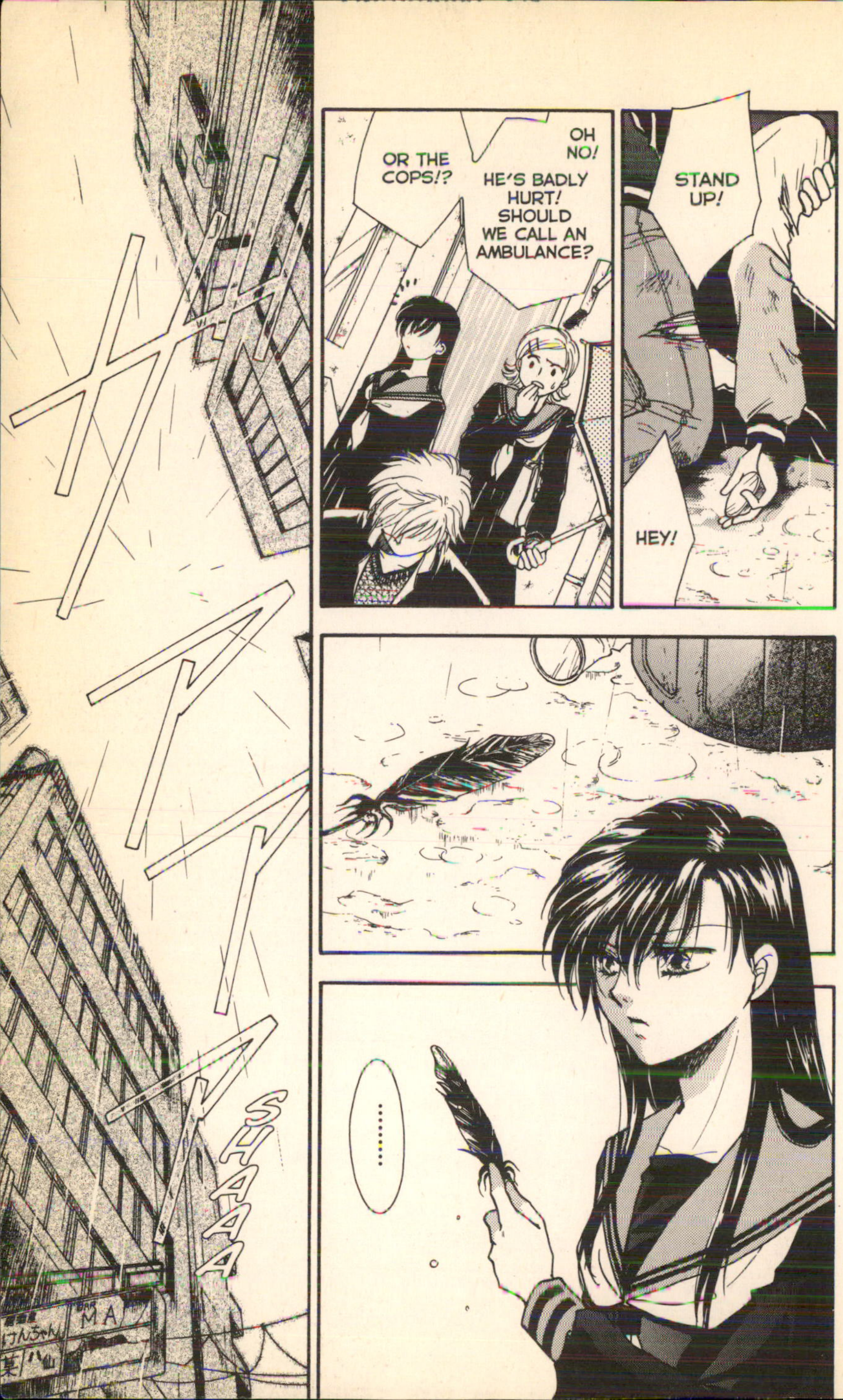
STAND UP!
HEY!
OH NO!
HE'S BADLY HURT! SHOULD WE CALL AN AMBULANCE?
OR THE COPS!?
......
SHAAAA

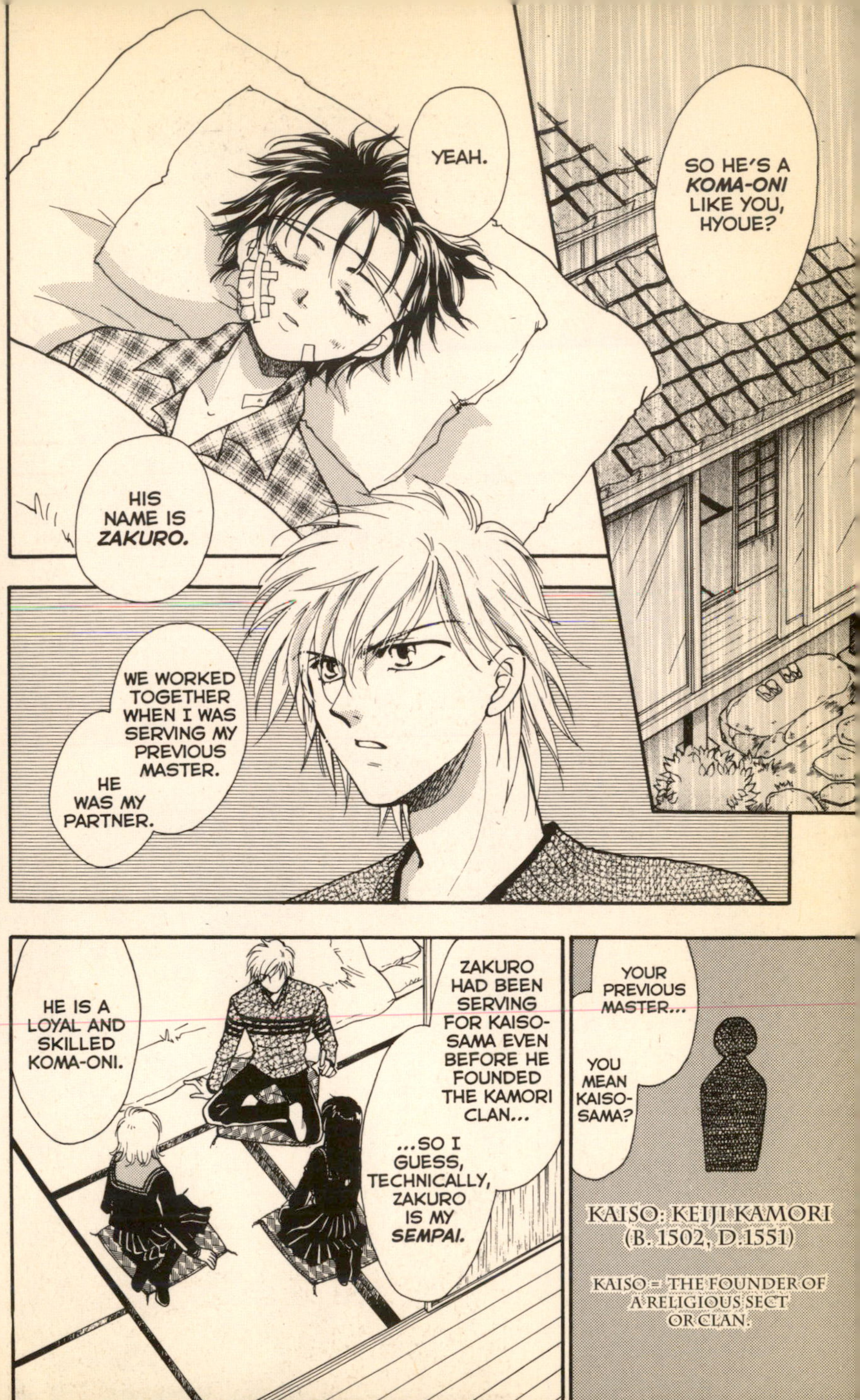
SO HE'S A KOMA-ONI LIKE YOU, HYOUE?
YEAH.
HIS NAME IS ZAKURO.
WE WORKED TOGETHER WHEN I WAS SERVING MY PREVIOUS MASTER.
HE WAS MY PARTNER.
YOUR PREVIOUS MASTER...
YOU MEAN KAISO-SAMA?
KAISO: KEIJI KAMORI (B. 1502, D.1551)
KAISO = THE FOUNDER OF A RELIGIOUS SECT OR CLAN.
ZAKURO HAD BEEN SERVING FOR KAISO-SAMA EVEN BEFORE HE FOUNDED THE KAMORI CLAN...
...SO I GUESS, TECHNICALLY, ZAKURO IS MY SEMPAI.
HE IS A LOYAL AND SKILLED KOMA-ONI.

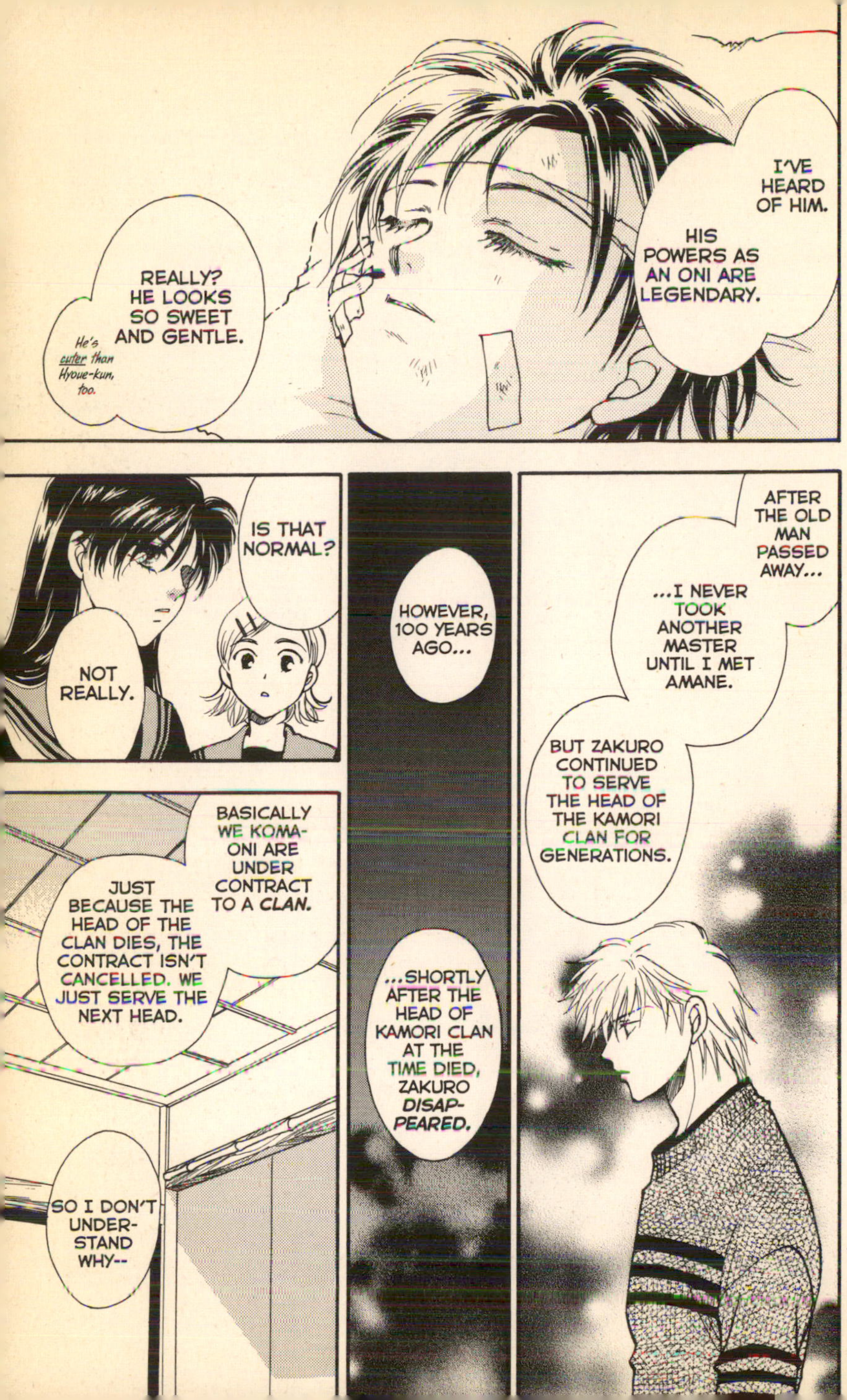
I'VE HEARD OF HIM.
HIS POWERS AS AN ONI ARE LEGENDARY.
REALLY? HE LOOKS SO SWEET AND GENTLE.
He's cuter than Hyoue-kun, too.
AFTER THE OLD MAN PASSED AWAY...
...I NEVER TOOK ANOTHER MASTER UNTIL I MET AMANE.
BUT ZAKURO CONTINUED TO SERVE THE HEAD OF THE KAMORI CLAN FOR GENERATIONS.
HOWEVER, 100 YEARS AGO...
...SHORTLY AFTER THE HEAD OF KAMORI CLAN AT THE TIME DIED, ZAKURO DISAPPEARED.
IS THAT NORMAL?
NOT REALLY.
BASICALLY WE KOMA-ONI ARE UNDER CONTRACT TO A CLAN.
JUST BECAUSE THE HEAD OF THE CLAN DIES, THE CONTRACT ISN'T CANCELLED. WE JUST SERVE THE NEXT HEAD.
SO I DON'T UNDERSTAND WHY--

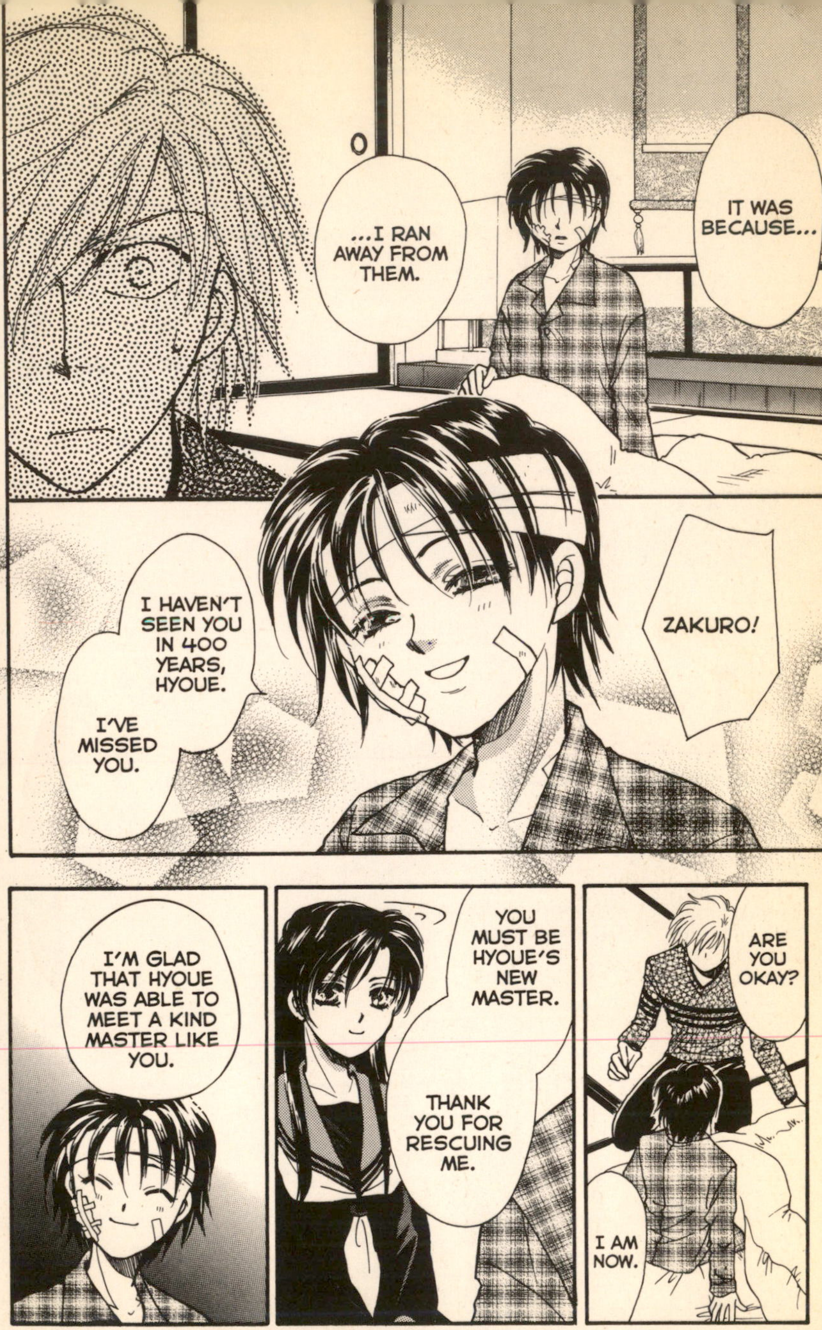
IT WAS BECAUSE...
...I RAN AWAY FROM THEM.
ZAKURO!
I HAVEN'T SEEN YOU IN 400 YEARS, HYOUE.
I'VE MISSED YOU.
ARE YOU OKAY?
I AM NOW.
YOU MUST BE HYOUE'S NEW MASTER.
THANK YOU FOR RESCUING ME.
I'M GLAD THAT HYOUE WAS ABLE TO MEET A KIND MASTER LIKE YOU.

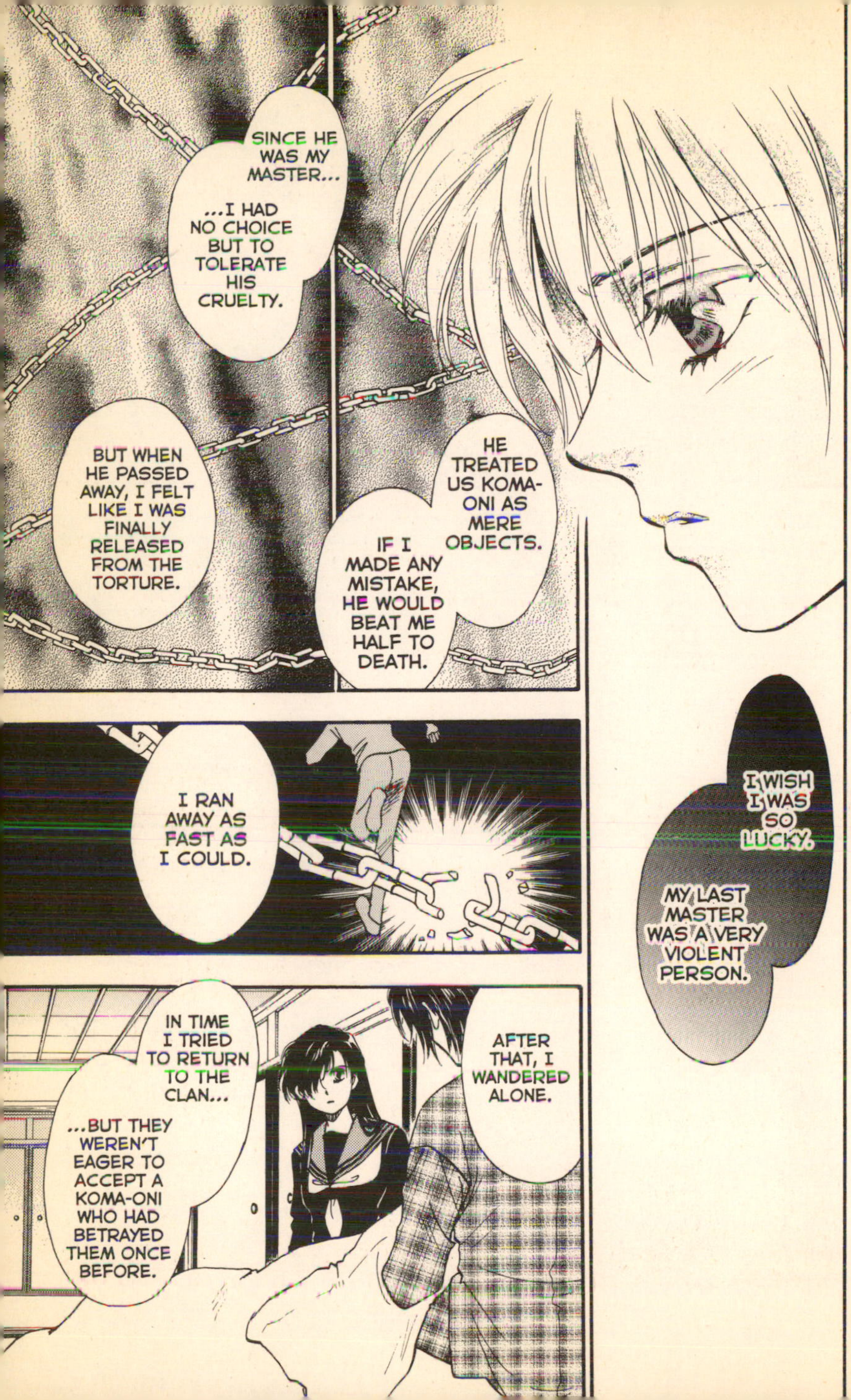
I WISH I WAS SO LUCKY.
MY LAST MASTER WAS A VERY VIOLENT PERSON.
HE TREATED US KOMA-ONI AS MERE OBJECTS.
IF I MADE ANY MISTAKE, HE WOULD BEAT ME HALF TO DEATH.
SINCE HE WAS MY MASTER...
...I HAD NO CHOICE BUT TO TOLERATE HIS CRUELTY.
BUT WHEN HE PASSED AWAY, I FELT LIKE I WAS FINALLY RELEASED FROM THE TORTURE.
I RAN AWAY AS FAST AS I COULD.
AFTER THAT, I WANDERED ALONE.
IN TIME I TRIED TO RETURN TO THE CLAN...
...BUT THEY WEREN'T EAGER TO ACCEPT A KOMA-ONI WHO HAD BETRAYED THEM ONCE BEFORE.

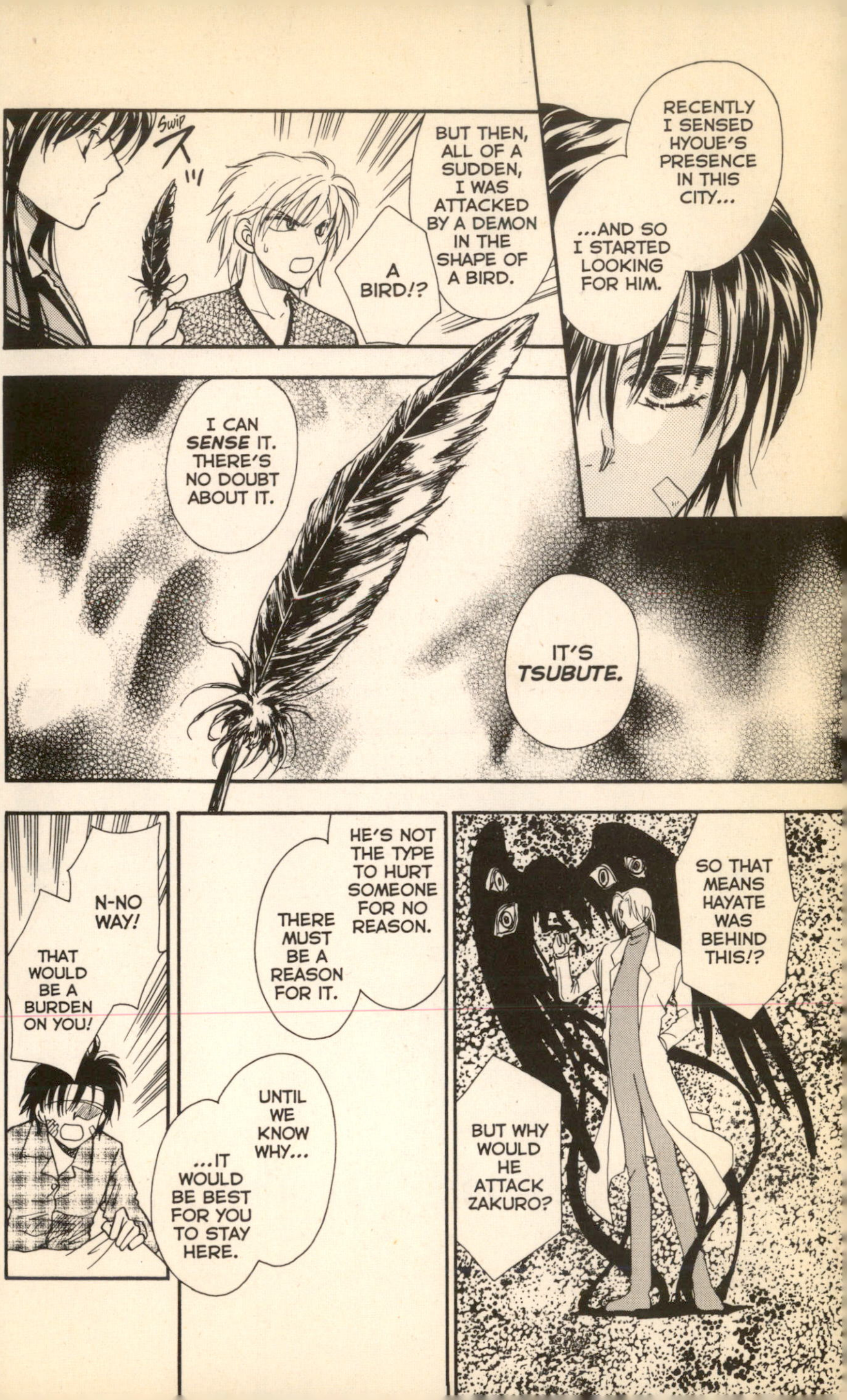
RECENTLY I SENSED HYOUE'S PRESENCE IN THIS CITY...
...AND SO I STARTED LOOKING FOR HIM.
BUT THEN, ALL OF A SUDDEN, I WAS ATTACKED BY A DEMON IN THE SHAPE OF A BIRD.
A BIRD!?
Swip
I CAN SENSE IT. THERE'S NO DOUBT ABOUT IT.
IT'S TSUBUTE.
SO THAT MEANS HAYATE WAS BEHIND THIS!?
BUT WHY WOULD HE ATTACK ZAKURO?
HE'S NOT THE TYPE TO HURT SOMEONE FOR NO REASON.
THERE MUST BE A REASON FOR IT.
UNTIL WE KNOW WHY...
...IT WOULD BE BEST FOR YOU TO STAY HERE.
N-NO WAY!
THAT WOULD BE A BURDEN ON YOU!

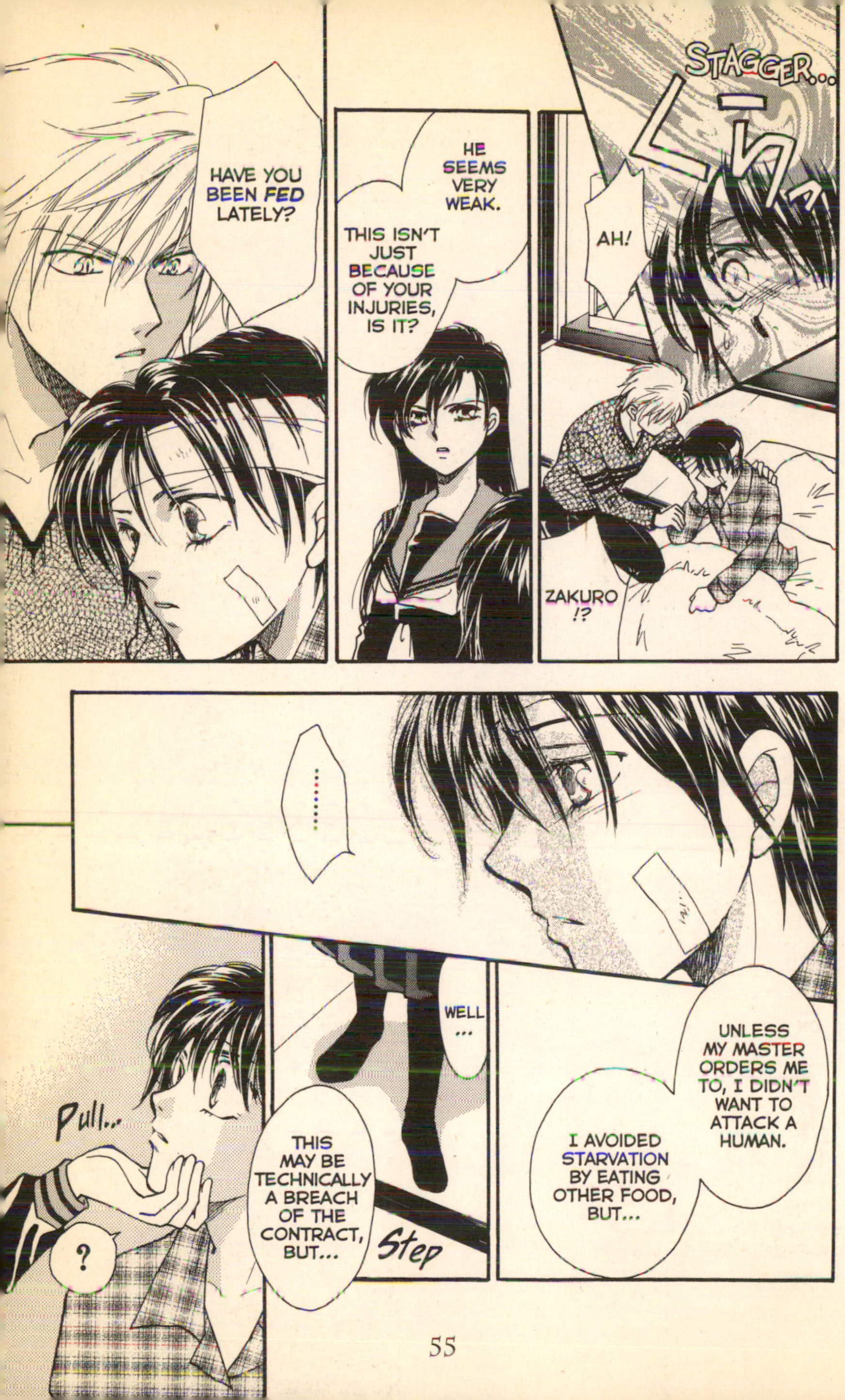
STAGGER...
AH!
ZAKURO !?
HE SEEMS VERY WEAK.
THIS ISN'T JUST BECAUSE OF YOUR INJURIES, IS IT?
HAVE YOU BEEN FED LATELY?
......
UNLESS MY MASTER ORDERS ME TO, I DIDN'T WANT TO ATTACK A HUMAN.
I AVOIDED STARVATION BY EATING OTHER FOOD, BUT...
WELL...
THIS MAY BE TECHNICALLY A BREACH OF THE CONTRACT, BUT...
Step
Pull...
?

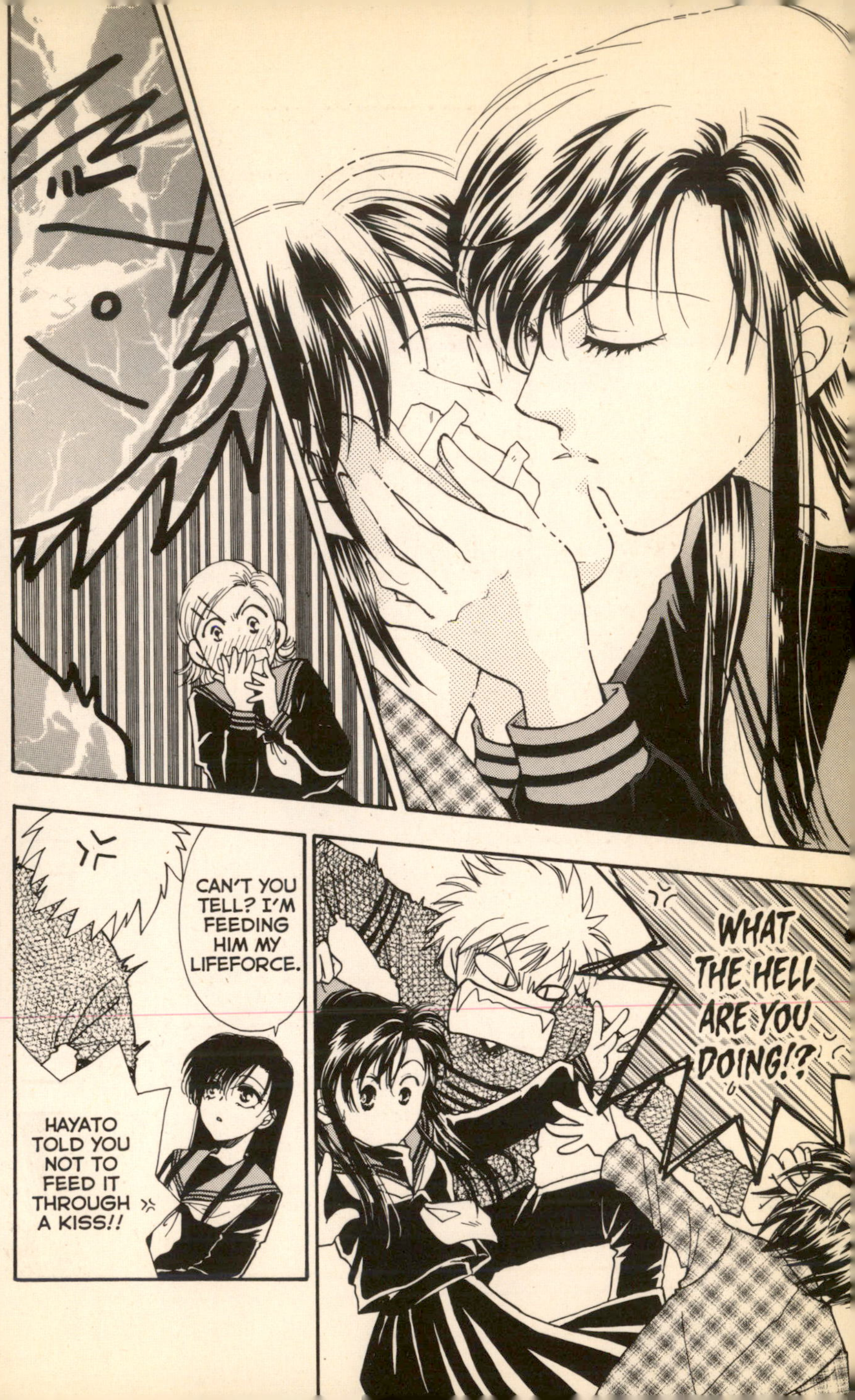
WHAT THE HELL ARE YOU DOING!?
CAN'T YOU TELL? I'M FEEDING HIM MY LIFEFORCE.
HAYATO TOLD YOU NOT TO FEED IT THROUGH A KISS!!

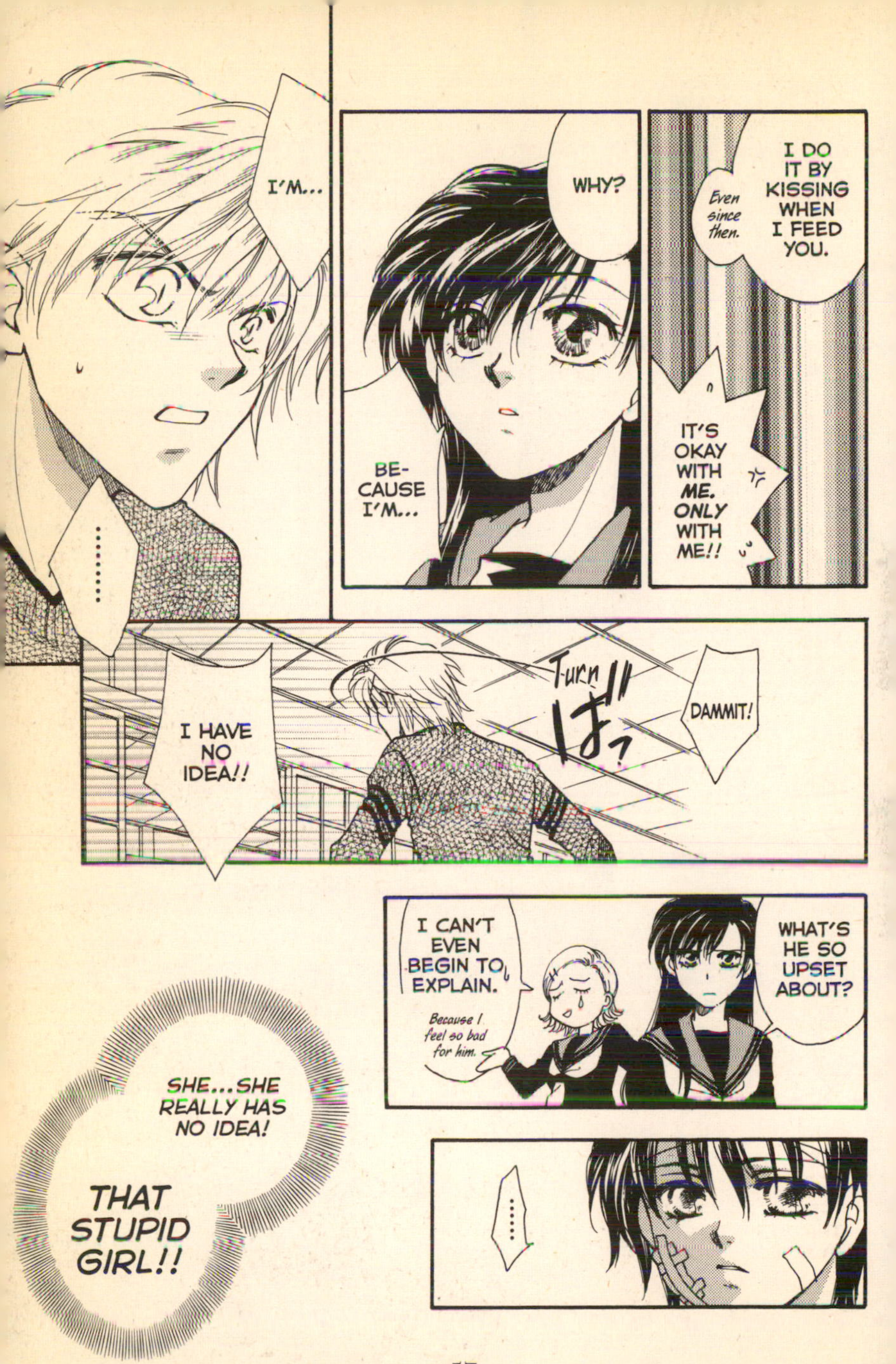
I DO IT BY KISSING WHEN I FEED YOU.
Even since then.
IT'S OKAY WITH ME. ONLY WITH ME!!
WHY?
BECAUSE I'M...
I'M...
......
DAMMIT!
Turn ばっ
I HAVE NO IDEA!!
WHAT'S HE SO UPSET ABOUT?
I CAN'T EVEN BEGIN TO EXPLAIN.
Because I feel so bad for him.
......
SHE...SHE REALLY HAS NO IDEA!
THAT STUPID GIRL!!

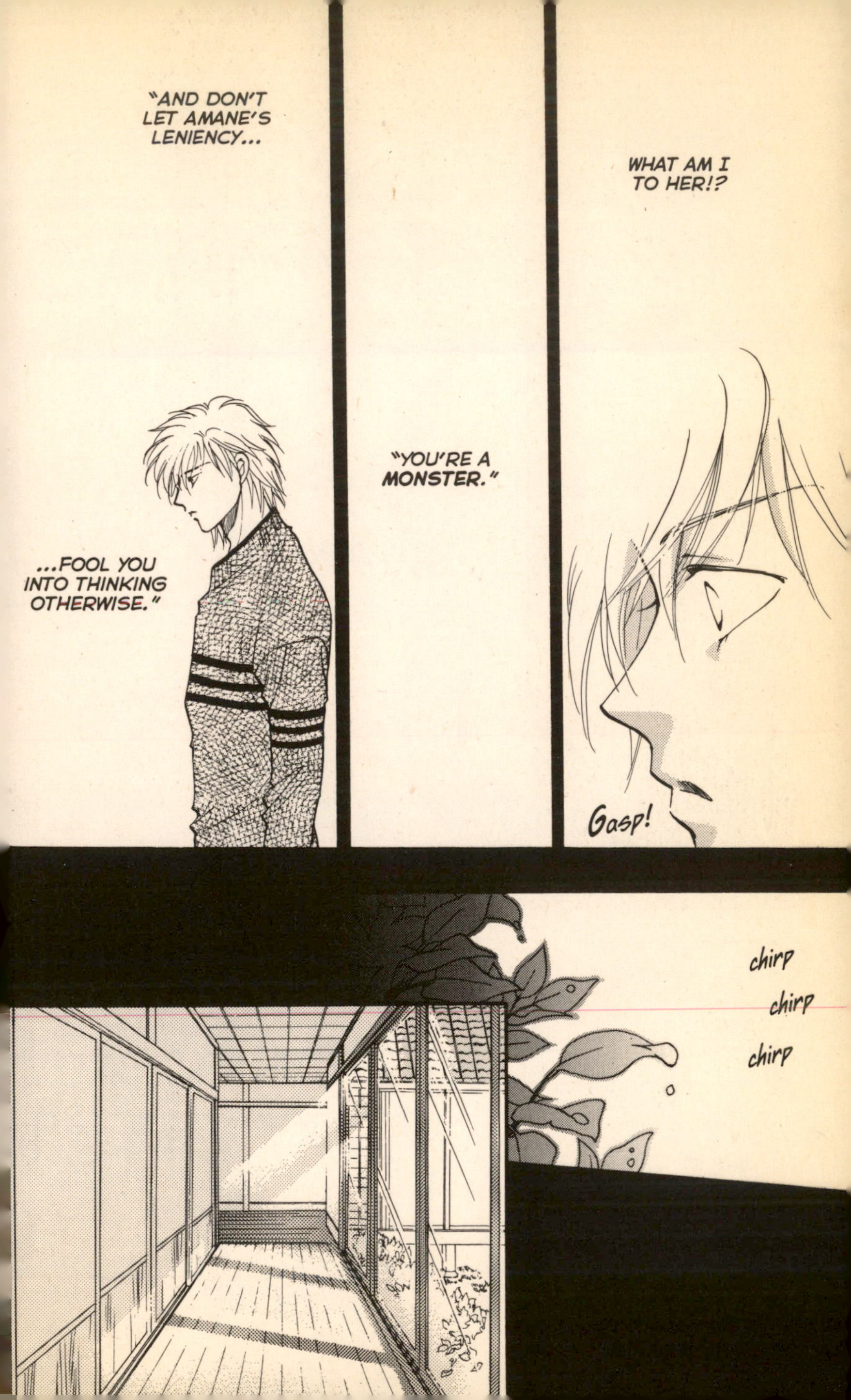
WHAT AM I TO HER!?
Gasp!
"YOU'RE A MONSTER."
"AND DON'T LET AMANE'S LENIENCY...
...FOOL YOU INTO THINKING OTHERWISE."
chirp
chirp
chirp

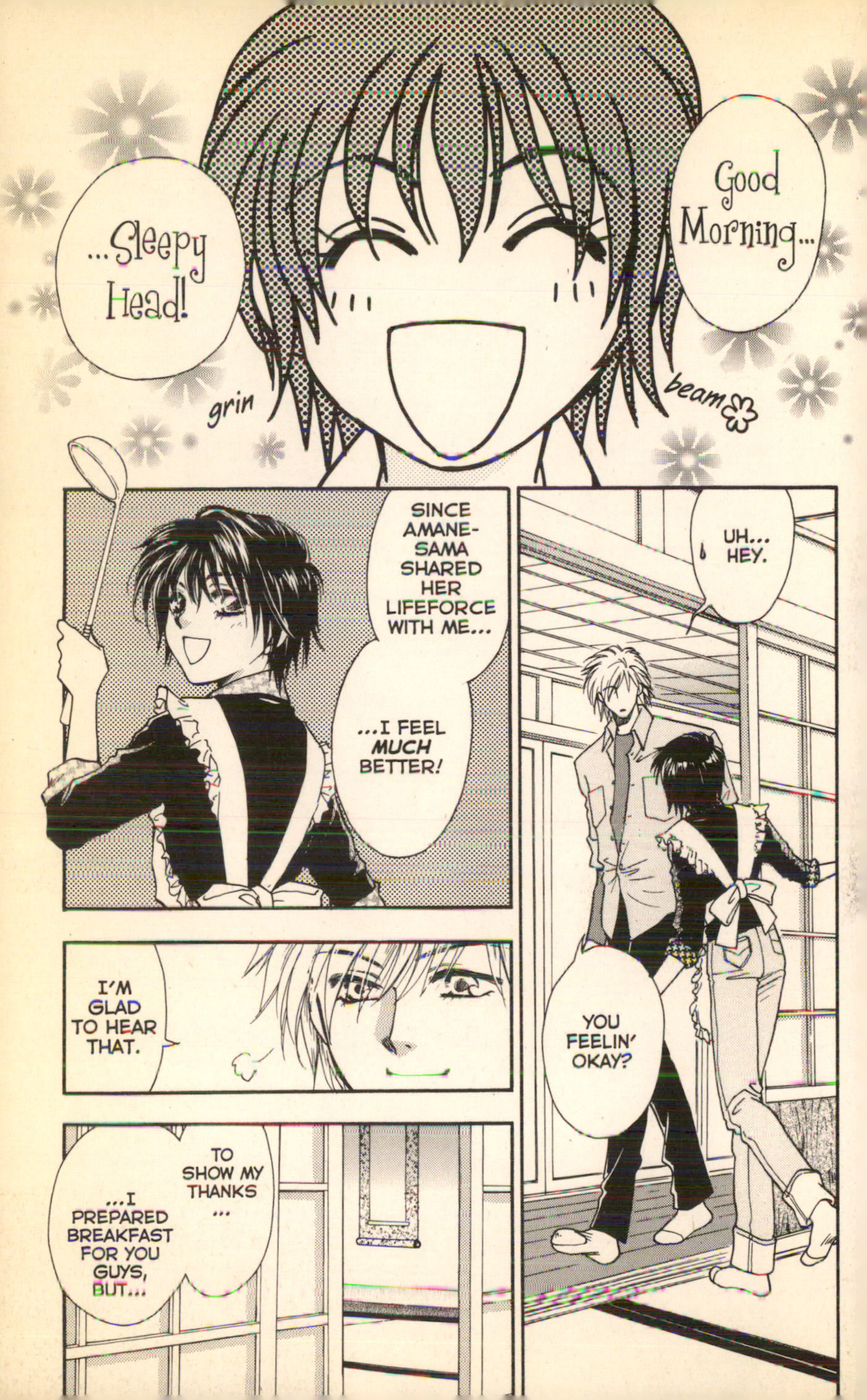
Good Morning...
beam
...Sleepy Head!
grin
UH... HEY.
YOU FEELIN' OKAY?
SINCE AMANE-SAMA SHARED HER LIFEFORCE WITH ME...
...I FEEL *MUCH* BETTER!
I'M GLAD TO HEAR THAT.
TO SHOW MY THANKS...
...I PREPARED BREAKFAST FOR YOU GUYS, BUT...

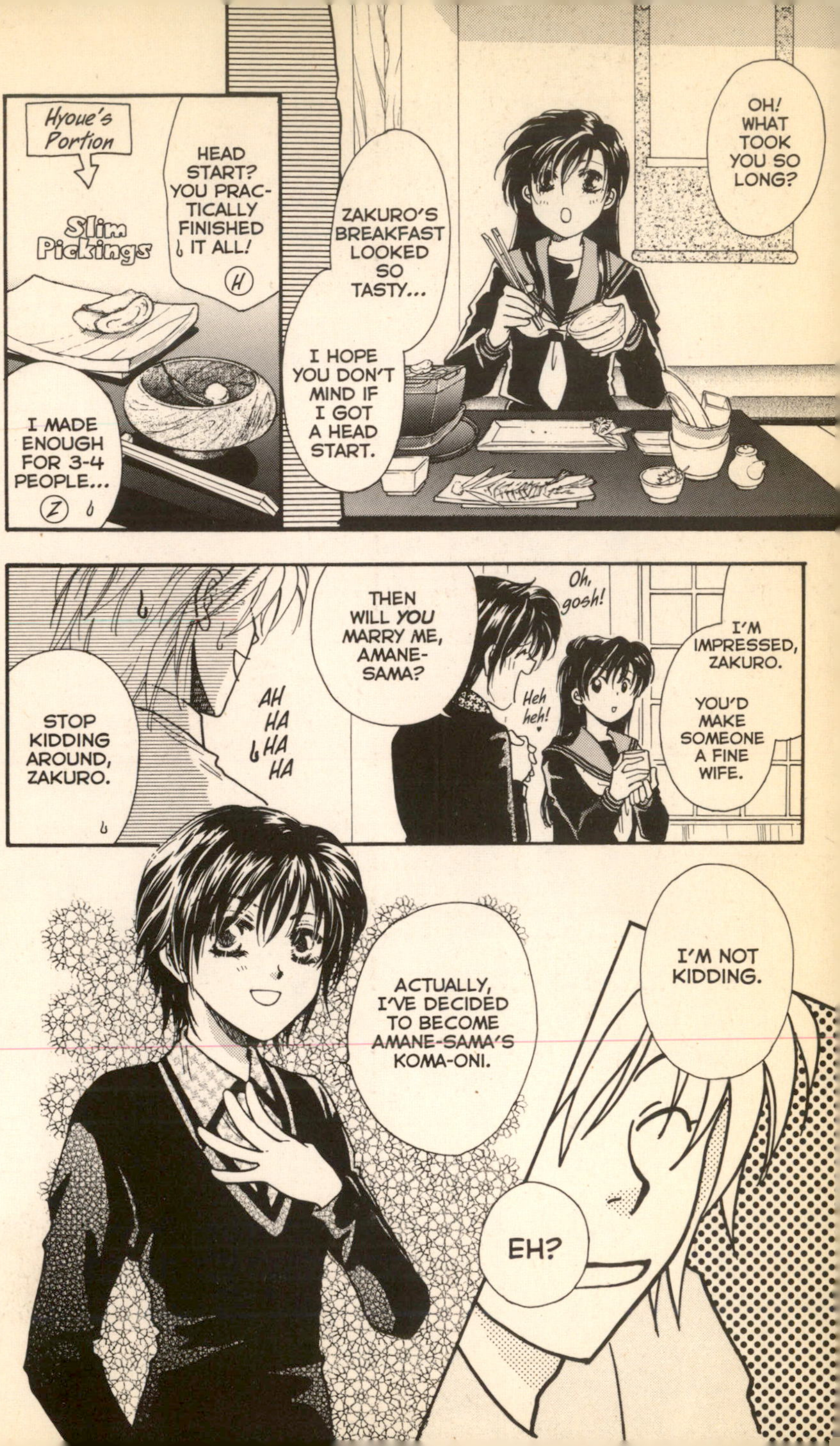
OH! WHAT TOOK YOU SO LONG?
ZAKURO'S BREAKFAST LOOKED SO TASTY...
I HOPE YOU DON'T MIND IF I GOT A HEAD START.
HEAD START? YOU PRACTICALLY FINISHED IT ALL!
H
Hyoue's Portion
Slim Pickings
I MADE ENOUGH FOR 3-4 PEOPLE...
Z
I'M IMPRESSED, ZAKURO.
YOU'D MAKE SOMEONE A FINE WIFE.
Oh, gosh!
Heh heh!
THEN WILL *YOU* MARRY ME, AMANE-SAMA?
AH HA HA HA
STOP KIDDING AROUND, ZAKURO.
I'M NOT KIDDING.
ACTUALLY, I'VE DECIDED TO BECOME AMANE-SAMA'S KOMA-ONI.
EH?

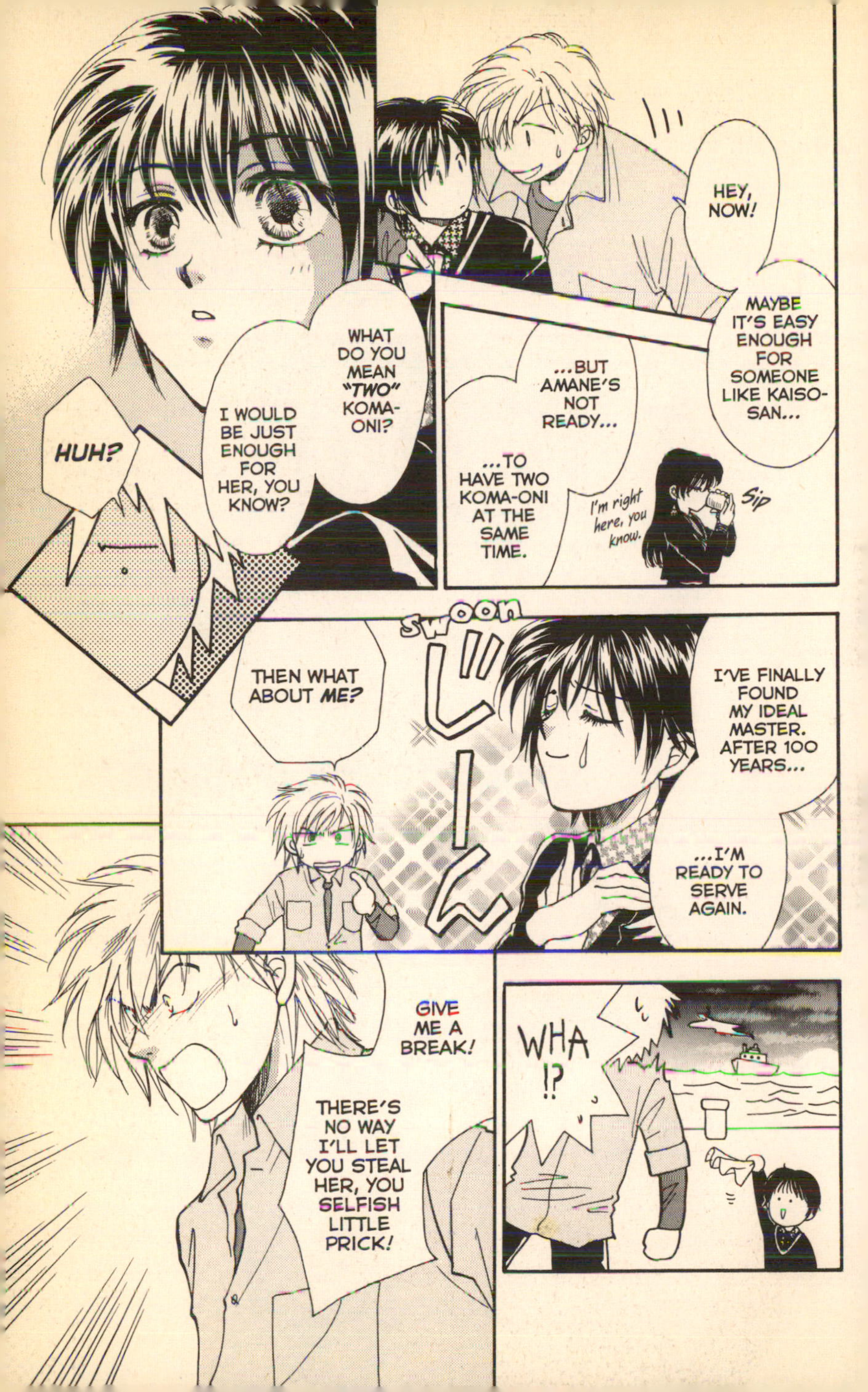

HEY, NOW!
MAYBE IT'S EASY ENOUGH FOR SOMEONE LIKE KAISO-SAN...
...BUT AMANE'S NOT READY...
...TO HAVE TWO KOMA-ONI AT THE SAME TIME.
I'm right here, you know.
Sip
WHAT DO YOU MEAN "TWO" KOMA-ONI?
I WOULD BE JUST ENOUGH FOR HER, YOU KNOW?
HUH?
SWOON
I'VE FINALLY FOUND MY IDEAL MASTER. AFTER 100 YEARS...
...I'M READY TO SERVE AGAIN.
じ〜ん
THEN WHAT ABOUT ME?
WHA !?
GIVE ME A BREAK!
THERE'S NO WAY I'LL LET YOU STEAL HER, YOU SELFISH LITTLE PRICK!

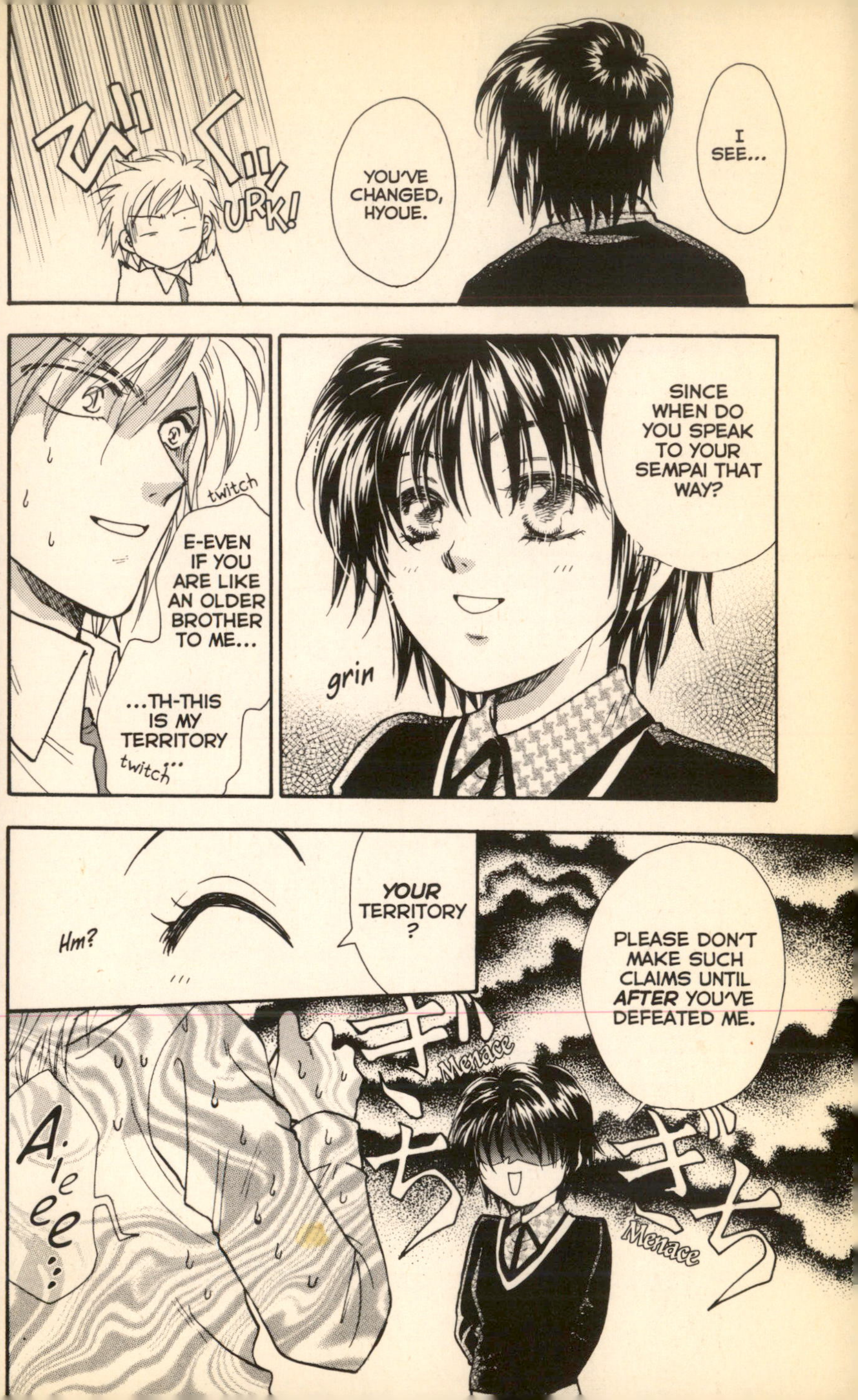
I SEE...
YOU'VE CHANGED, HYOUE.
URK!
SINCE WHEN DO YOU SPEAK TO YOUR SEMPAI THAT WAY?
grin
twitch
E-EVEN IF YOU ARE LIKE AN OLDER BROTHER TO ME...
...TH-THIS IS MY TERRITORY...
twitch
YOUR TERRITORY?
Hm?
PLEASE DON'T MAKE SUCH CLAIMS UNTIL *AFTER* YOU'VE DEFEATED ME.
Menace
Menace
Aieee...

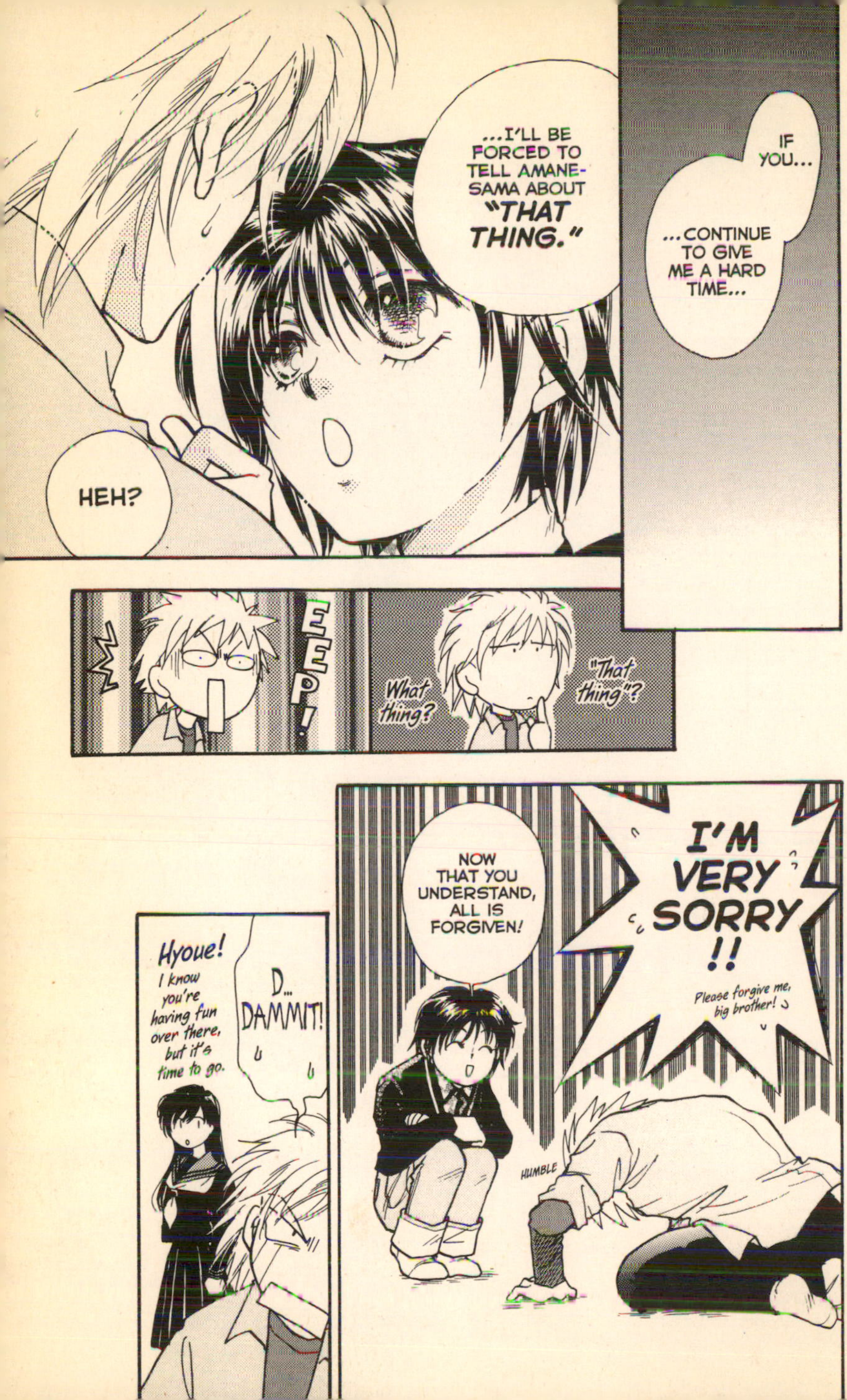
IF YOU...
...CONTINUE TO GIVE ME A HARD TIME...
...I'LL BE FORCED TO TELL AMANE-SAMA ABOUT "THAT THING."
HEH?
"That thing"?
What thing?
EEEP!
I'M VERY SORRY!!
Please forgive me, big brother!
NOW THAT YOU UNDERSTAND, ALL IS FORGIVEN!
HUMBLE
D... DAMMIT!
Hyoue! I know you're having fun over there, but it's time to go.

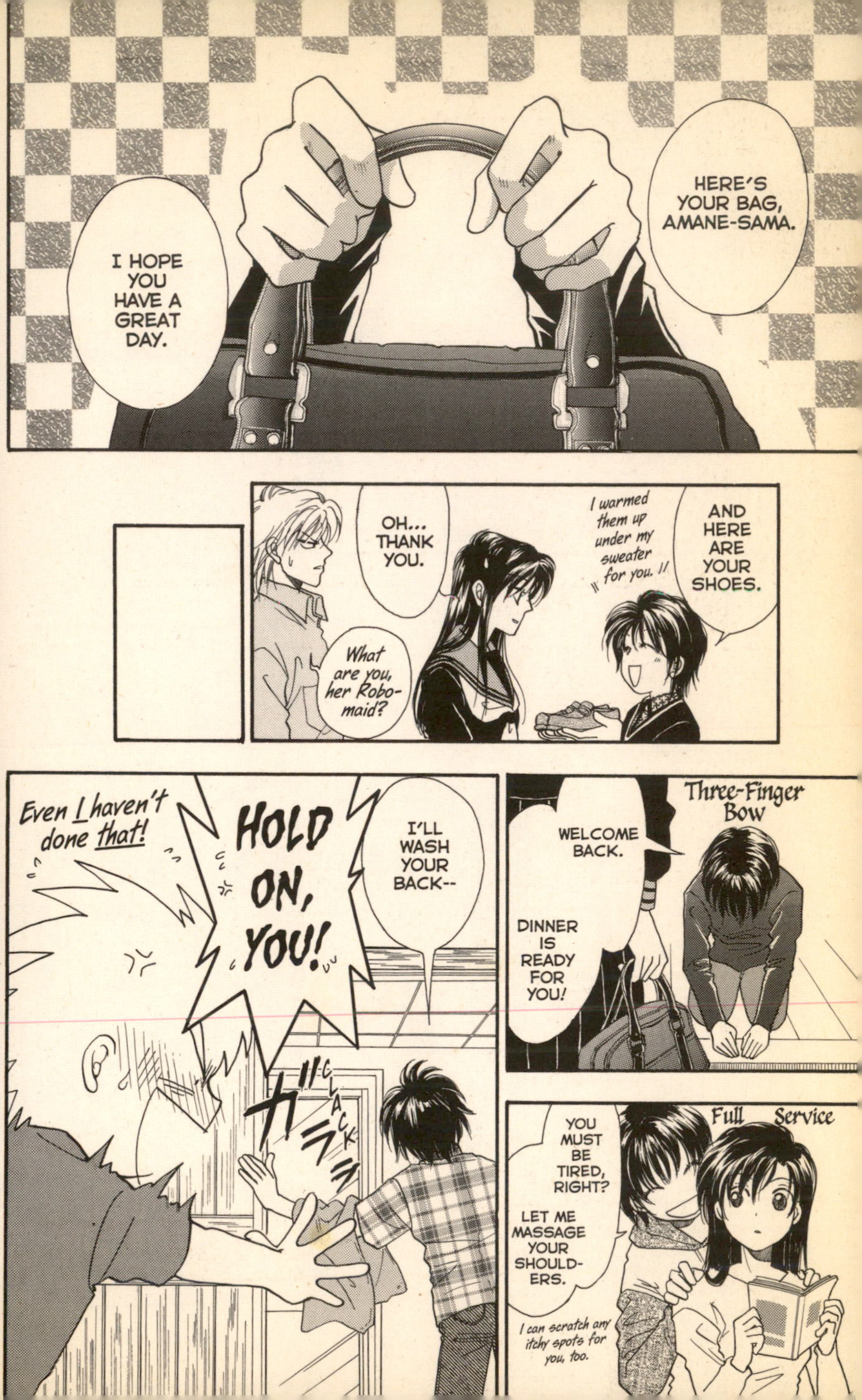
HERE'S YOUR BAG, AMANE-SAMA.
I HOPE YOU HAVE A GREAT DAY.
AND HERE ARE YOUR SHOES.
I warmed them up under my sweater for you.
OH... THANK YOU.
What are you, her Robo-maid?
Three-Finger Bow
WELCOME BACK.
DINNER IS READY FOR YOU!
Full Service
YOU MUST BE TIRED, RIGHT?
LET ME MASSAGE YOUR SHOULDERS.
I can scratch any itchy spots for you, too.
I'LL WASH YOUR BACK--
HOLD ON, YOU!
Even I haven't done that!
CLACK

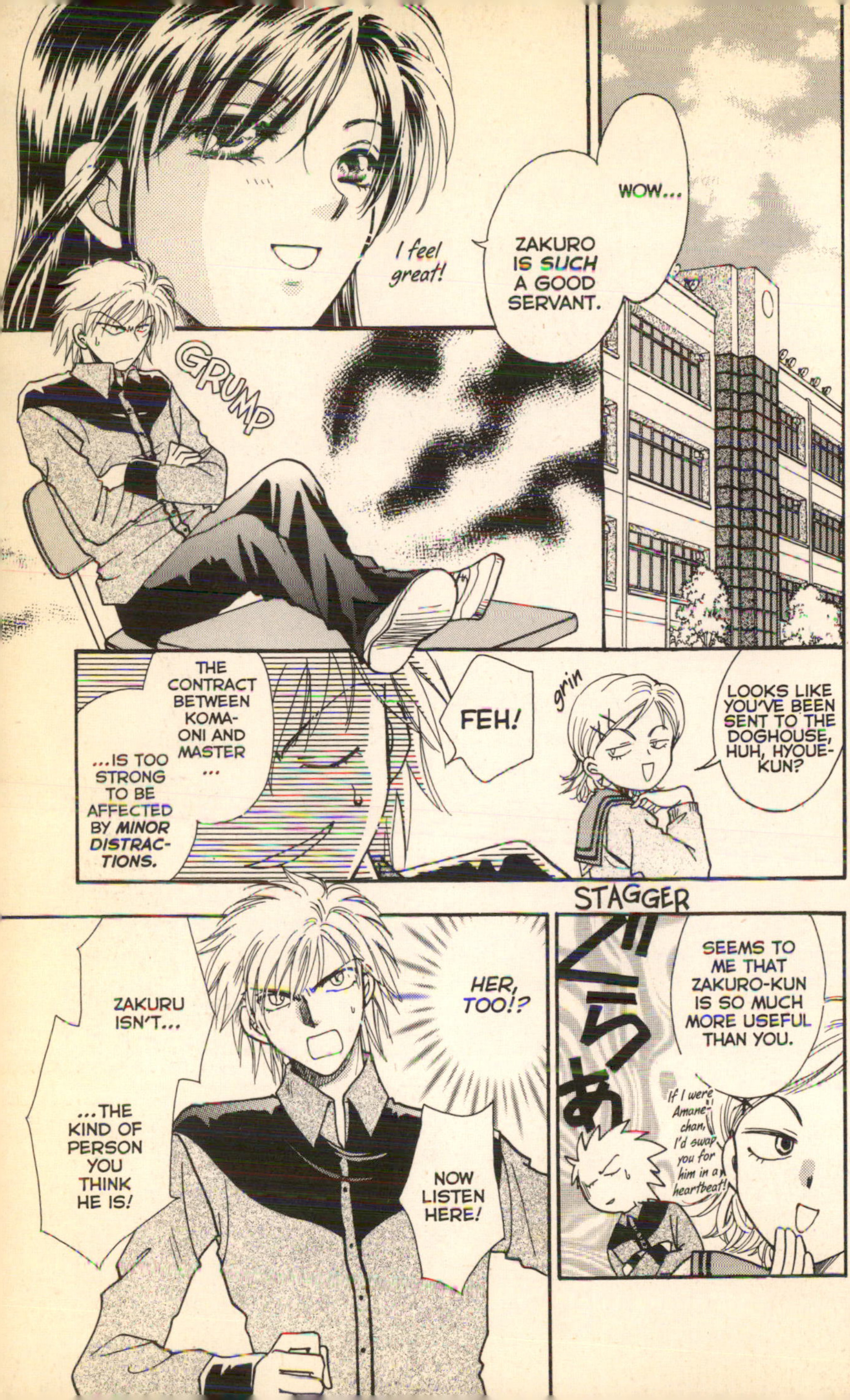
WOW...
ZAKURO IS SUCH A GOOD SERVANT.
I feel great!
GRUMP
grin
LOOKS LIKE YOU'VE BEEN SENT TO THE DOGHOUSE, HUH, HYOUE-KUN?
FEH!
THE CONTRACT BETWEEN KOMA-ONI AND MASTER...
...IS TOO STRONG TO BE AFFECTED BY MINOR DISTRACTIONS.
STAGGER
SEEMS TO ME THAT ZAKURO-KUN IS SO MUCH MORE USEFUL THAN YOU.
If I were Amane-chan, I'd swap you for him in a heartbeat!
HER, TOO!?
NOW LISTEN HERE!
ZAKURU ISN'T...
...THE KIND OF PERSON YOU THINK HE IS!

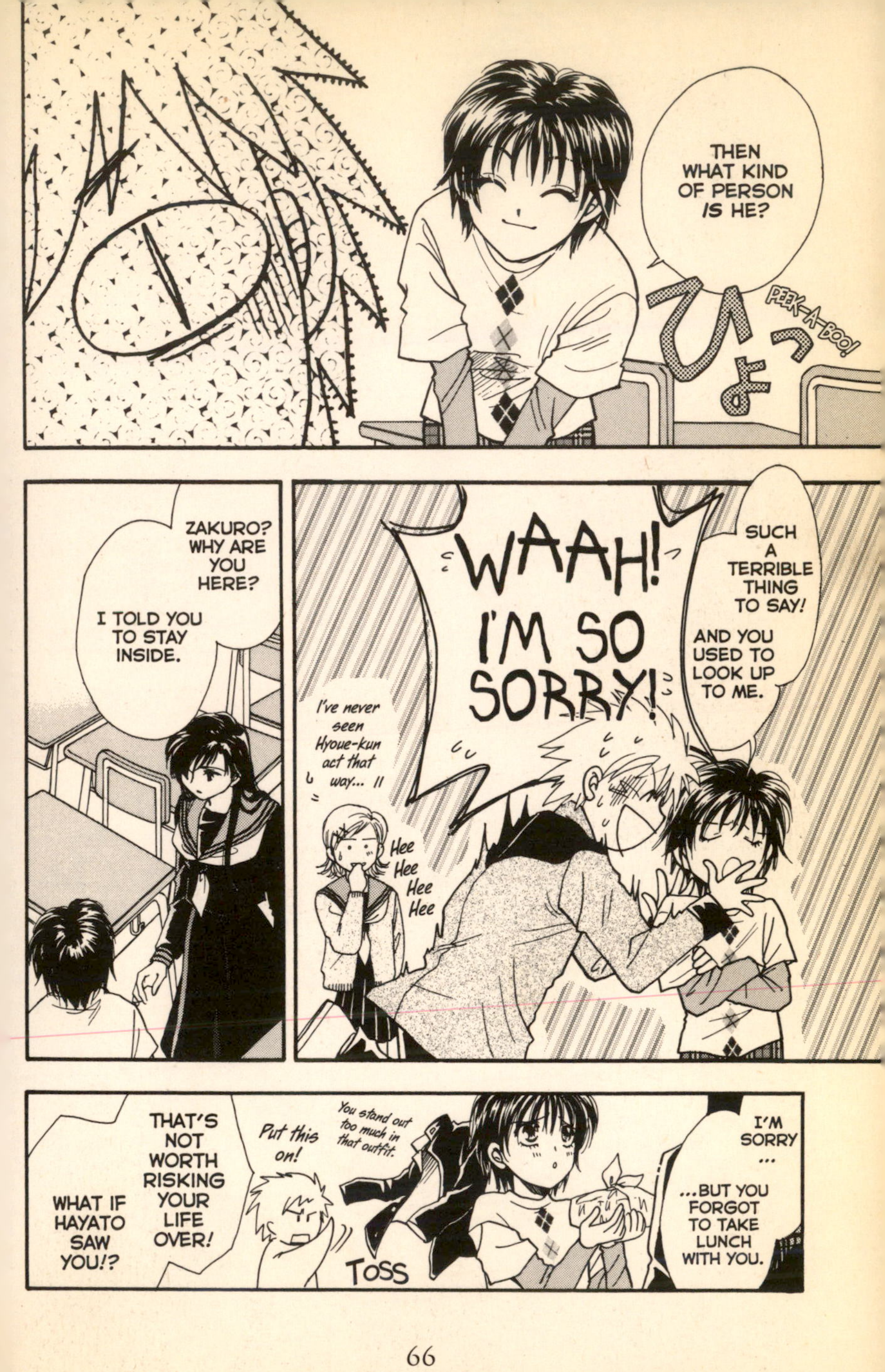
THEN WHAT KIND OF PERSON IS HE?
ひょっ
PEEK-A-BOO!
SUCH A TERRIBLE THING TO SAY!
AND YOU USED TO LOOK UP TO ME.
WAAH! I'M SO SORRY!
I've never seen Hyoue-kun act that way...
Hee Hee Hee Hee
ZAKURO? WHY ARE YOU HERE?
I TOLD YOU TO STAY INSIDE.
I'M SORRY...
...BUT YOU FORGOT TO TAKE LUNCH WITH YOU.
You stand out too much in that outfit.
Put this on!
TOSS
THAT'S NOT WORTH RISKING YOUR LIFE OVER!
WHAT IF HAYATO SAW YOU!?

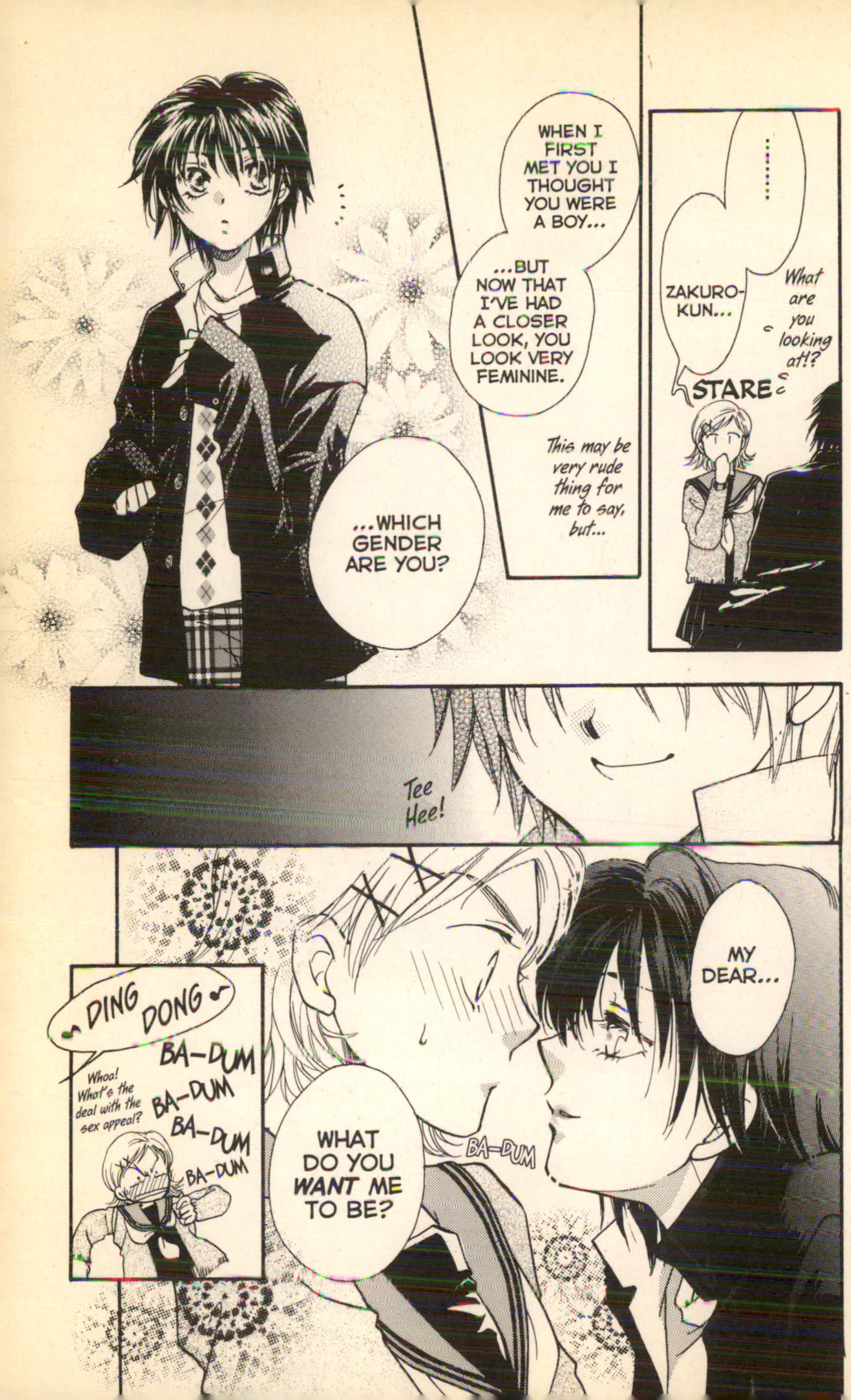
......
ZAKURO-KUN...
What are you looking at!?
STARE
WHEN I FIRST MET YOU I THOUGHT YOU WERE A BOY...
...BUT NOW THAT I'VE HAD A CLOSER LOOK, YOU LOOK VERY FEMININE.
This may be very rude thing for me to say, but...
...WHICH GENDER ARE YOU?
Tee Hee!
MY DEAR...
WHAT DO YOU WANT ME TO BE?
BA-DUM
DING DONG
BA-DUM
BA-DUM
BA-DUM
BA-DUM
Whoa! What's the deal with the sex appeal?

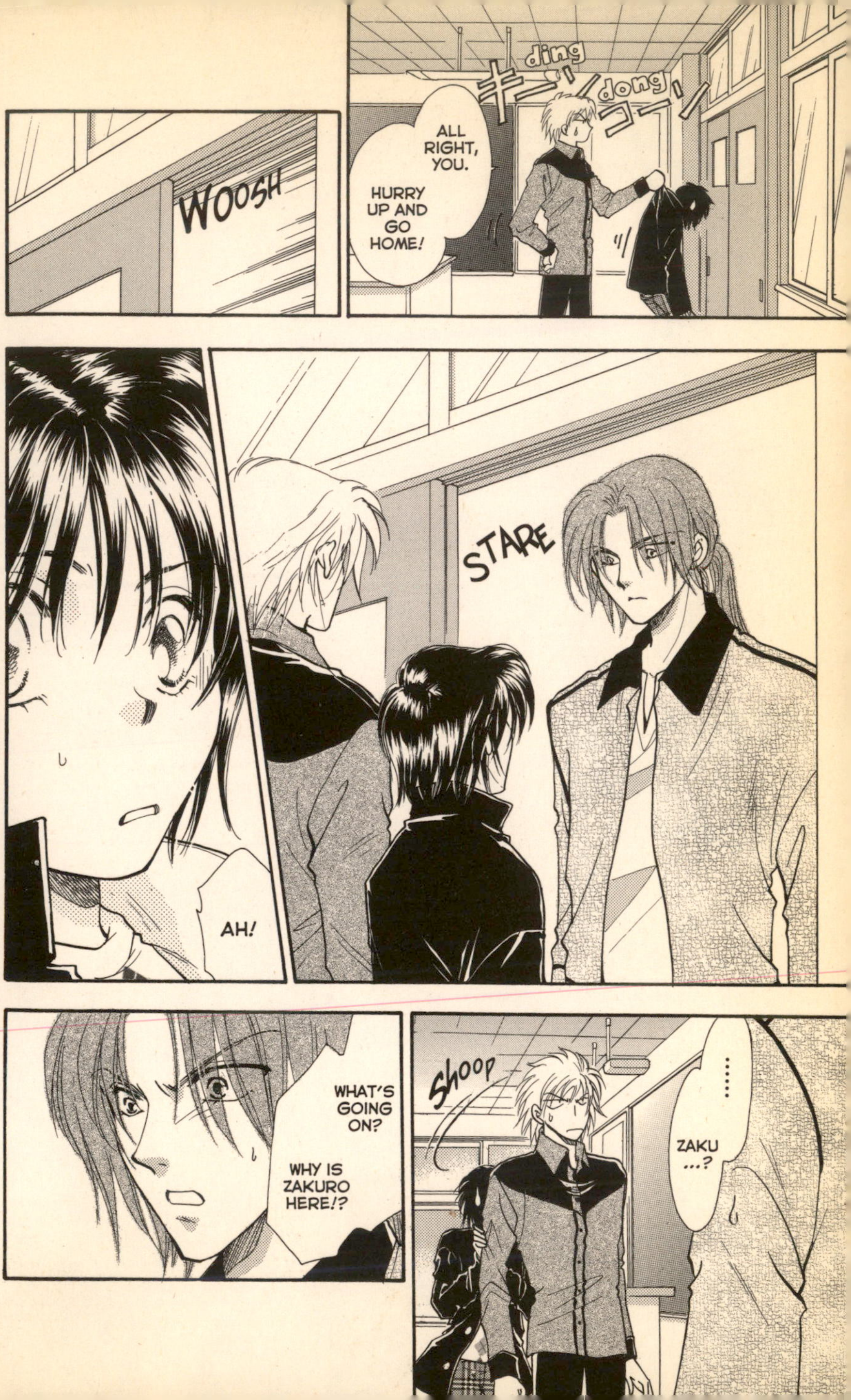
ding
dong
ALL RIGHT, YOU.
HURRY UP AND GO HOME!
WOOSH
STARE
AH!
......
ZAKU ...?
Shoop
WHAT'S GOING ON?
WHY IS ZAKURO HERE!?

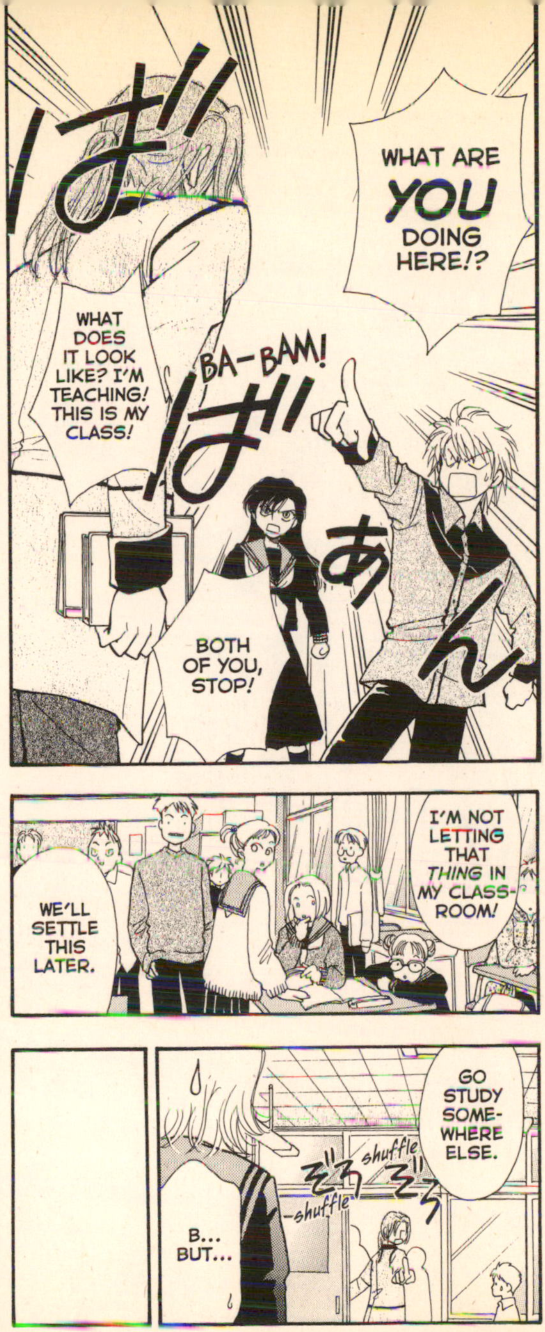
WHAT ARE YOU DOING HERE!?
ばっ
BA-BAM!
ばっ
あん
WHAT DOES IT LOOK LIKE? I'M TEACHING! THIS IS MY CLASS!
BOTH OF YOU, STOP!
I'M NOT LETTING THAT THING IN MY CLASS-ROOM!
WE'LL SETTLE THIS LATER.
GO STUDY SOME-WHERE ELSE.
ぞろ shuffle
ぞろ -shuffle
B... BUT...

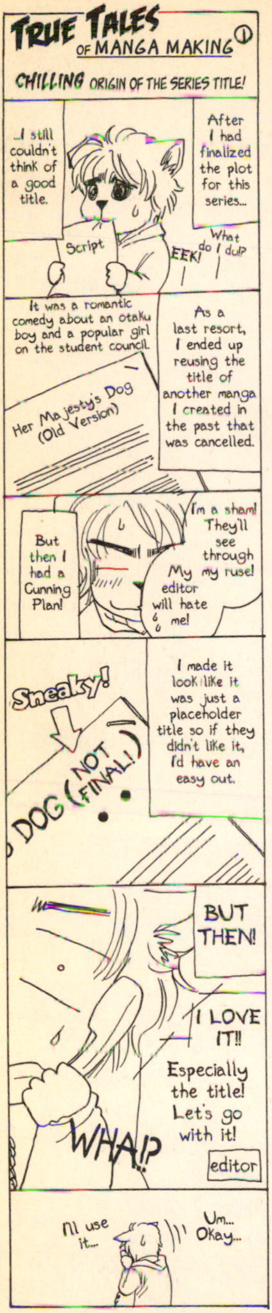
TRUE TALES OF MANGA MAKING ①
CHILLING ORIGIN OF THE SERIES TITLE!
After I had finalized the plot for this series...
...I still couldn't think of a good title.
What do I do!?
EEK!
Script
As a last resort, I ended up reusing the title of another manga I created in the past that was cancelled.
It was a romantic comedy about an otaku boy and a popular girl on the student council.
Her Majesty's Dog (Old Version)
I'm a sham! They'll see through my ruse! My editor will hate me!
But then I had a Cunning Plan!
I made it look like it was just a placeholder title so if they didn't like it, I'd have an easy out.
Sneaky!
DOG (NOT FINAL!)
BUT THEN!
I LOVE IT!! Especially the title! Let's go with it!
editor
WHA!?
Um... Okay...
I'll use it...

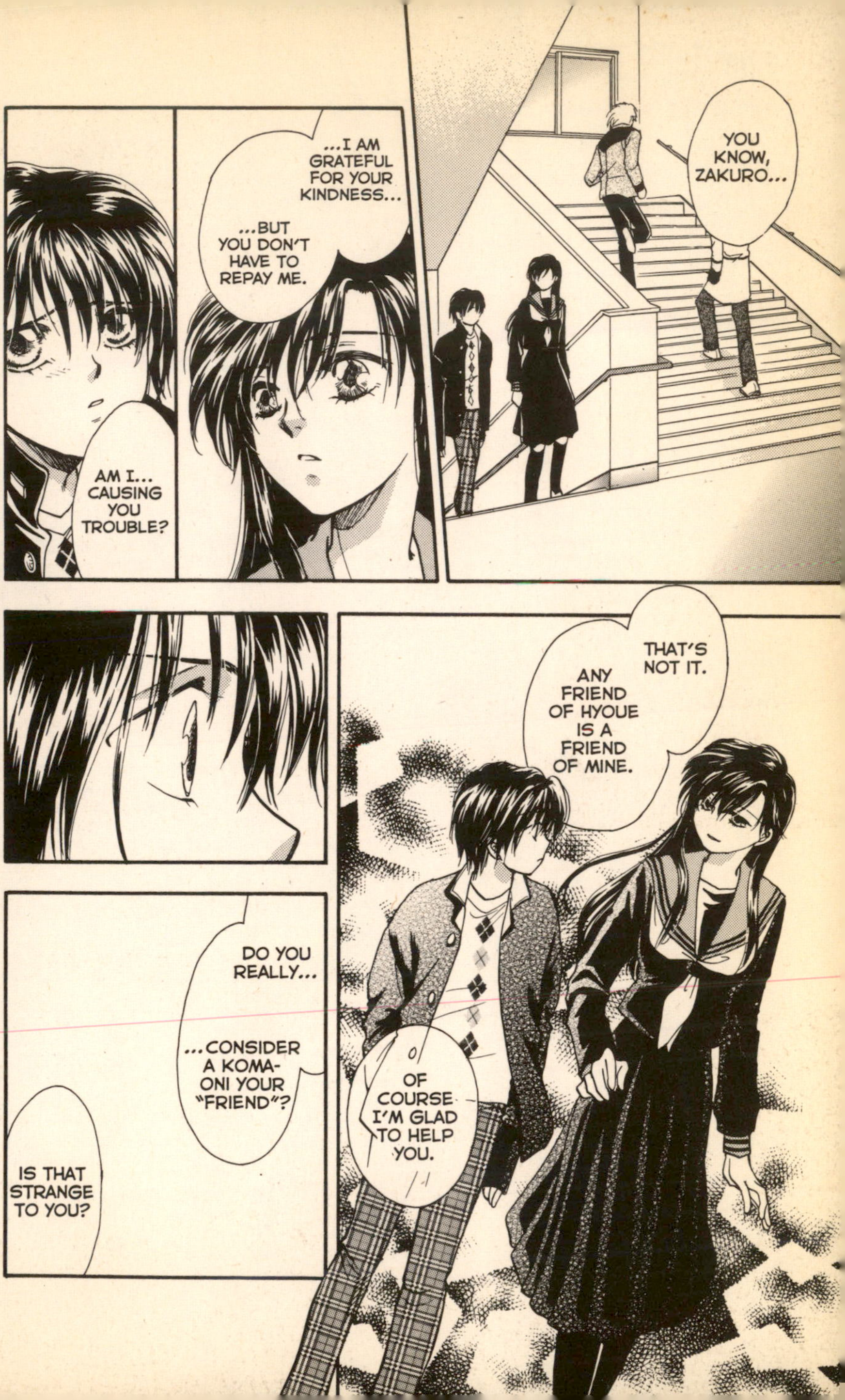
YOU KNOW, ZAKURO...
...I AM GRATEFUL FOR YOUR KINDNESS...
...BUT YOU DON'T HAVE TO REPAY ME.
AM I... CAUSING YOU TROUBLE?
THAT'S NOT IT.
ANY FRIEND OF HYOUE IS A FRIEND OF MINE.
OF COURSE I'M GLAD TO HELP YOU.
DO YOU REALLY...
...CONSIDER A KOMA-ONI YOUR "FRIEND"?
IS THAT STRANGE TO YOU?

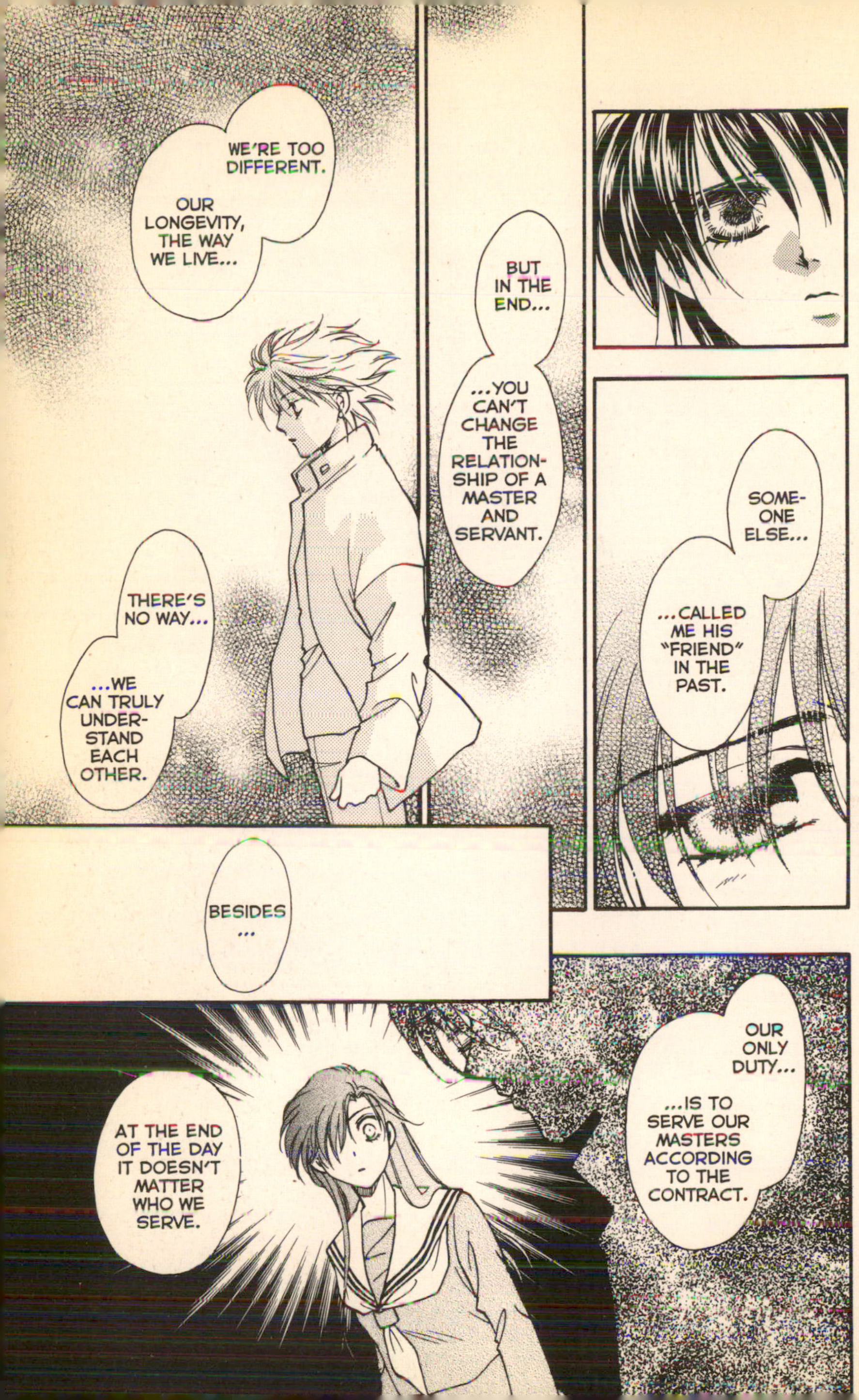
SOME-ONE ELSE...
...CALLED ME HIS "FRIEND" IN THE PAST.
BUT IN THE END...
...YOU CAN'T CHANGE THE RELATION-SHIP OF A MASTER AND SERVANT.
WE'RE TOO DIFFERENT.
OUR LONGEVITY, THE WAY WE LIVE...
THERE'S NO WAY...
...WE CAN TRULY UNDER-STAND EACH OTHER.
BESIDES...
OUR ONLY DUTY...
...IS TO SERVE OUR MASTERS ACCORDING TO THE CONTRACT.
AT THE END OF THE DAY IT DOESN'T MATTER WHO WE SERVE.

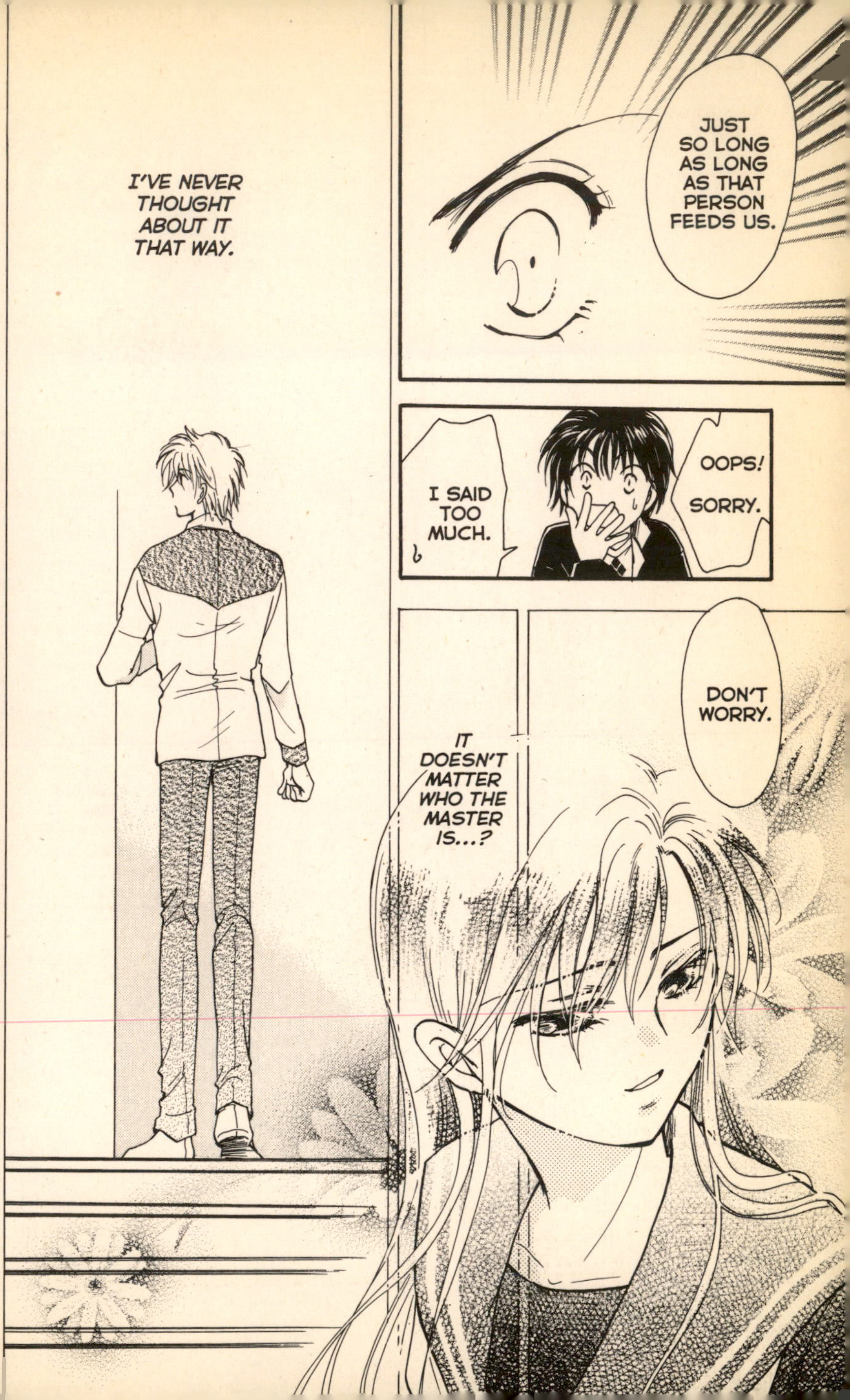
JUST SO LONG AS LONG AS THAT PERSON FEEDS US.
OOPS! SORRY.
I SAID TOO MUCH.
DON'T WORRY.
IT DOESN'T MATTER WHO THE MASTER IS...?
I'VE NEVER THOUGHT ABOUT IT THAT WAY.

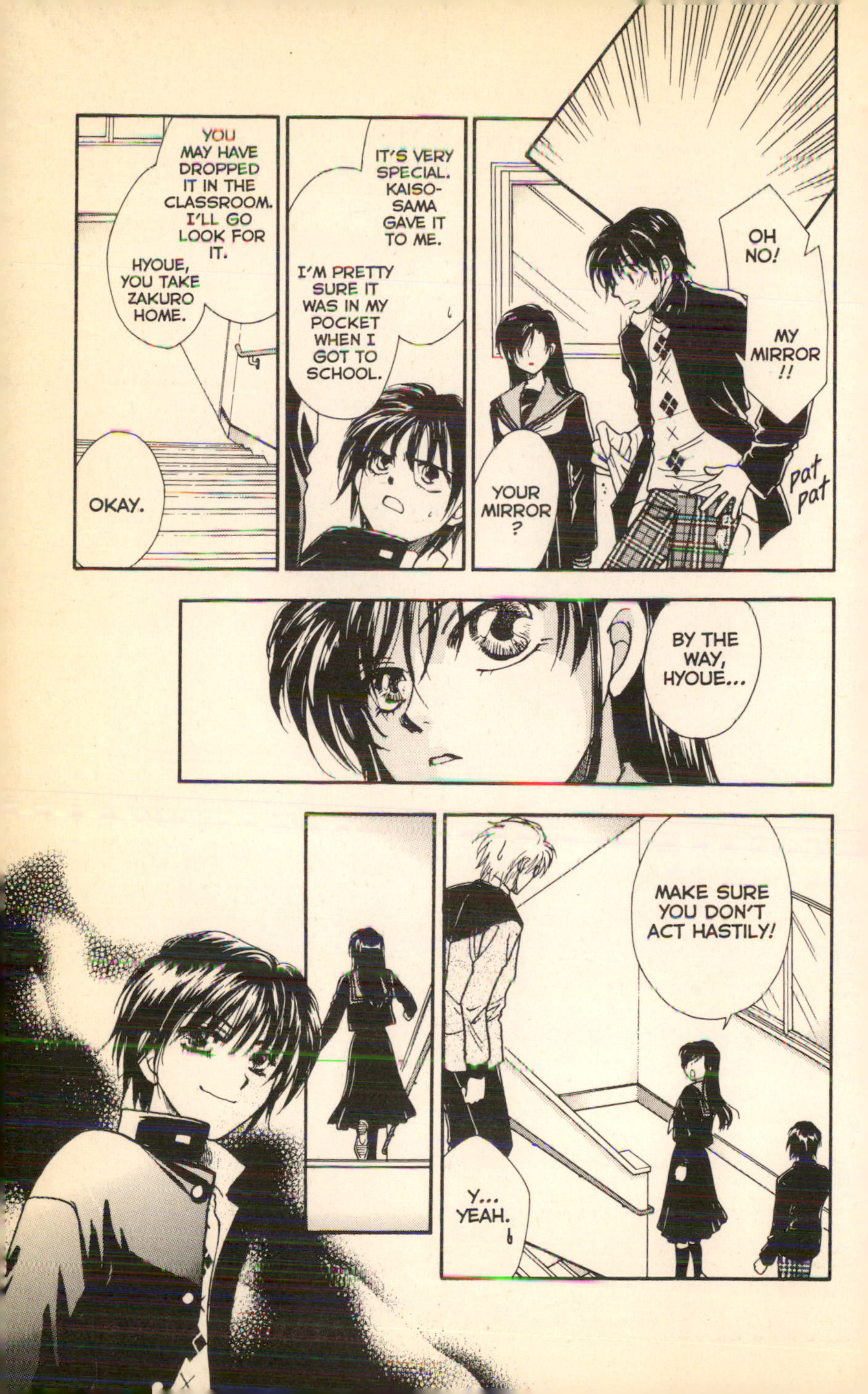
OH NO!
MY MIRROR!!
Pat pat
YOUR MIRROR?
IT'S VERY SPECIAL. KAISO-SAMA GAVE IT TO ME.
I'M PRETTY SURE IT WAS IN MY POCKET WHEN I GOT TO SCHOOL.
YOU MAY HAVE DROPPED IT IN THE CLASSROOM. I'LL GO LOOK FOR IT.
HYOUE, YOU TAKE ZAKURO HOME.
OKAY.
BY THE WAY, HYOUE...
MAKE SURE YOU DON'T ACT HASTILY!
Y... YEAH.

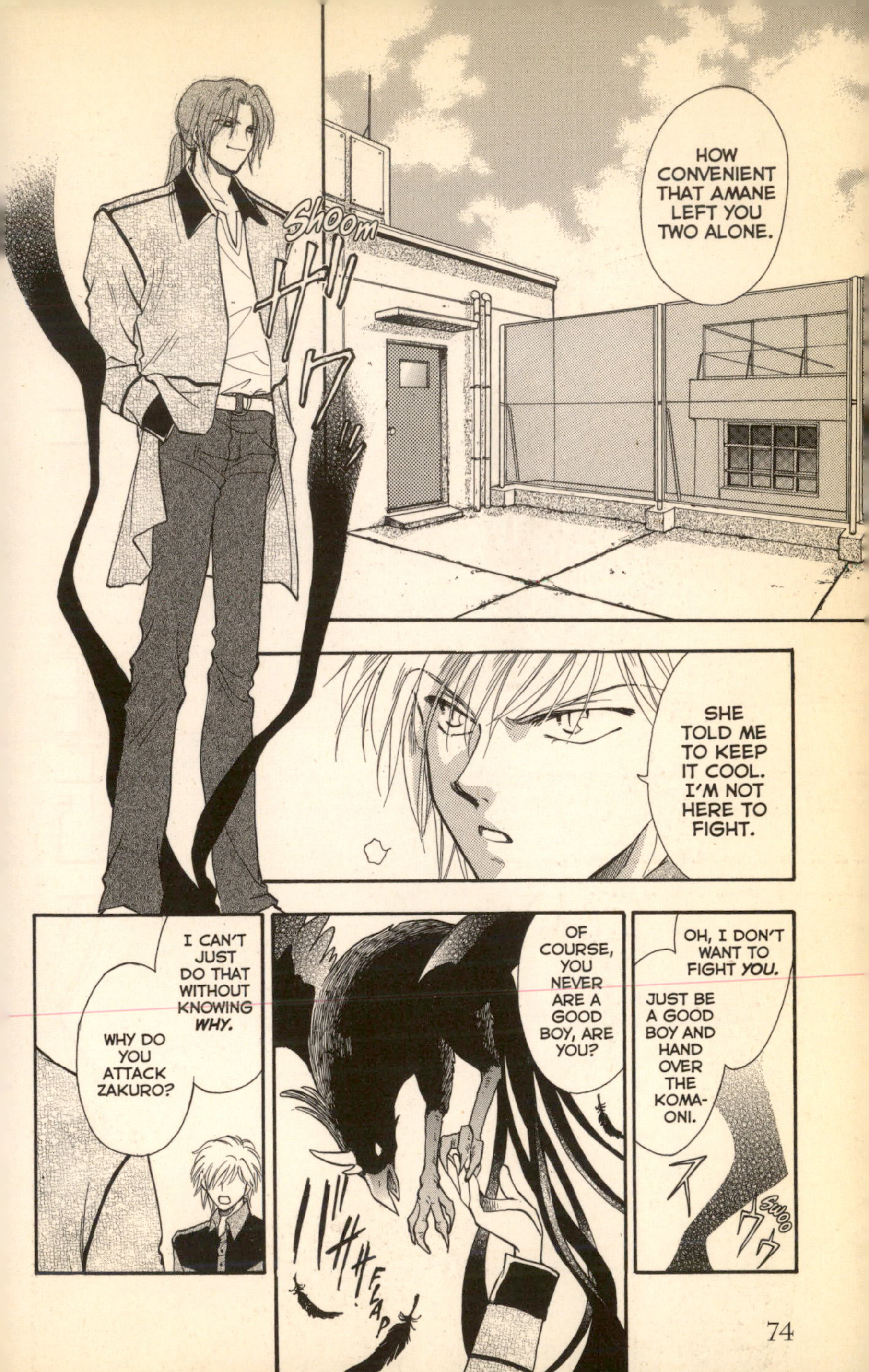
HOW CONVENIENT THAT AMANE LEFT YOU TWO ALONE.
SHE TOLD ME TO KEEP IT COOL. I'M NOT HERE TO FIGHT.
Shoom
OH, I DON'T WANT TO FIGHT *YOU.*
JUST BE A GOOD BOY AND HAND OVER THE KOMA-ONI.
SWOO
OF COURSE, YOU NEVER ARE A GOOD BOY, ARE YOU?
FLAP
I CAN'T JUST DO THAT WITHOUT KNOWING *WHY.*
WHY DO YOU ATTACK ZAKURO?

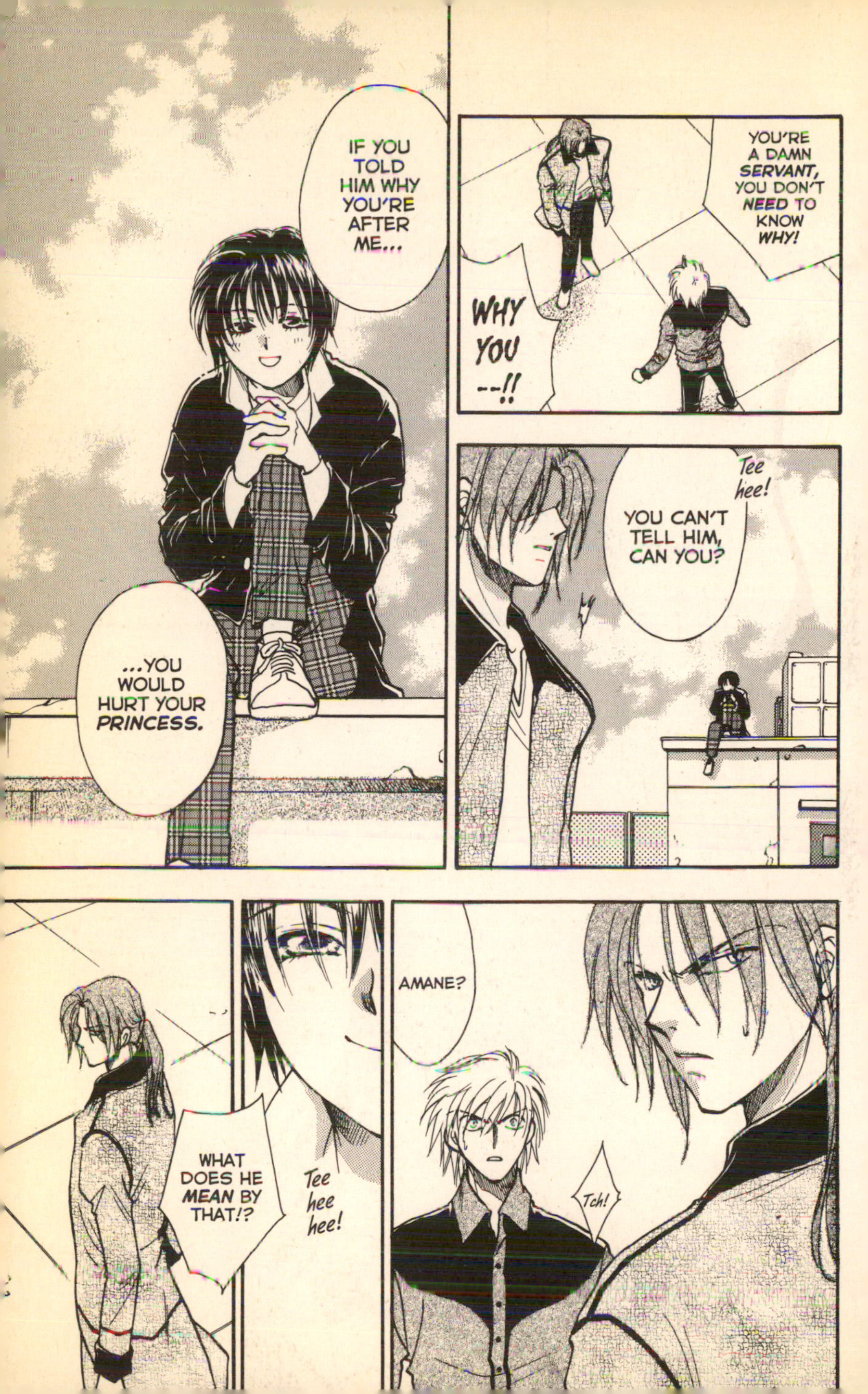
YOU'RE A DAMN SERVANT, YOU DON'T NEED TO KNOW WHY!
WHY YOU --!!
Tee hee!
YOU CAN'T TELL HIM, CAN YOU?
IF YOU TOLD HIM WHY YOU'RE AFTER ME...
...YOU WOULD HURT YOUR PRINCESS.
AMANE?
Tch!
Tee hee hee!
WHAT DOES HE MEAN BY THAT!?

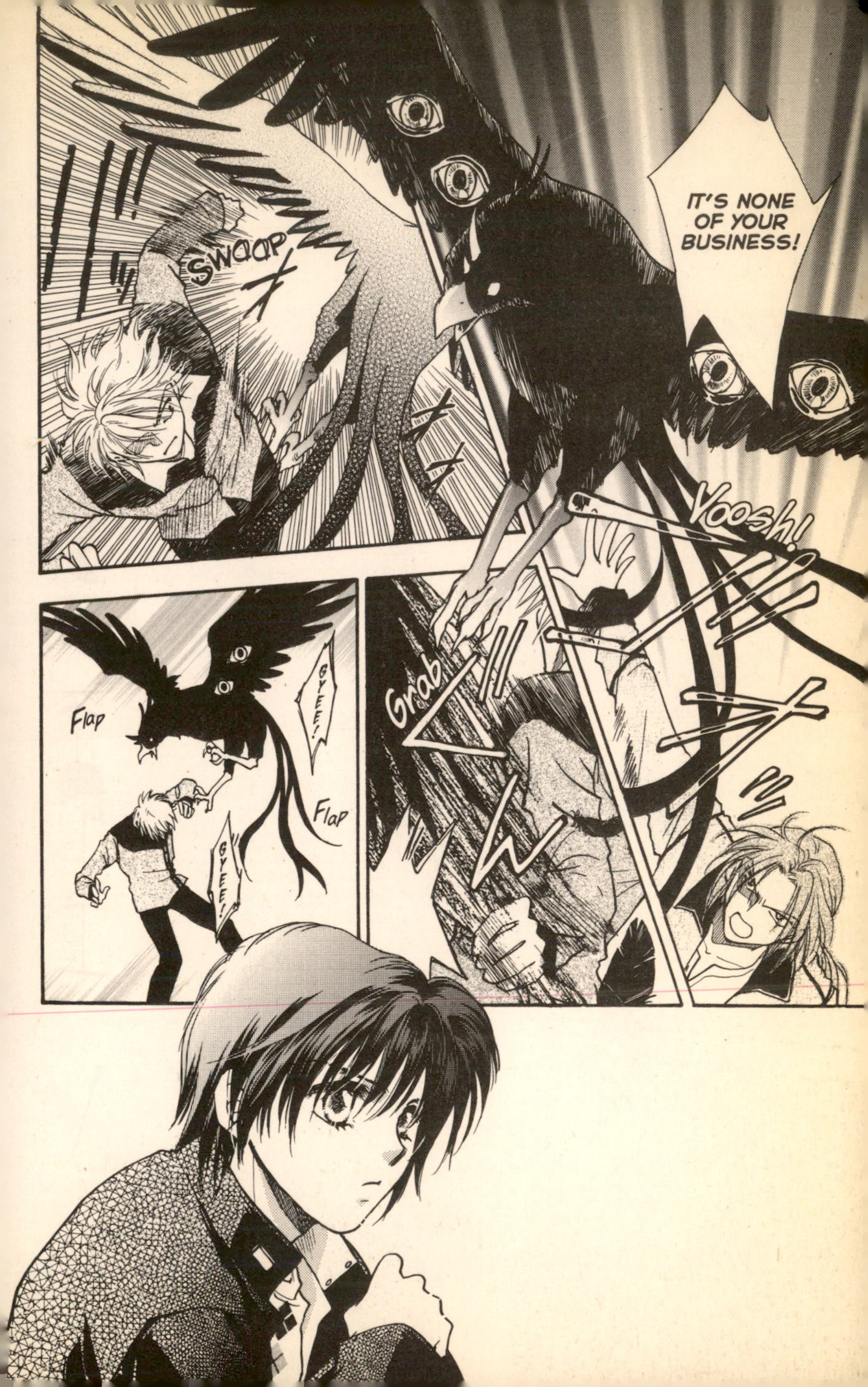
IT'S NONE OF YOUR BUSINESS!
SWAAP
Voosh!
Grab
GYEE!
Flap
Flap
GYEE!

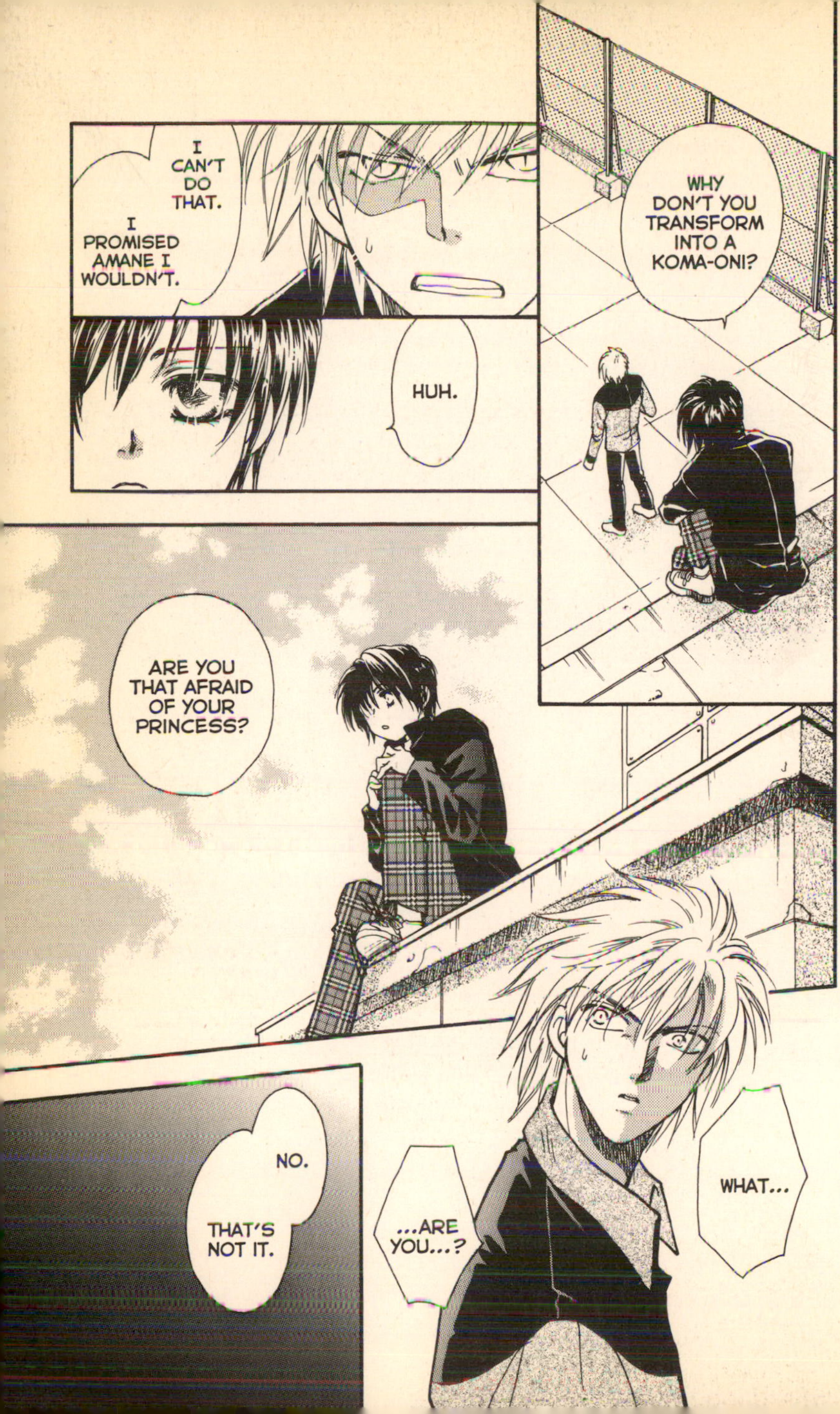
WHY DON'T YOU TRANSFORM INTO A KOMA-ONI?
I CAN'T DO THAT.
I PROMISED AMANE I WOULDN'T.
HUH.
ARE YOU THAT AFRAID OF YOUR PRINCESS?
WHAT...
...ARE YOU...?
NO.
THAT'S NOT IT.

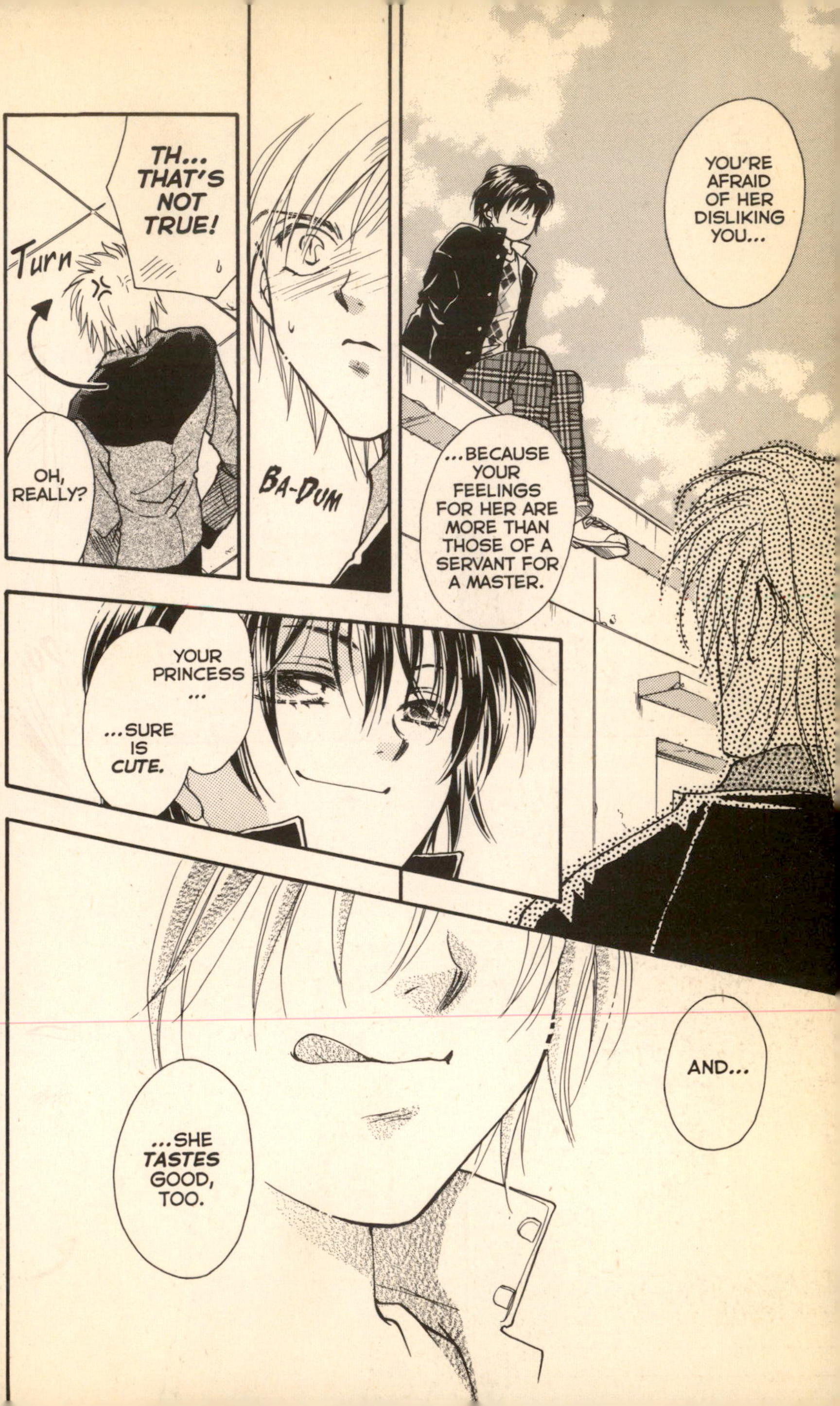
YOU'RE AFRAID OF HER DISLIKING YOU...
...BECAUSE YOUR FEELINGS FOR HER ARE MORE THAN THOSE OF A SERVANT FOR A MASTER.
BA-DUM
TH... THAT'S NOT TRUE!
Turn
OH, REALLY?
YOUR PRINCESS ... ...SURE IS *CUTE.*
AND...
...SHE *TASTES* GOOD, TOO.

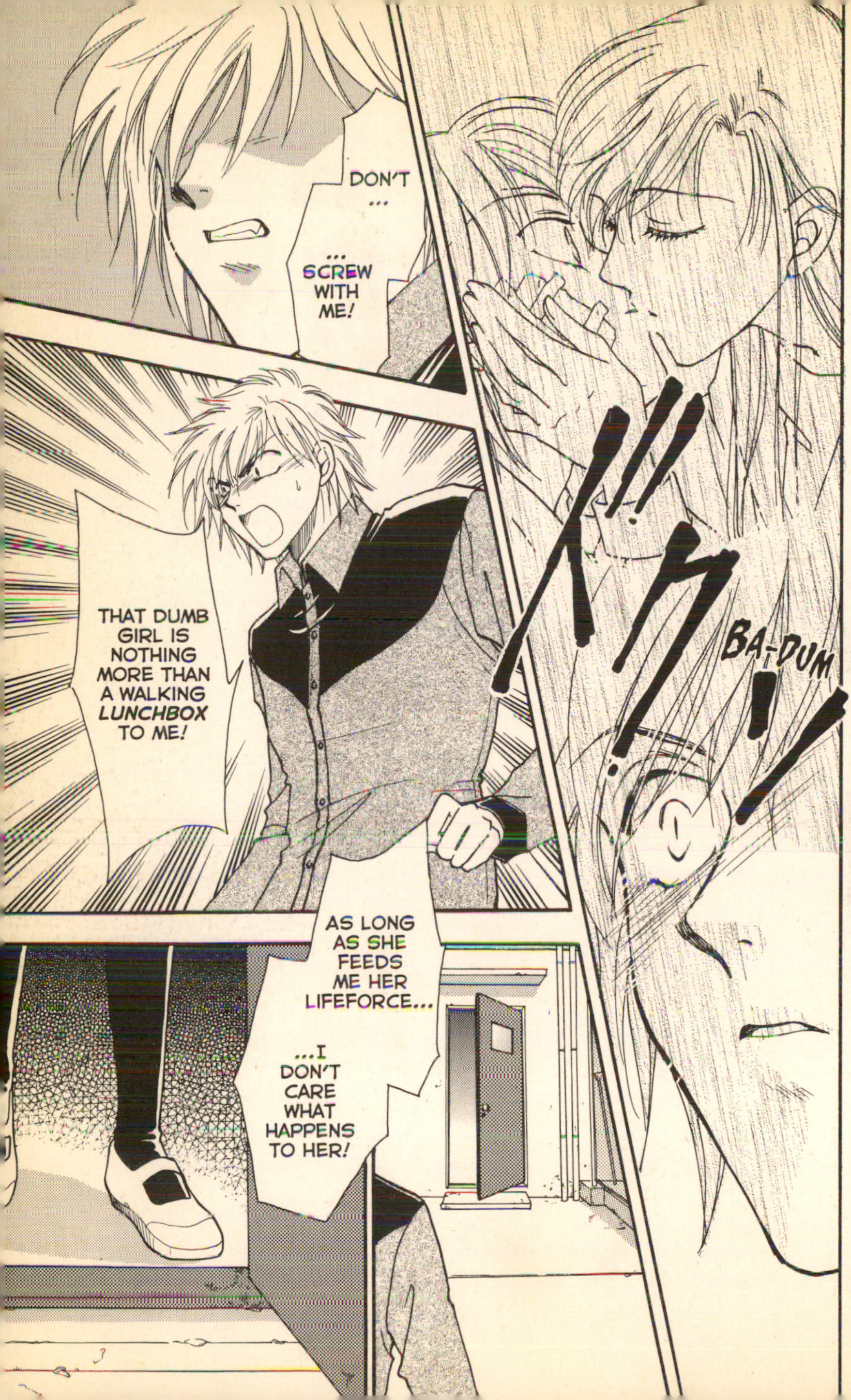
BA-DUM
DON'T ...
... SCREW WITH ME!
THAT DUMB GIRL IS NOTHING MORE THAN A WALKING *LUNCHBOX* TO ME!
AS LONG AS SHE FEEDS ME HER LIFEFORCE...
...I DON'T CARE WHAT HAPPENS TO HER!

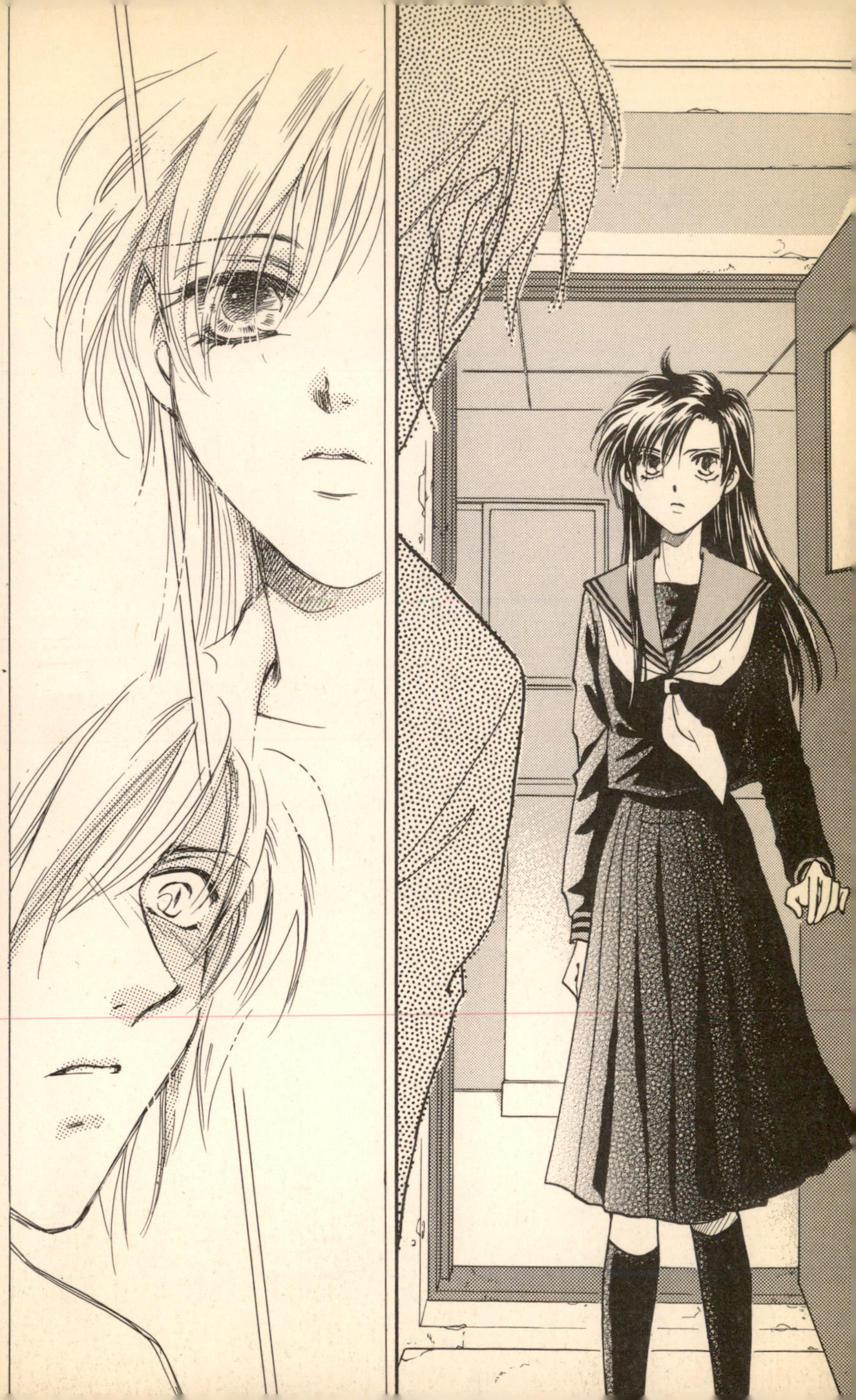

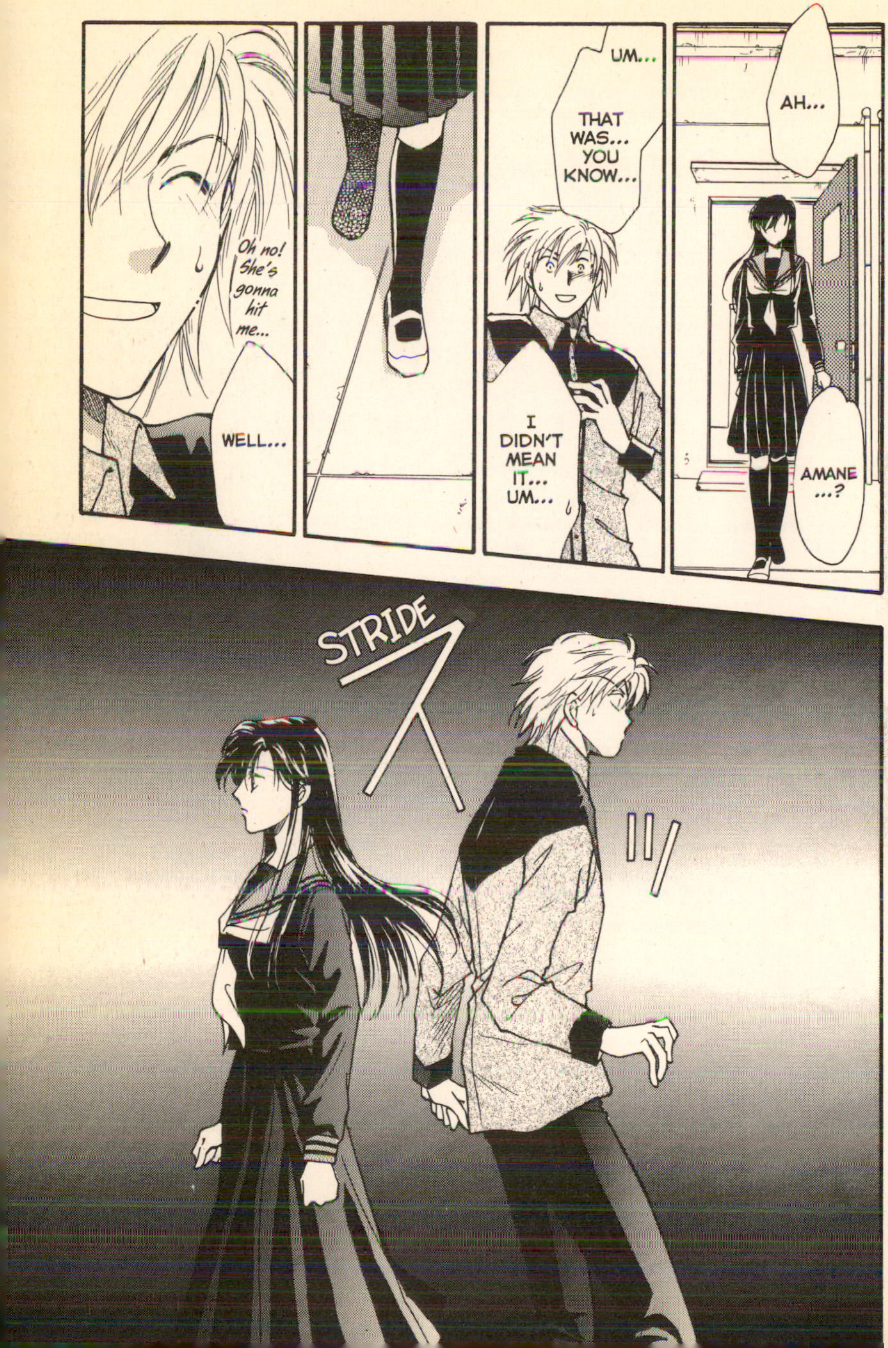
AH...
AMANE ...?
UM...
THAT WAS... YOU KNOW...
I DIDN'T MEAN IT... UM...
Oh no! She's gonna hit me...
WELL...
STRIDE

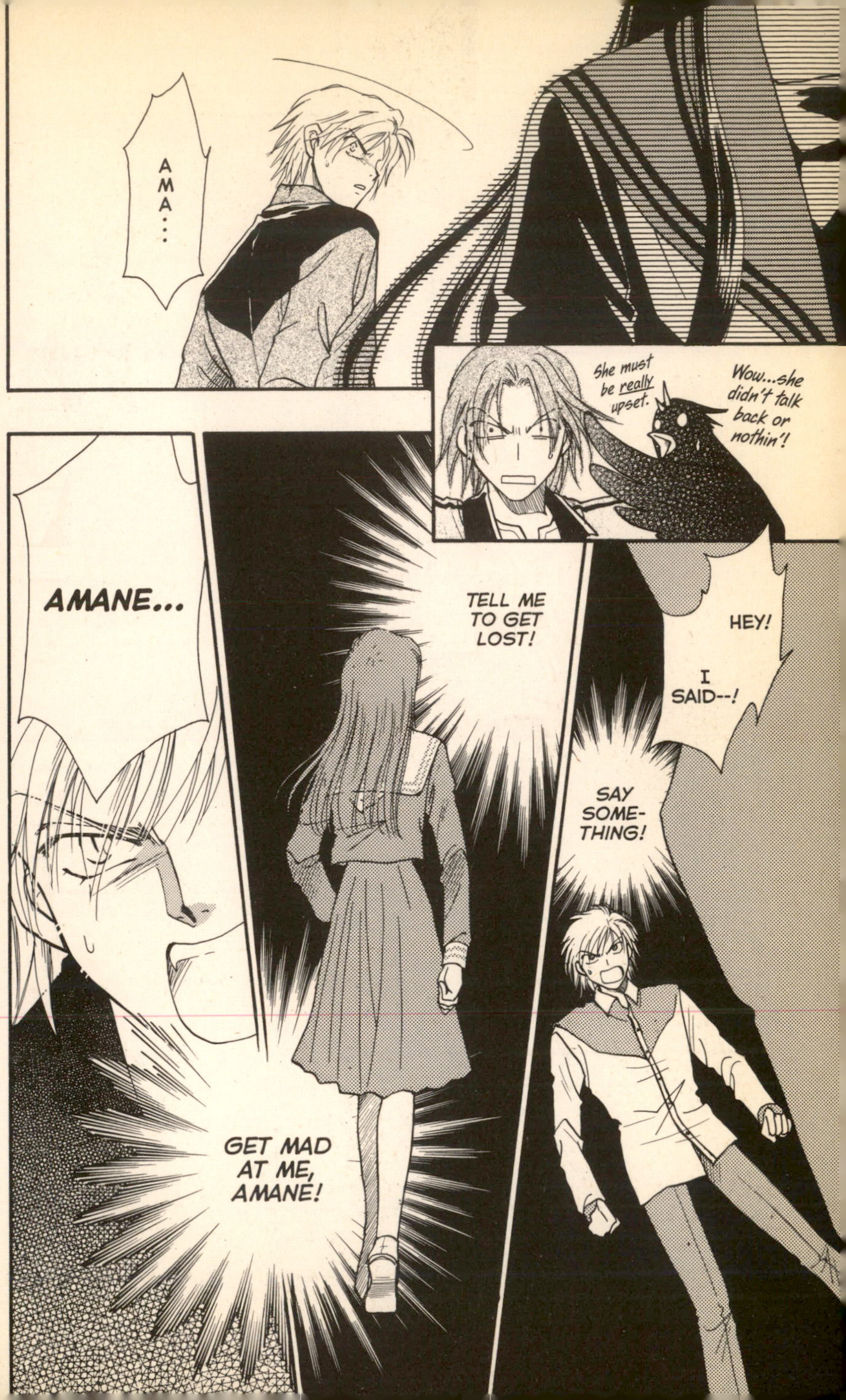
AMA...
Wow...she didn't talk back or nothin'!
She must be really upset.
HEY!
I SAID--!
SAY SOME-THING!
TELL ME TO GET LOST!
AMANE...
GET MAD AT ME, AMANE!

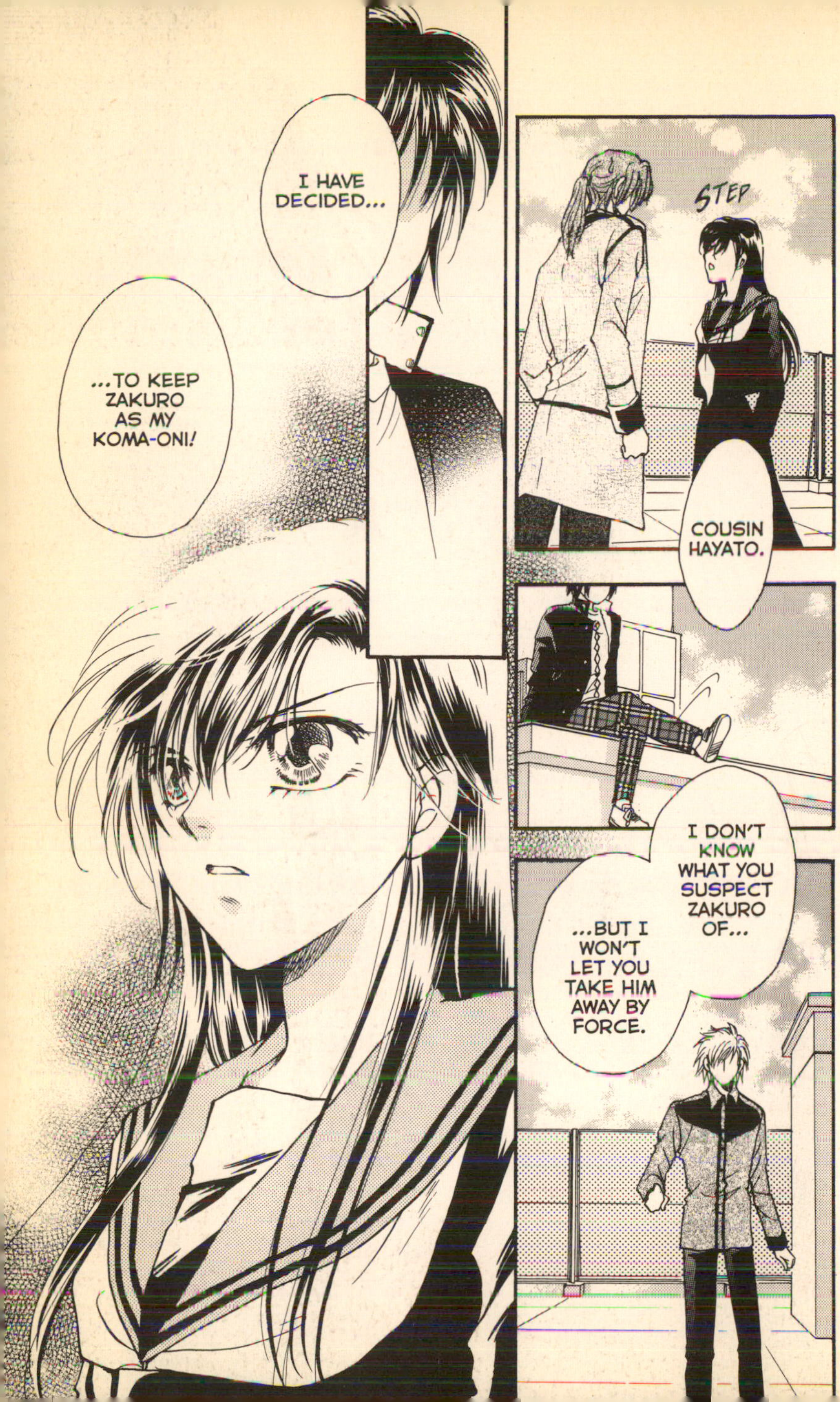
STEP
COUSIN HAYATO.
I DON'T KNOW WHAT YOU SUSPECT ZAKURO OF...
...BUT I WON'T LET YOU TAKE HIM AWAY BY FORCE.
I HAVE DECIDED...
...TO KEEP ZAKURO AS MY KOMA-ONI!

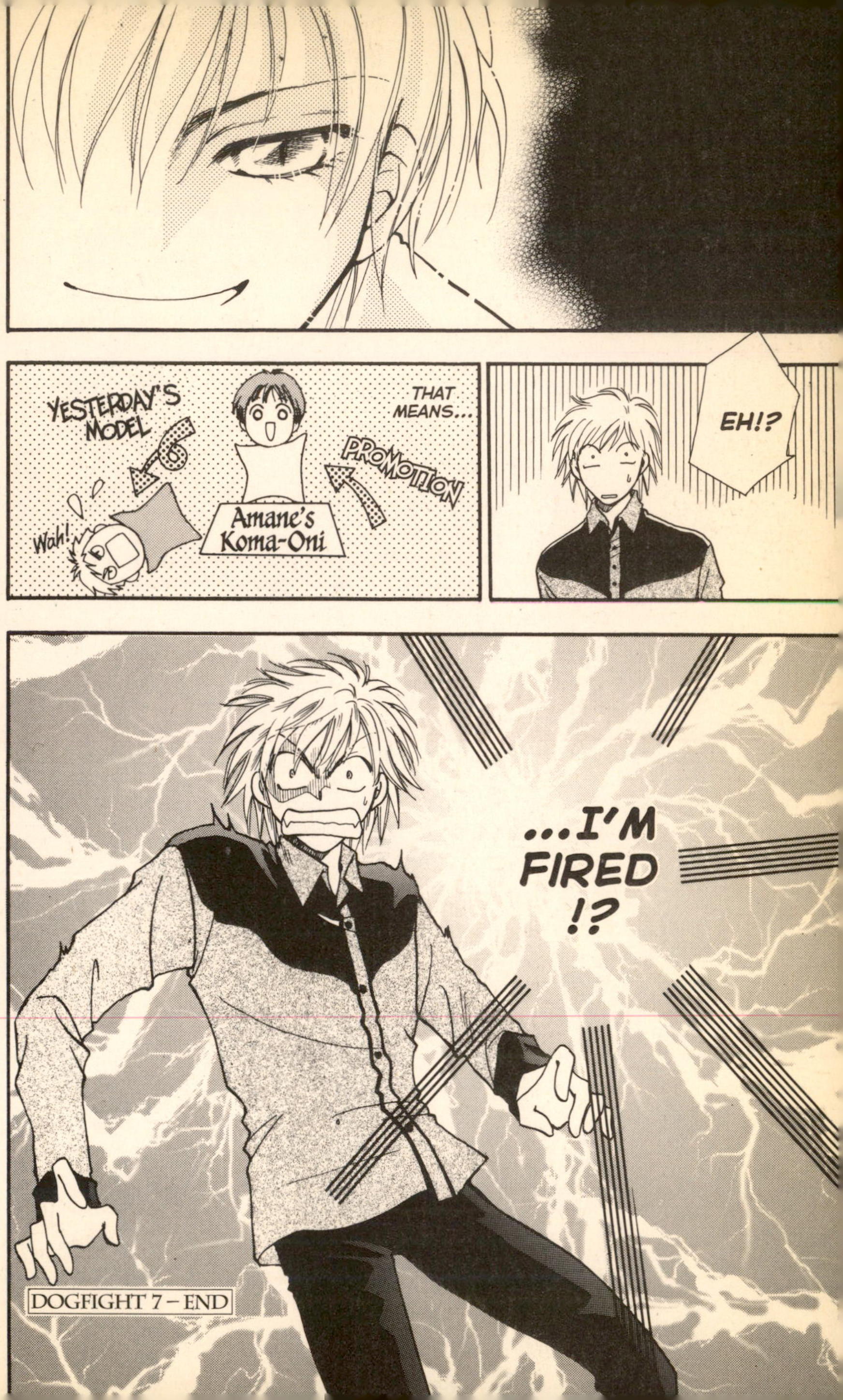
EH!?
THAT MEANS...
YESTERDAY'S MODEL
PROMOTION
Amane's Koma-Oni
Wah!
...I'M FIRED !?
DOGFIGHT 7 – END

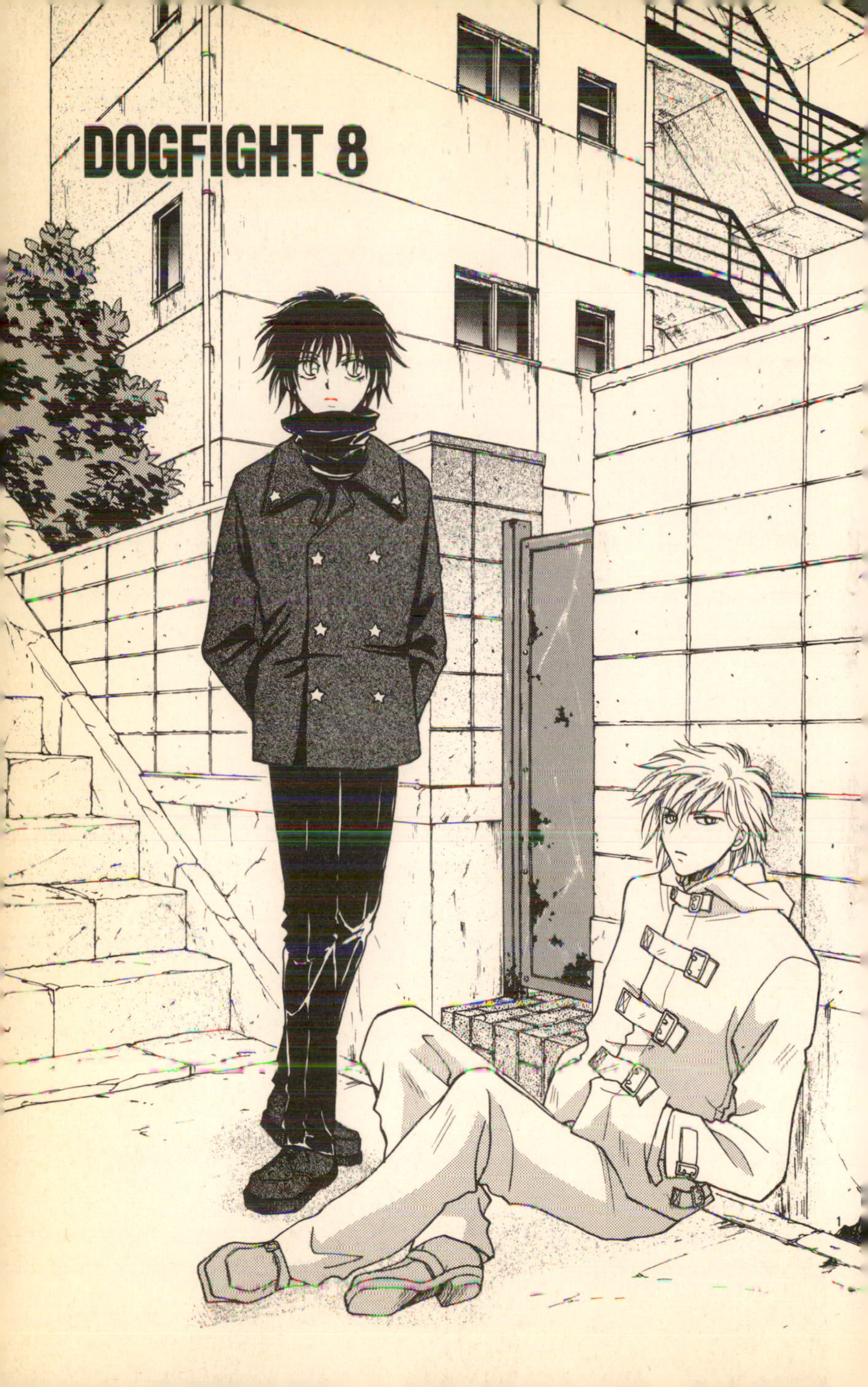
DOGFIGHT 8

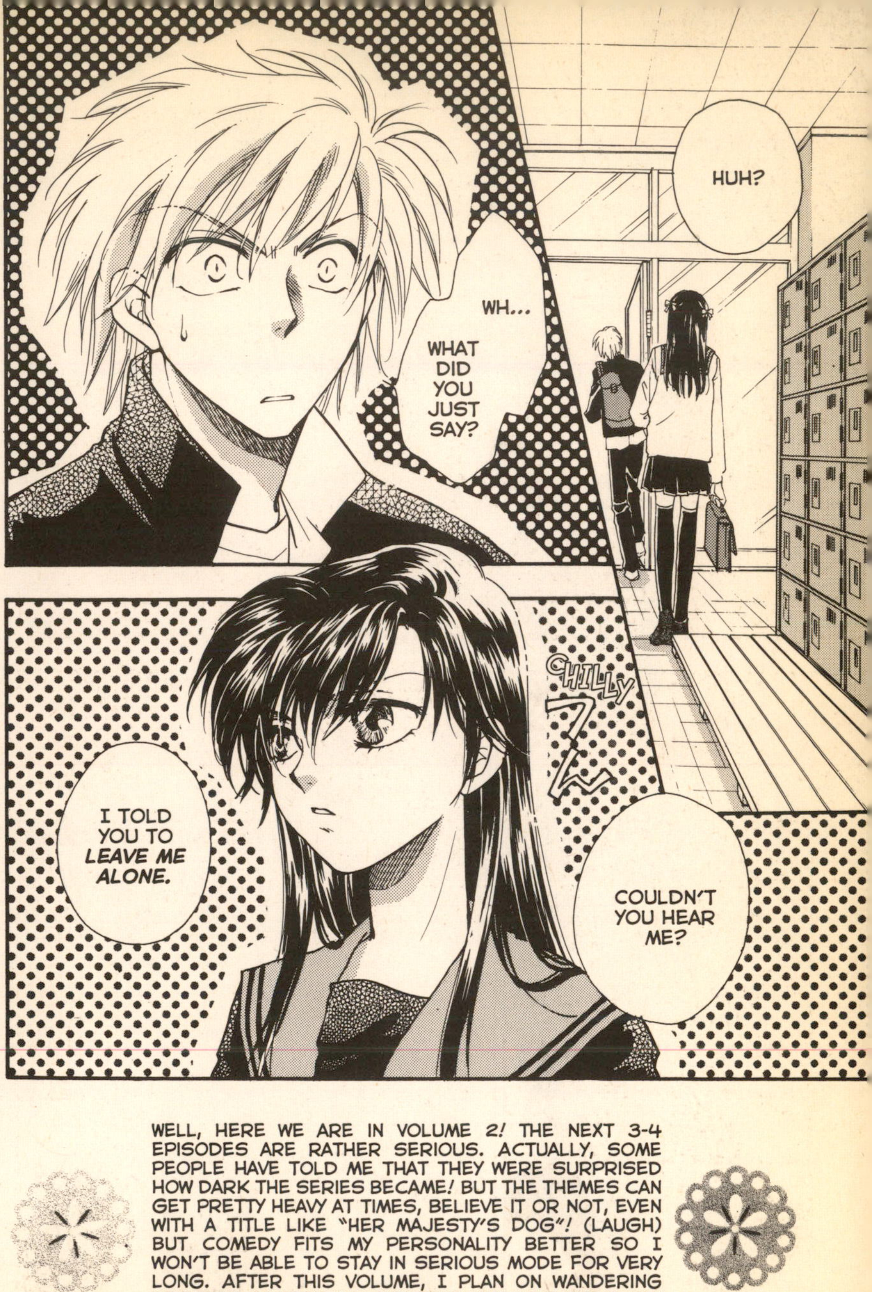
HUH?
WH...
WHAT DID YOU JUST SAY?
CHILLY
I TOLD YOU TO ***LEAVE ME ALONE.***
COULDN'T YOU HEAR ME?

WELL, HERE WE ARE IN VOLUME 2! THE NEXT 3-4 EPISODES ARE RATHER SERIOUS. ACTUALLY, SOME PEOPLE HAVE TOLD ME THAT THEY WERE SURPRISED HOW DARK THE SERIES BECAME! BUT THE THEMES CAN GET PRETTY HEAVY AT TIMES, BELIEVE IT OR NOT, EVEN WITH A TITLE LIKE "HER MAJESTY'S DOG"! (LAUGH) BUT COMEDY FITS MY PERSONALITY BETTER SO I WON'T BE ABLE TO STAY IN SERIOUS MODE FOR VERY LONG. AFTER THIS VOLUME, I PLAN ON WANDERING BETWEEN COMEDY AND SERIOUS STORIES BUT I MAY ALSO WANT TO GET INTO ROMANTIC THEMES, TOO... (LAUGH) PLEASE LOOK FORWARD TO IT! (PLEASE?)

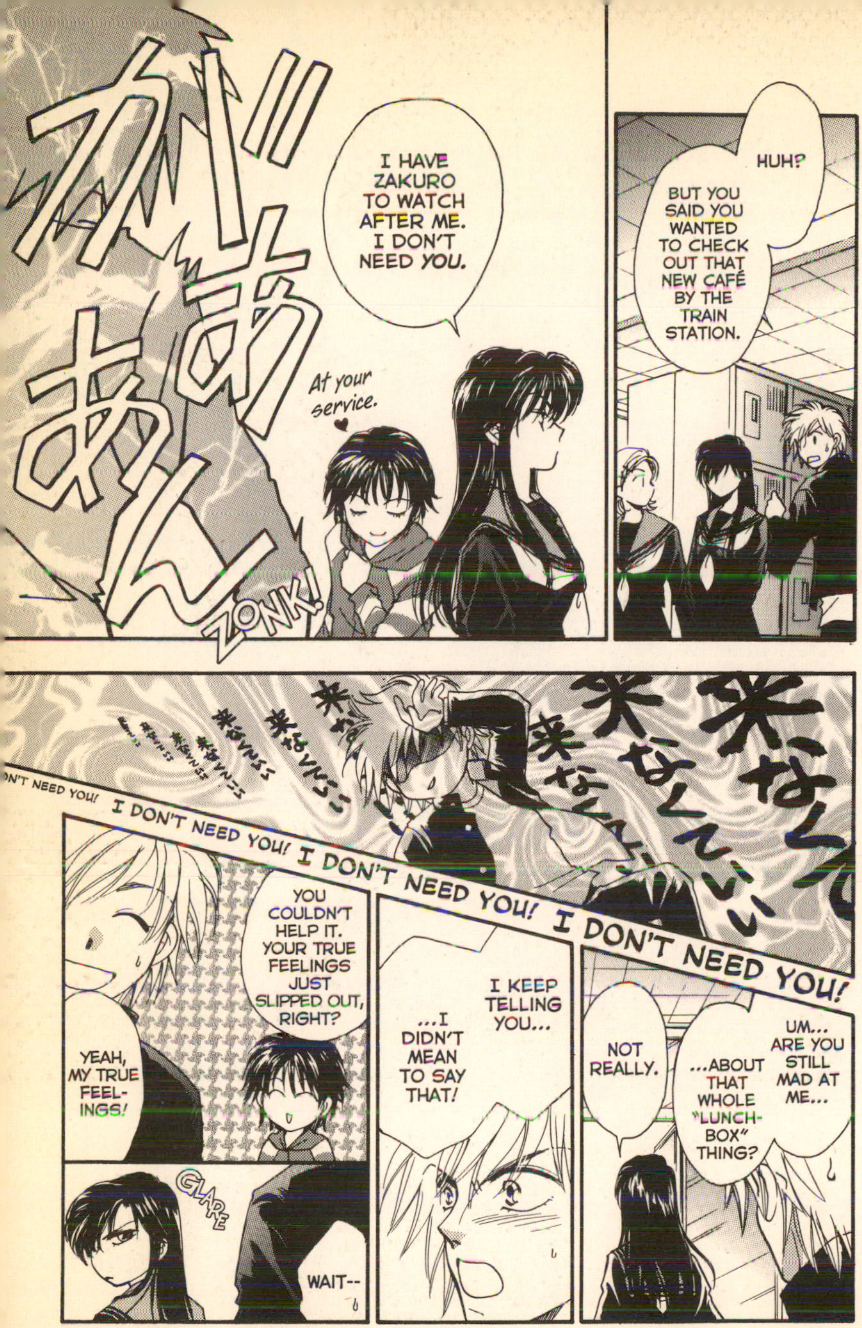
HUH?
BUT YOU SAID YOU WANTED TO CHECK OUT THAT NEW CAFÉ BY THE TRAIN STATION.
I HAVE ZAKURO TO WATCH AFTER ME. I DON'T NEED *YOU.*
At your service.
があああん
ZONK!
来なくていい
来なくていい
I DON'T NEED YOU! I DON'T NEED YOU! I DON'T NEED YOU! I DON'T NEED YOU!
UM... ARE YOU STILL MAD AT ME...
...ABOUT THAT WHOLE "LUNCHBOX" THING?
NOT REALLY.
I KEEP TELLING YOU...
...I DIDN'T MEAN TO SAY THAT!
YOU COULDN'T HELP IT. YOUR TRUE FEELINGS JUST SLIPPED OUT, RIGHT?
YEAH, MY TRUE FEEL-INGS!
GLARE
WAIT--

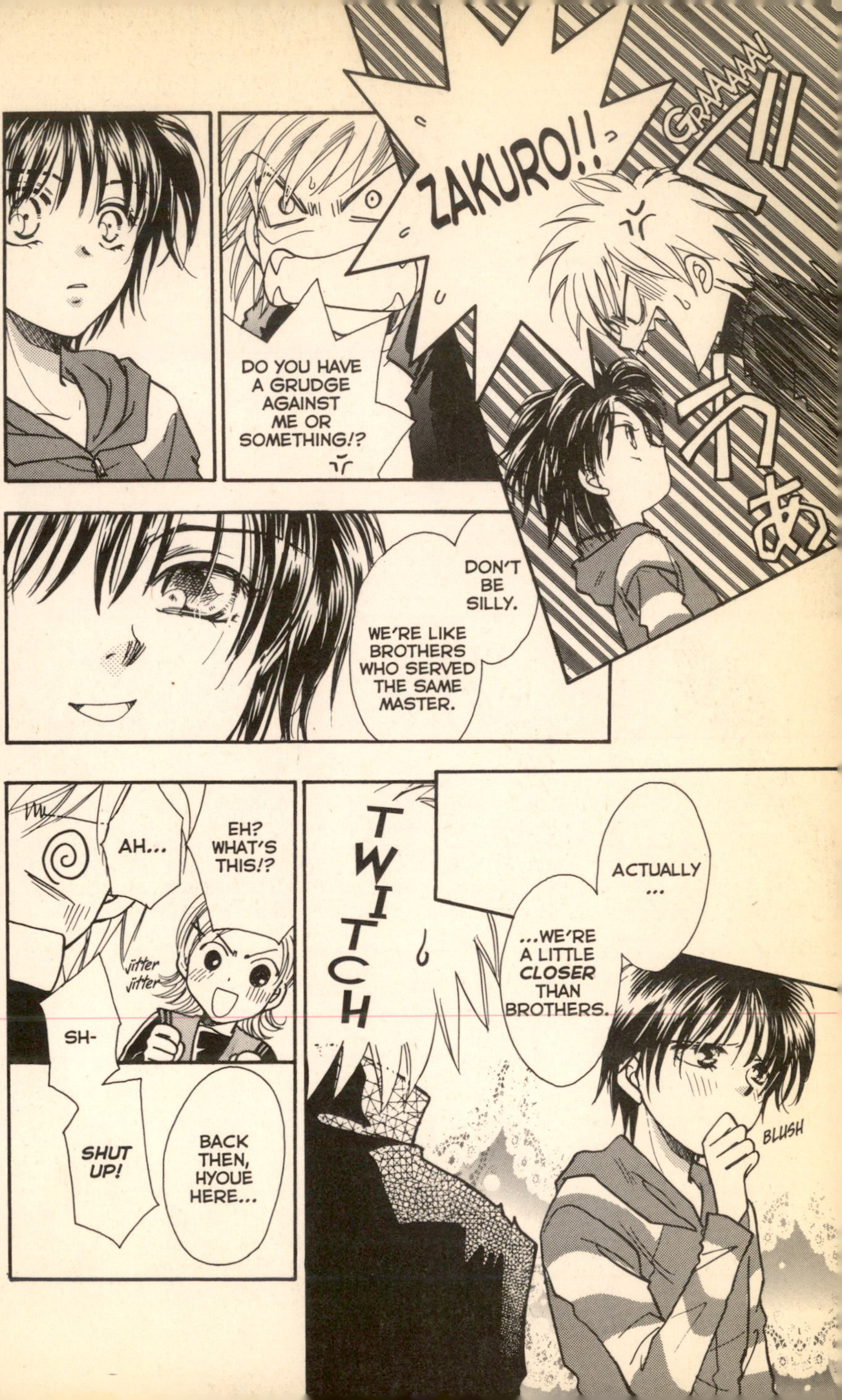
ZAKURO!!
GRAAAA!
DO YOU HAVE A GRUDGE AGAINST ME OR SOMETHING!?
DON'T BE SILLY.
WE'RE LIKE BROTHERS WHO SERVED THE SAME MASTER.
ACTUALLY...
...WE'RE A LITTLE *CLOSER* THAN BROTHERS.
TWITCH
BLUSH
EH? WHAT'S THIS!?
AH...
jitter jitter
SH-
BACK THEN, HYOUE HERE...
SHUT UP!

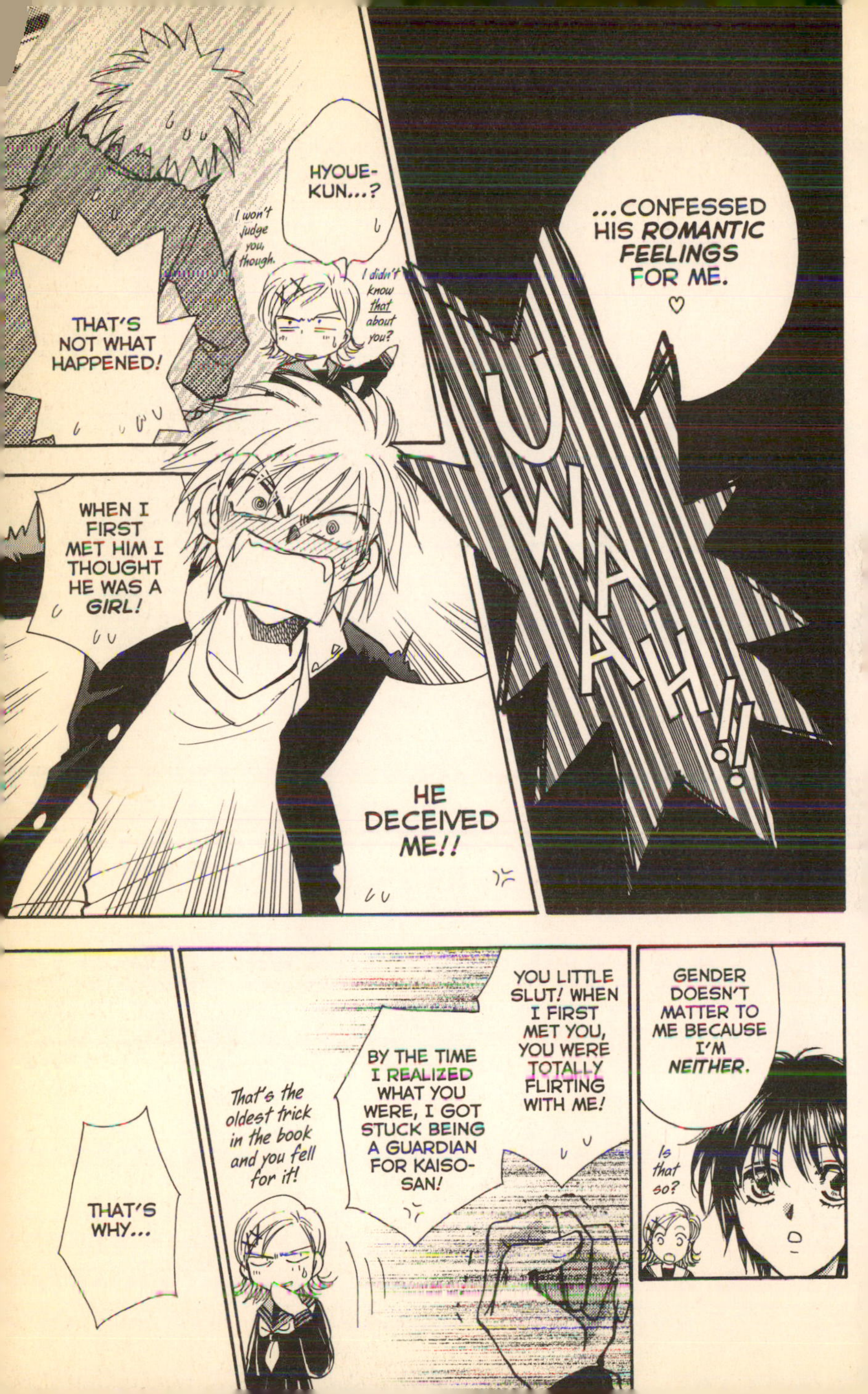

...CONFESSED HIS ROMANTIC FEELINGS FOR ME. ♡
UWAAH!!
HYOUE-KUN...?
I didn't know that about you?
I won't judge you, though.
THAT'S NOT WHAT HAPPENED!
WHEN I FIRST MET HIM I THOUGHT HE WAS A GIRL!
HE DECEIVED ME!!
GENDER DOESN'T MATTER TO ME BECAUSE I'M NEITHER.
Is that so?
YOU LITTLE SLUT! WHEN I FIRST MET YOU, YOU WERE TOTALLY FLIRTING WITH ME!
BY THE TIME I REALIZED WHAT YOU WERE, I GOT STUCK BEING A GUARDIAN FOR KAISO-SAN!
That's the oldest trick in the book and you fell for it!
THAT'S WHY...

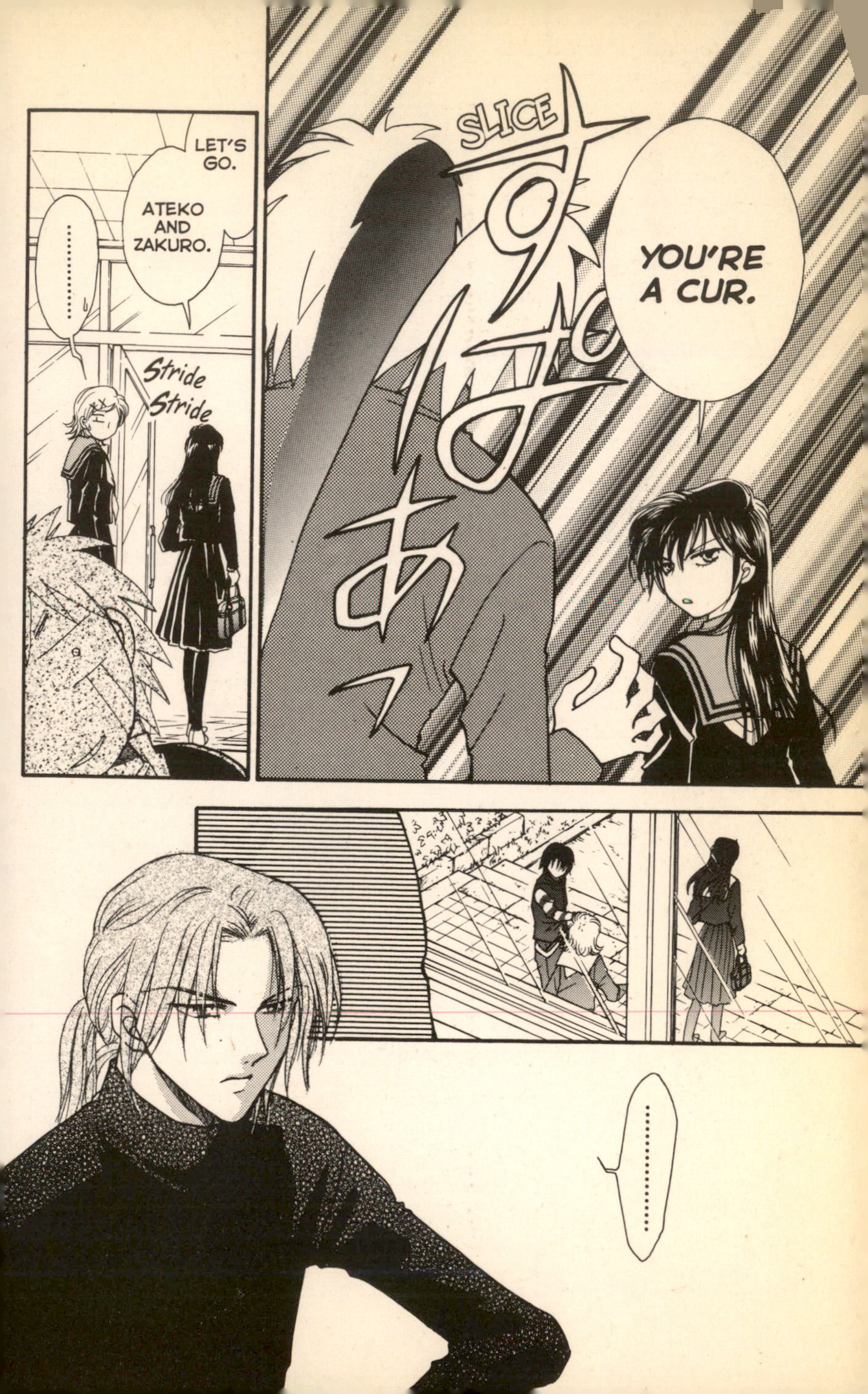
SLICE
YOU'RE A CUR.
LET'S GO.
ATEKO AND ZAKURO.
......
Stride
Stride
......

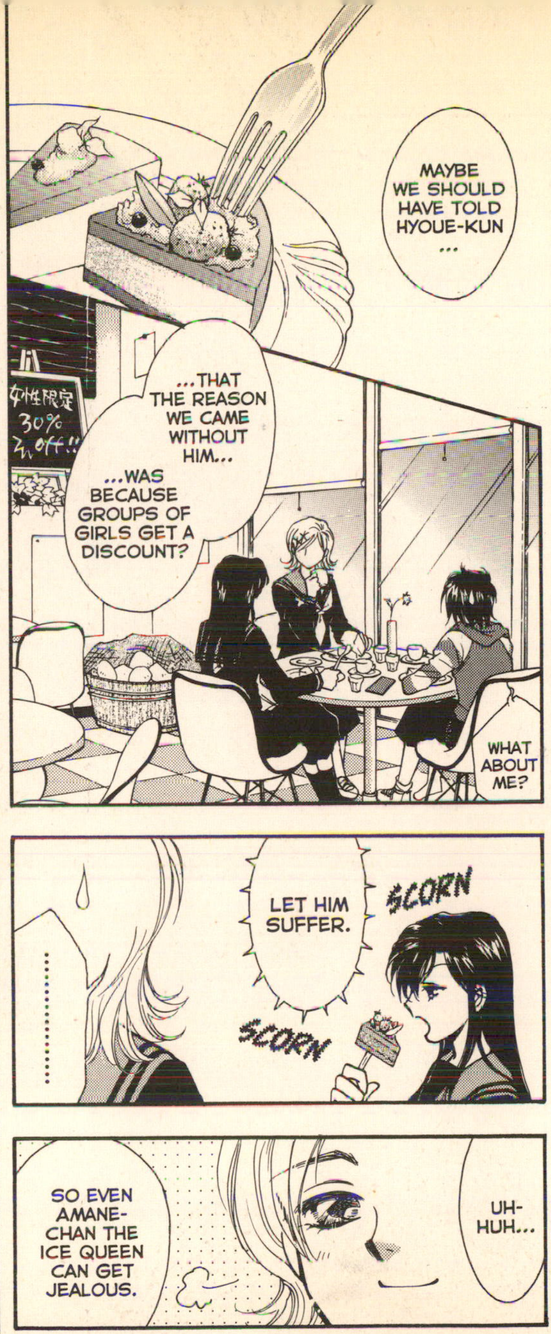
MAYBE WE SHOULD HAVE TOLD HYOUE-KUN...
...THAT THE REASON WE CAME WITHOUT HIM...
...WAS BECAUSE GROUPS OF GIRLS GET A DISCOUNT?
女性限定 30%
WHAT ABOUT ME?
LET HIM SUFFER.
SCORN
SCORN
UH-HUH...
SO EVEN AMANE-CHAN THE ICE QUEEN CAN GET JEALOUS.

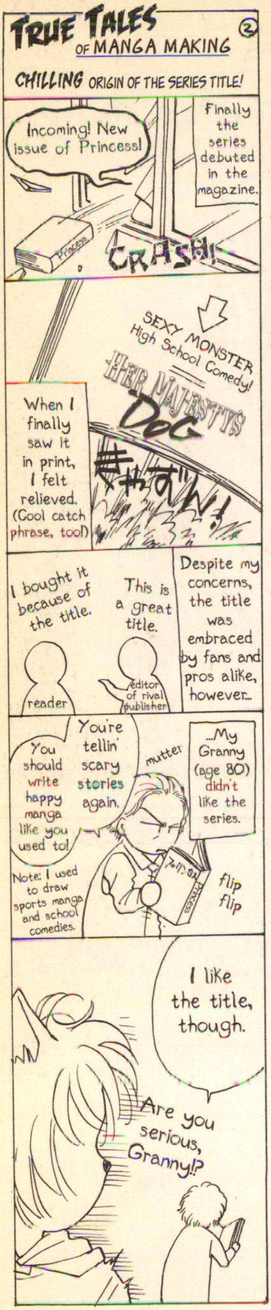
TRUE TALES OF MANGA MAKING ②
CHILLING ORIGIN OF THE SERIES TITLE!
Finally the series debuted in the magazine.
Incoming! New issue of Princess!
CRASH!
Princess
SEXY MONSTER High School Comedy!
HER MAJESTY'S DOG
When I finally saw it in print, I felt relieved. (Cool catch phrase, too!)
Despite my concerns, the title was embraced by fans and pros alike, however...
This is a great title.
editor of rival publisher
I bought it because of the title.
reader
...My Granny (age 80) didn't like the series.
mutter
You're tellin' scary stories again.
You should write happy manga like you used to!
Note: I used to draw sports manga and school comedies.
flip flip
I like the title, though.
Are you serious, Granny!?

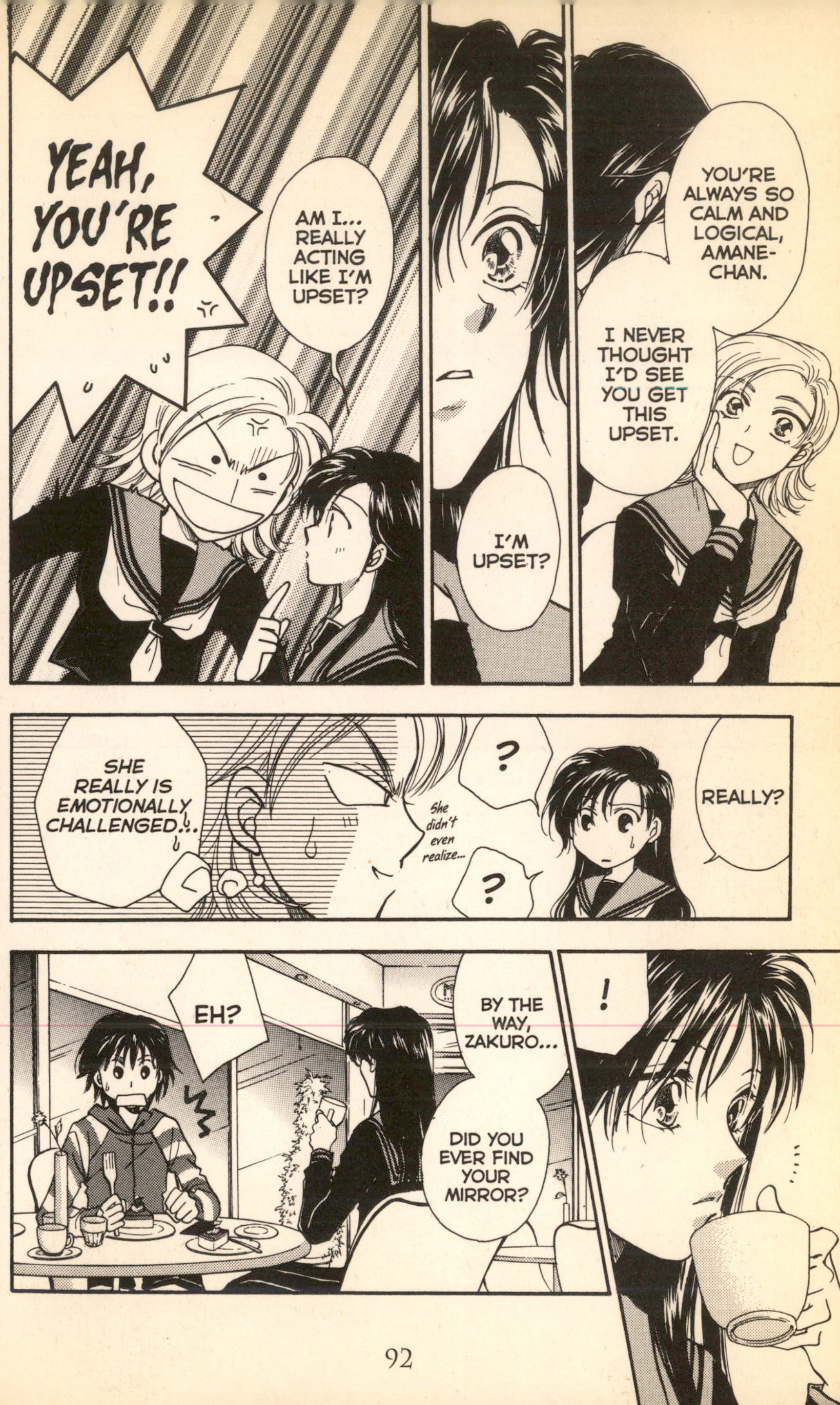
YOU'RE ALWAYS SO CALM AND LOGICAL, AMANE-CHAN.
I NEVER THOUGHT I'D SEE YOU GET THIS UPSET.
I'M UPSET?
AM I... REALLY ACTING LIKE I'M UPSET?
YEAH, YOU'RE UPSET!!
REALLY?
?
?
She didn't even realize...
SHE REALLY IS EMOTIONALLY CHALLENGED...
!
BY THE WAY, ZAKURO...
DID YOU EVER FIND YOUR MIRROR?
EH?

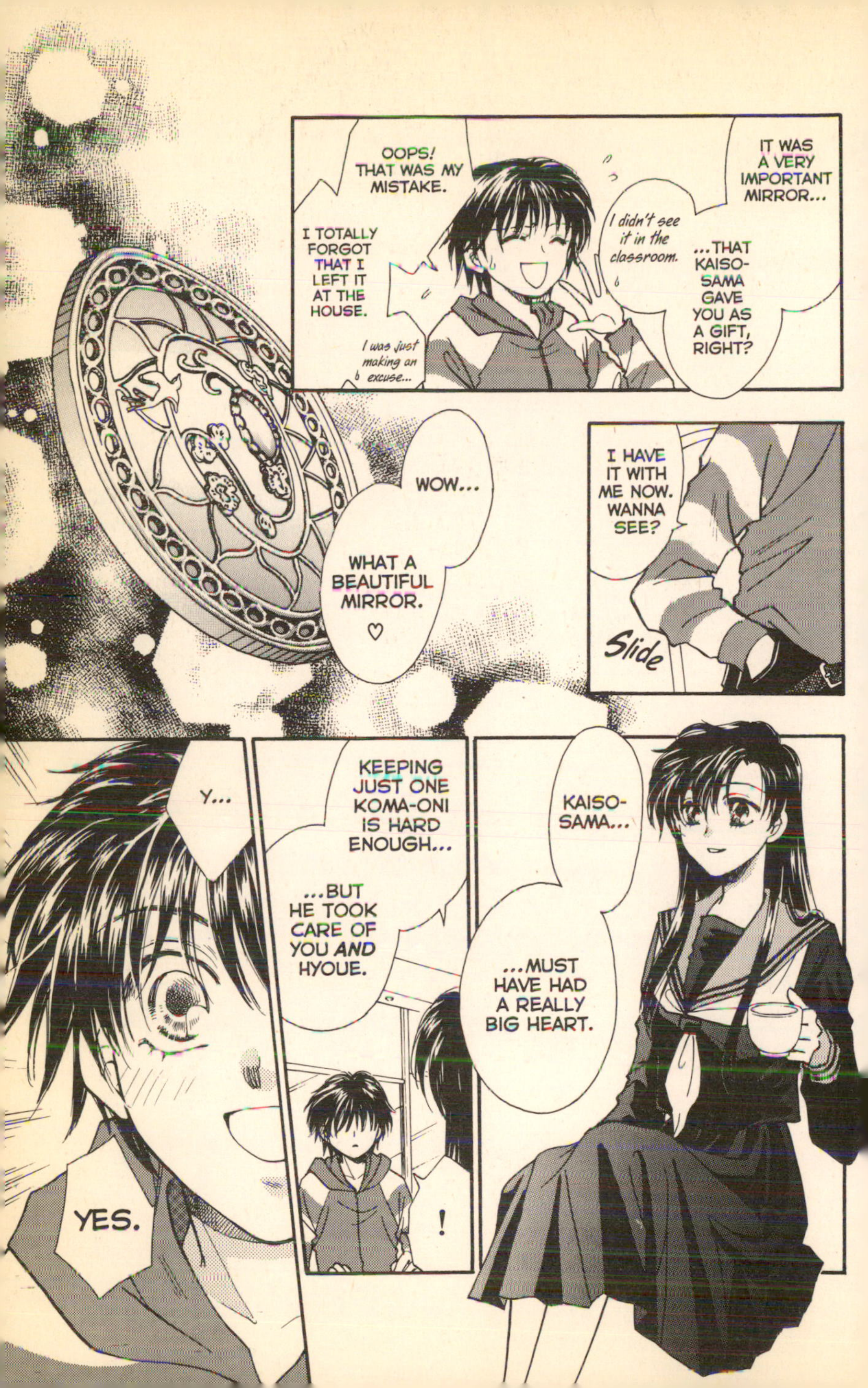
IT WAS A VERY IMPORTANT MIRROR...
...THAT KAISO-SAMA GAVE YOU AS A GIFT, RIGHT?
I didn't see it in the classroom.
OOPS! THAT WAS MY MISTAKE.
I TOTALLY FORGOT THAT I LEFT IT AT THE HOUSE.
I was just making an excuse...
I HAVE IT WITH ME NOW. WANNA SEE?
Slide
WOW...
WHAT A BEAUTIFUL MIRROR. ♡
KAISO-SAMA...
...MUST HAVE HAD A REALLY BIG HEART.
KEEPING JUST ONE KOMA-ONI IS HARD ENOUGH...
...BUT HE TOOK CARE OF YOU *AND* HYOUE.
!
Y...
YES.

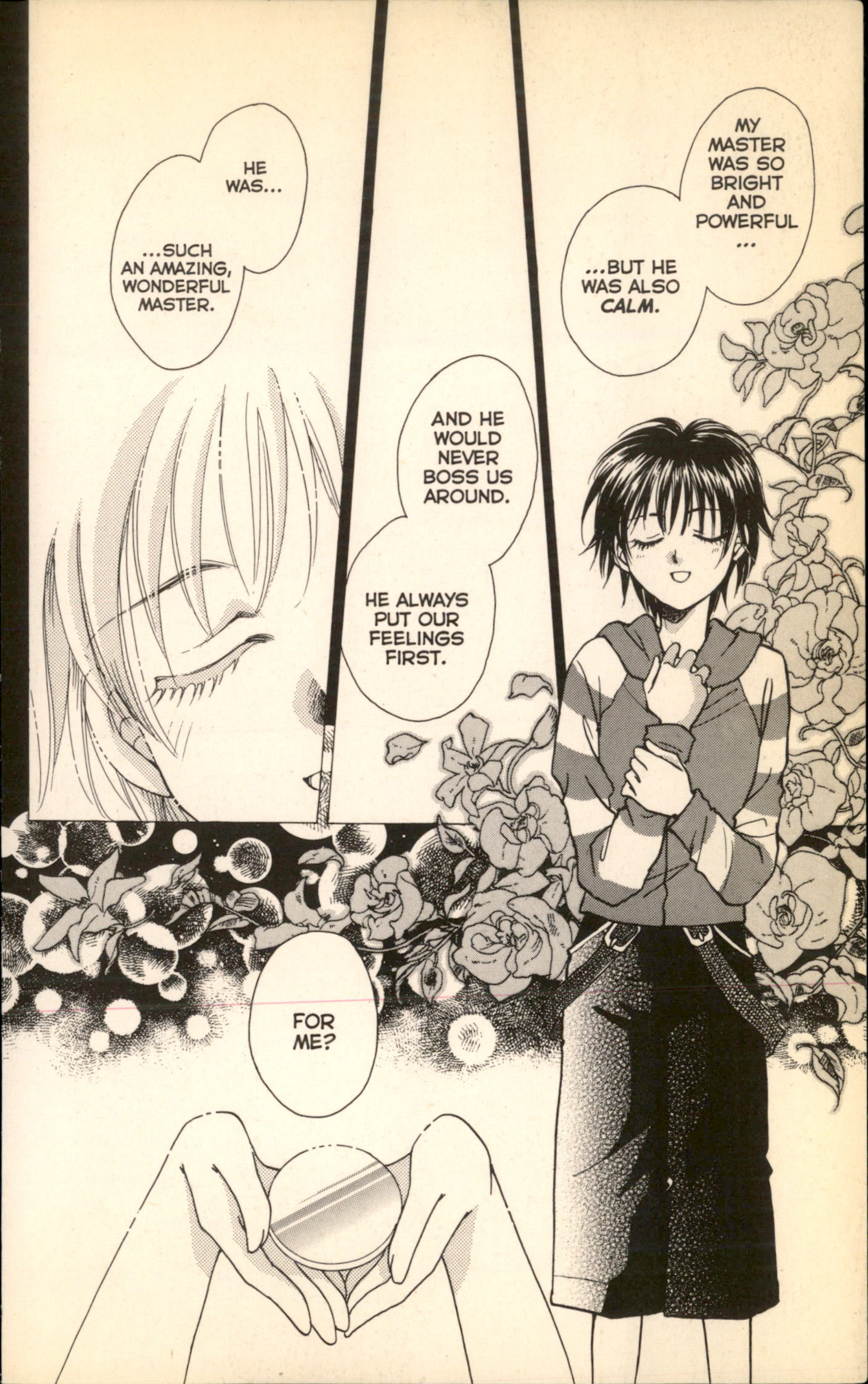
MY MASTER WAS SO BRIGHT AND POWERFUL ...
...BUT HE WAS ALSO *CALM*.
AND HE WOULD NEVER BOSS US AROUND.
HE ALWAYS PUT OUR FEELINGS FIRST.
HE WAS...
...SUCH AN AMAZING, WONDERFUL MASTER.
FOR ME?

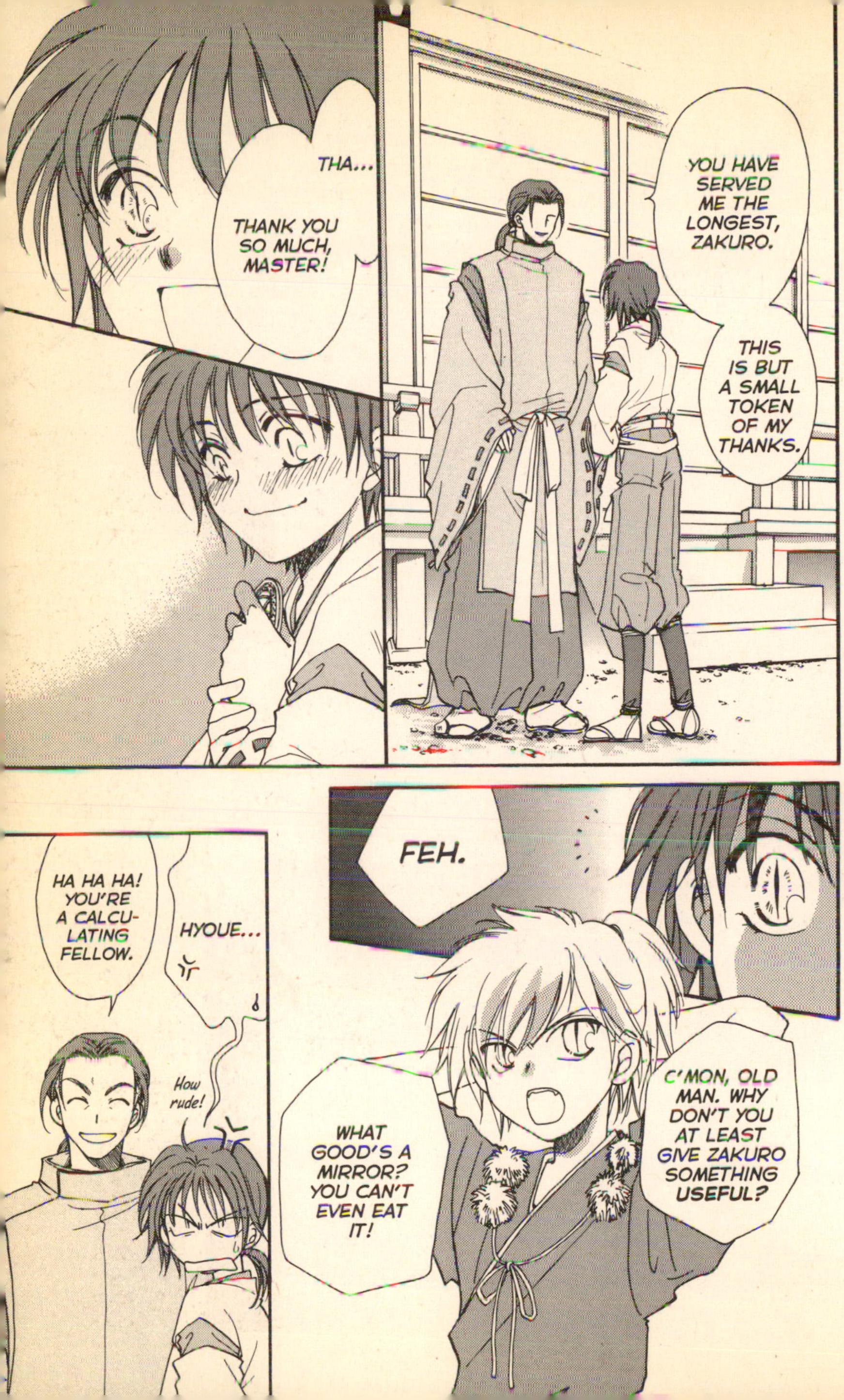
YOU HAVE SERVED ME THE LONGEST, ZAKURO.
THIS IS BUT A SMALL TOKEN OF MY THANKS.
THA...
THANK YOU SO MUCH, MASTER!
FEH.
C'MON, OLD MAN. WHY DON'T YOU AT LEAST GIVE ZAKURO SOMETHING USEFUL?
WHAT GOOD'S A MIRROR? YOU CAN'T EVEN EAT IT!
HYOUE...
HA HA HA! YOU'RE A CALCULATING FELLOW.
How rude!

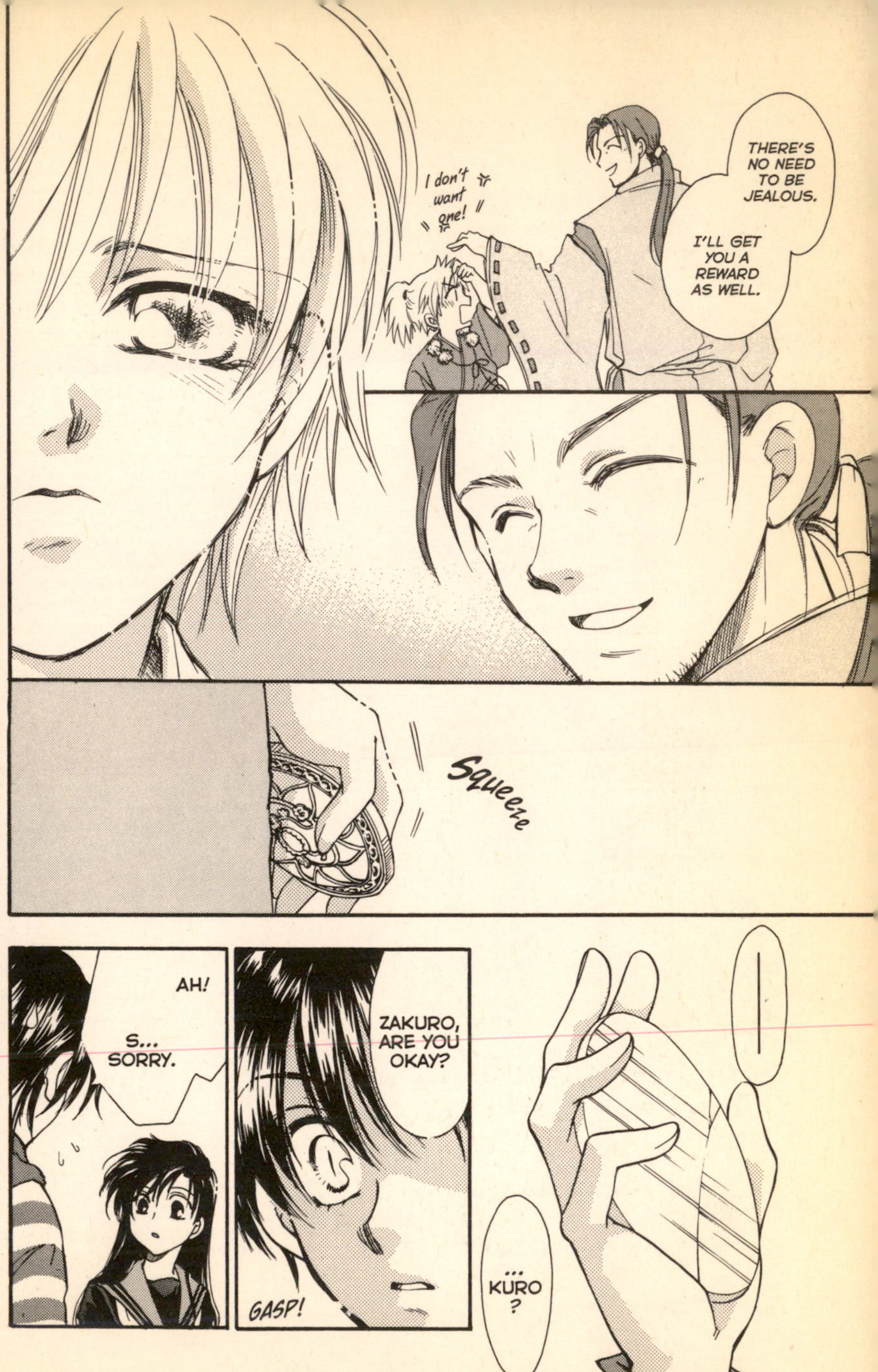
THERE'S NO NEED TO BE JEALOUS.
I'LL GET YOU A REWARD AS WELL.
I don't want one!
Squeeze
... KURO ?
ZAKURO, ARE YOU OKAY?
GASP!
AH!
S... SORRY.

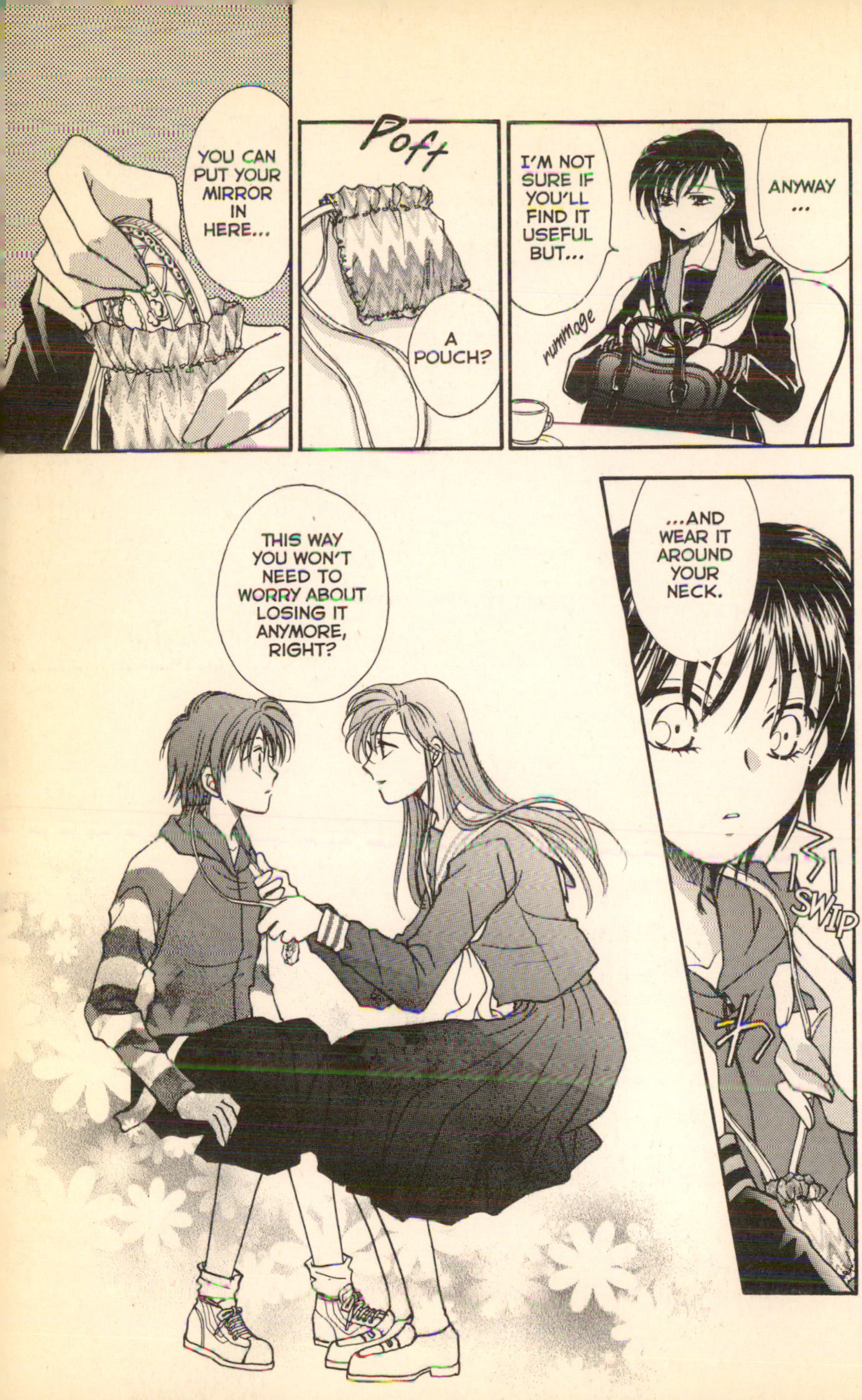
ANYWAY ...
I'M NOT SURE IF YOU'LL FIND IT USEFUL BUT...
rummage
Poff
A POUCH?
YOU CAN PUT YOUR MIRROR IN HERE...
...AND WEAR IT AROUND YOUR NECK.
SWIP
THIS WAY YOU WON'T NEED TO WORRY ABOUT LOSING IT ANYMORE, RIGHT?

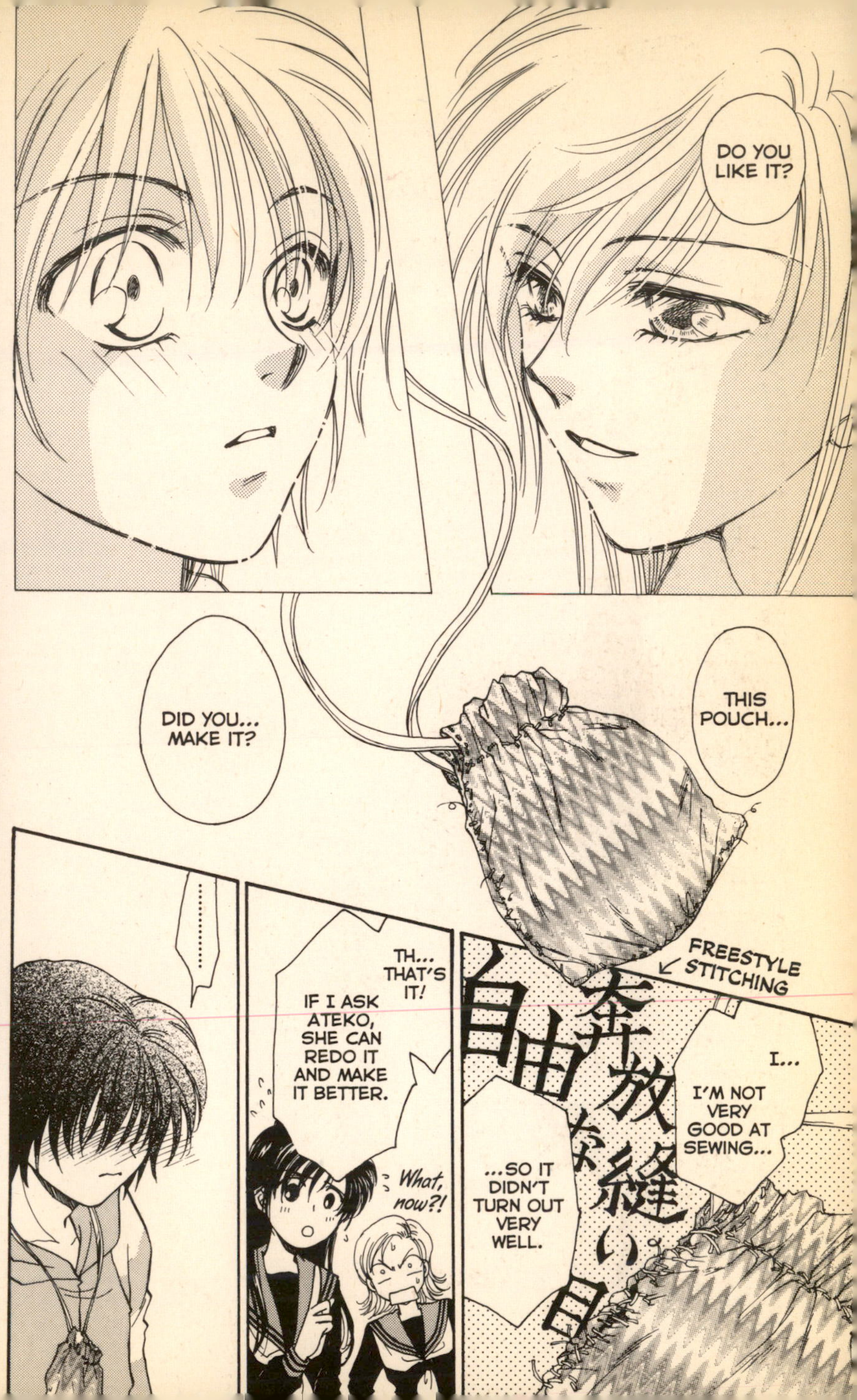
DO YOU LIKE IT?
THIS POUCH...
DID YOU... MAKE IT?
FREESTYLE STITCHING
自由奔放な縫い目
I...
I'M NOT VERY GOOD AT SEWING...
...SO IT DIDN'T TURN OUT VERY WELL.
TH... THAT'S IT!
IF I ASK ATEKO, SHE CAN REDO IT AND MAKE IT BETTER.
What, now?!
......

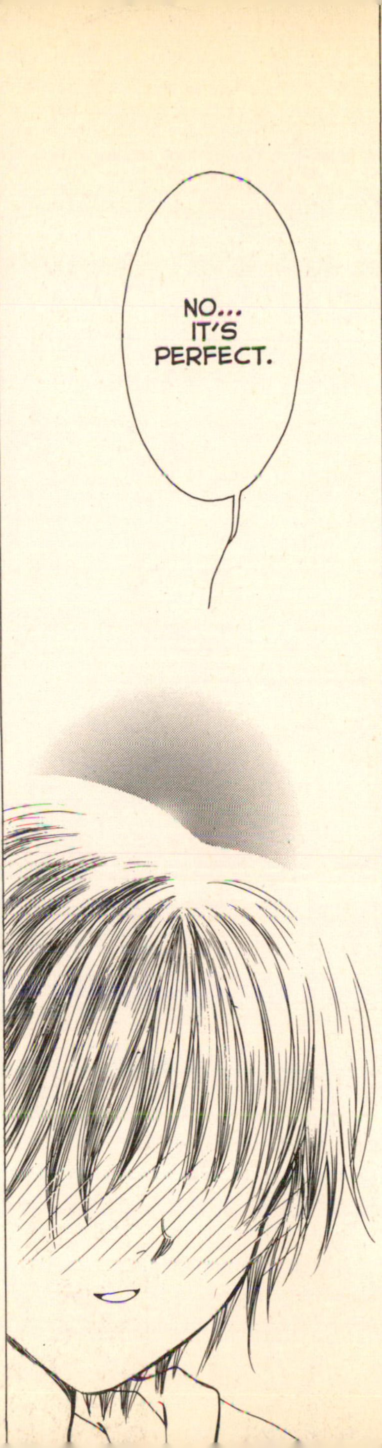
NO... IT'S PERFECT.

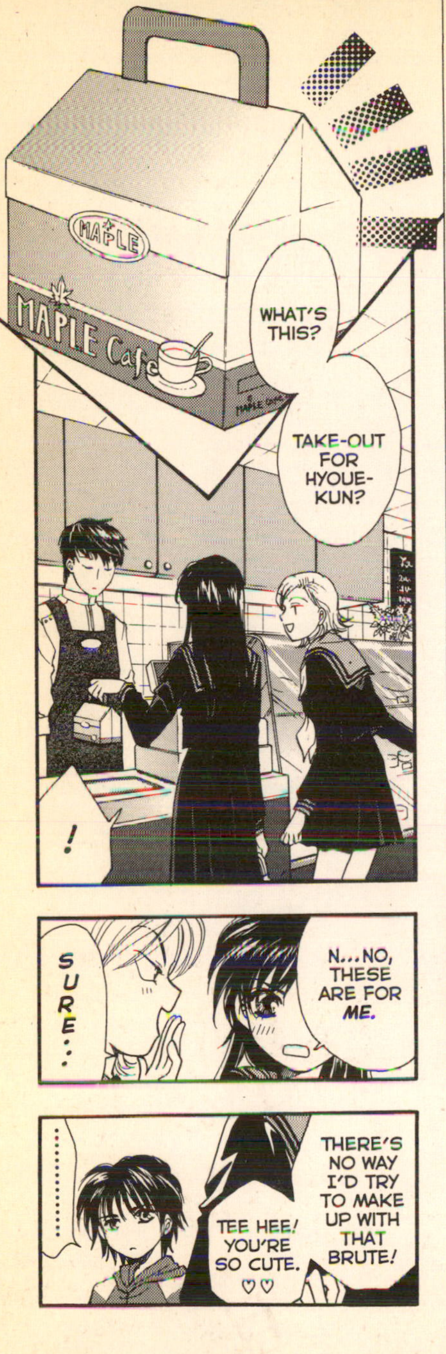
MAPLE
MAPLE Café
WHAT'S THIS?
TAKE-OUT FOR HYOUE-KUN?
!
N...NO, THESE ARE FOR *ME.*
SURE...
THERE'S NO WAY I'D TRY TO MAKE UP WITH THAT BRUTE!
TEE HEE! YOU'RE SO CUTE. ♡♡
....

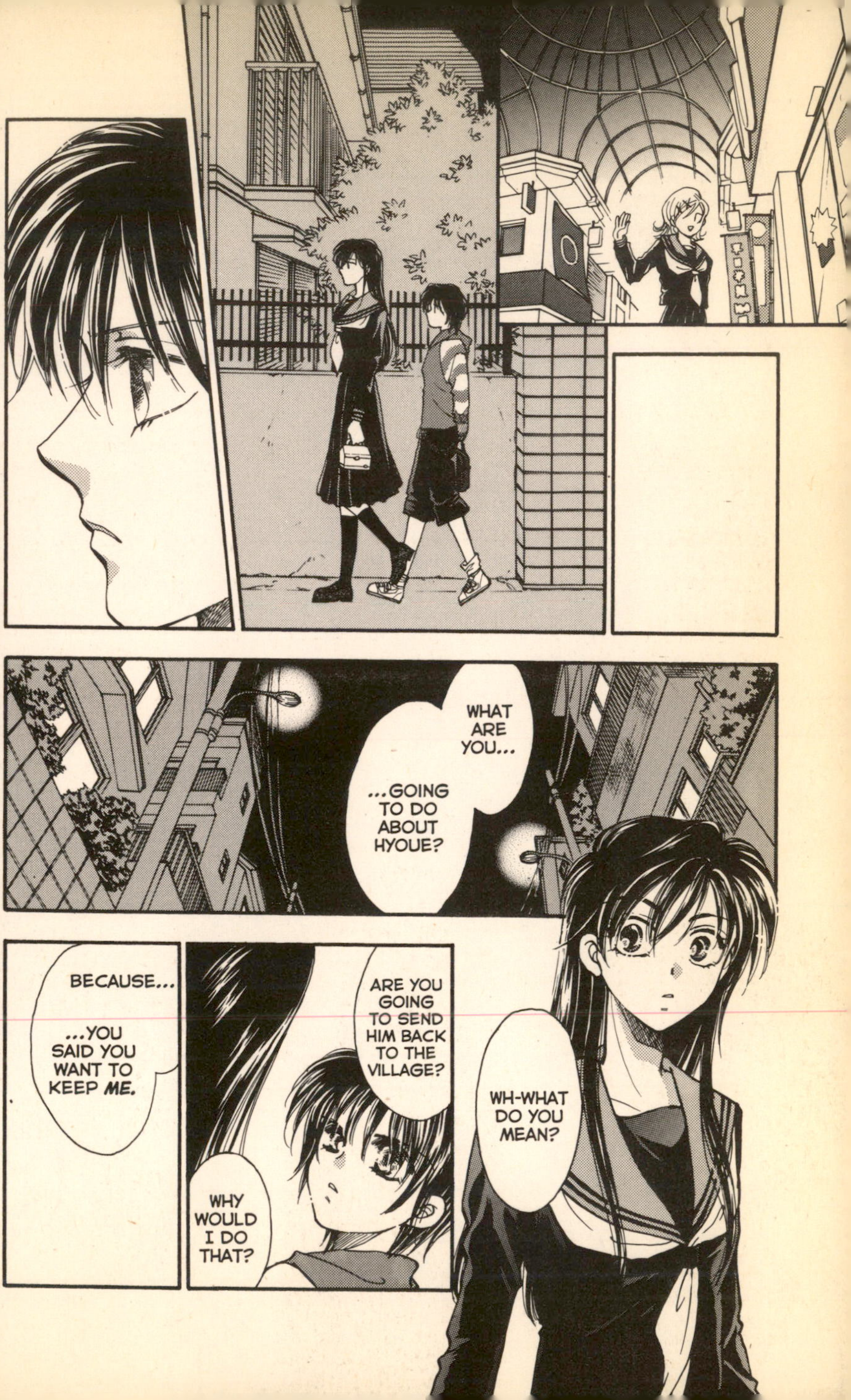
WHAT ARE YOU...
...GOING TO DO ABOUT HYOUE?
WH-WHAT DO YOU MEAN?
ARE YOU GOING TO SEND HIM BACK TO THE VILLAGE?
WHY WOULD I DO THAT?
BECAUSE...
...YOU SAID YOU WANT TO KEEP *ME.*

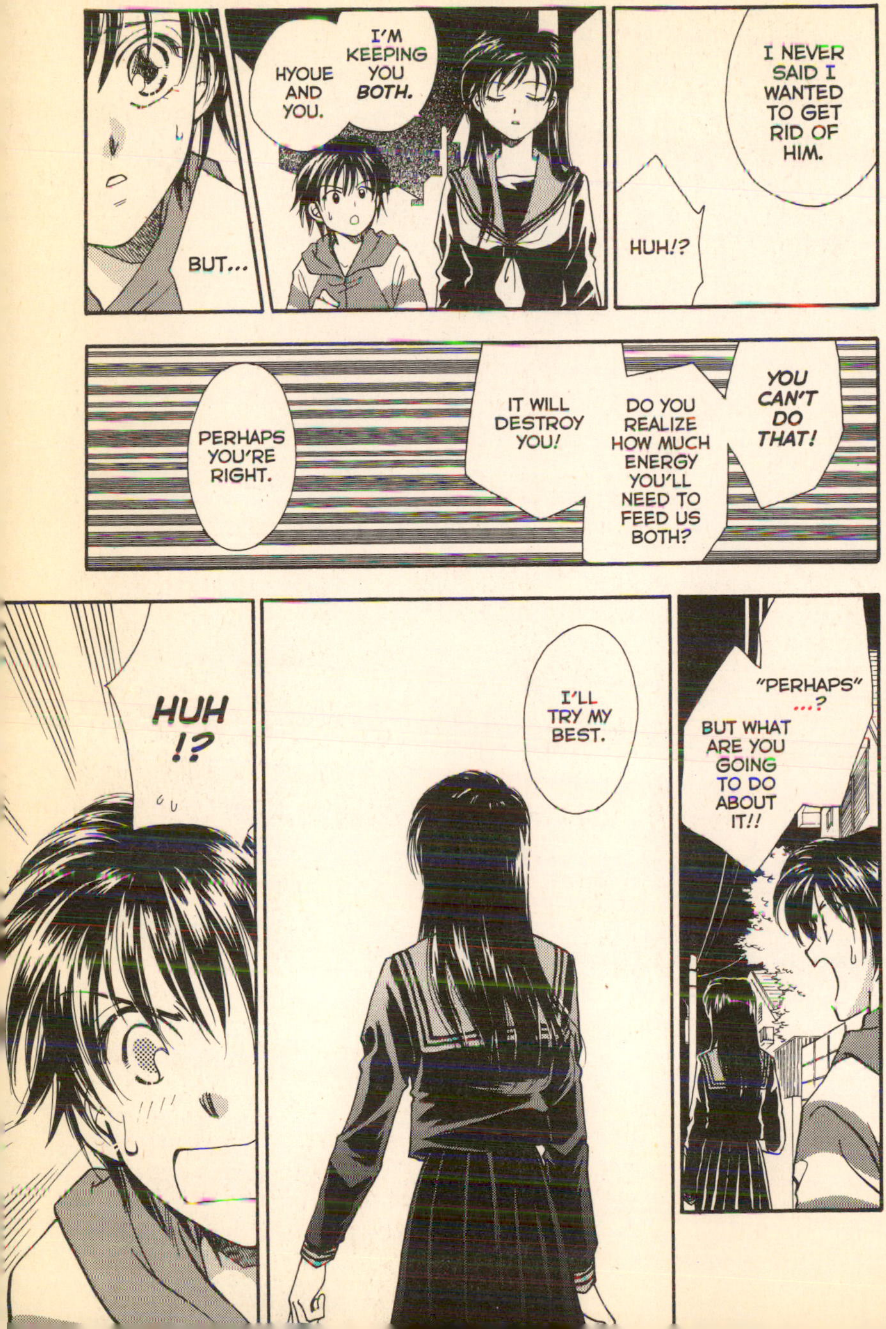
I NEVER SAID I WANTED TO GET RID OF HIM.
HUH!?
I'M KEEPING YOU BOTH.
HYOUE AND YOU.
BUT...
YOU CAN'T DO THAT!
DO YOU REALIZE HOW MUCH ENERGY YOU'LL NEED TO FEED US BOTH?
IT WILL DESTROY YOU!
PERHAPS YOU'RE RIGHT.
"PERHAPS" ...?
BUT WHAT ARE YOU GOING TO DO ABOUT IT!!
I'LL TRY MY BEST.
HUH !?

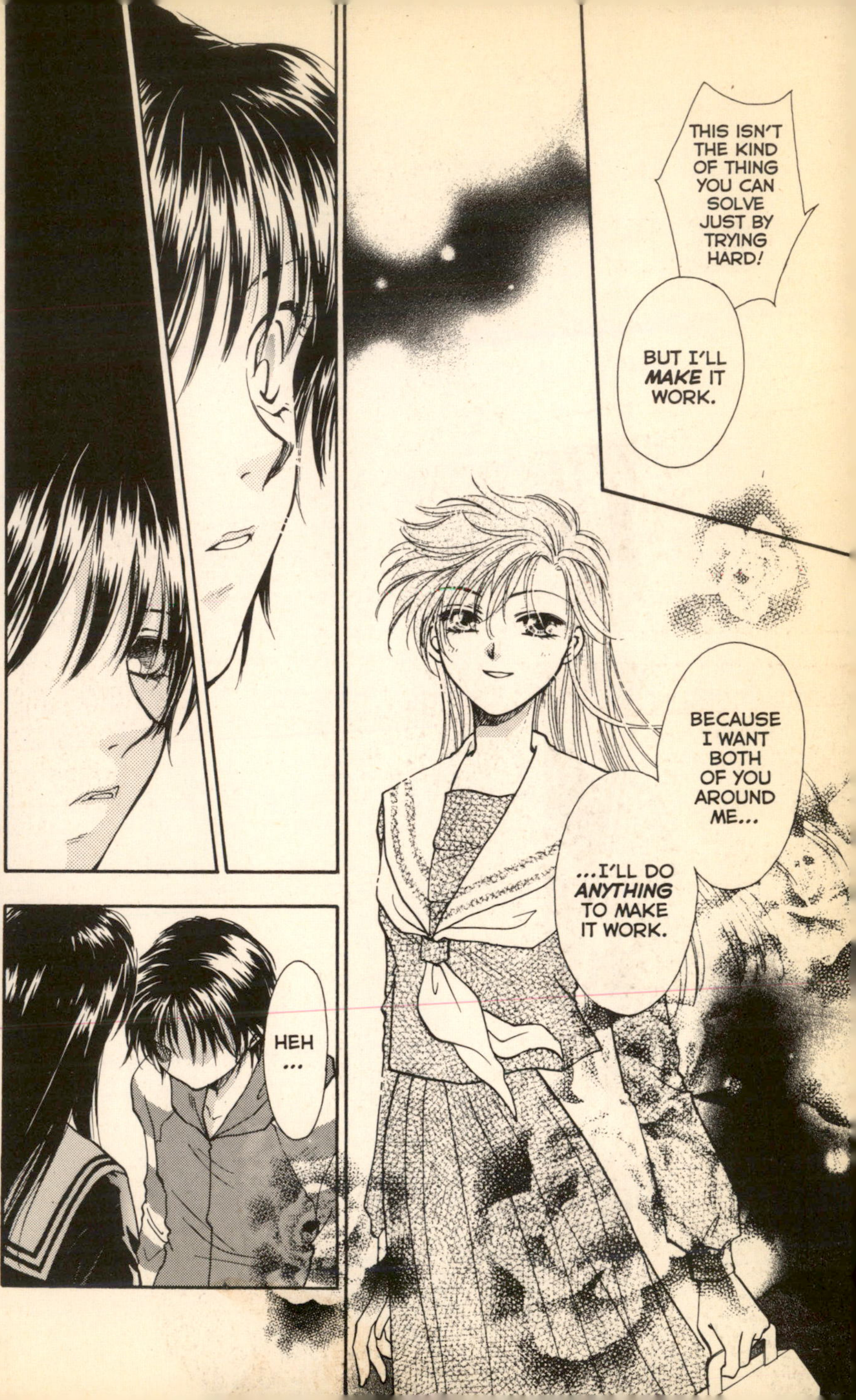
THIS ISN'T THE KIND OF THING YOU CAN SOLVE JUST BY TRYING HARD!
BUT I'LL *MAKE* IT WORK.
BECAUSE I WANT BOTH OF YOU AROUND ME...
...I'LL DO *ANYTHING* TO MAKE IT WORK.
HEH ...

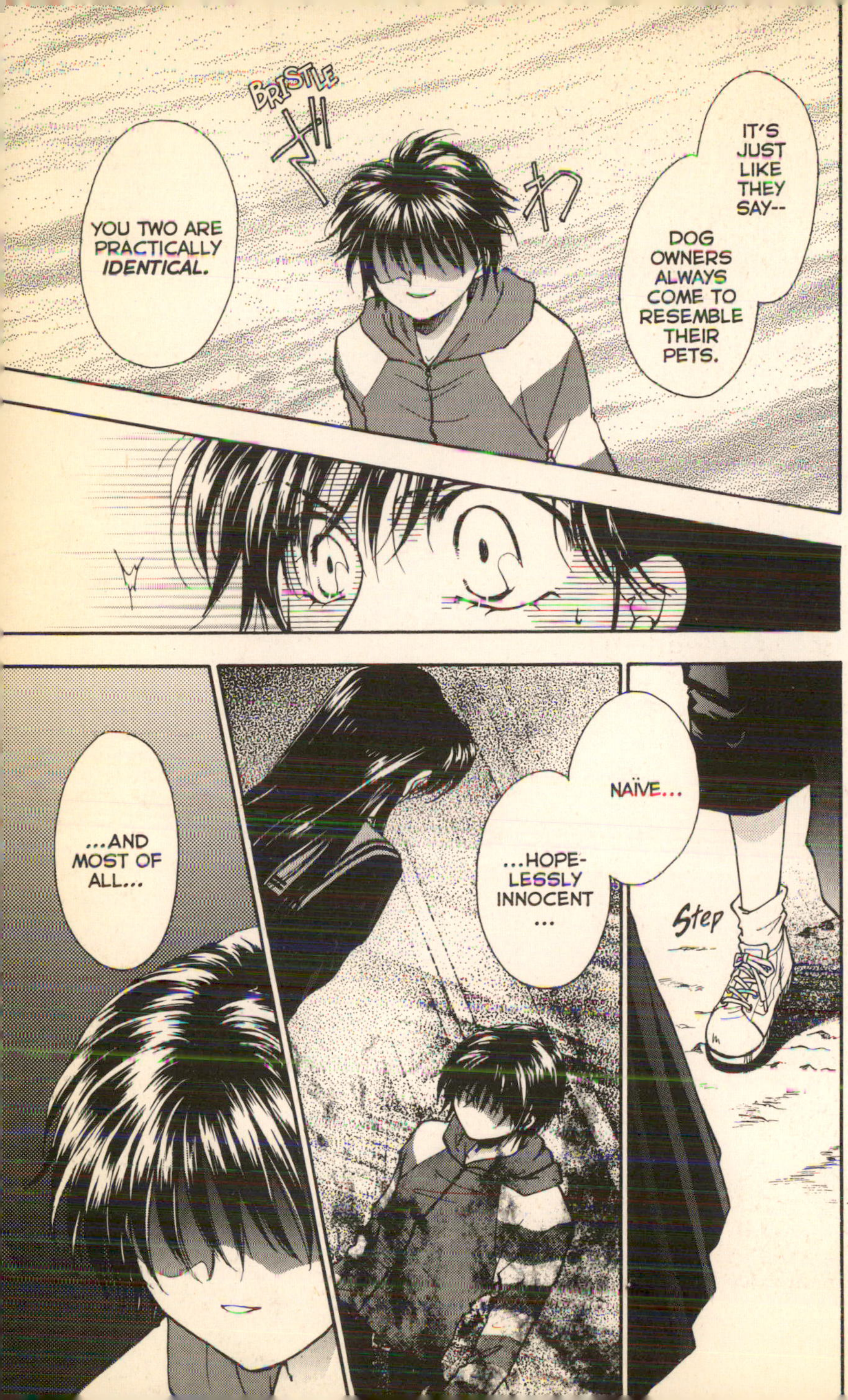
IT'S JUST LIKE THEY SAY--
DOG OWNERS ALWAYS COME TO RESEMBLE THEIR PETS.
BRISTLE
YOU TWO ARE PRACTICALLY *IDENTICAL.*
Step
NAÏVE...
...HOPE-LESSLY INNOCENT ...
...AND MOST OF ALL...

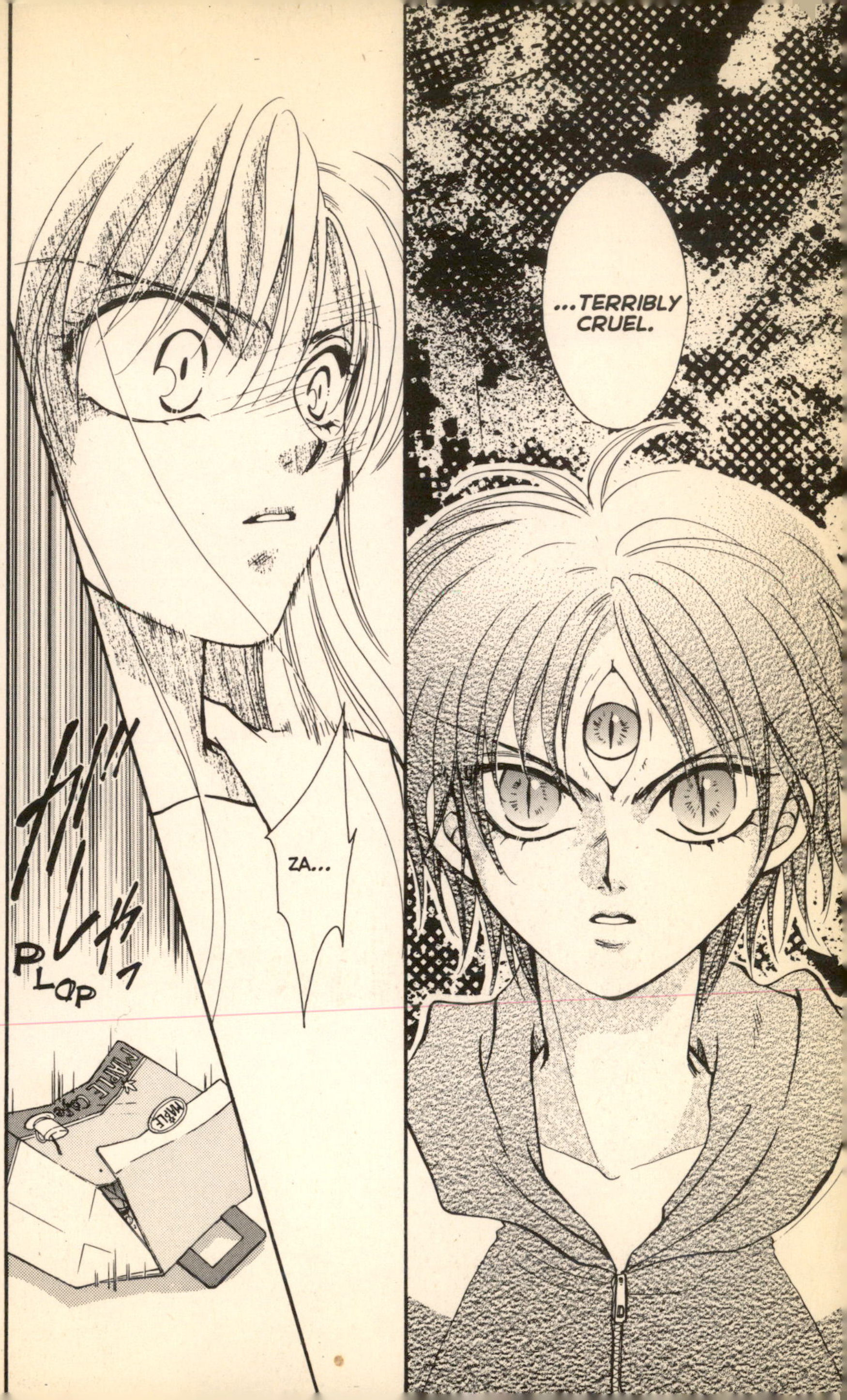
...TERRIBLY CRUEL.
ZA...
PLOP
MAPLE Cafe

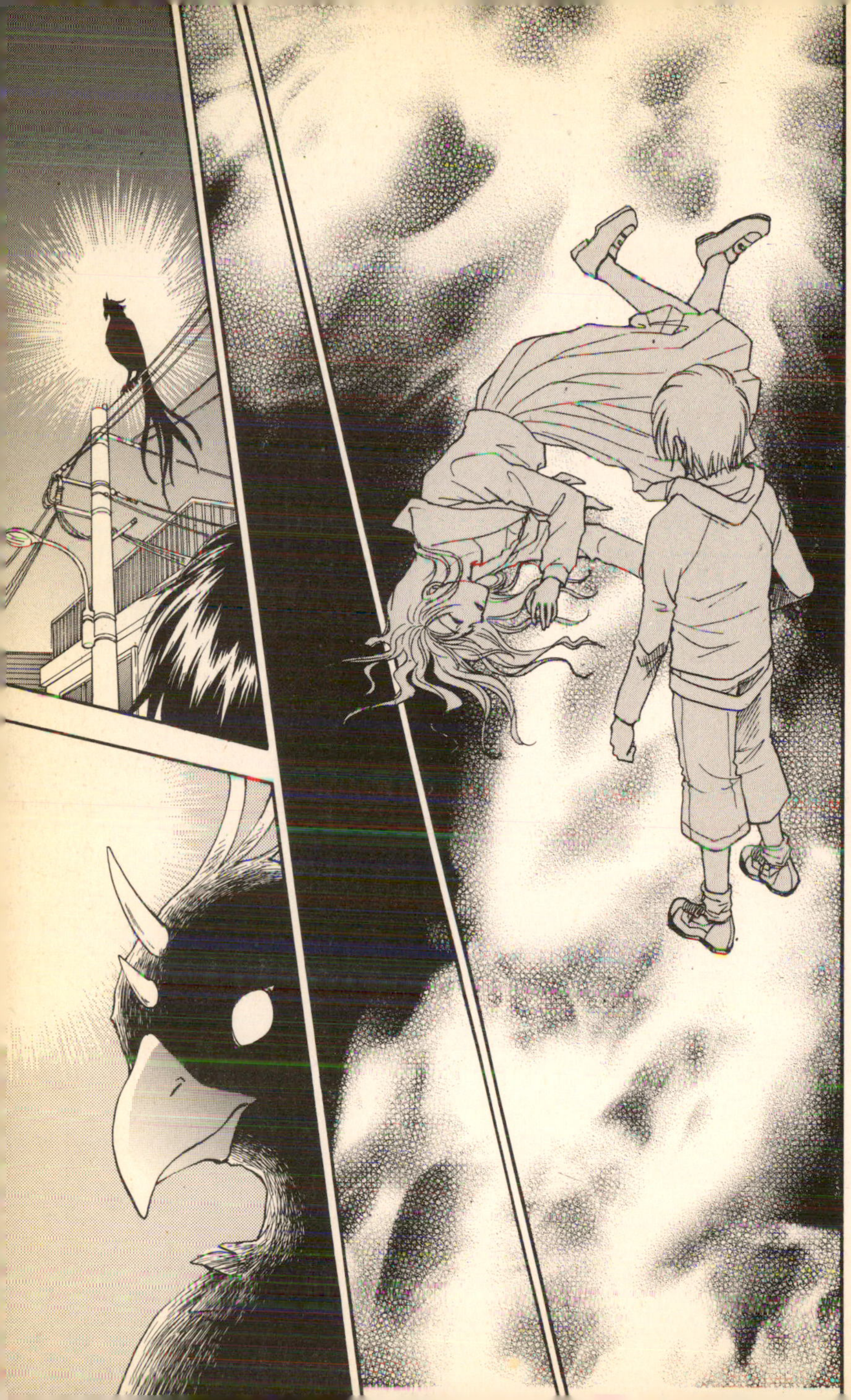

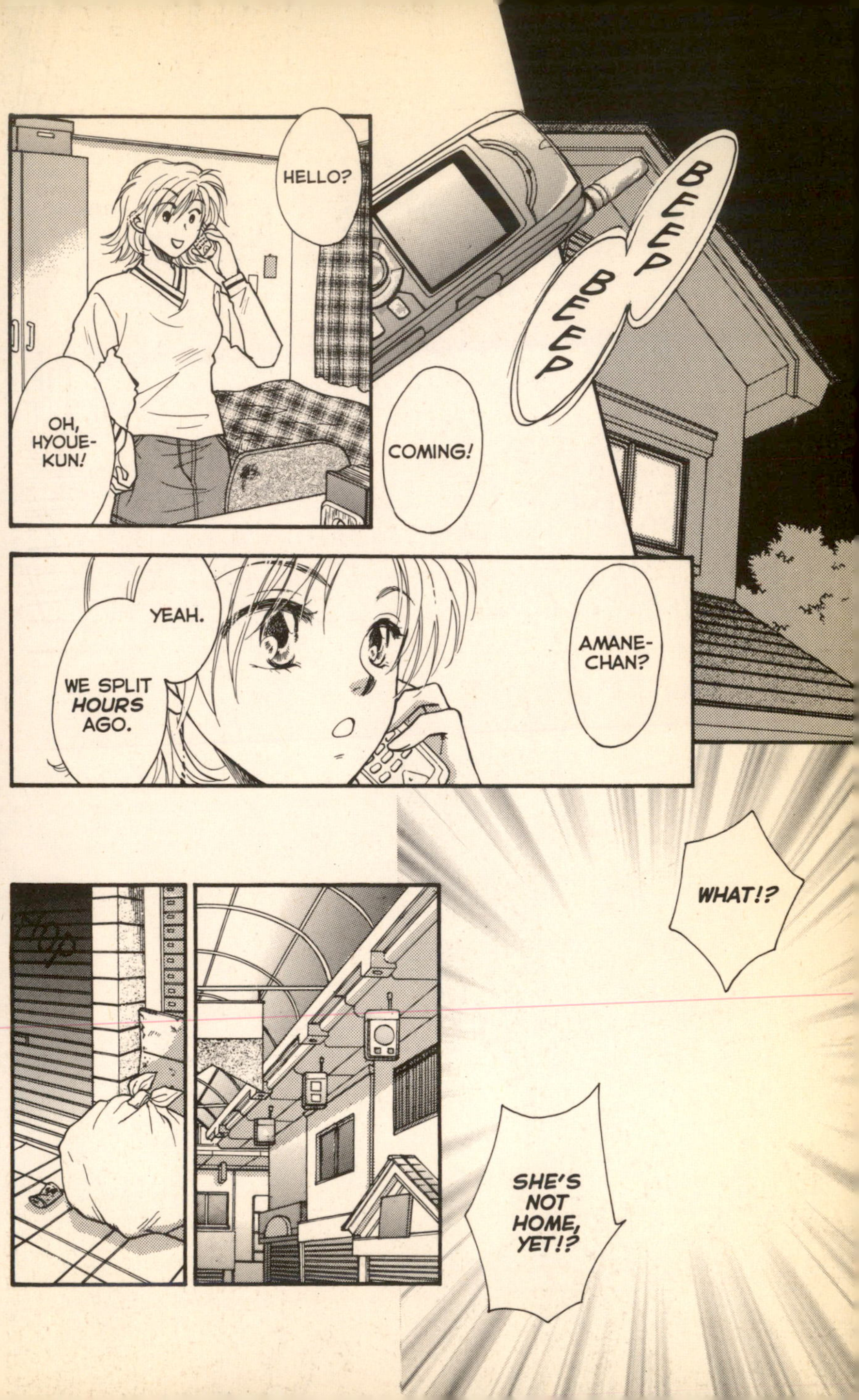
BEEP BEEP
COMING!
HELLO?
OH, HYOUE-KUN!
AMANE-CHAN?
YEAH.
WE SPLIT *HOURS* AGO.
WHAT!?
SHE'S NOT HOME, YET!?

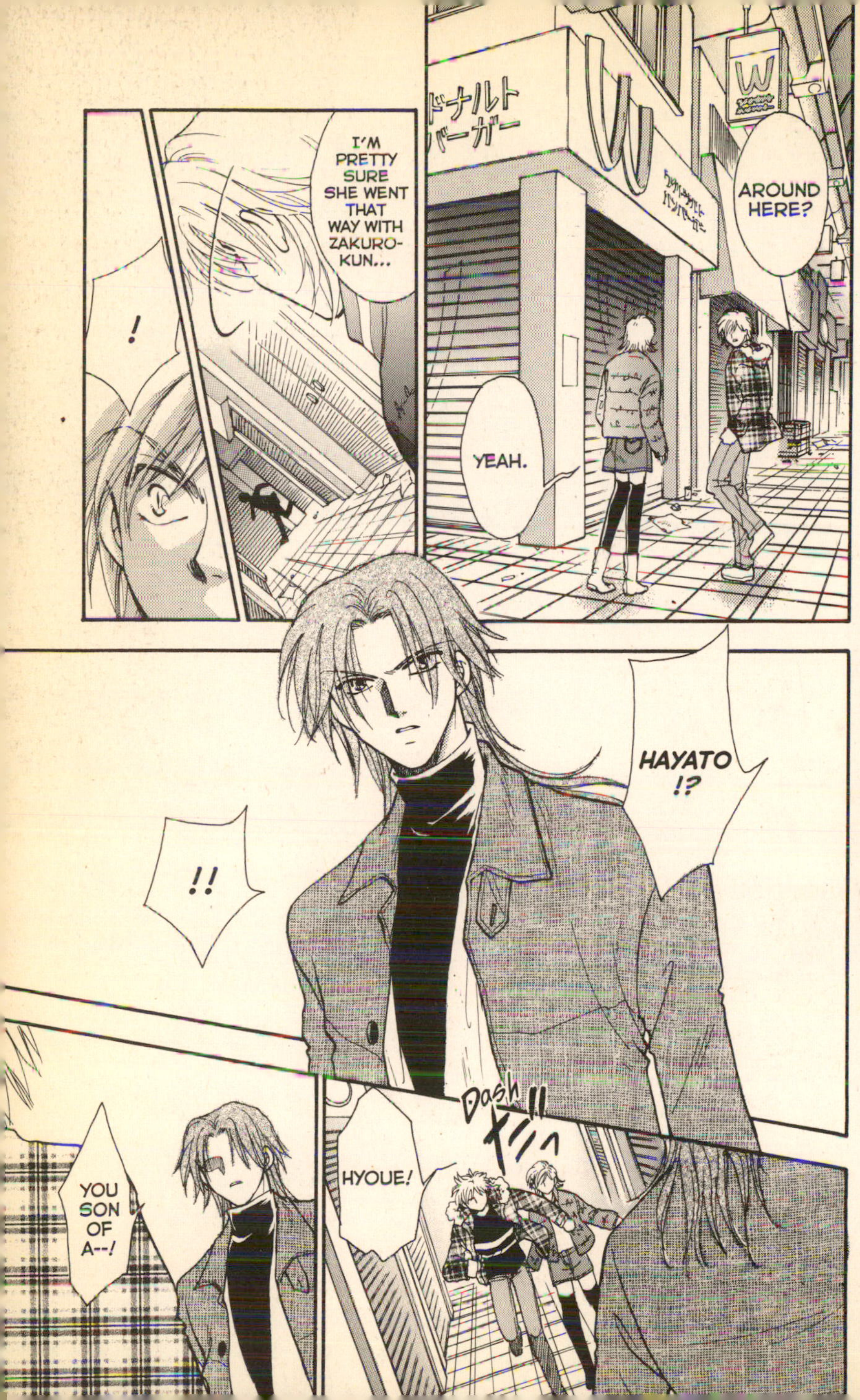
AROUND HERE?
YEAH.
I'M PRETTY SURE SHE WENT THAT WAY WITH ZAKURO-KUN...
!
HAYATO !?
!!
Dash
HYOUE!
YOU SON OF A--!

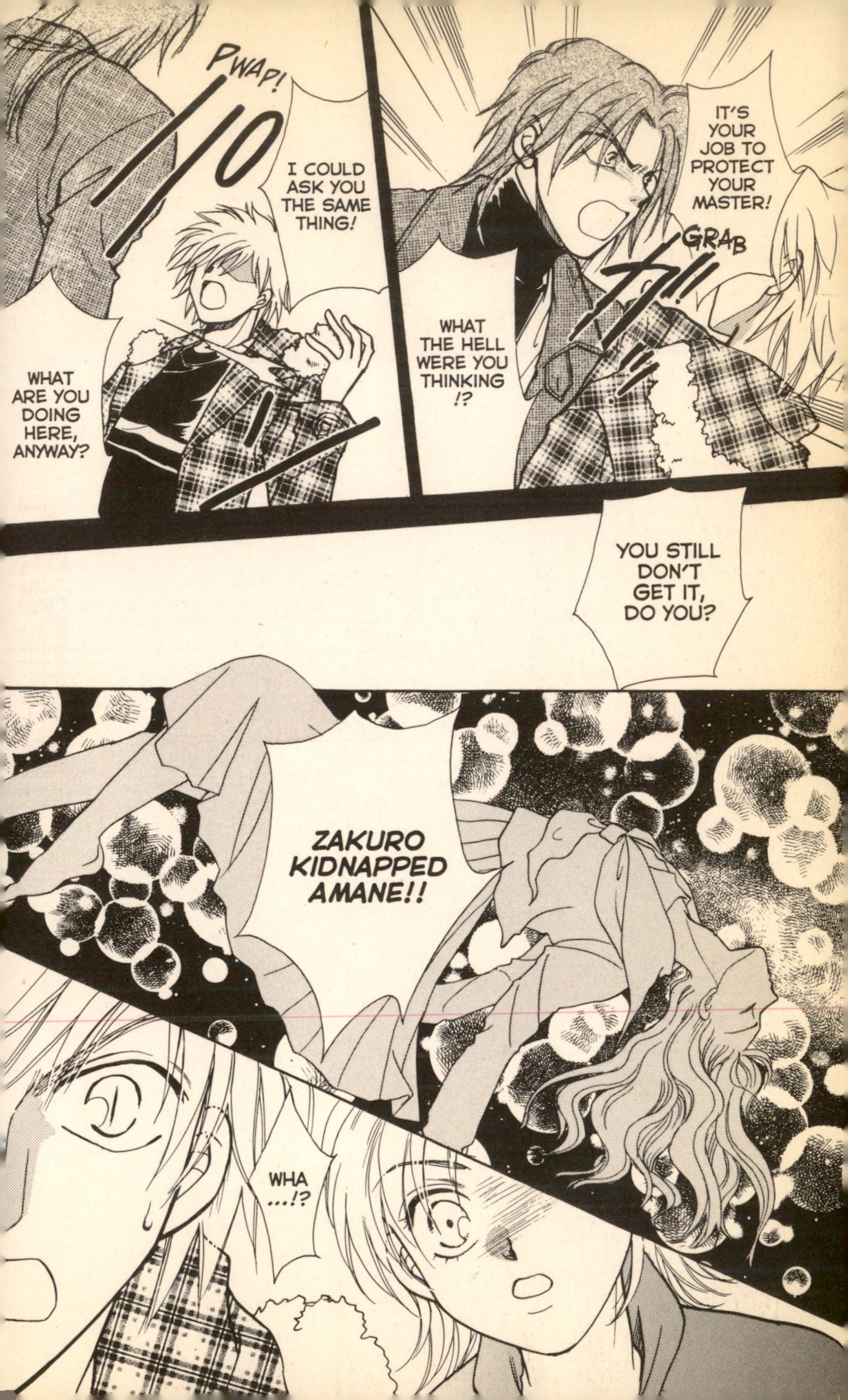

IT'S YOUR JOB TO PROTECT YOUR MASTER!
GRAB
WHAT THE HELL WERE YOU THINKING !?
PWAP!
I COULD ASK YOU THE SAME THING!
WHAT ARE YOU DOING HERE, ANYWAY?
YOU STILL DON'T GET IT, DO YOU?
ZAKURO KIDNAPPED AMANE!!
WHA ...!?

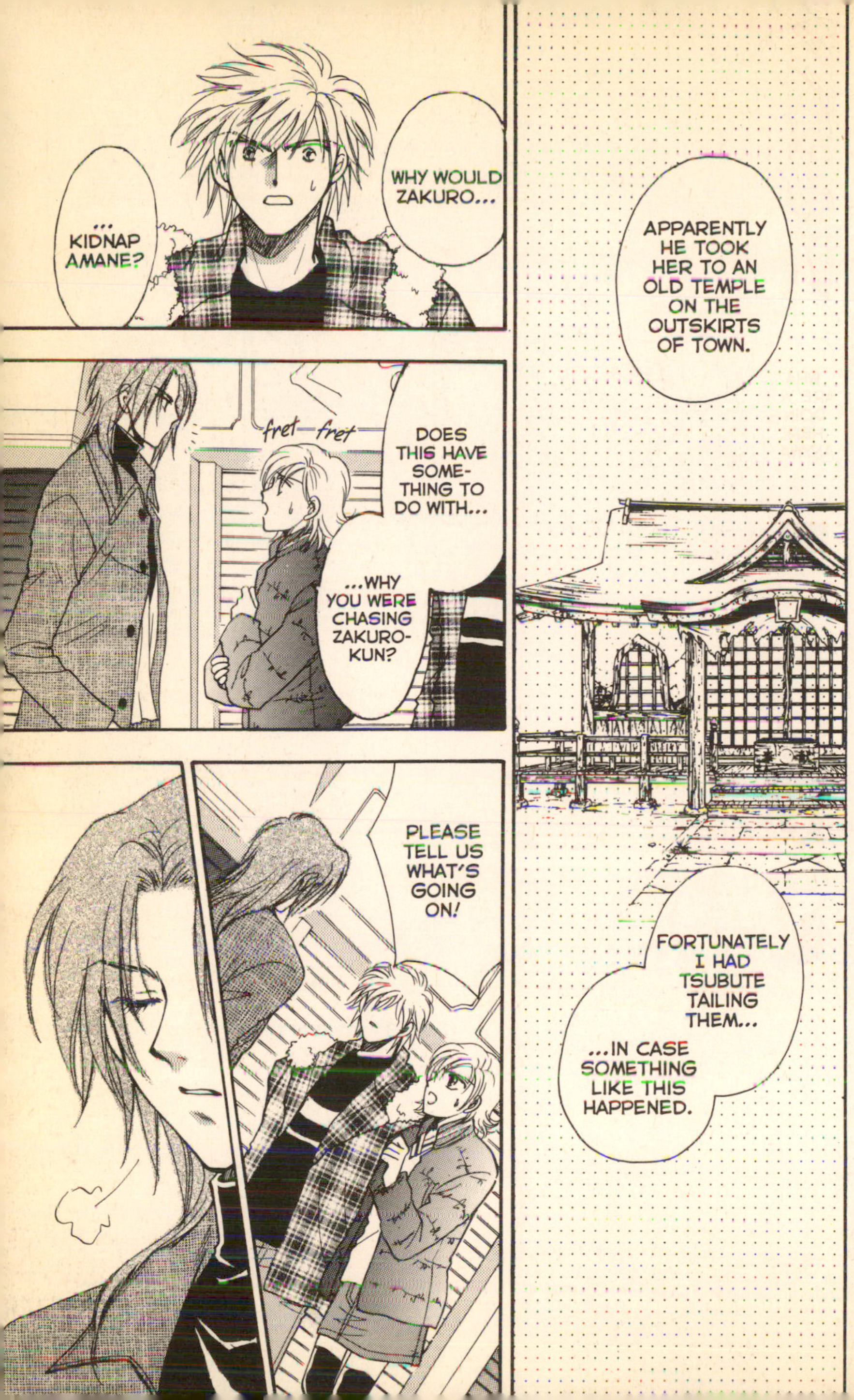
APPARENTLY HE TOOK HER TO AN OLD TEMPLE ON THE OUTSKIRTS OF TOWN.
FORTUNATELY I HAD TSUBUTE TAILING THEM...
...IN CASE SOMETHING LIKE THIS HAPPENED.
WHY WOULD ZAKURO...
... KIDNAP AMANE?
fret fret
DOES THIS HAVE SOME-THING TO DO WITH...
...WHY YOU WERE CHASING ZAKURO-KUN?
PLEASE TELL US WHAT'S GOING ON!

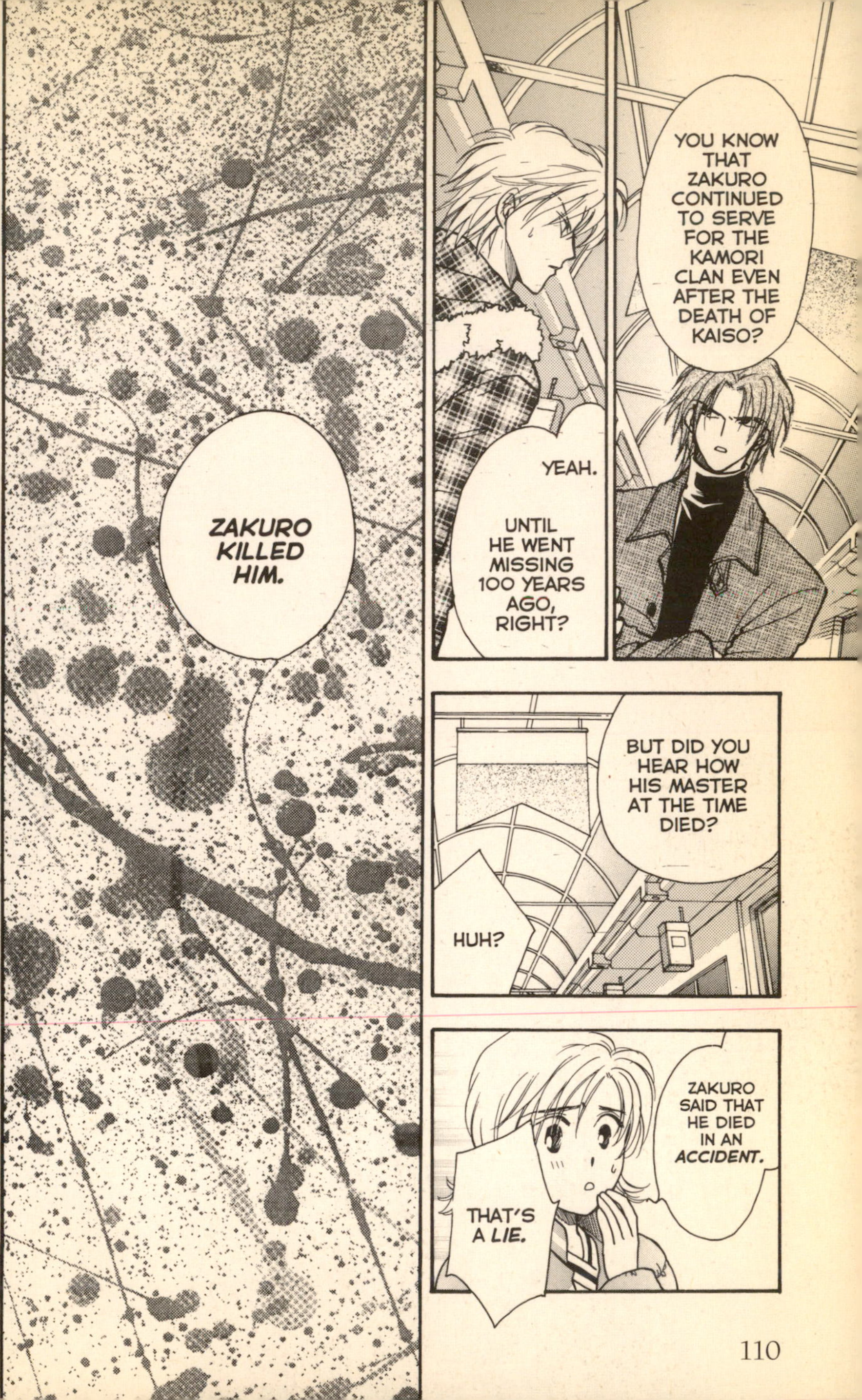
YOU KNOW THAT ZAKURO CONTINUED TO SERVE FOR THE KAMORI CLAN EVEN AFTER THE DEATH OF KAISO?
YEAH.
UNTIL HE WENT MISSING 100 YEARS AGO, RIGHT?
BUT DID YOU HEAR HOW HIS MASTER AT THE TIME DIED?
HUH?
ZAKURO SAID THAT HE DIED IN AN *ACCIDENT*.
THAT'S A *LIE*.
ZAKURO KILLED HIM.

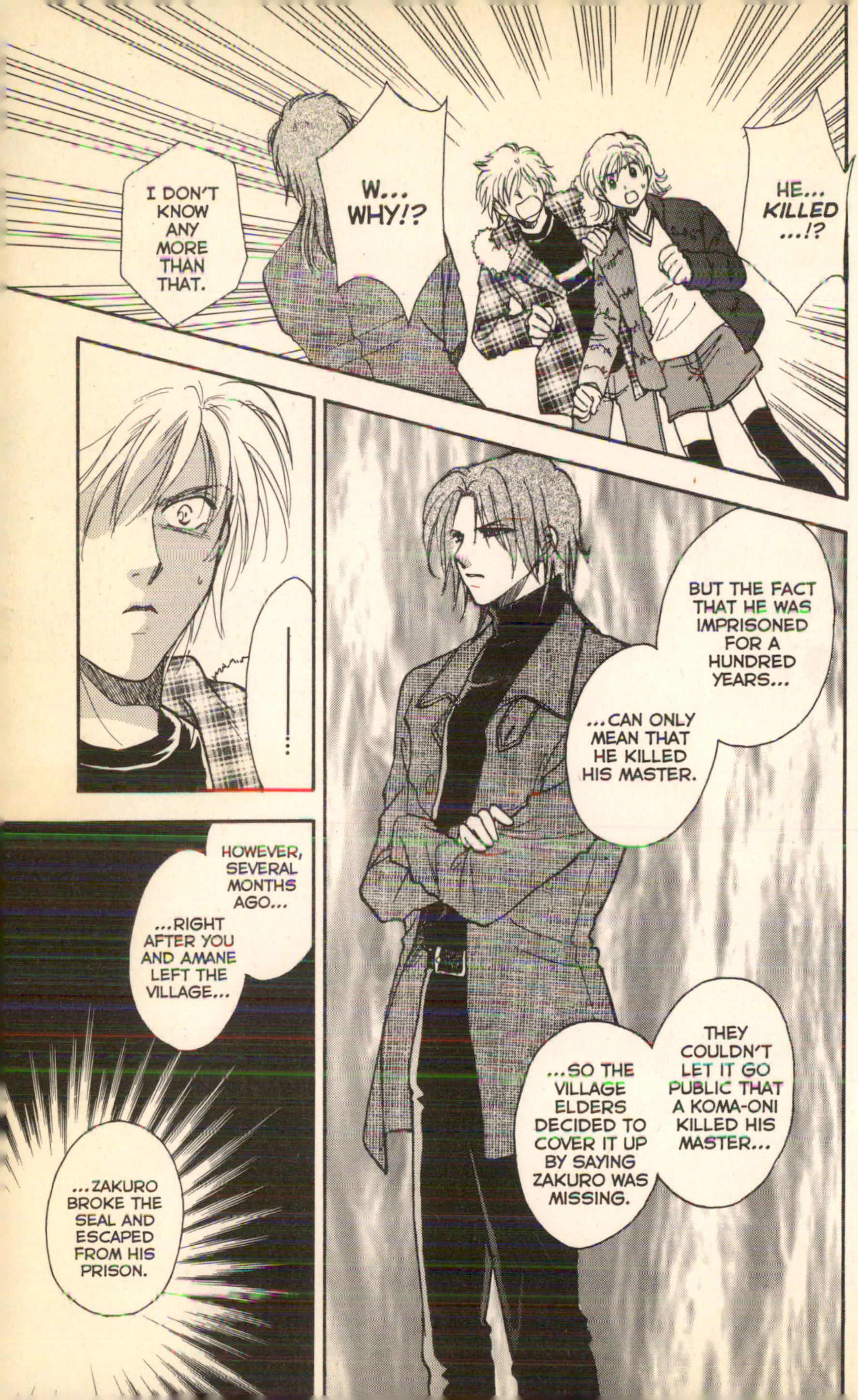
HE... KILLED ...!?
W... WHY!?
I DON'T KNOW ANY MORE THAN THAT.
BUT THE FACT THAT HE WAS IMPRISONED FOR A HUNDRED YEARS...
...CAN ONLY MEAN THAT HE KILLED HIS MASTER.
THEY COULDN'T LET IT GO PUBLIC THAT A KOMA-ONI KILLED HIS MASTER...
...SO THE VILLAGE ELDERS DECIDED TO COVER IT UP BY SAYING ZAKURO WAS MISSING.
HOWEVER, SEVERAL MONTHS AGO...
...RIGHT AFTER YOU AND AMANE LEFT THE VILLAGE...
...ZAKURO BROKE THE SEAL AND ESCAPED FROM HIS PRISON.

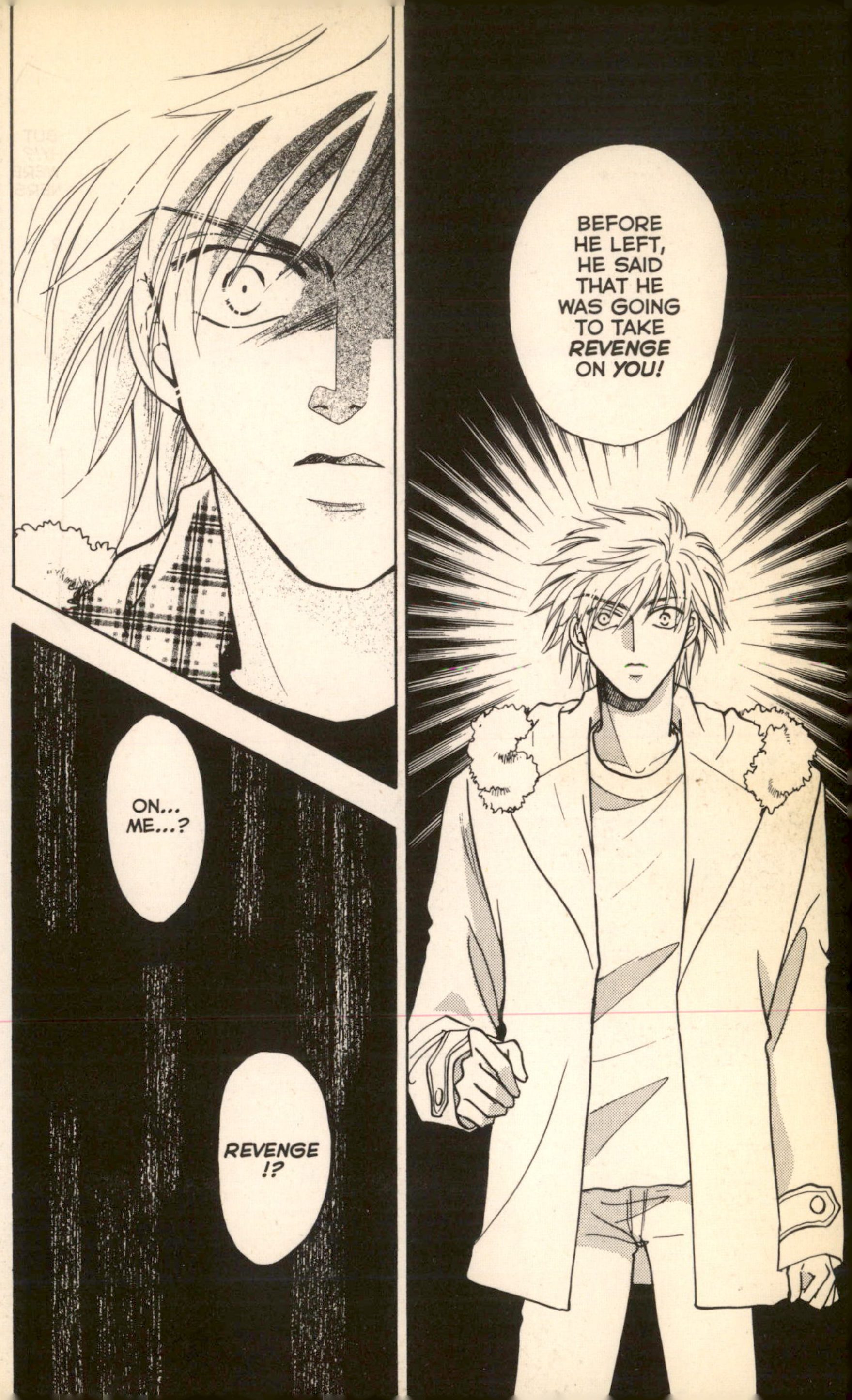
BEFORE HE LEFT, HE SAID THAT HE WAS GOING TO TAKE *REVENGE* ON *YOU!*
ON... ME...?
REVENGE !?

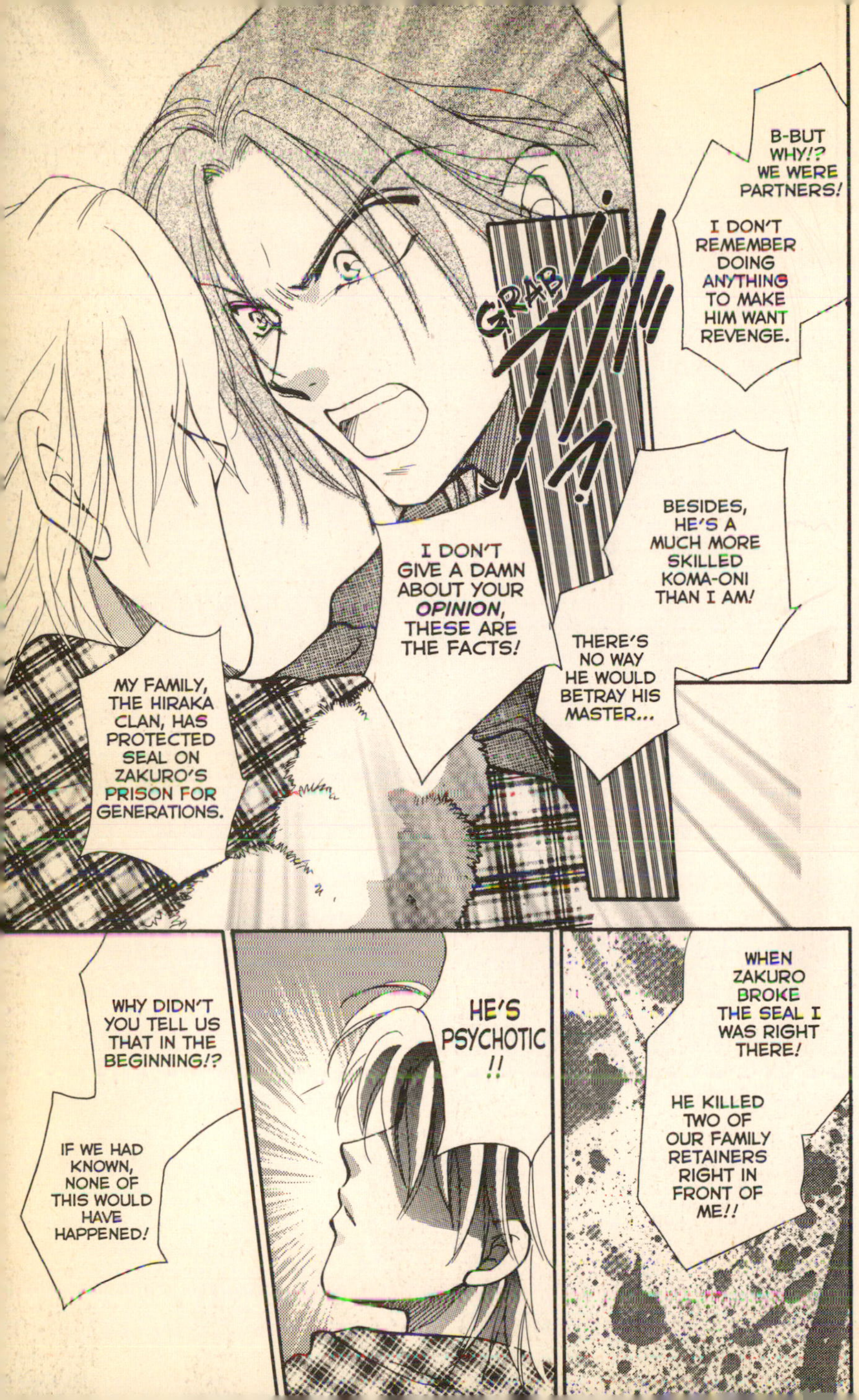
B-BUT WHY!? WE WERE PARTNERS!
I DON'T REMEMBER DOING ANYTHING TO MAKE HIM WANT REVENGE.
GRAB
BESIDES, HE'S A MUCH MORE SKILLED KOMA-ONI THAN I AM!
THERE'S NO WAY HE WOULD BETRAY HIS MASTER...
I DON'T GIVE A DAMN ABOUT YOUR *OPINION*, THESE ARE THE FACTS!
MY FAMILY, THE HIRAKA CLAN, HAS PROTECTED SEAL ON ZAKURO'S PRISON FOR GENERATIONS.
WHEN ZAKURO BROKE THE SEAL I WAS RIGHT THERE!
HE KILLED TWO OF OUR FAMILY RETAINERS RIGHT IN FRONT OF ME!!
HE'S PSYCHOTIC!!
WHY DIDN'T YOU TELL US THAT IN THE BEGINNING!?
IF WE HAD KNOWN, NONE OF THIS WOULD HAVE HAPPENED!

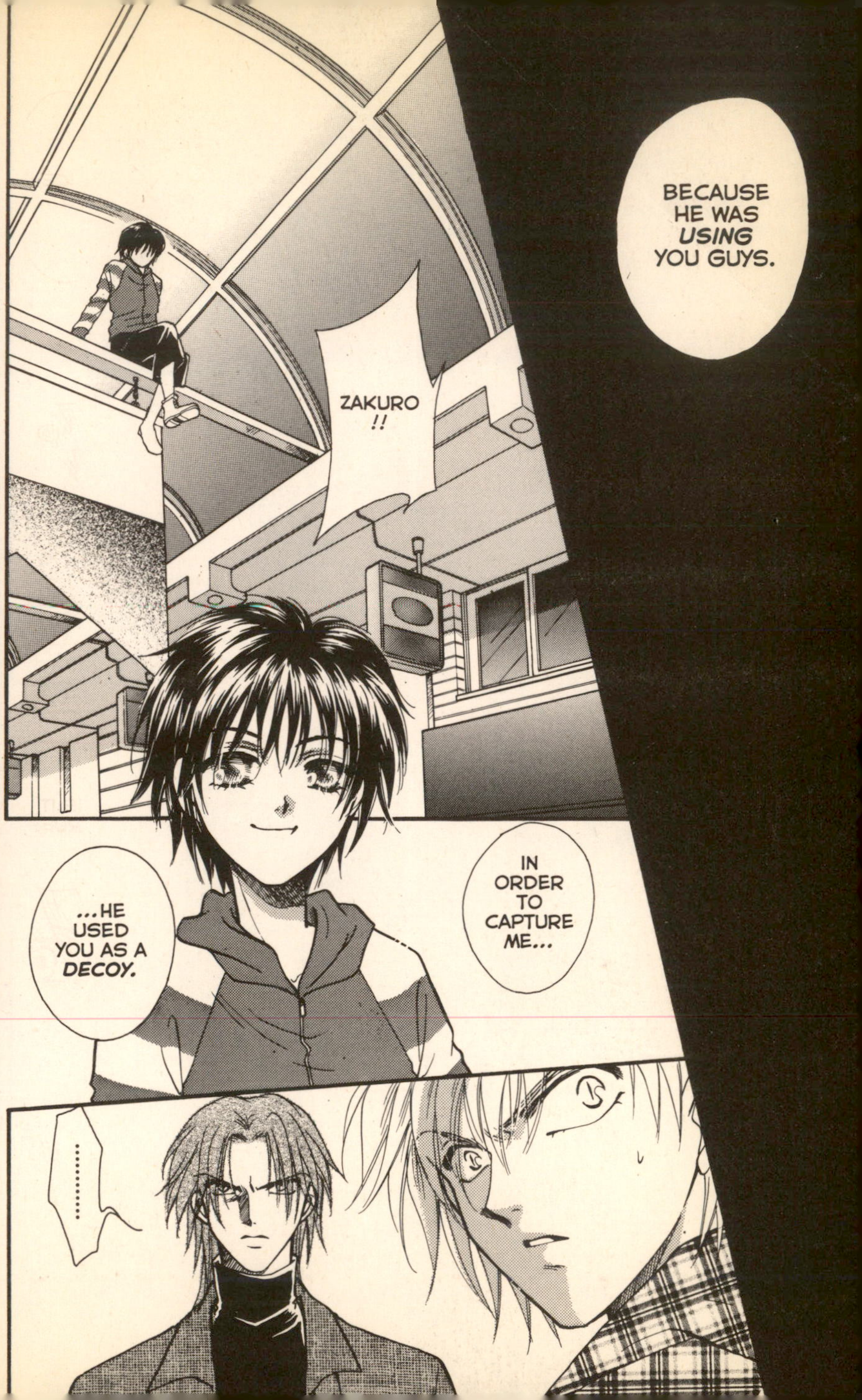
BECAUSE HE WAS *USING* YOU GUYS.
ZAKURO !!
IN ORDER TO CAPTURE ME...
...HE USED YOU AS A *DECOY.*
......

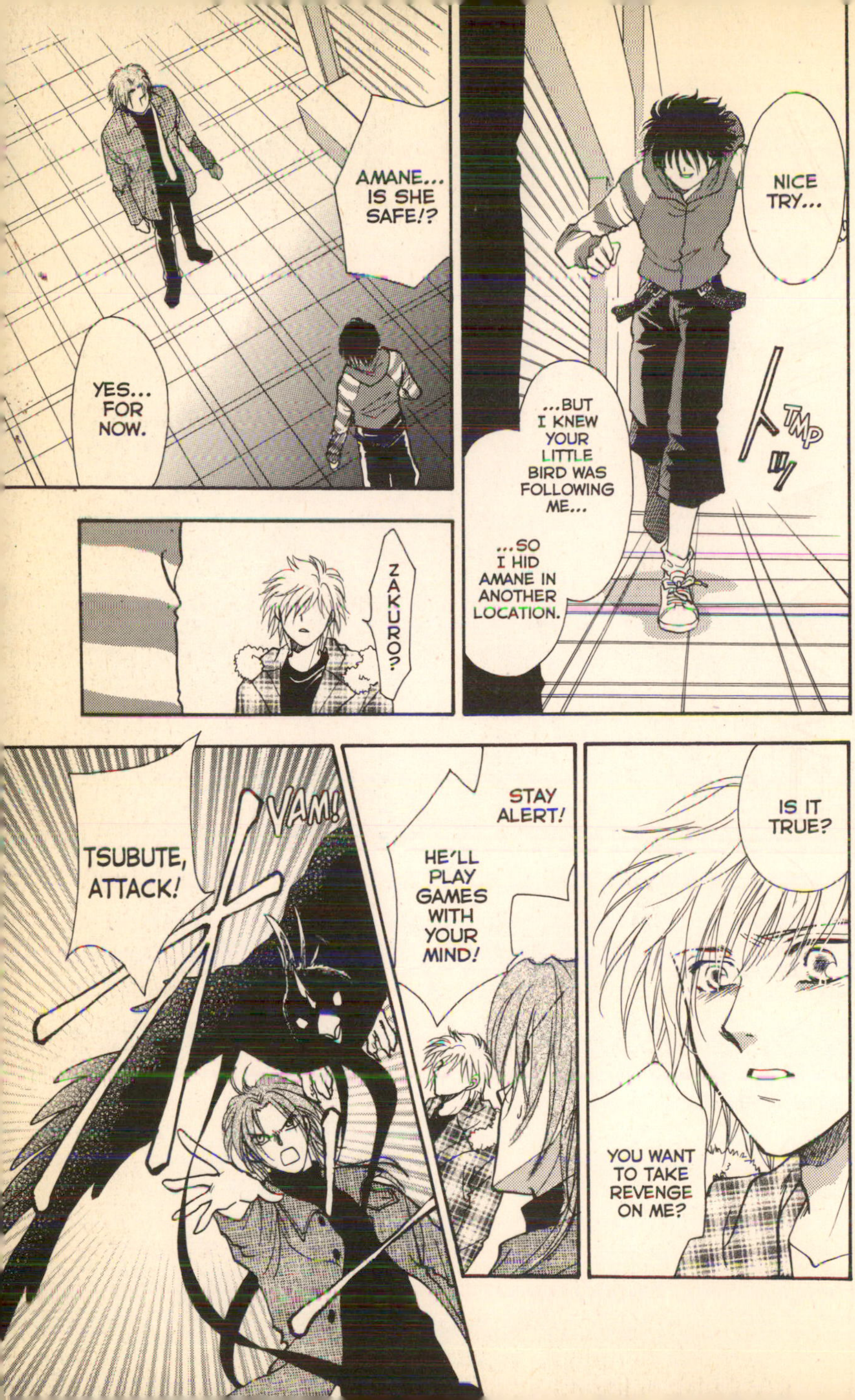
NICE TRY...
...BUT I KNEW YOUR LITTLE BIRD WAS FOLLOWING ME...
...SO I HID AMANE IN ANOTHER LOCATION.
TMP
AMANE... IS SHE SAFE!?
YES... FOR NOW.
ZAKURO?
IS IT TRUE?
YOU WANT TO TAKE REVENGE ON ME?
STAY ALERT!
HE'LL PLAY GAMES WITH YOUR MIND!
VAM!
TSUBUTE, ATTACK!

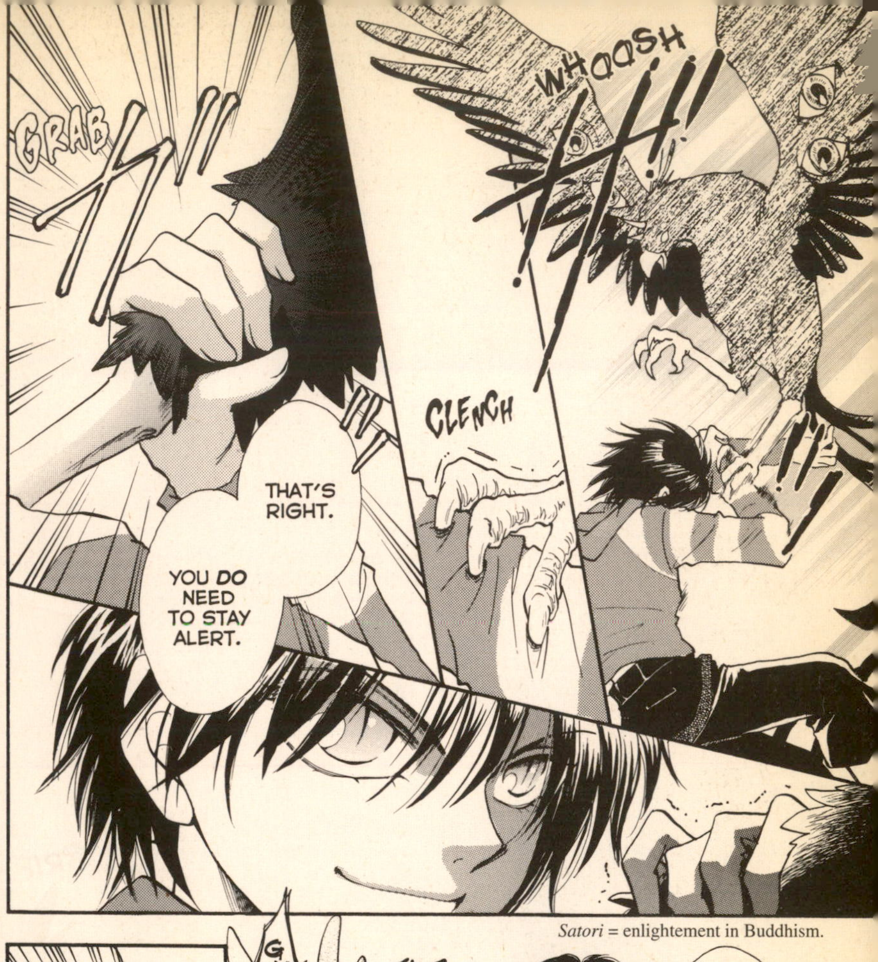
WHOOSH
CLENCH
GRAB
THAT'S RIGHT.
YOU *DO* NEED TO STAY ALERT.

Satori = enlightement in Buddhism.

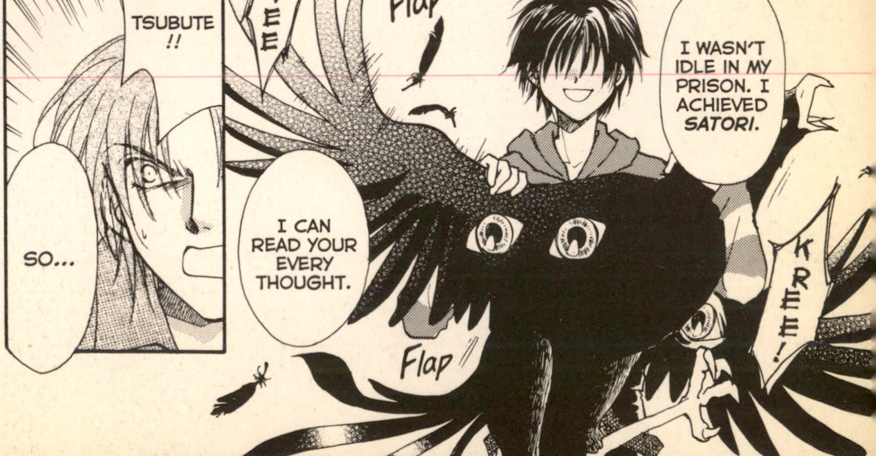
I WASN'T IDLE IN MY PRISON. I ACHIEVED *SATORI*.
KREE!
Flap
GYEE
I CAN READ YOUR EVERY THOUGHT.
Flap
TSUBUTE!!
SO...

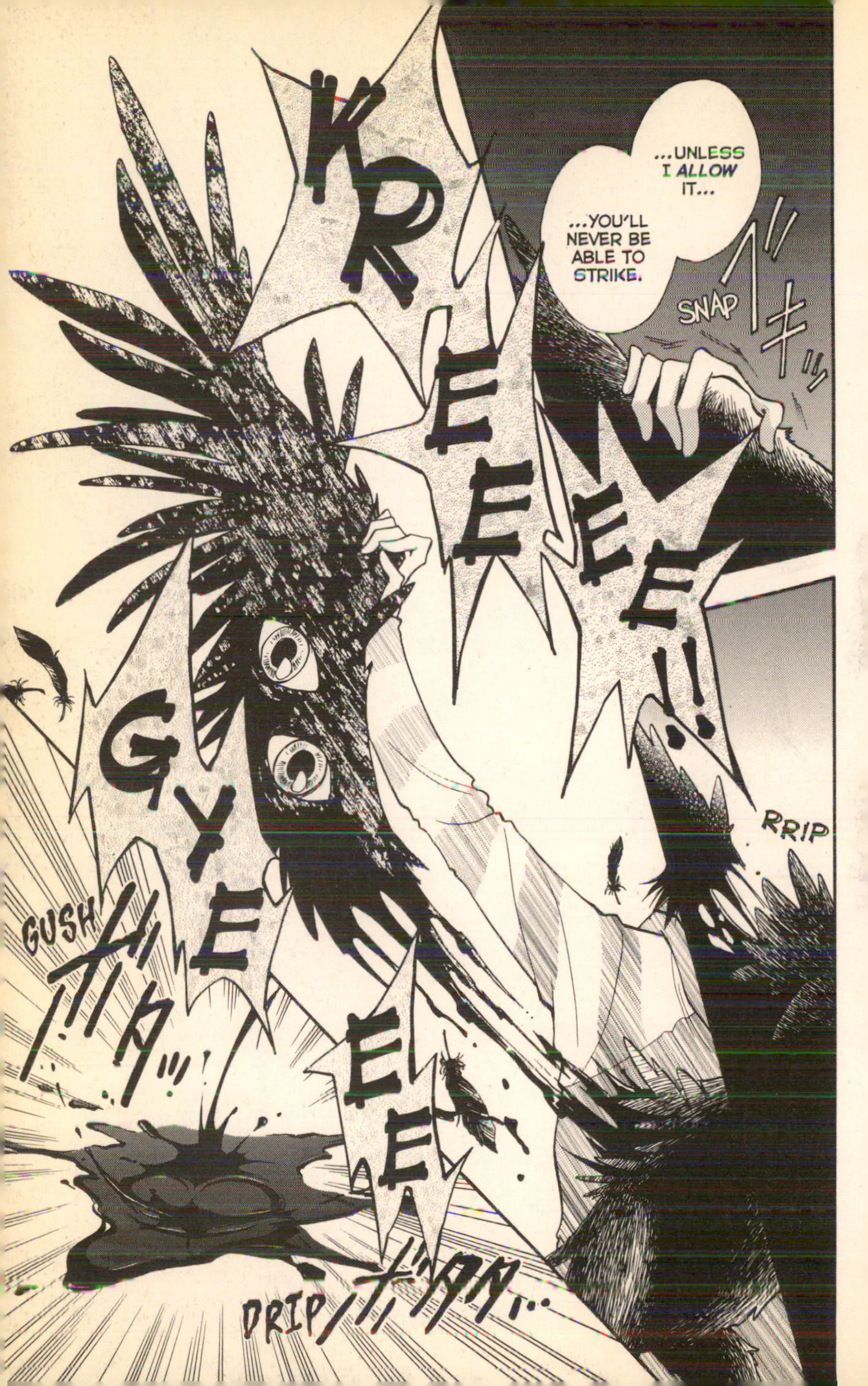

...UNLESS I ALLOW IT...
...YOU'LL NEVER BE ABLE TO STRIKE.
SNAP
KREEEE!!
RRIP
GYEEE
GUSH
DRIP

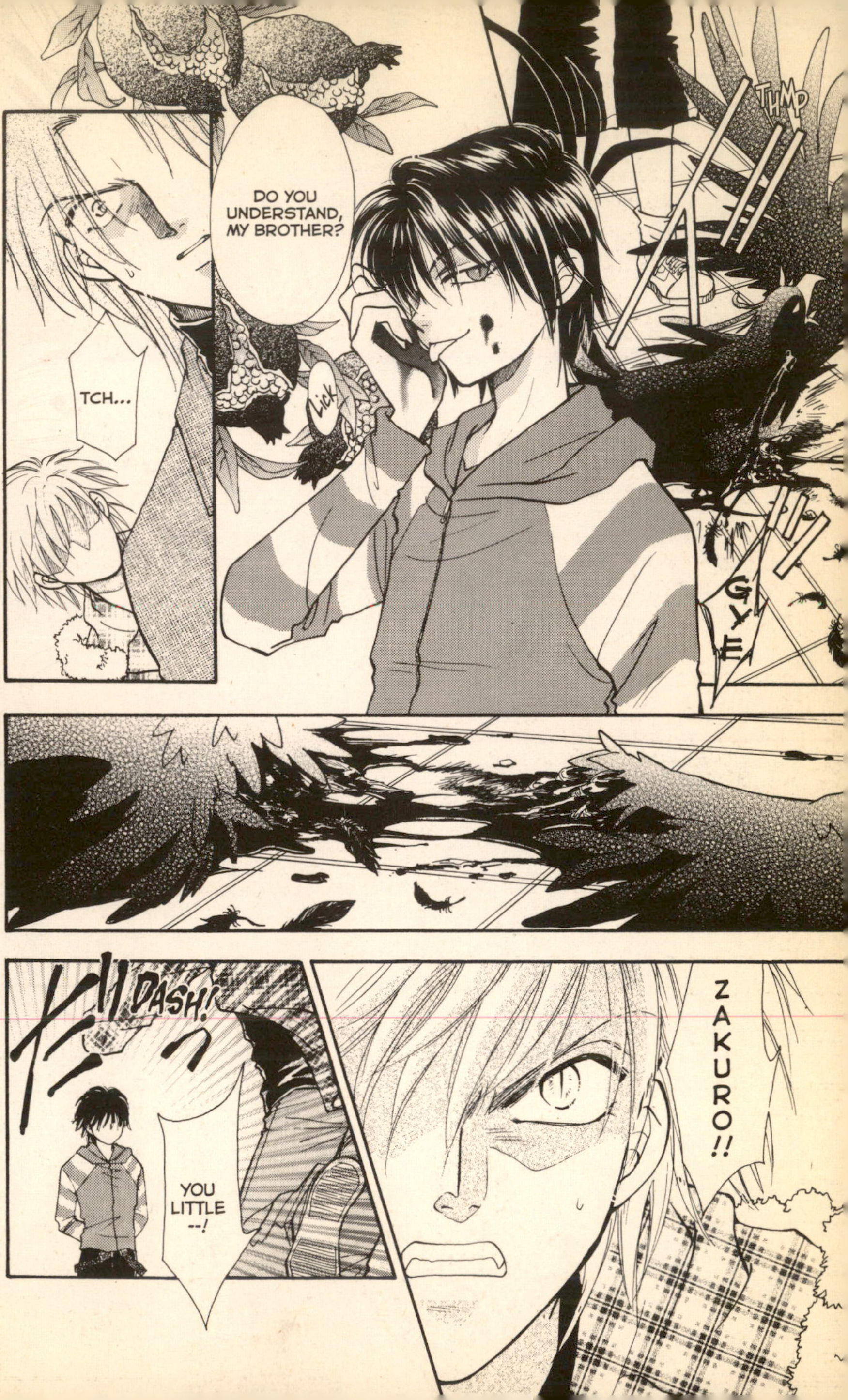
THMP
DO YOU UNDERSTAND, MY BROTHER?
Lick
GYE
TCH...
ZAKURO!!
YOU LITTLE --!
DASH!

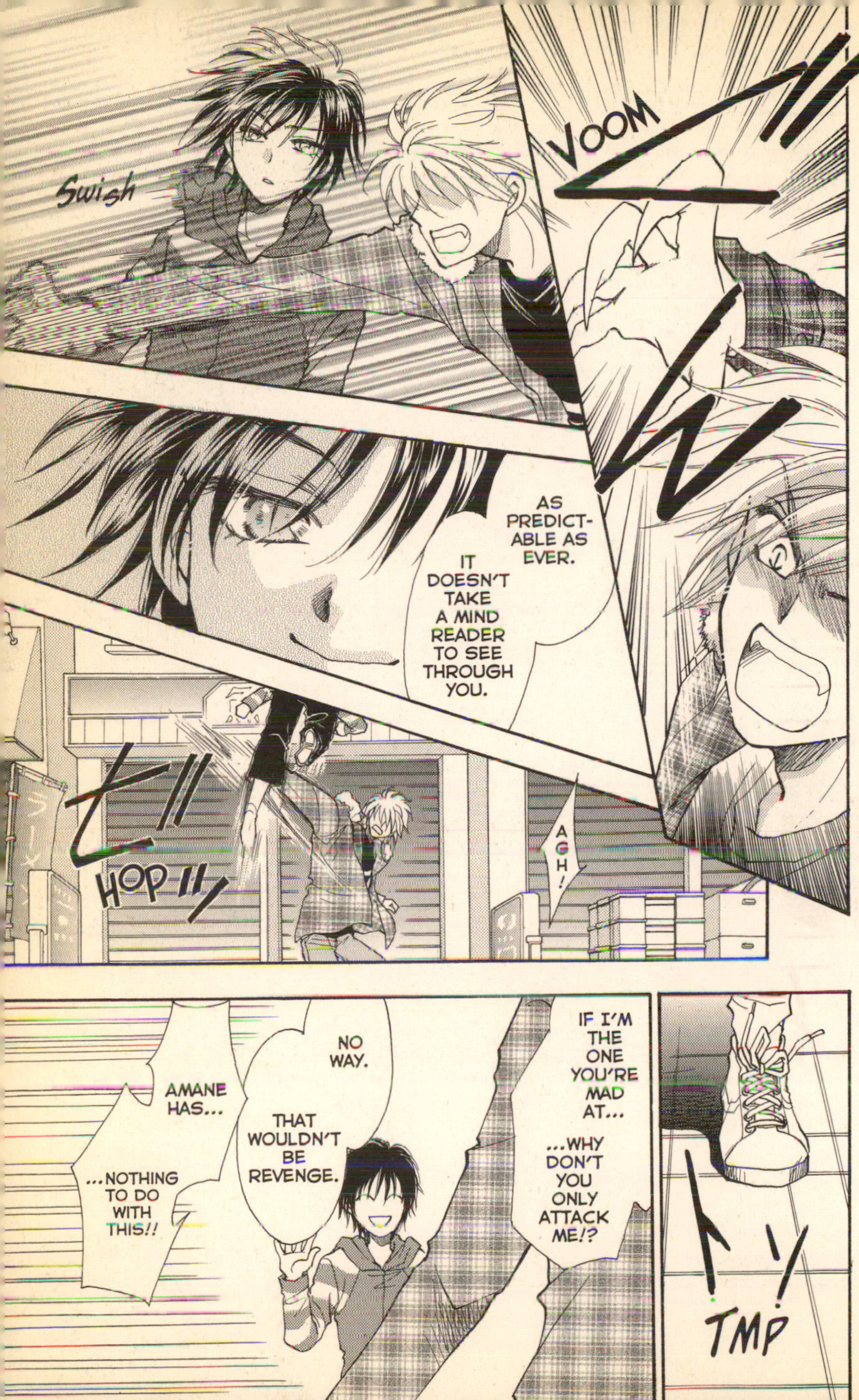
VOOM
Swish
AS PREDICTABLE AS EVER.
IT DOESN'T TAKE A MIND READER TO SEE THROUGH YOU.
AGH!
HOP!!
TMP
IF I'M THE ONE YOU'RE MAD AT...
...WHY DON'T YOU ONLY ATTACK ME!?
NO WAY.
THAT WOULDN'T BE REVENGE.
AMANE HAS...
...NOTHING TO DO WITH THIS!!

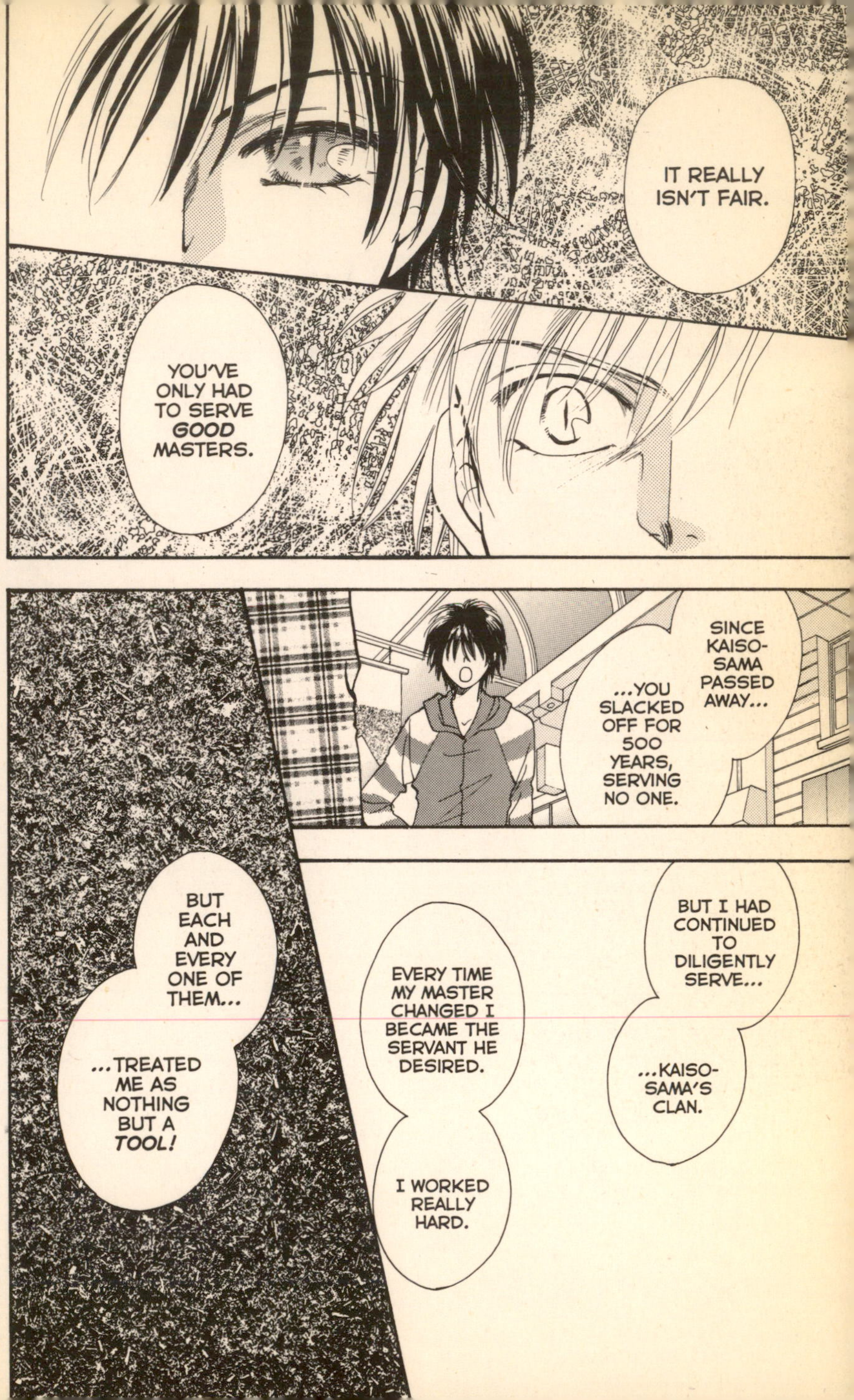
IT REALLY ISN'T FAIR.
YOU'VE ONLY HAD TO SERVE *GOOD* MASTERS.
SINCE KAISO-SAMA PASSED AWAY...
...YOU SLACKED OFF FOR 500 YEARS, SERVING NO ONE.
BUT I HAD CONTINUED TO DILIGENTLY SERVE...
...KAISO-SAMA'S CLAN.
EVERY TIME MY MASTER CHANGED I BECAME THE SERVANT HE DESIRED.
I WORKED REALLY HARD.
BUT EACH AND EVERY ONE OF THEM...
...TREATED ME AS NOTHING BUT A *TOOL!*

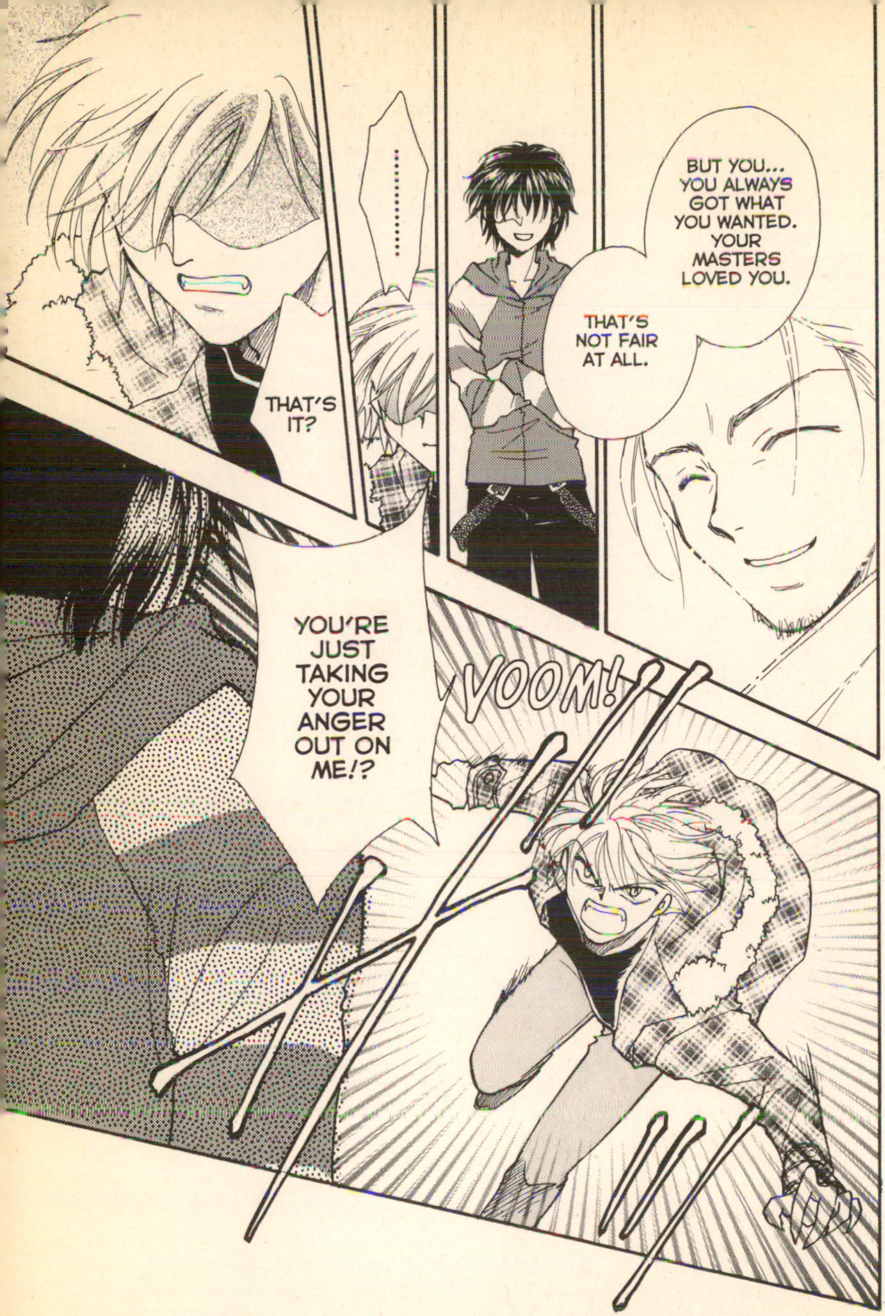
BUT YOU... YOU ALWAYS GOT WHAT YOU WANTED. YOUR MASTERS LOVED YOU.
THAT'S NOT FAIR AT ALL.
......
THAT'S IT?
YOU'RE JUST TAKING YOUR ANGER OUT ON ME!?
VOOM!

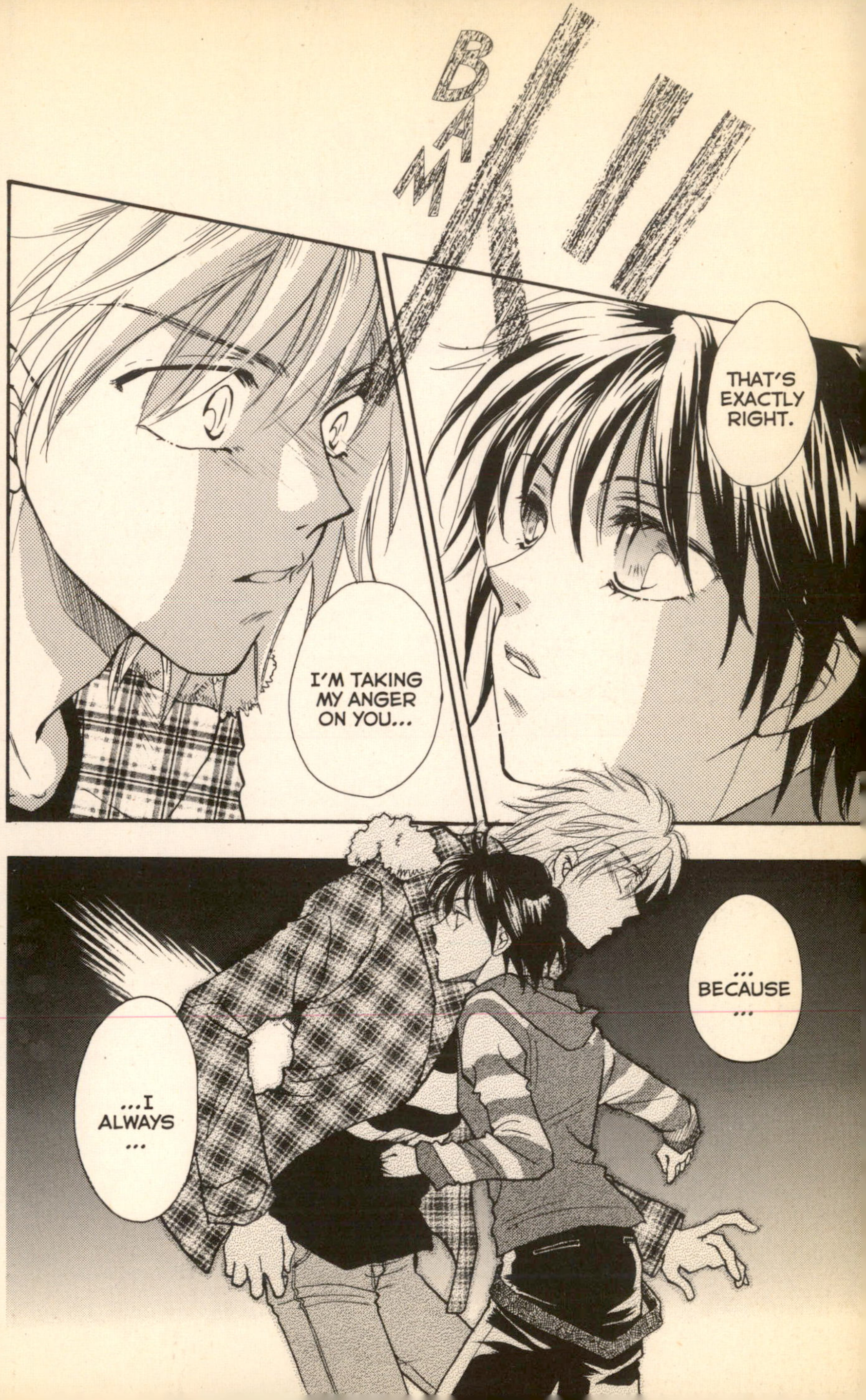
BAM
THAT'S EXACTLY RIGHT.
I'M TAKING MY ANGER ON YOU...
...BECAUSE...
...I ALWAYS...

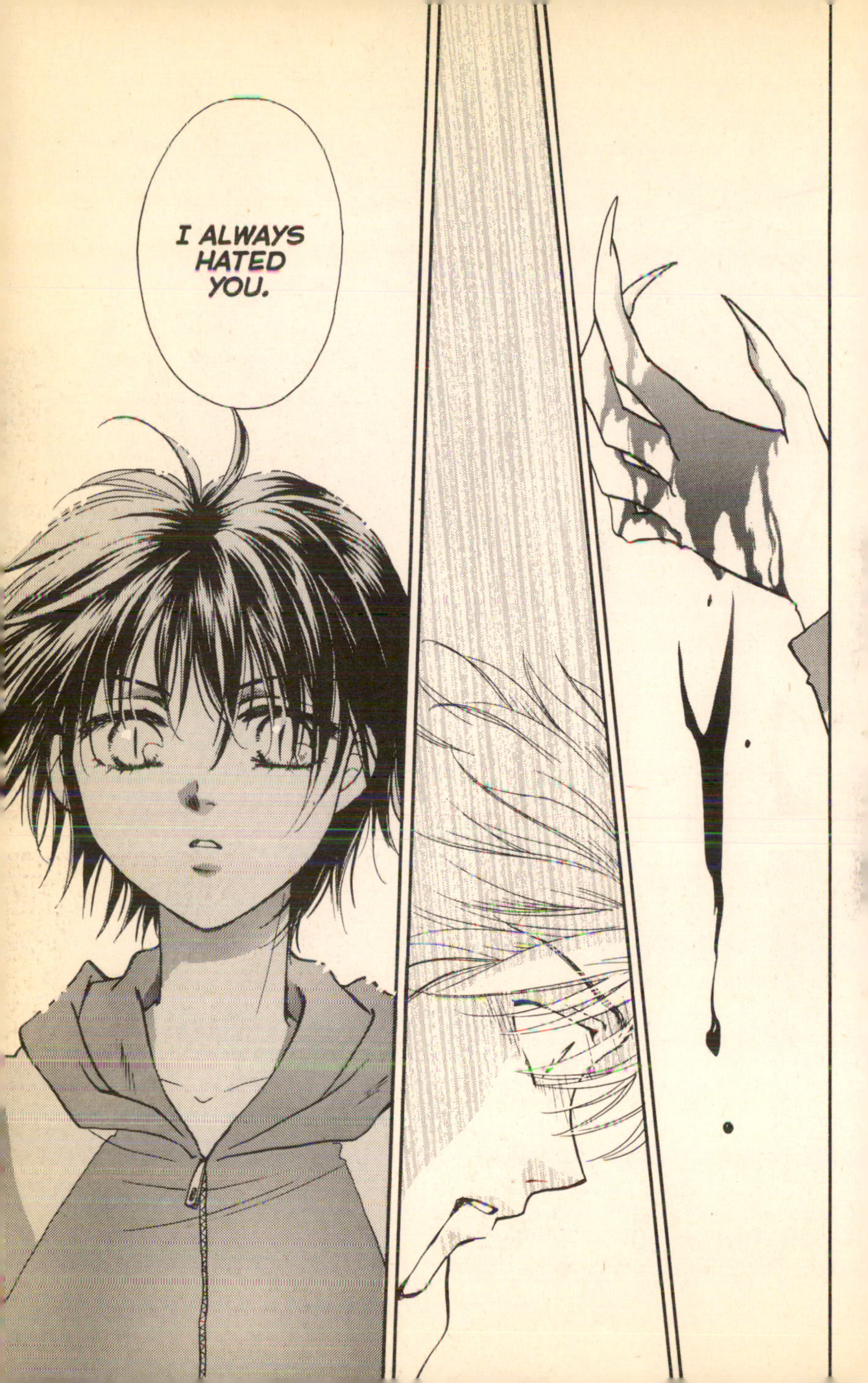
I ALWAYS HATED YOU.

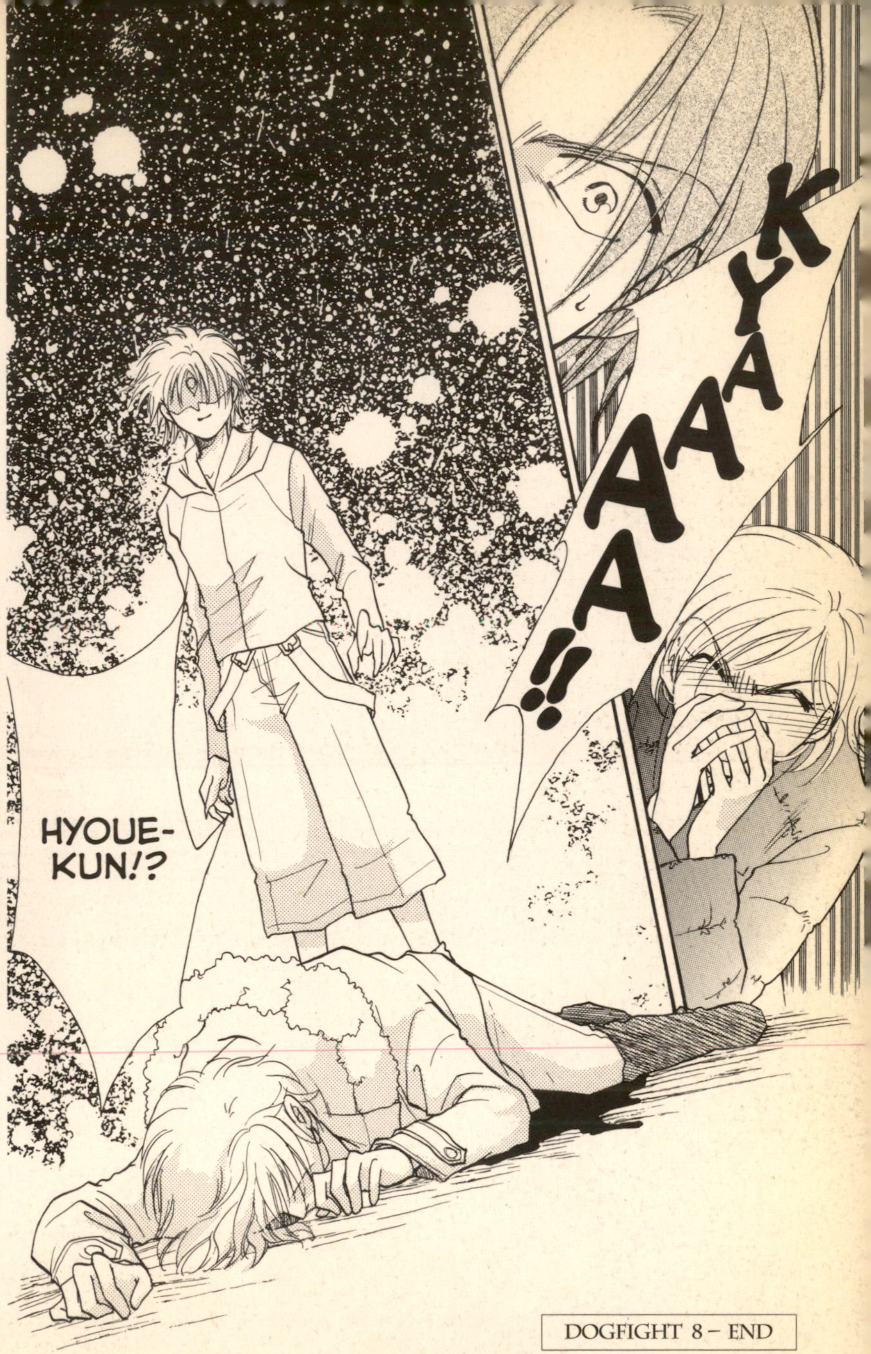
KYAAAAA!!
HYOUE-KUN!?

DOGFIGHT 8 – END

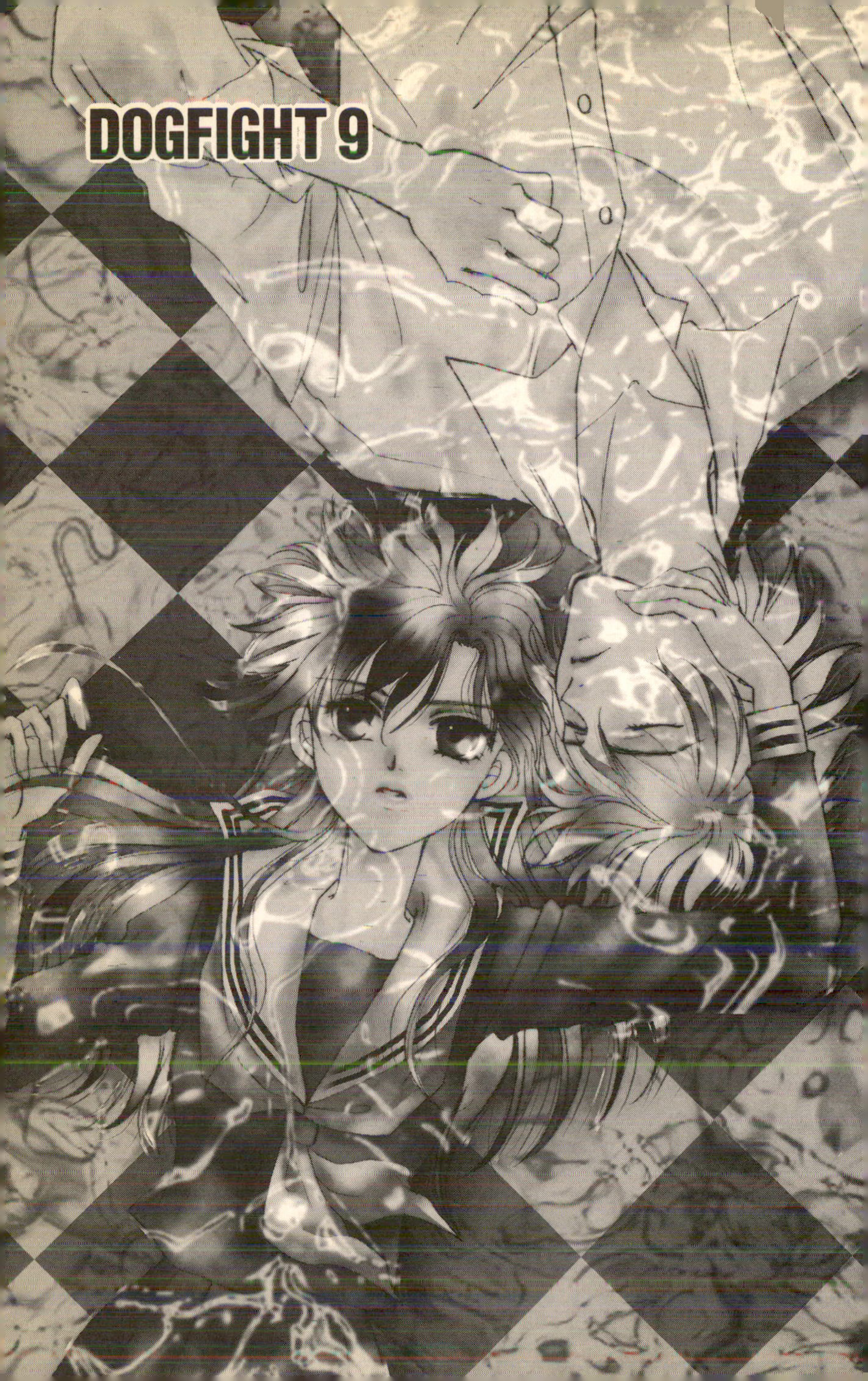
DOGFIGHT 9

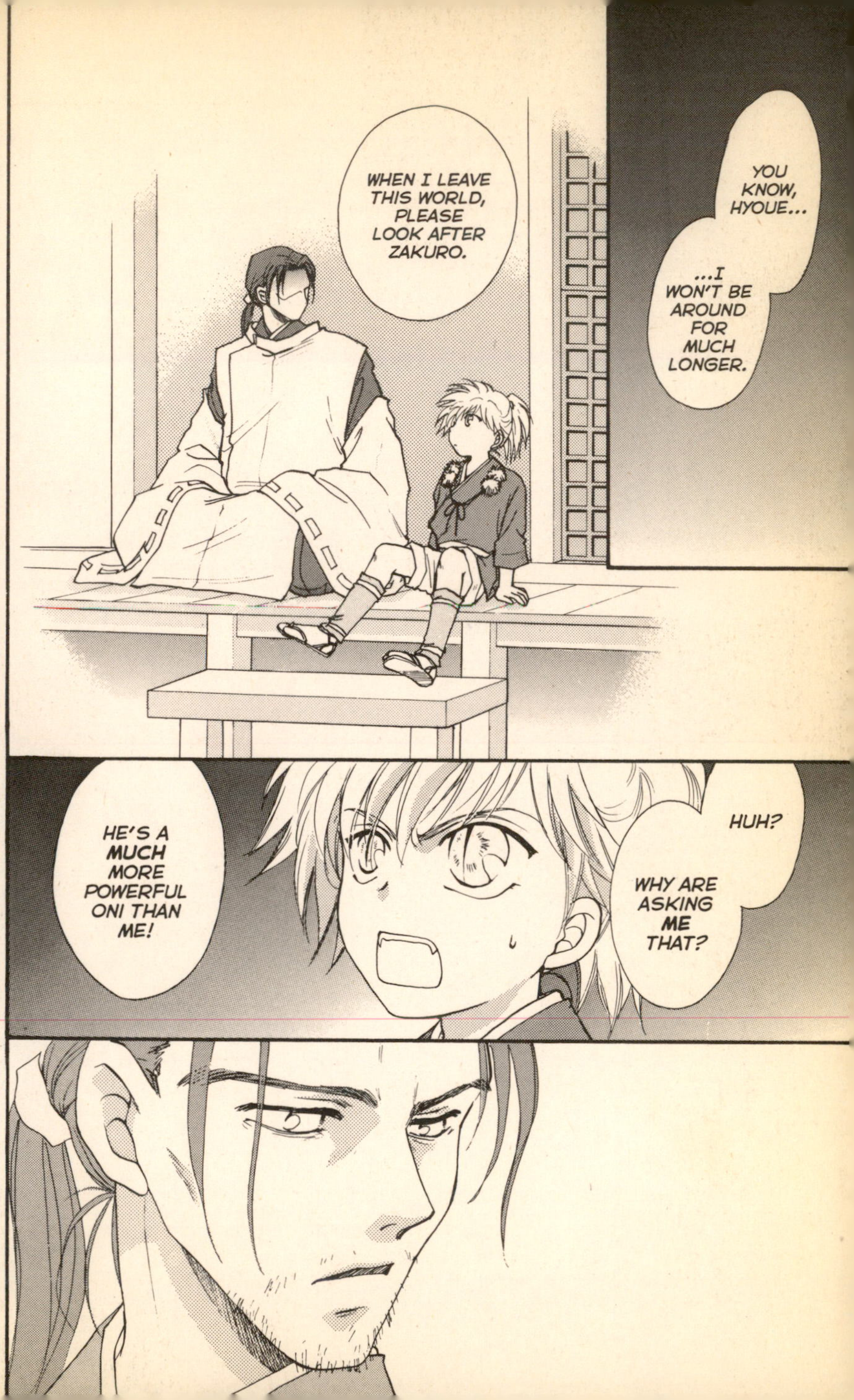
YOU KNOW, HYOUE...
...I WON'T BE AROUND FOR MUCH LONGER.
WHEN I LEAVE THIS WORLD, PLEASE LOOK AFTER ZAKURO.
HUH?
WHY ARE ASKING ME THAT?
HE'S A MUCH MORE POWERFUL ONI THAN ME!

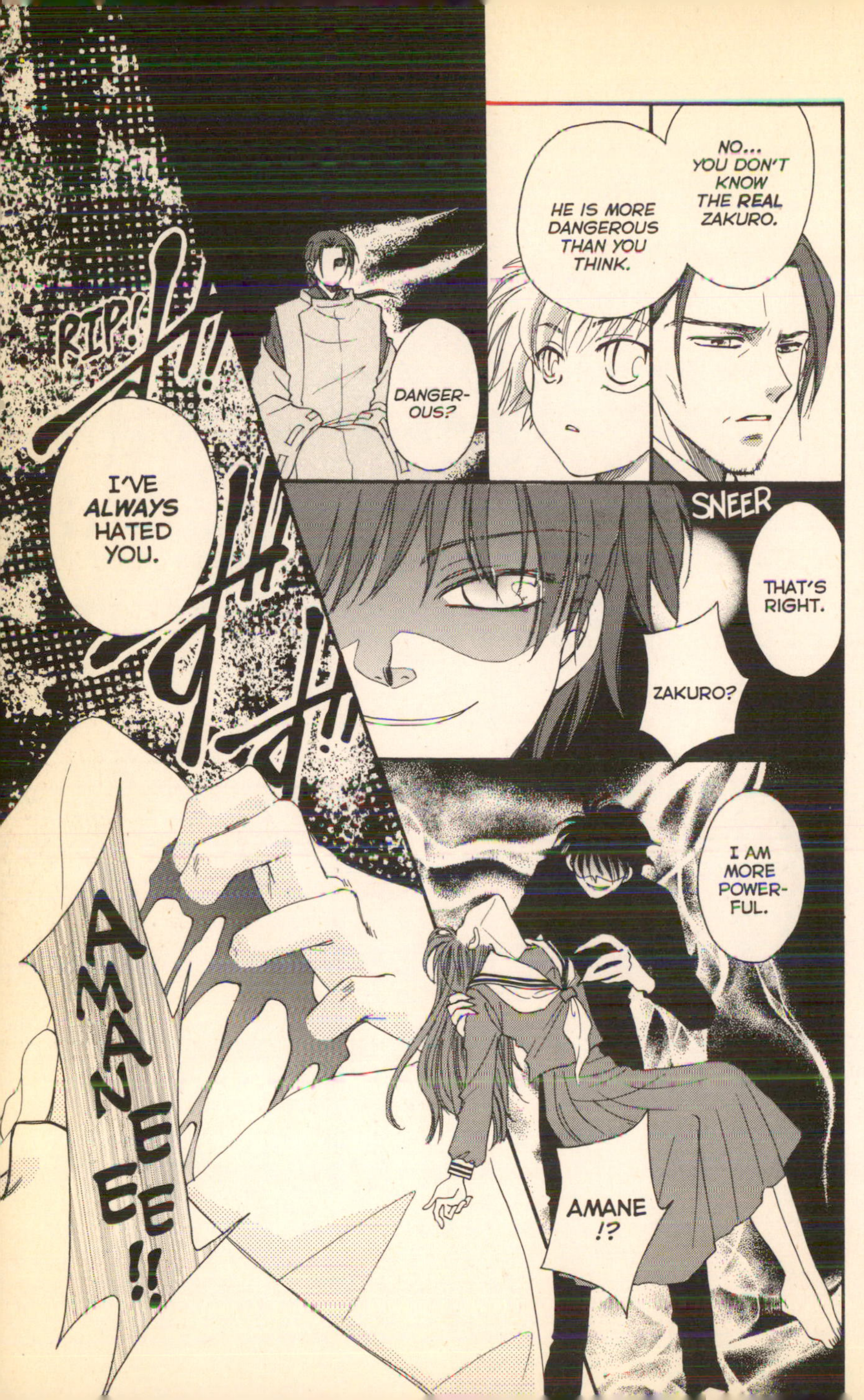
NO... YOU DON'T KNOW THE REAL ZAKURO.
HE IS MORE DANGEROUS THAN YOU THINK.
DANGER-OUS?
RIP!!
SNEER
THAT'S RIGHT.
ZAKURO?
I'VE ALWAYS HATED YOU.
I AM MORE POWER-FUL.
AMANE !?
AMANEEE!!

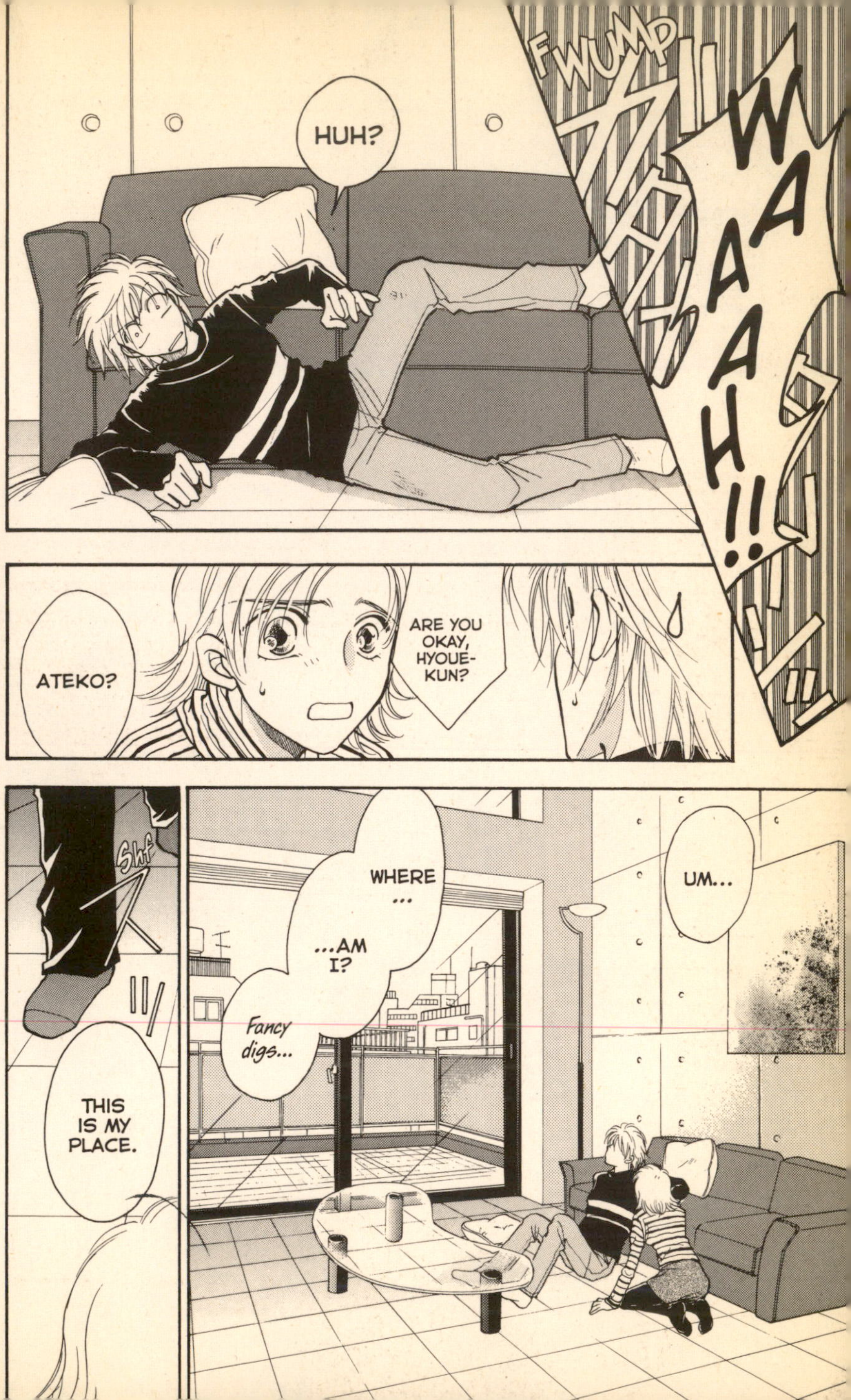
FWUMP
WAAAH!!
HUH?
ARE YOU OKAY, HYOUE-KUN?
ATEKO?
UM...
WHERE ...
...AM I?
Fancy digs...
Shf
THIS IS MY PLACE.

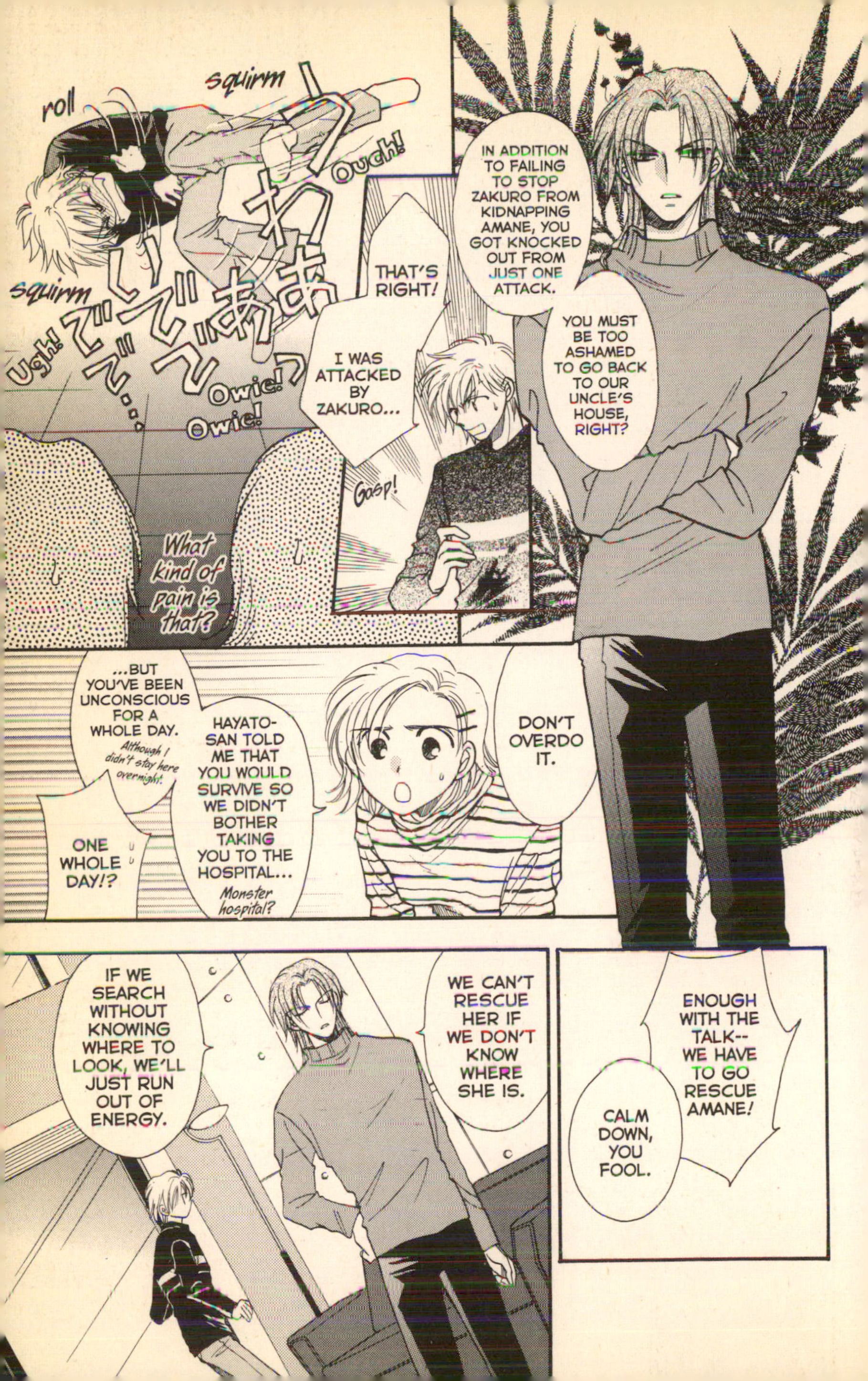
IN ADDITION TO FAILING TO STOP ZAKURO FROM KIDNAPPING AMANE, YOU GOT KNOCKED OUT FROM JUST ONE ATTACK.
YOU MUST BE TOO ASHAMED TO GO BACK TO OUR UNCLE'S HOUSE, RIGHT?
THAT'S RIGHT!
I WAS ATTACKED BY ZAKURO...
Gasp!
roll
squirm
Ouch!
squirm
Ugh!
Owie!?
Owie!
What kind of pain is that?
DON'T OVERDO IT.
HAYATO-SAN TOLD ME THAT YOU WOULD SURVIVE SO WE DIDN'T BOTHER TAKING YOU TO THE HOSPITAL...
Monster hospital?
...BUT YOU'VE BEEN UNCONSCIOUS FOR A WHOLE DAY.
Although I didn't stay here overnight.
ONE WHOLE DAY!?
ENOUGH WITH THE TALK-- WE HAVE TO GO RESCUE AMANE!
CALM DOWN, YOU FOOL.
WE CAN'T RESCUE HER IF WE DON'T KNOW WHERE SHE IS.
IF WE SEARCH WITHOUT KNOWING WHERE TO LOOK, WE'LL JUST RUN OUT OF ENERGY.

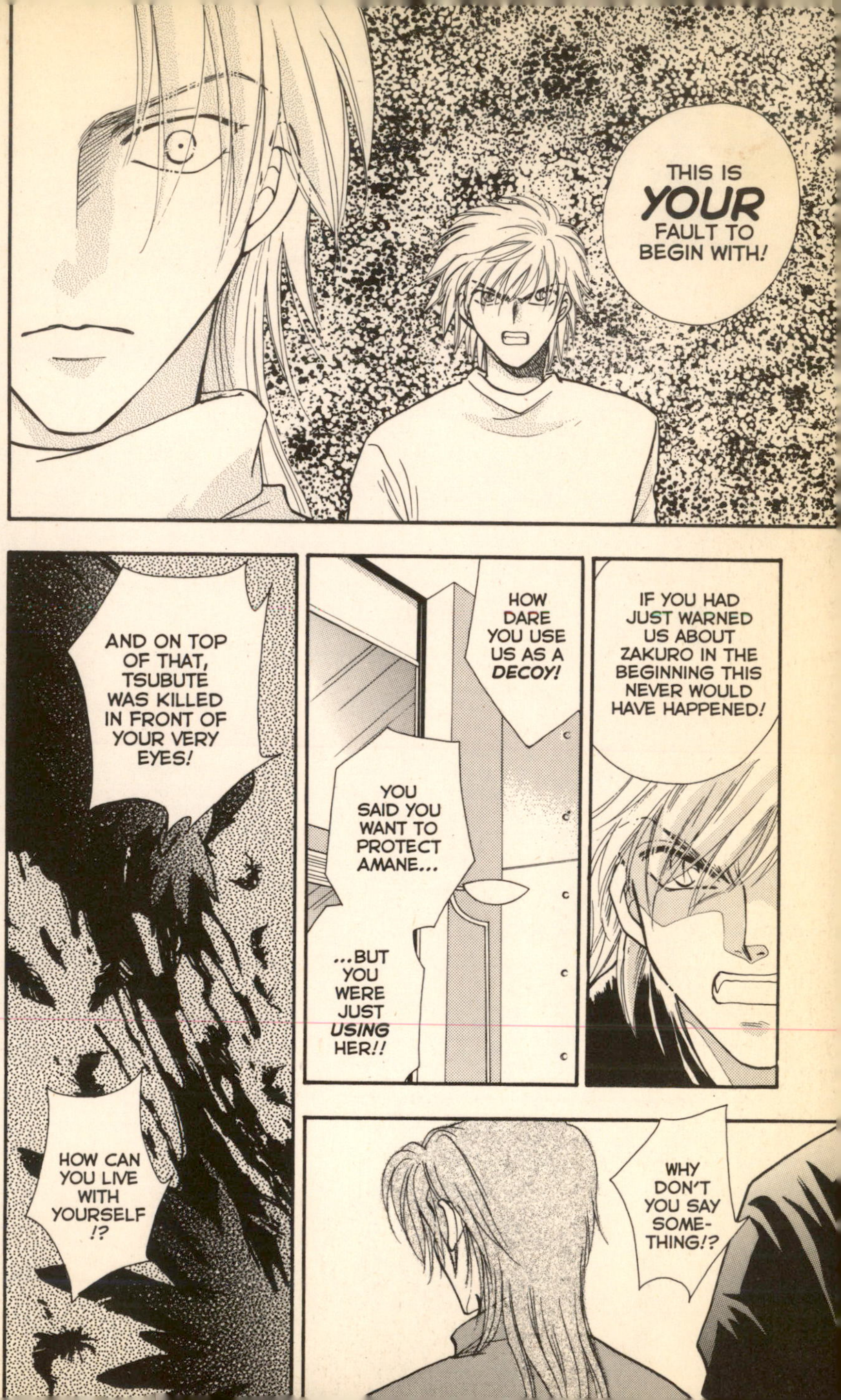
THIS IS YOUR FAULT TO BEGIN WITH!
IF YOU HAD JUST WARNED US ABOUT ZAKURO IN THE BEGINNING THIS NEVER WOULD HAVE HAPPENED!
HOW DARE YOU USE US AS A DECOY!
YOU SAID YOU WANT TO PROTECT AMANE...
...BUT YOU WERE JUST USING HER!!
WHY DON'T YOU SAY SOME-THING!?
AND ON TOP OF THAT, TSUBUTE WAS KILLED IN FRONT OF YOUR VERY EYES!
HOW CAN YOU LIVE WITH YOURSELF!?

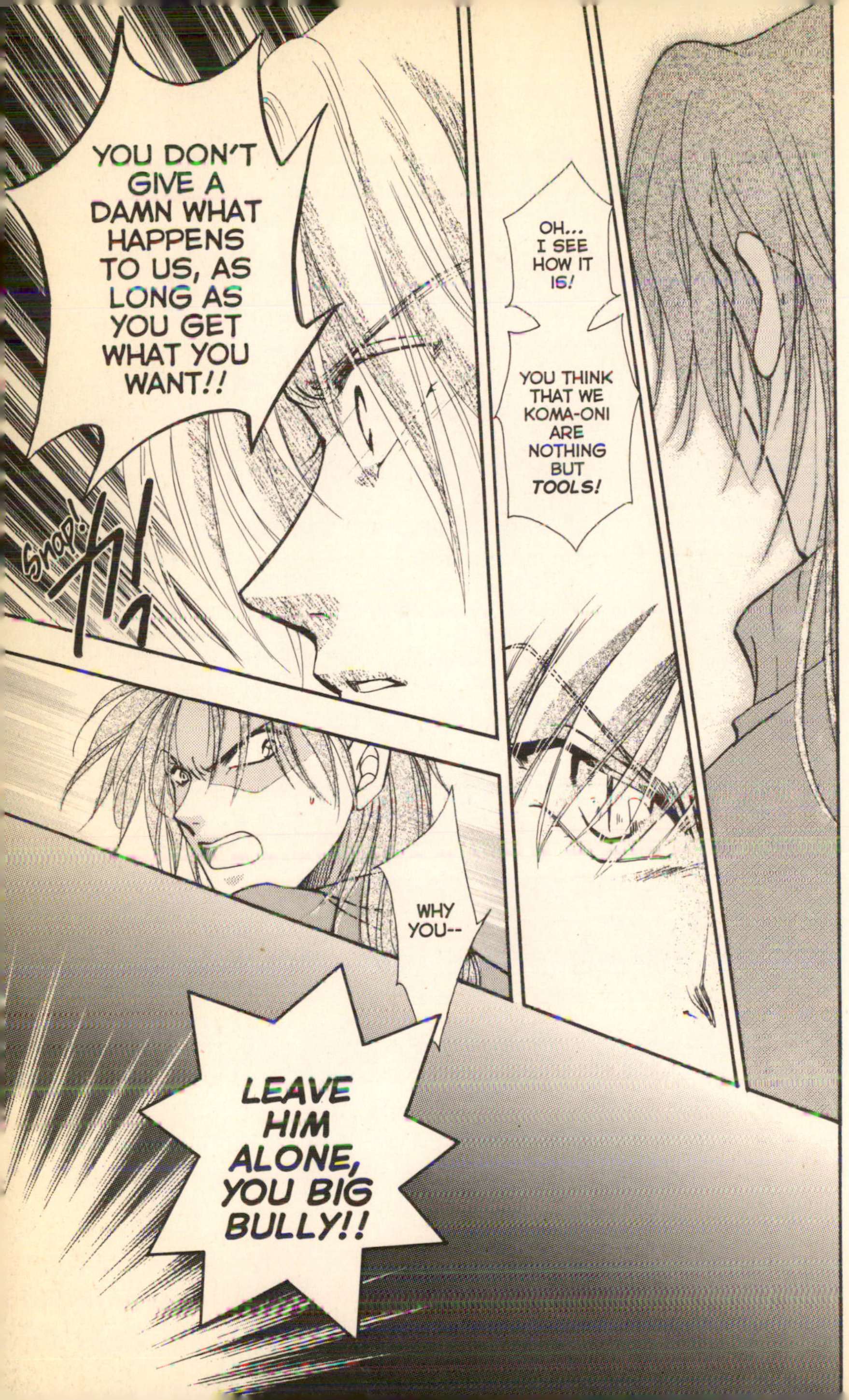
OH... I SEE HOW IT IS!
YOU THINK THAT WE KOMA-ONI ARE NOTHING BUT *TOOLS!*
YOU DON'T GIVE A DAMN WHAT HAPPENS TO US, AS LONG AS YOU GET WHAT YOU WANT!!
Snap!
WHY YOU--
LEAVE HIM ALONE, YOU BIG BULLY!!

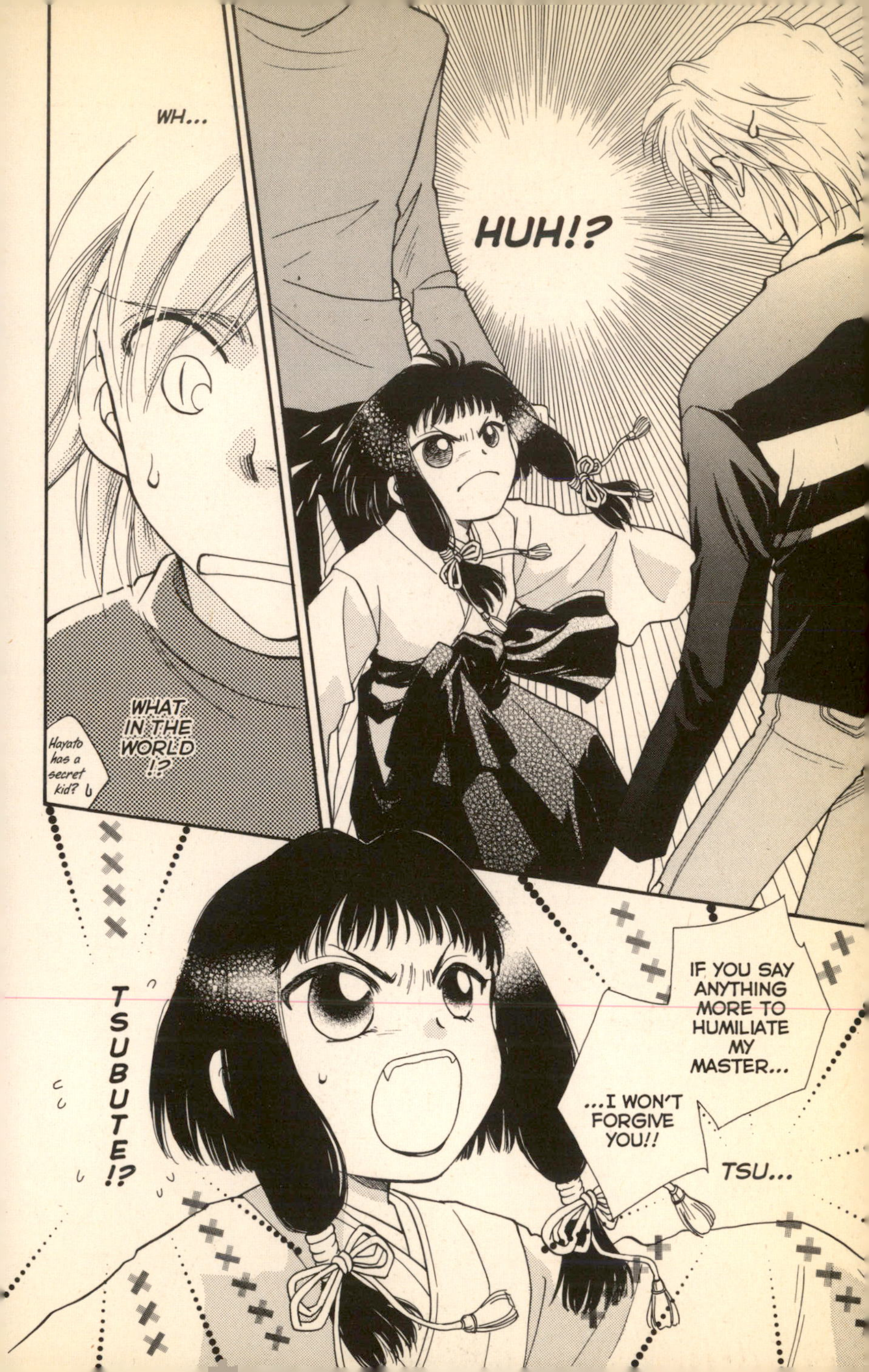
HUH!?
WH...
WHAT IN THE WORLD !?
Hayato has a secret kid?
IF YOU SAY ANYTHING MORE TO HUMILIATE MY MASTER...
...I WON'T FORGIVE YOU!!
TSU...
TSUBUTE!?

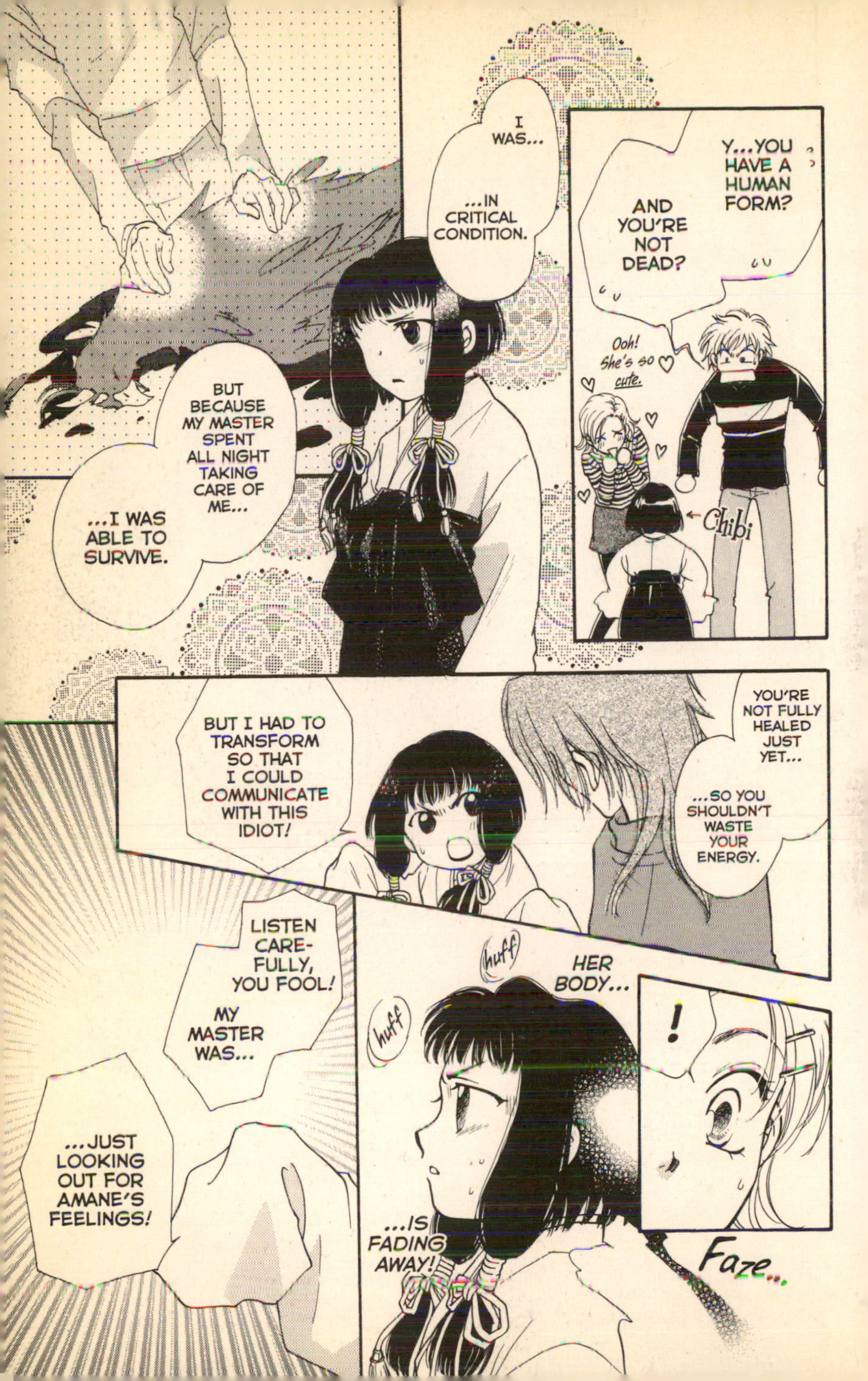
Y...YOU HAVE A HUMAN FORM?
AND YOU'RE NOT DEAD?
Ooh! She's so cute.
Chibi
I WAS...
...IN CRITICAL CONDITION.
BUT BECAUSE MY MASTER SPENT ALL NIGHT TAKING CARE OF ME...
...I WAS ABLE TO SURVIVE.
YOU'RE NOT FULLY HEALED JUST YET...
...SO YOU SHOULDN'T WASTE YOUR ENERGY.
BUT I HAD TO TRANSFORM SO THAT I COULD COMMUNICATE WITH THIS IDIOT!
!
huff
HER BODY...
huff
...IS FADING AWAY!
Faze...
LISTEN CARE-FULLY, YOU FOOL!
MY MASTER WAS...
...JUST LOOKING OUT FOR AMANE'S FEELINGS!

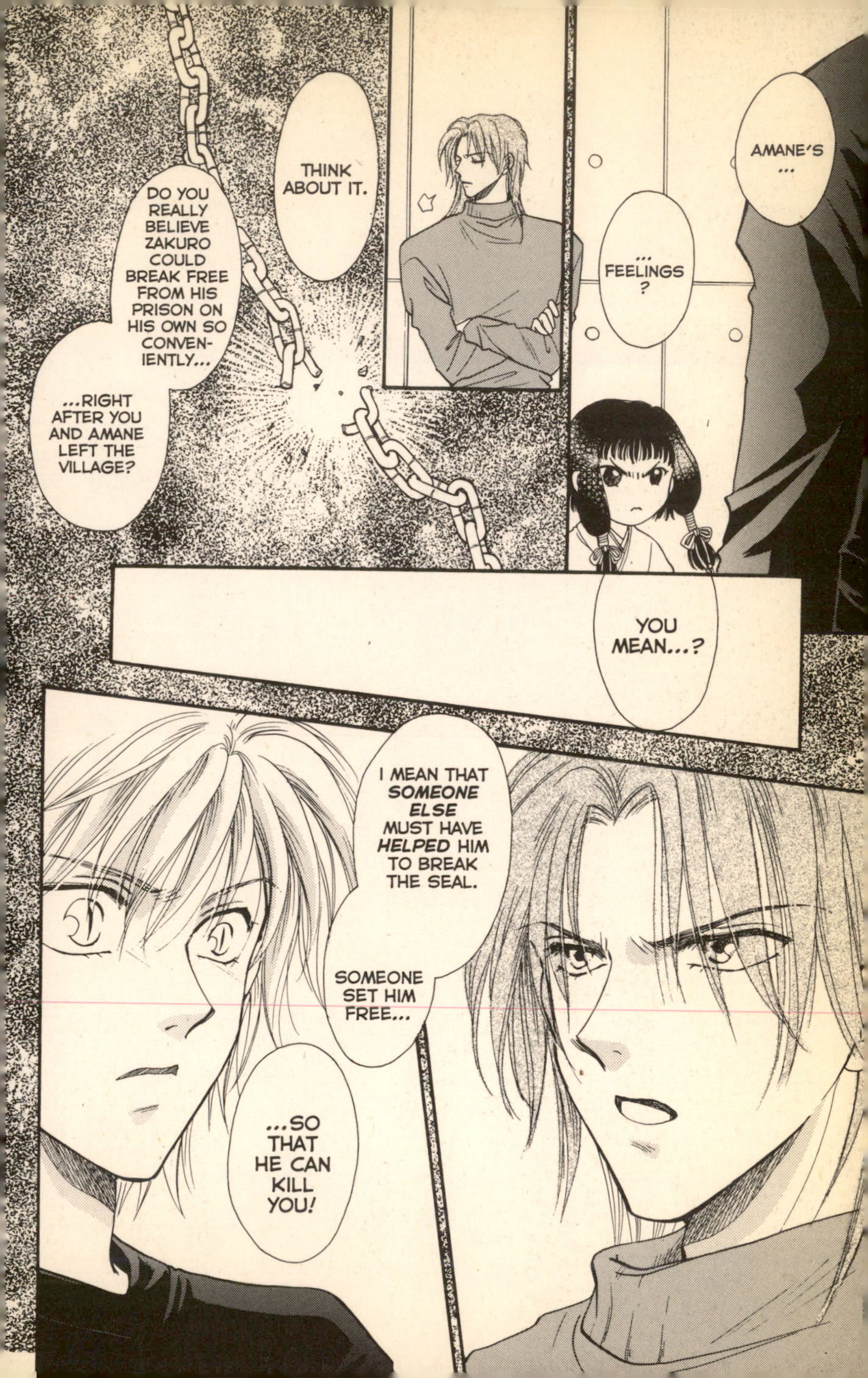
AMANE'S ...
... FEELINGS ?
THINK ABOUT IT.
DO YOU REALLY BELIEVE ZAKURO COULD BREAK FREE FROM HIS PRISON ON HIS OWN SO CONVENIENTLY...
...RIGHT AFTER YOU AND AMANE LEFT THE VILLAGE?
YOU MEAN...?
I MEAN THAT *SOMEONE ELSE* MUST HAVE *HELPED* HIM TO BREAK THE SEAL.
SOMEONE SET HIM FREE...
...SO THAT HE CAN KILL YOU!

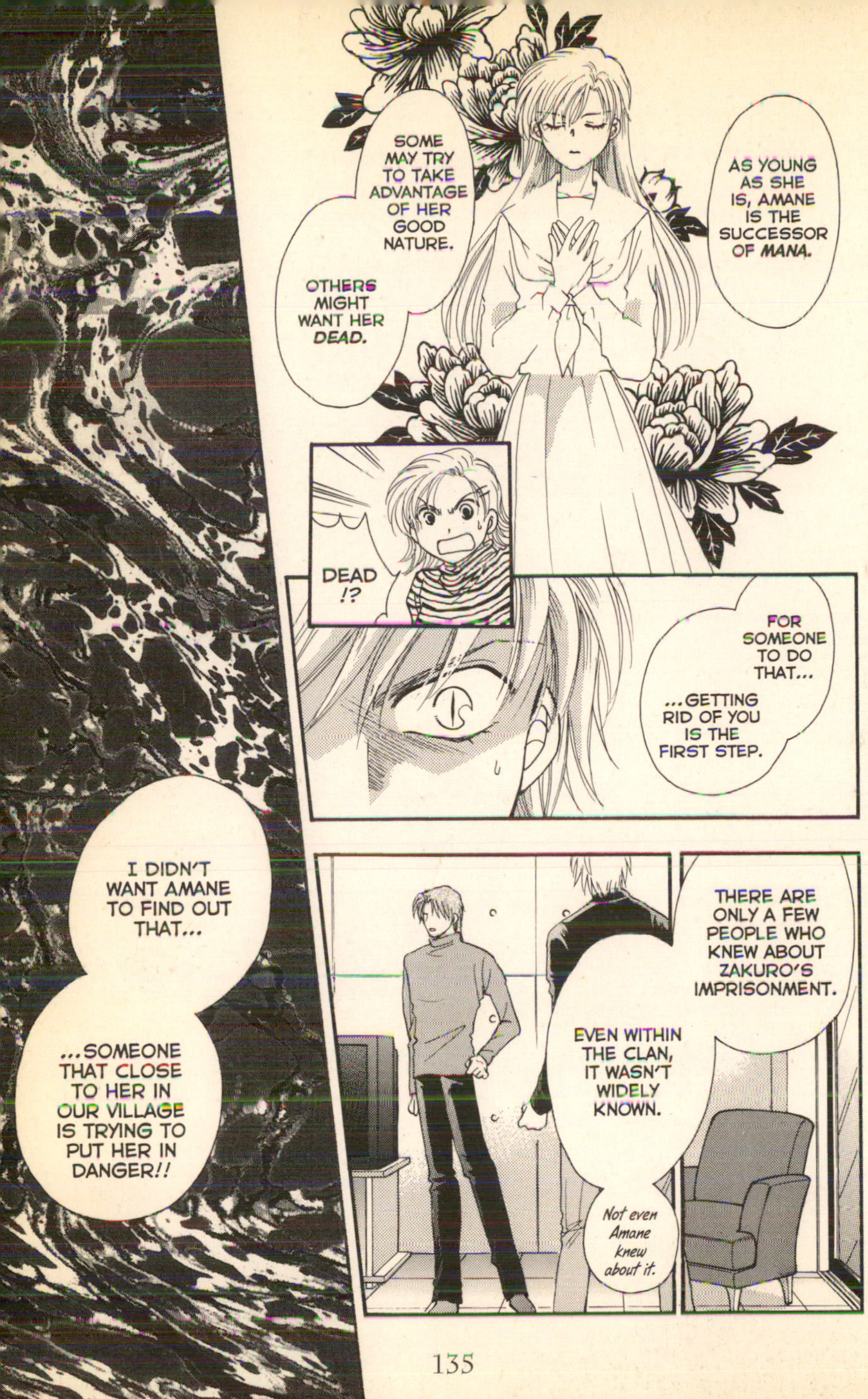
AS YOUNG AS SHE IS, AMANE IS THE SUCCESSOR OF *MANA.*
SOME MAY TRY TO TAKE ADVANTAGE OF HER GOOD NATURE.
OTHERS MIGHT WANT HER *DEAD.*
DEAD!?
FOR SOMEONE TO DO THAT...
...GETTING RID OF YOU IS THE FIRST STEP.
THERE ARE ONLY A FEW PEOPLE WHO KNEW ABOUT ZAKURO'S IMPRISONMENT.
EVEN WITHIN THE CLAN, IT WASN'T WIDELY KNOWN.
Not even Amane knew about it.
I DIDN'T WANT AMANE TO FIND OUT THAT...
...SOMEONE THAT CLOSE TO HER IN OUR VILLAGE IS TRYING TO PUT HER IN DANGER!!

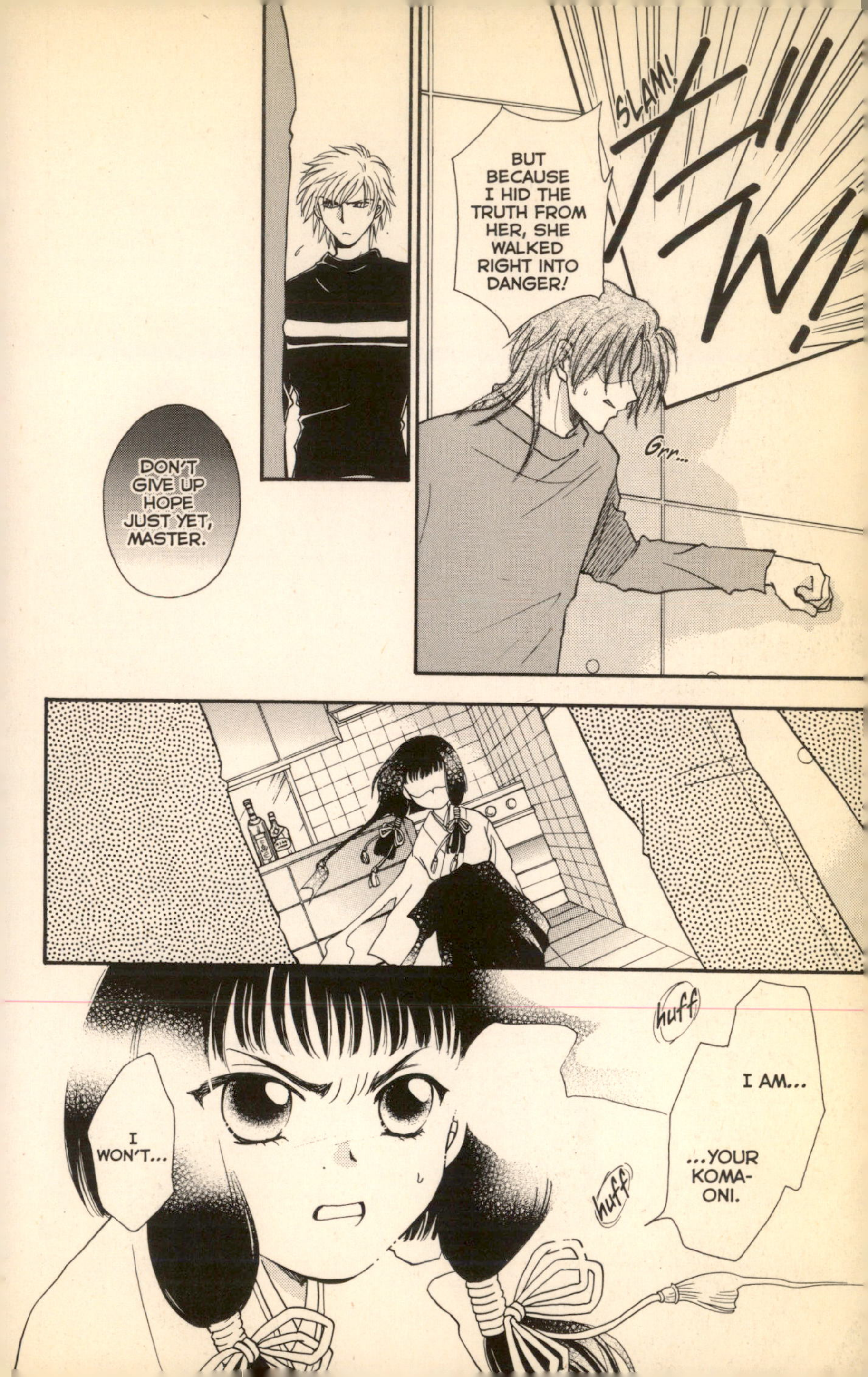
SLAM!
BUT BECAUSE I HID THE TRUTH FROM HER, SHE WALKED RIGHT INTO DANGER!
Grr...
DON'T GIVE UP HOPE JUST YET, MASTER.
huff
I AM...
...YOUR KOMA-ONI.
huff
I WON'T...

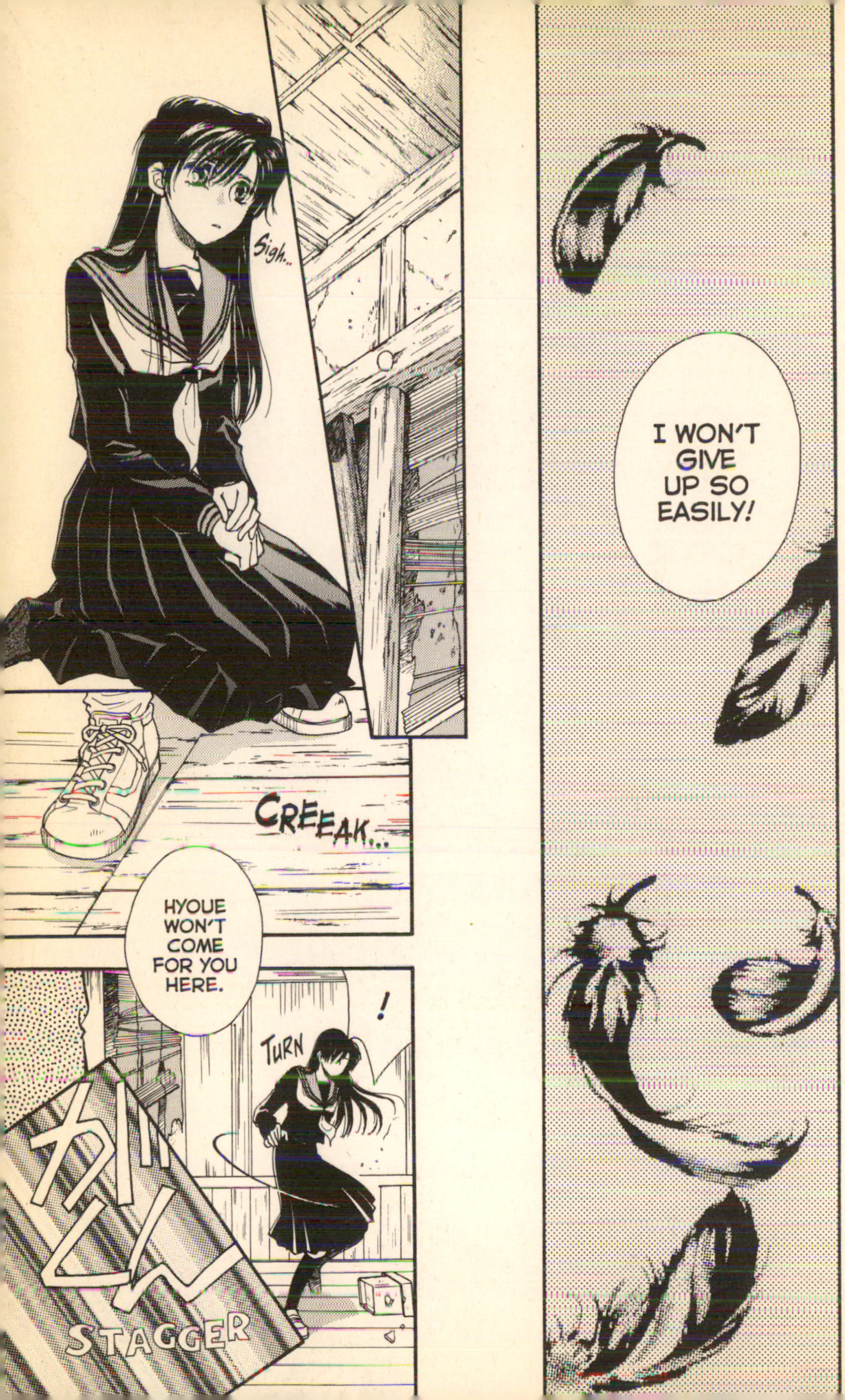
I WON'T GIVE UP SO EASILY!
Sigh..
CREEAK...
HYOUE WON'T COME FOR YOU HERE.
!
TURN
STAGGER

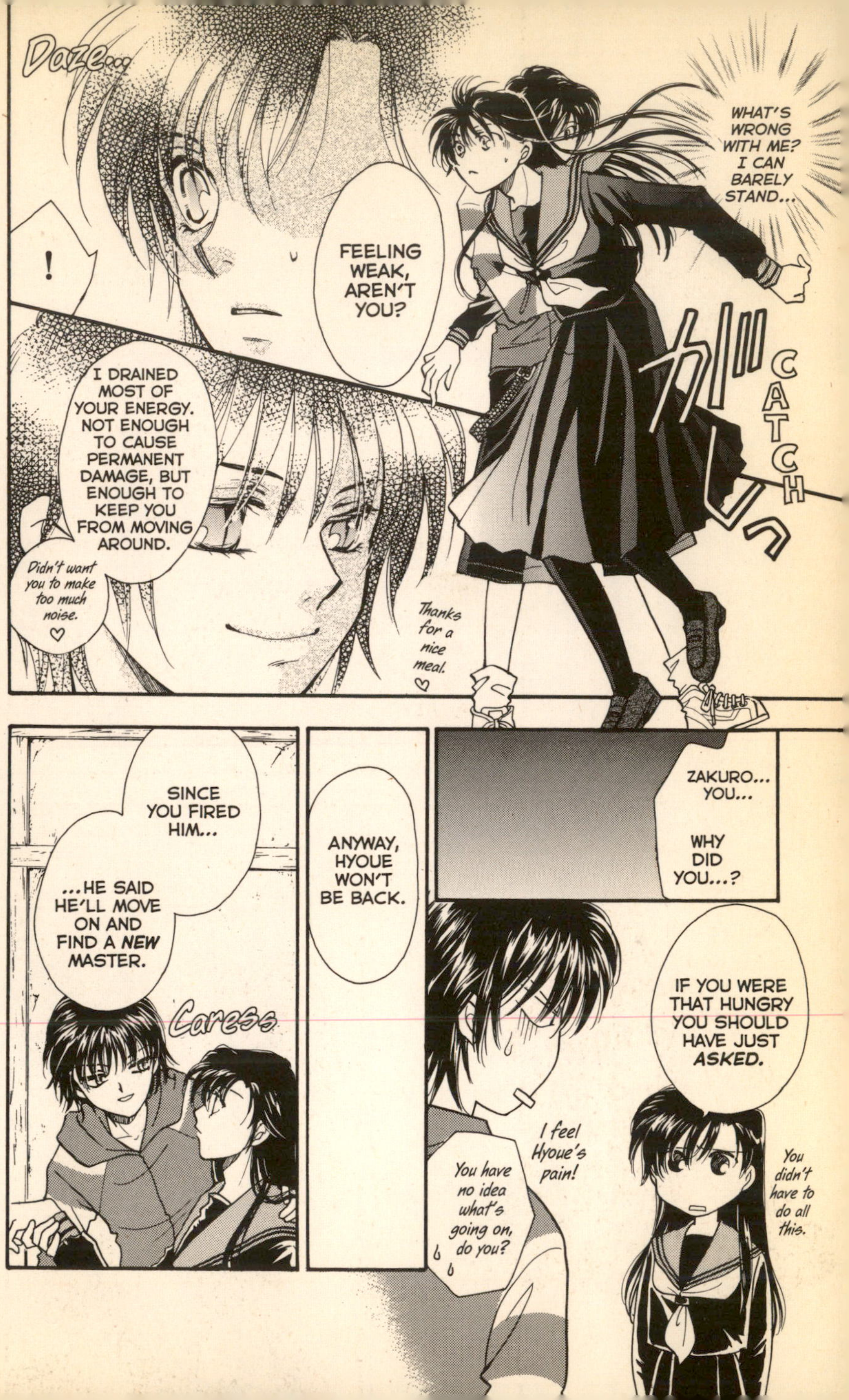
WHAT'S WRONG WITH ME? I CAN BARELY STAND...
FEELING WEAK, AREN'T YOU?
!
Daze...
CATCH
I DRAINED MOST OF YOUR ENERGY. NOT ENOUGH TO CAUSE PERMANENT DAMAGE, BUT ENOUGH TO KEEP YOU FROM MOVING AROUND.
Didn't want you to make too much noise. ♡
Thanks for a nice meal. ♡
ZAKURO... YOU...
WHY DID YOU...?
IF YOU WERE THAT HUNGRY YOU SHOULD HAVE JUST ASKED.
You didn't have to do all this.
I feel Hyoue's pain!
You have no idea what's going on, do you?
ANYWAY, HYOUE WON'T BE BACK.
SINCE YOU FIRED HIM...
...HE SAID HE'LL MOVE ON AND FIND A NEW MASTER.
Caress

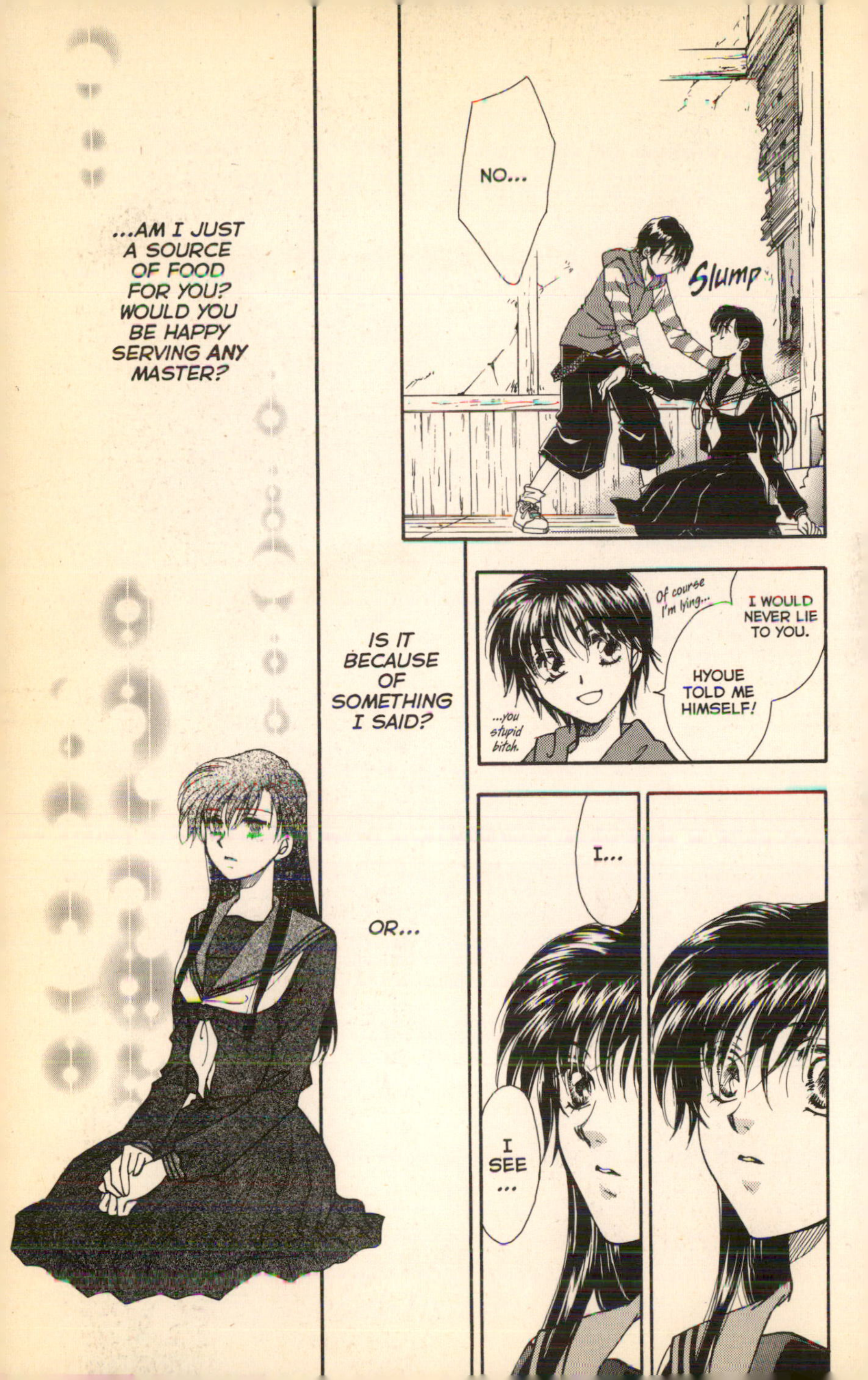
NO...
Slump
I WOULD NEVER LIE TO YOU.
HYOUE TOLD ME HIMSELF!
Of course I'm lying...
...you stupid bitch.
IS IT BECAUSE OF SOMETHING I SAID?
I...
I SEE...
OR...
...AM I JUST A SOURCE OF FOOD FOR YOU? WOULD YOU BE HAPPY SERVING ANY MASTER?

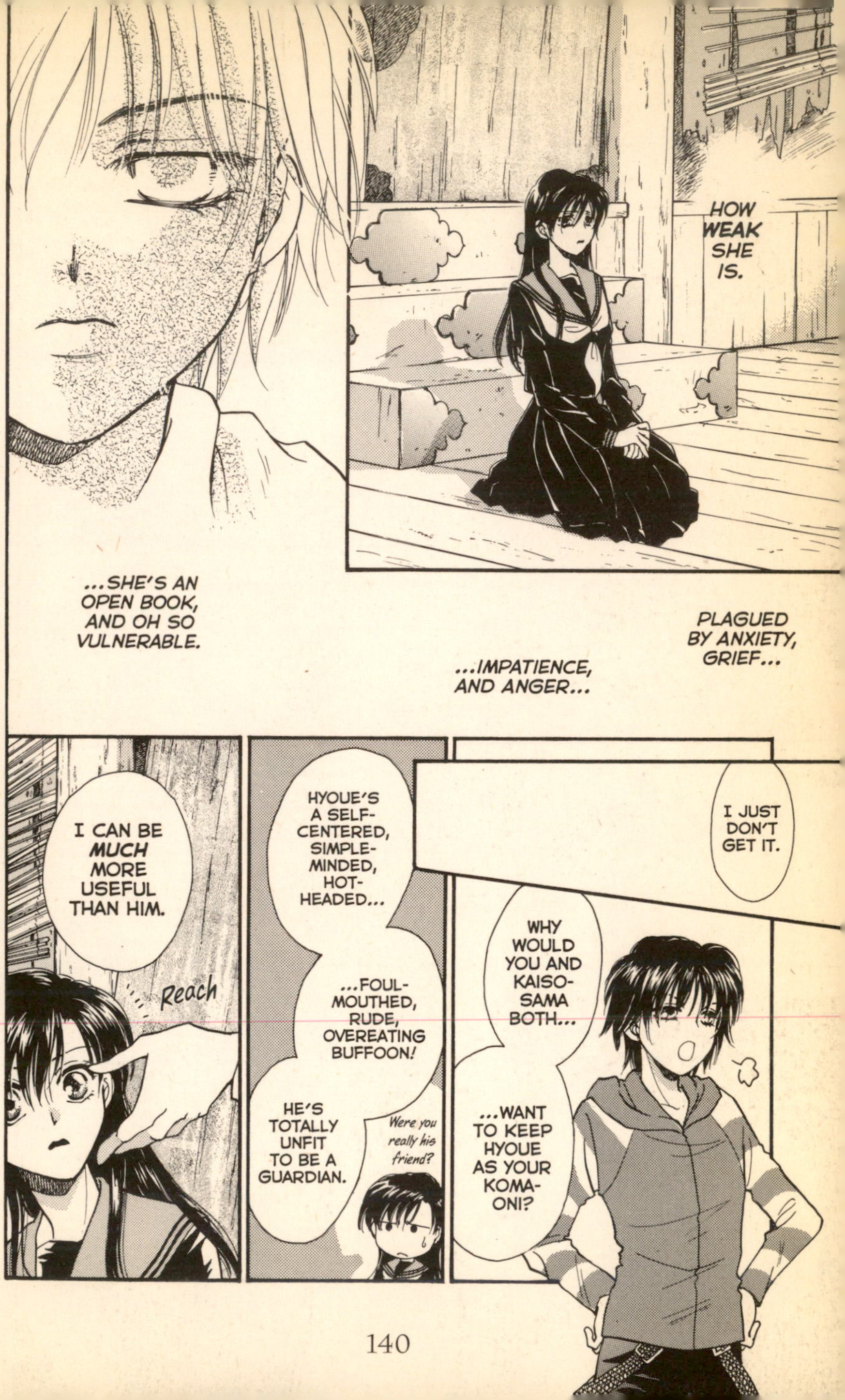
HOW WEAK SHE IS.
PLAGUED BY ANXIETY, GRIEF...
...IMPATIENCE, AND ANGER...
...SHE'S AN OPEN BOOK, AND OH SO VULNERABLE.
I JUST DON'T GET IT.
WHY WOULD YOU AND KAISO-SAMA BOTH...
...WANT TO KEEP HYOUE AS YOUR KOMA-ONI?
HYOUE'S A SELF-CENTERED, SIMPLE-MINDED, HOT-HEADED...
...FOUL-MOUTHED, RUDE, OVEREATING BUFFOON!
HE'S TOTALLY UNFIT TO BE A GUARDIAN.
Were you really his friend?
I CAN BE MUCH MORE USEFUL THAN HIM.
Reach

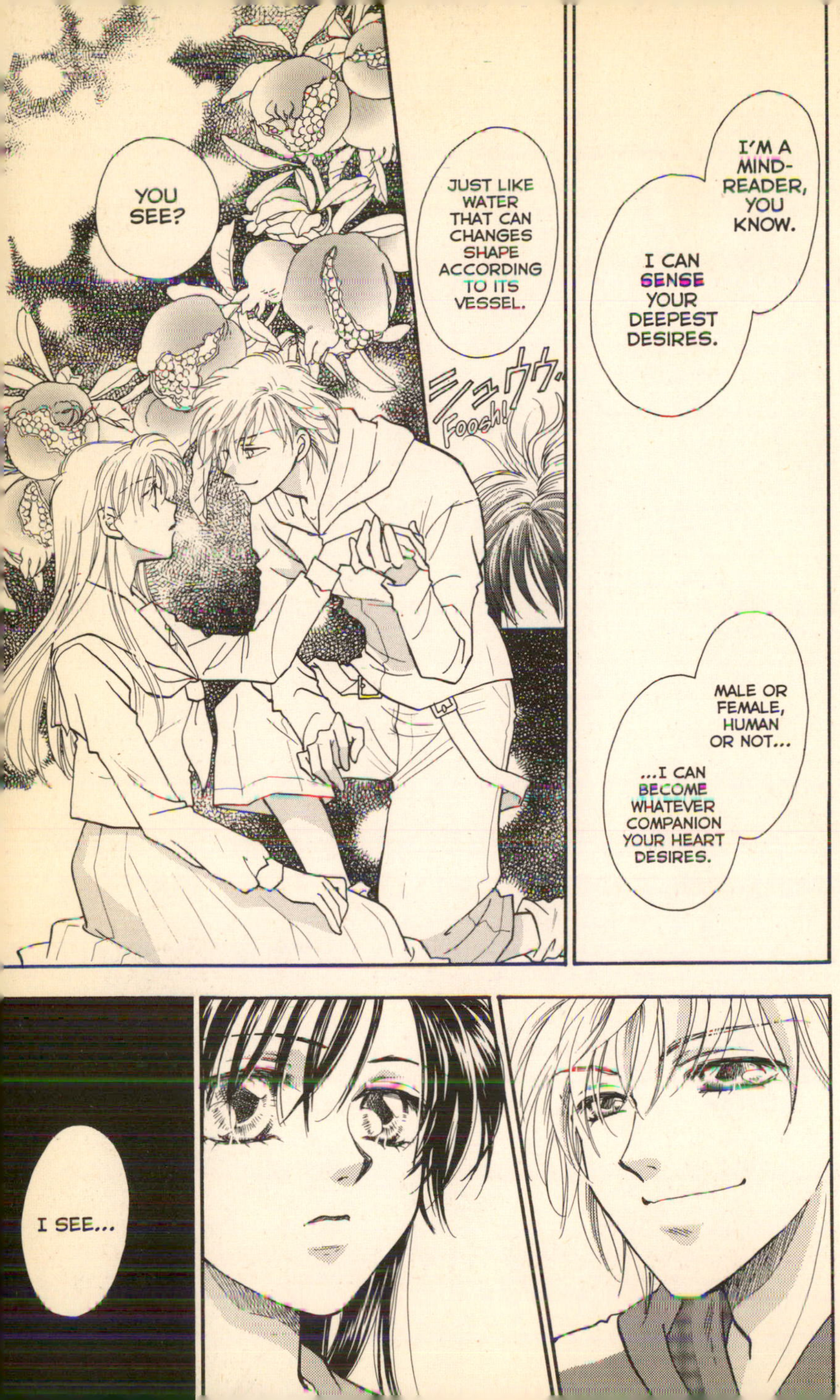
I'M A MIND-READER, YOU KNOW.
I CAN SENSE YOUR DEEPEST DESIRES.
MALE OR FEMALE, HUMAN OR NOT...
...I CAN BECOME WHATEVER COMPANION YOUR HEART DESIRES.
JUST LIKE WATER THAT CAN CHANGES SHAPE ACCORDING TO ITS VESSEL.
YOU SEE?
シュウウ
Foosh!
I SEE...

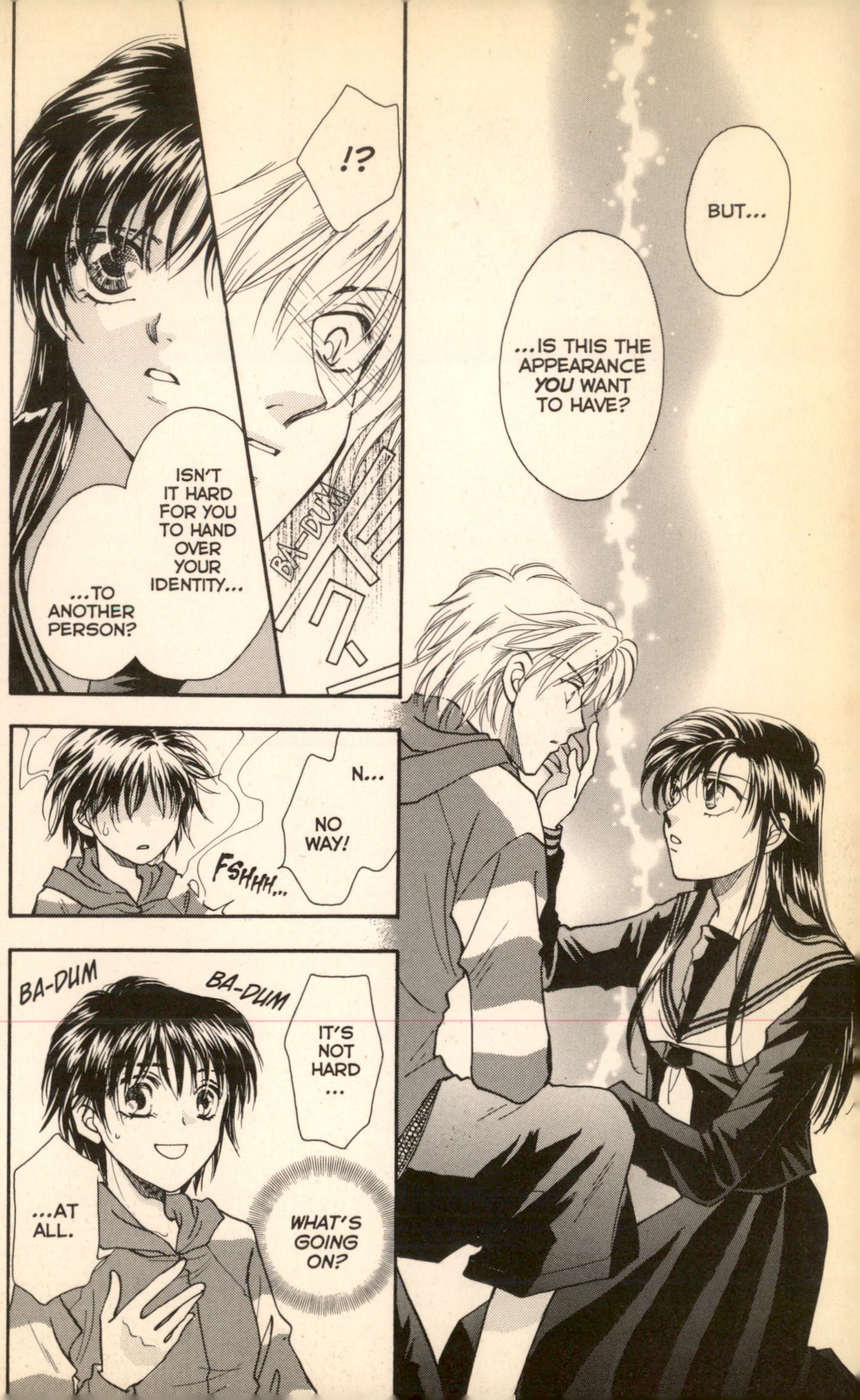
BUT...
...IS THIS THE APPEARANCE YOU WANT TO HAVE?
!?
ISN'T IT HARD FOR YOU TO HAND OVER YOUR IDENTITY...
...TO ANOTHER PERSON?
BA-DUM
N...
NO WAY!
FSHHH...
BA-DUM
BA-DUM
IT'S NOT HARD...
...AT ALL.
WHAT'S GOING ON?

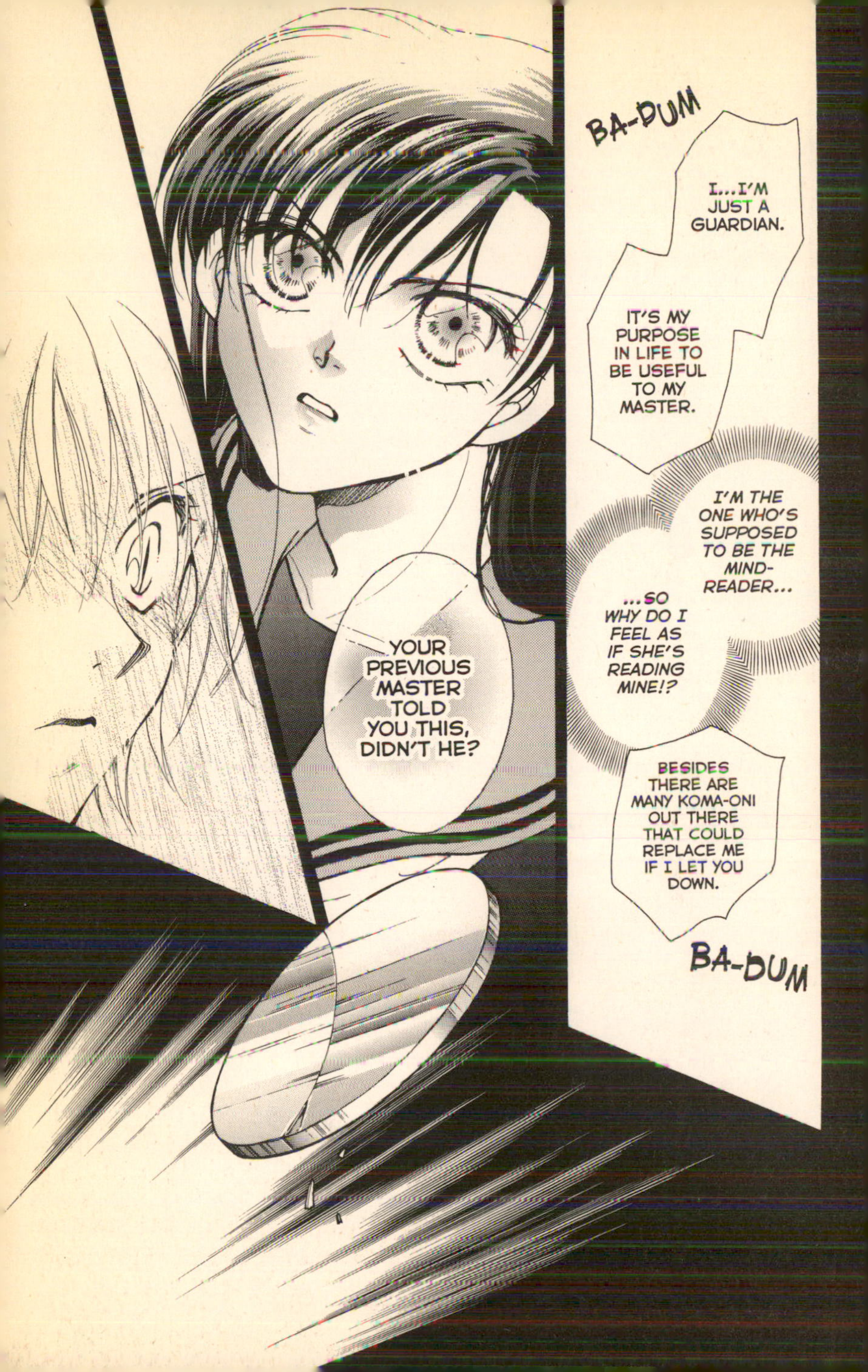
BA-DUM
I...I'M JUST A GUARDIAN.
IT'S MY PURPOSE IN LIFE TO BE USEFUL TO MY MASTER.
I'M THE ONE WHO'S SUPPOSED TO BE THE MIND-READER...
...SO WHY DO I FEEL AS IF SHE'S READING MINE!?
BESIDES THERE ARE MANY KOMA-ONI OUT THERE THAT COULD REPLACE ME IF I LET YOU DOWN.
BA-DUM
YOUR PREVIOUS MASTER TOLD YOU THIS, DIDN'T HE?

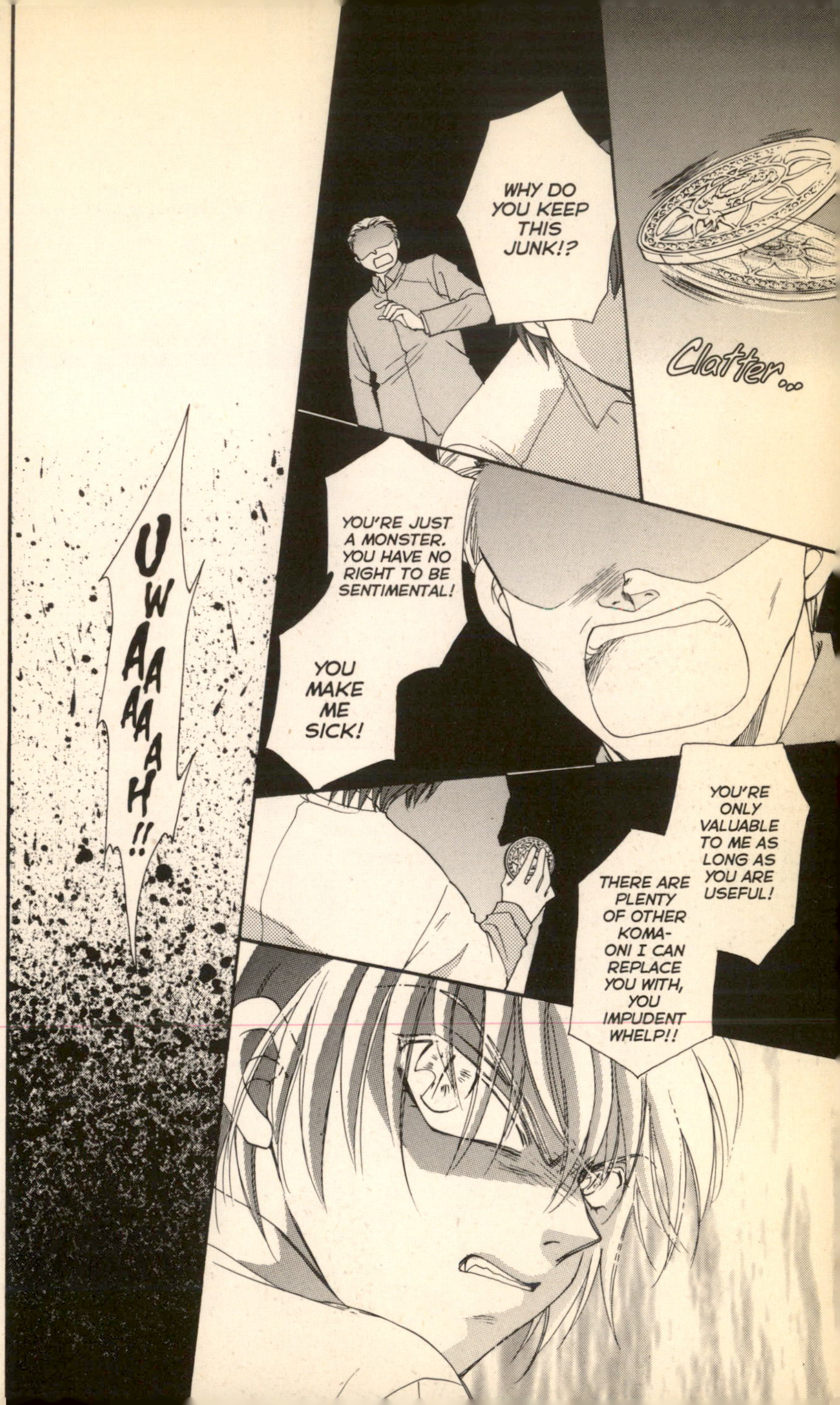
WHY DO YOU KEEP THIS JUNK!?
Clatter...
YOU'RE JUST A MONSTER. YOU HAVE NO RIGHT TO BE SENTIMENTAL!
YOU MAKE ME SICK!
YOU'RE ONLY VALUABLE TO ME AS LONG AS YOU ARE USEFUL!
THERE ARE PLENTY OF OTHER KOMA-ONI I CAN REPLACE YOU WITH, YOU IMPUDENT WHELP!!
UWAAAAAH!!

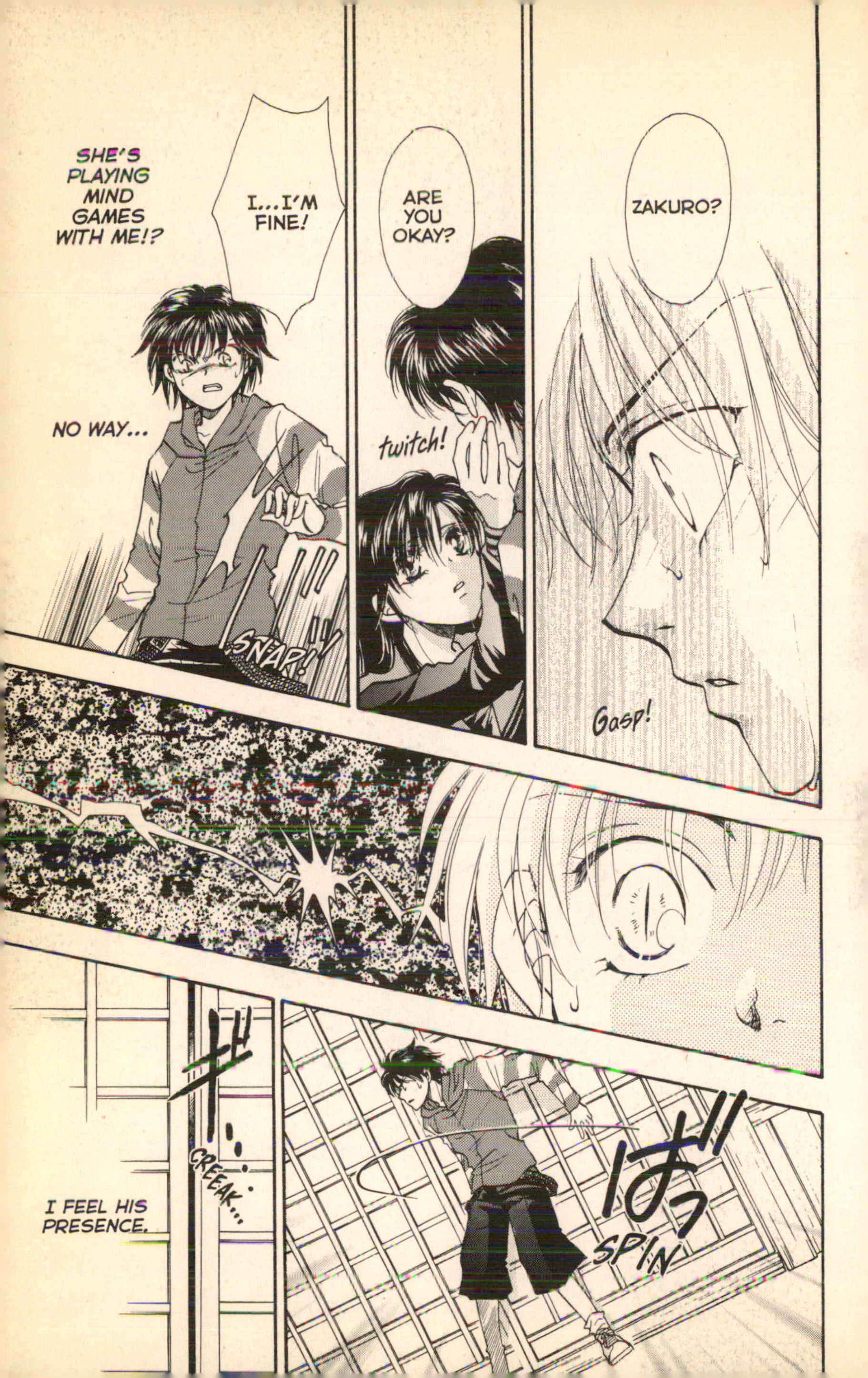
ZAKURO?
Gasp!
ARE YOU OKAY?
twitch!
I...I'M FINE!
SHE'S PLAYING MIND GAMES WITH ME!?
NO WAY...
SNAP!
ばっ
SPIN
CREEAK...
I FEEL HIS PRESENCE.

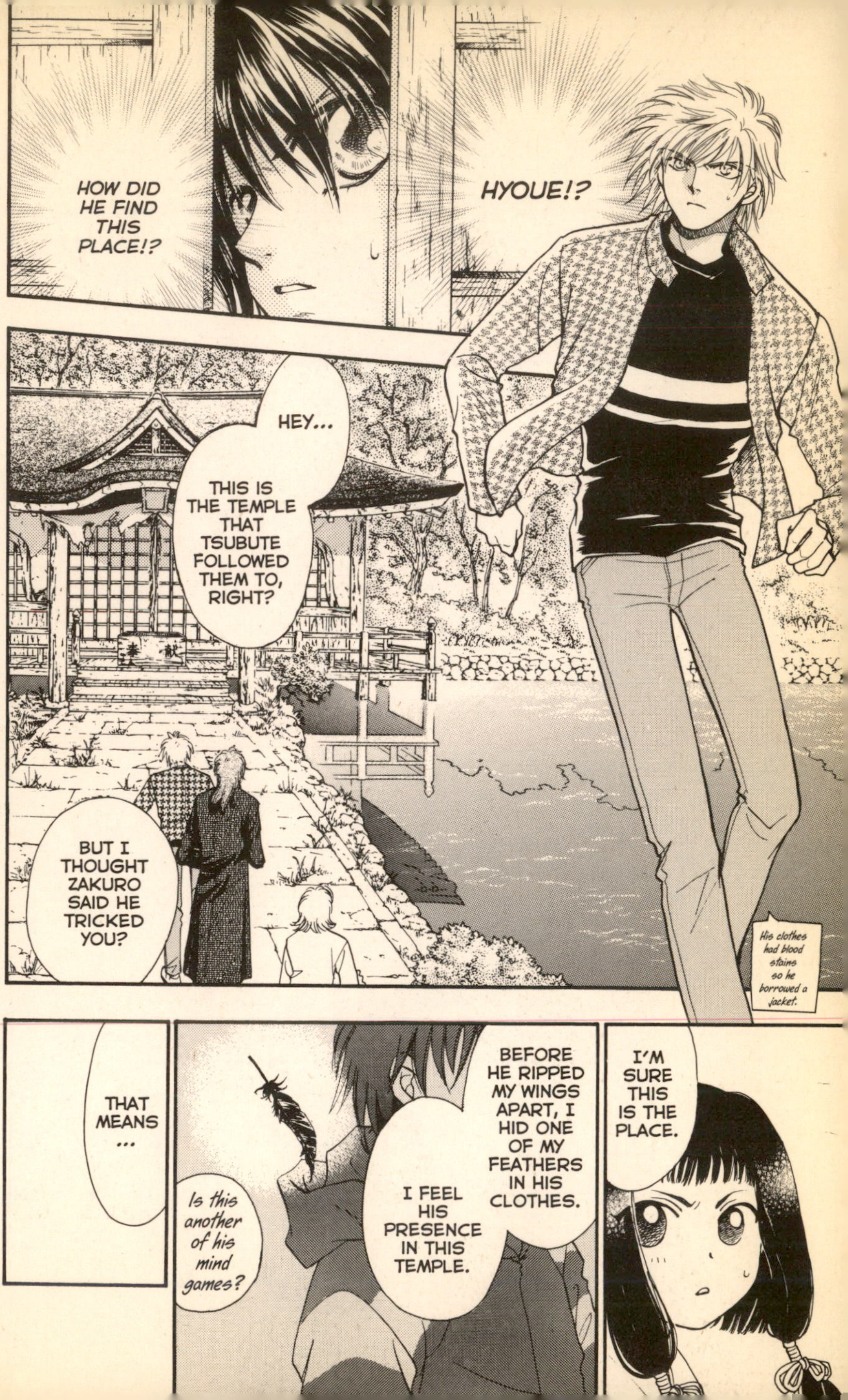
HYOUE!?
HOW DID HE FIND THIS PLACE!?
HEY...
THIS IS THE TEMPLE THAT TSUBUTE FOLLOWED THEM TO, RIGHT?
His clothes had blood stains so he borrowed a jacket.
BUT I THOUGHT ZAKURO SAID HE TRICKED YOU?
I'M SURE THIS IS THE PLACE.
BEFORE HE RIPPED MY WINGS APART, I HID ONE OF MY FEATHERS IN HIS CLOTHES.
I FEEL HIS PRESENCE IN THIS TEMPLE.
Is this another of his mind games?
THAT MEANS ...

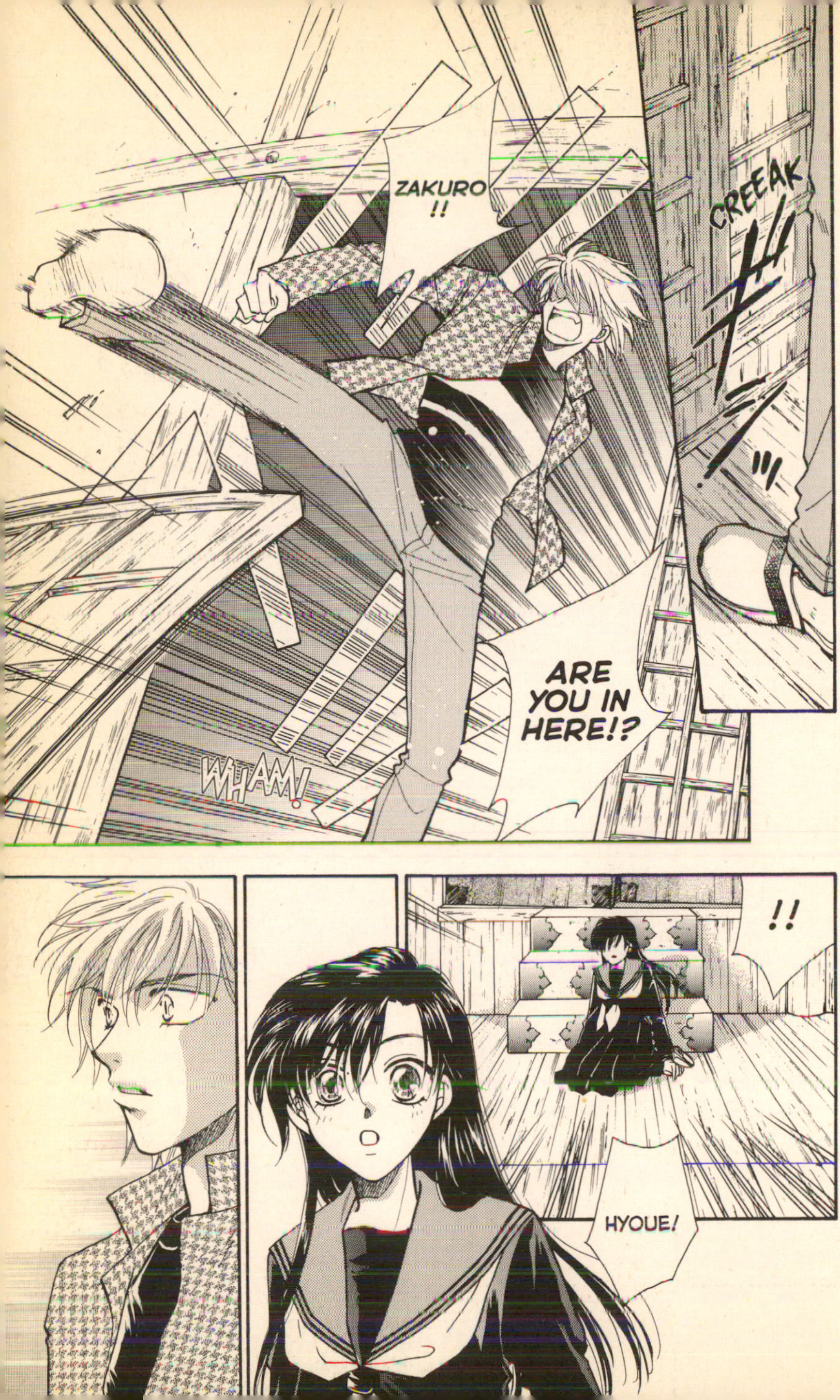
CREEAK
ZAKURO !!
ARE YOU IN HERE!?
WHAM!
!!
HYOUE!

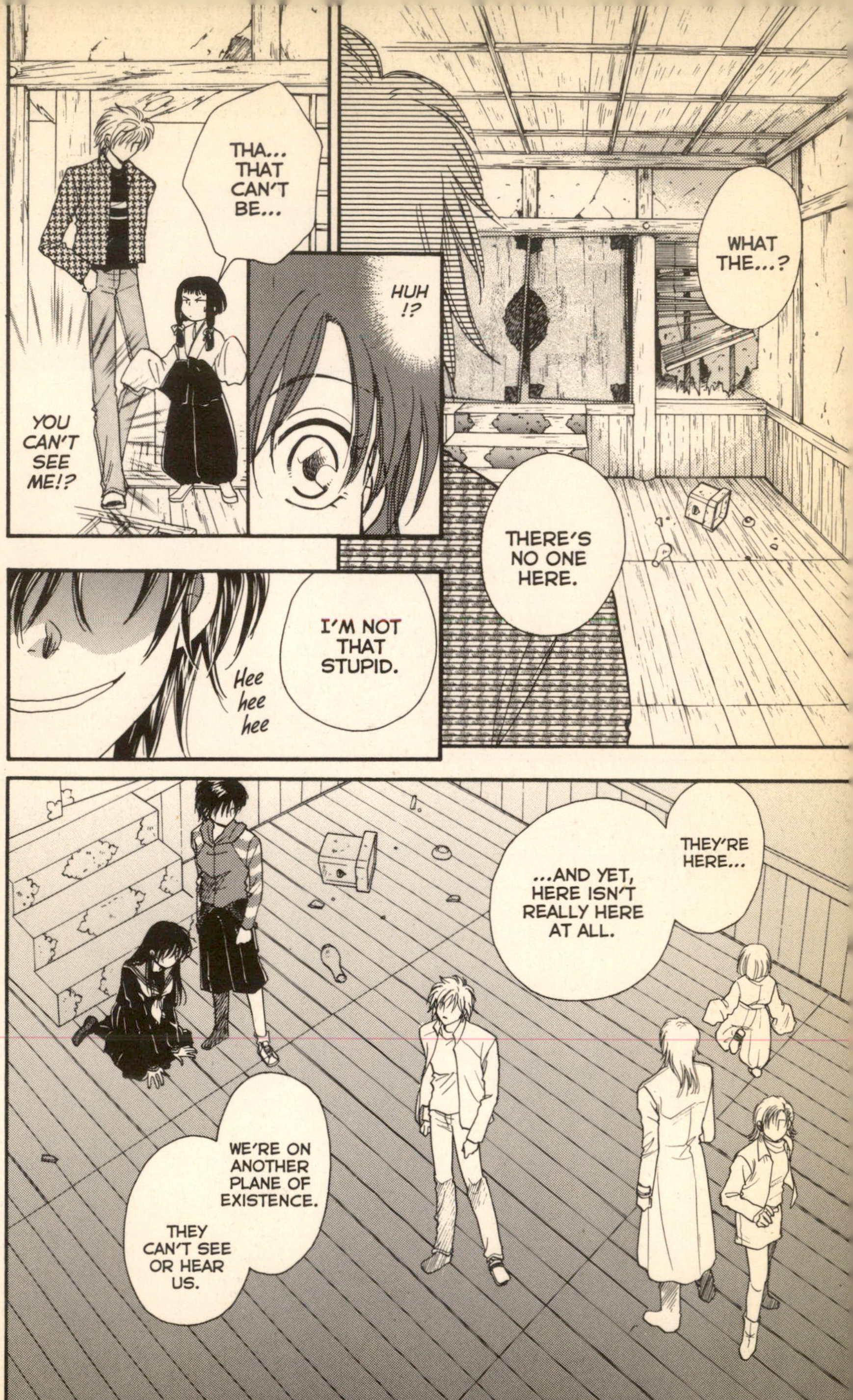
WHAT THE...?
THERE'S NO ONE HERE.
HUH !?
THA... THAT CAN'T BE...
YOU CAN'T SEE ME!?
I'M NOT THAT STUPID.
Hee hee hee
THEY'RE HERE...
...AND YET, HERE ISN'T REALLY HERE AT ALL.
WE'RE ON ANOTHER PLANE OF EXISTENCE.
THEY CAN'T SEE OR HEAR US.

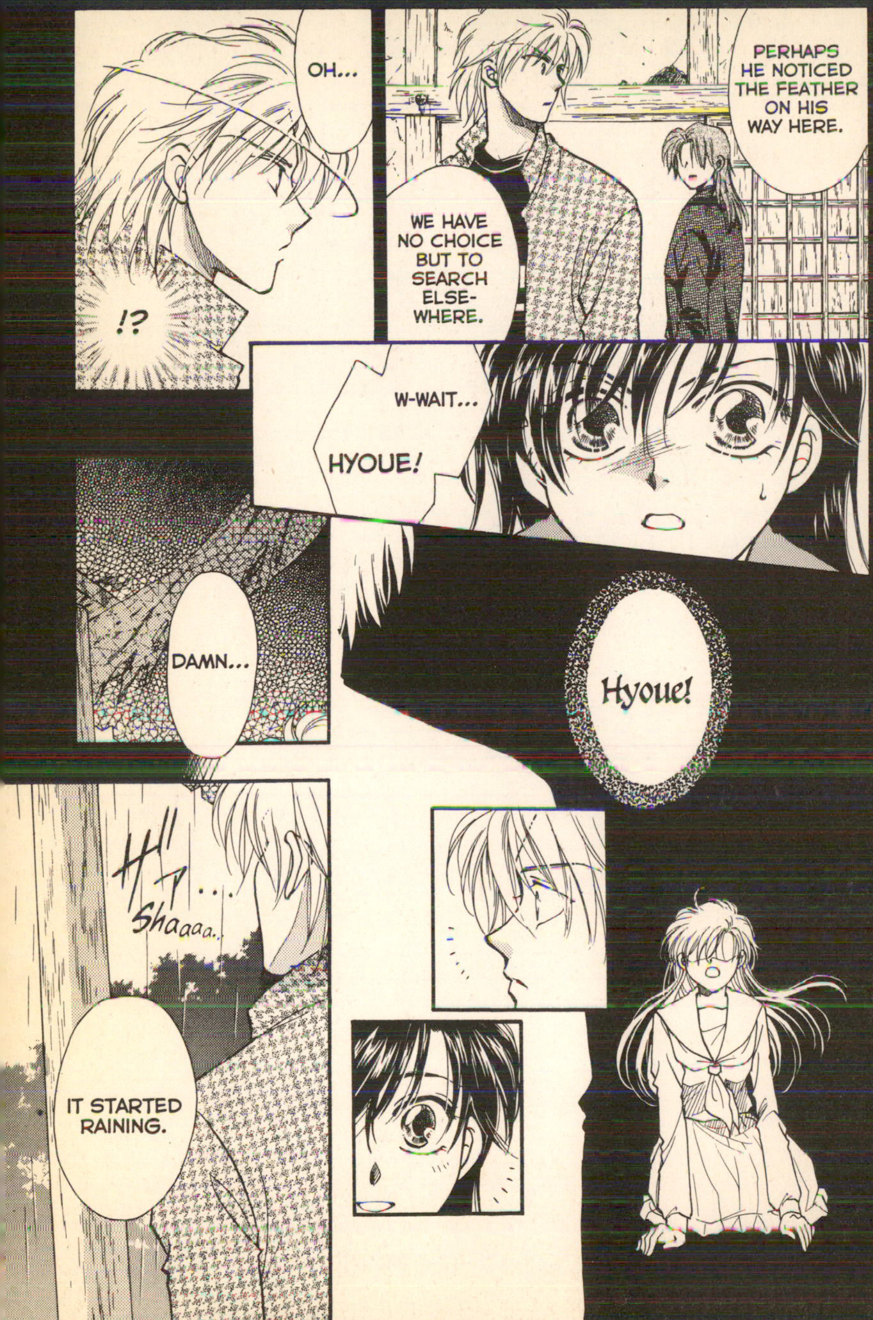
PERHAPS HE NOTICED THE FEATHER ON HIS WAY HERE.
WE HAVE NO CHOICE BUT TO SEARCH ELSE-WHERE.
OH...
!?
W-WAIT...
HYOUE!
Hyoue!
DAMN...
Shaaaa..
IT STARTED RAINING.

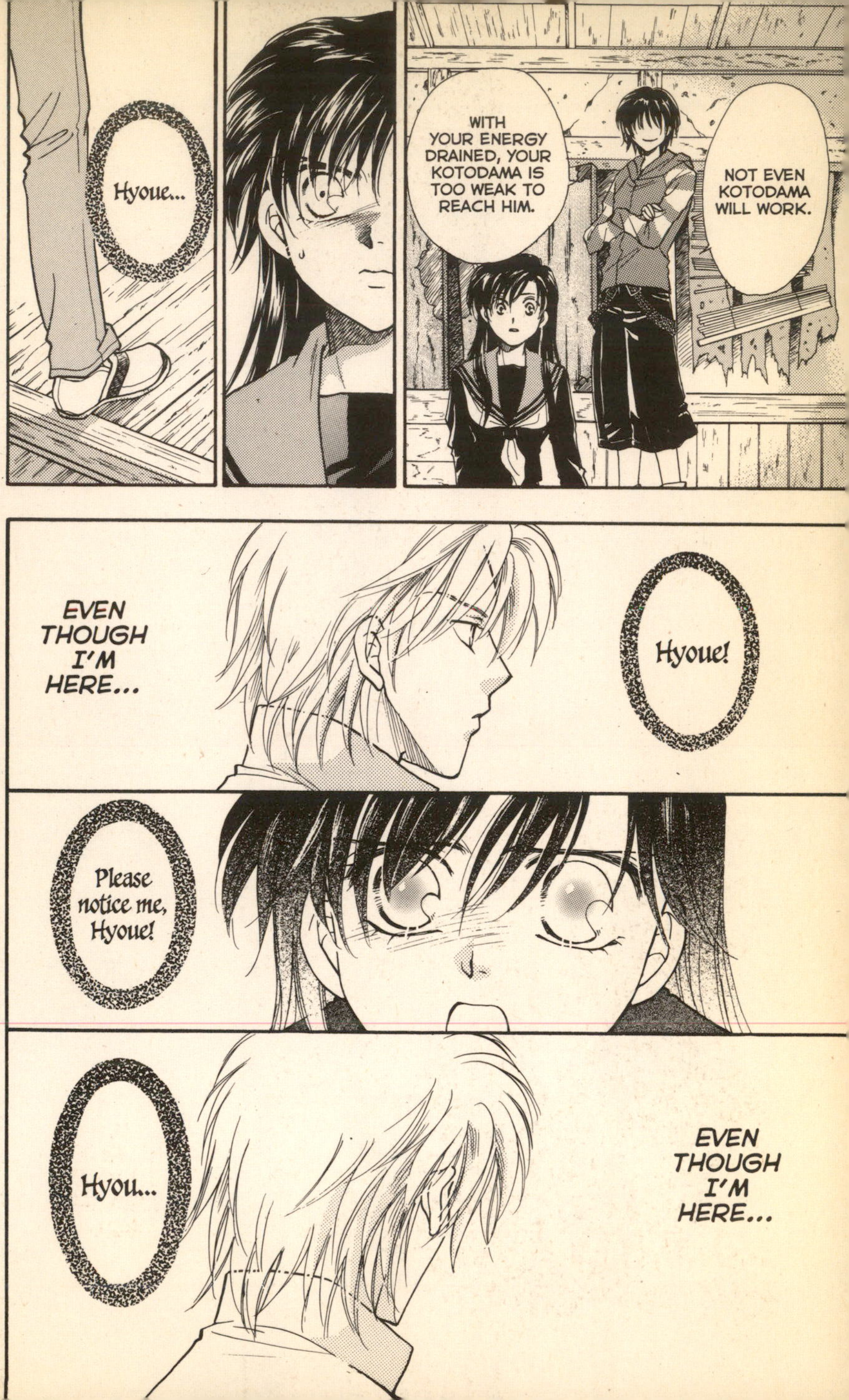
NOT EVEN KOTODAMA WILL WORK.
WITH YOUR ENERGY DRAINED, YOUR KOTODAMA IS TOO WEAK TO REACH HIM.
Hyoue...
Hyoue!
EVEN THOUGH I'M HERE...
Please notice me, Hyoue!
EVEN THOUGH I'M HERE...
Hyou...

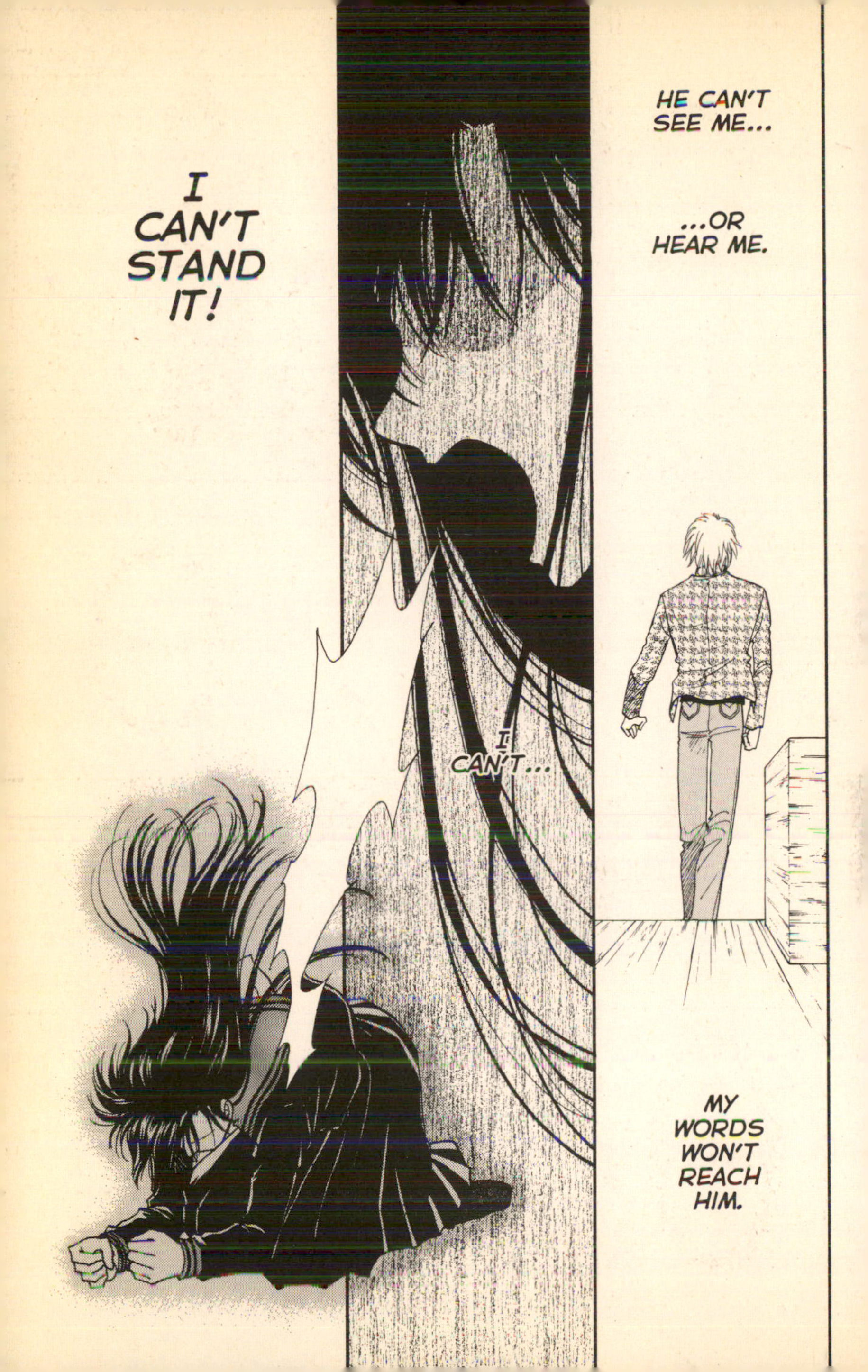
HE CAN'T SEE ME...
...OR HEAR ME.
MY WORDS WON'T REACH HIM.
I CAN'T...
I CAN'T STAND IT!

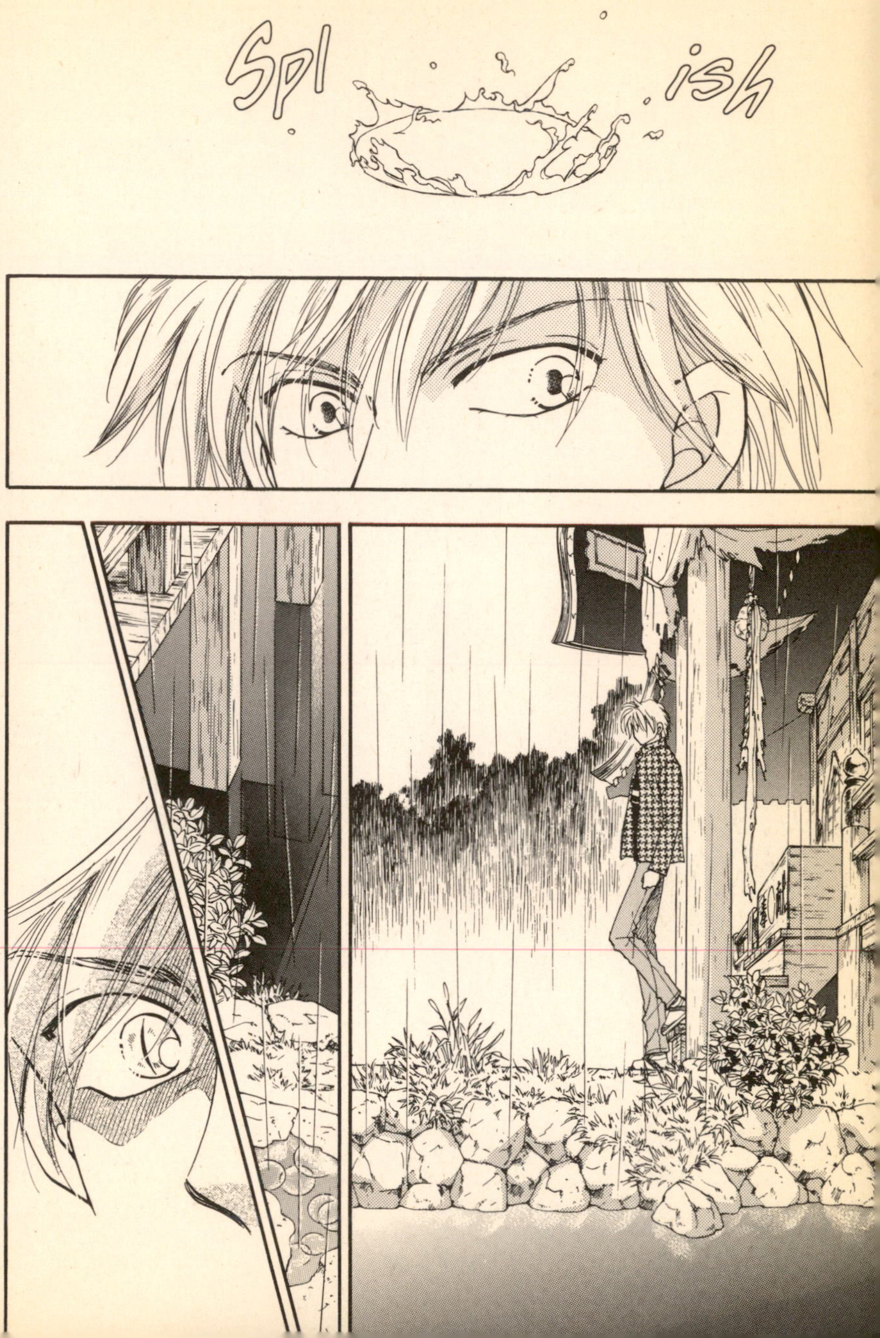
Spl ish

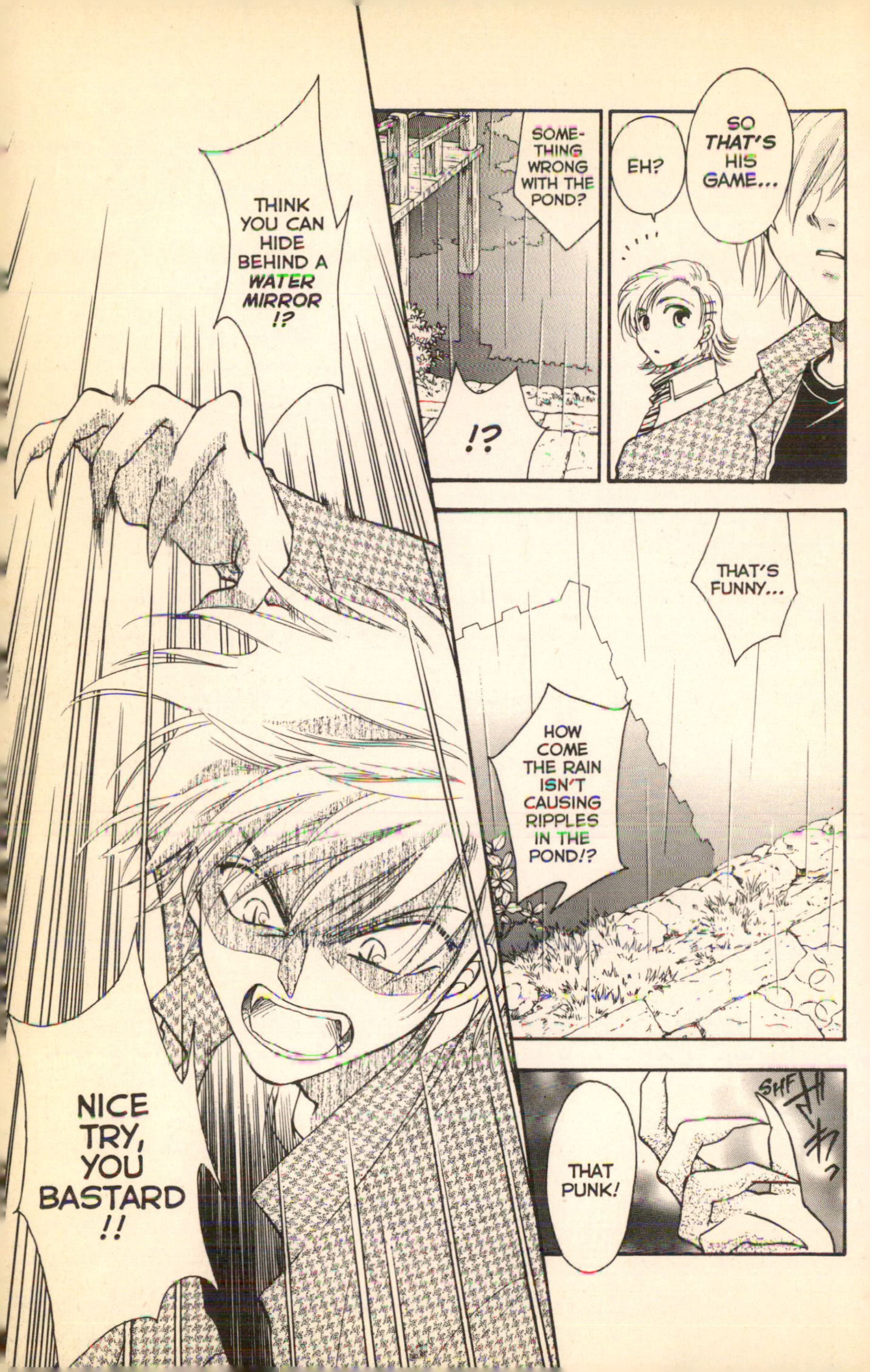
SO THAT'S HIS GAME...
EH?
SOME-THING WRONG WITH THE POND?
!?
THAT'S FUNNY...
HOW COME THE RAIN ISN'T CAUSING RIPPLES IN THE POND!?
SHF
THAT PUNK!
THINK YOU CAN HIDE BEHIND A WATER MIRROR !?
NICE TRY, YOU BASTARD !!

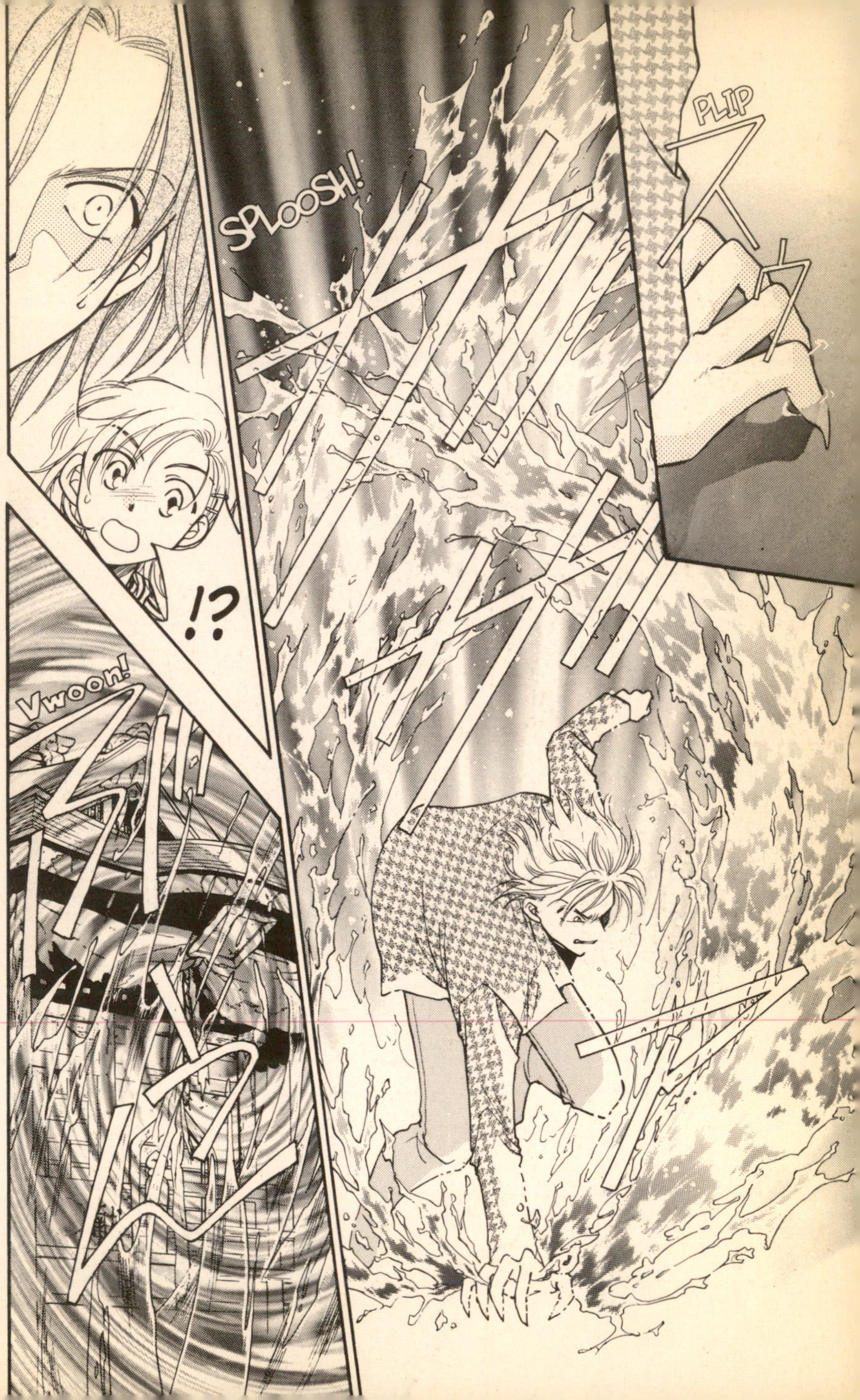
PLIP
SPLOOSH!
!?
Vwoon!

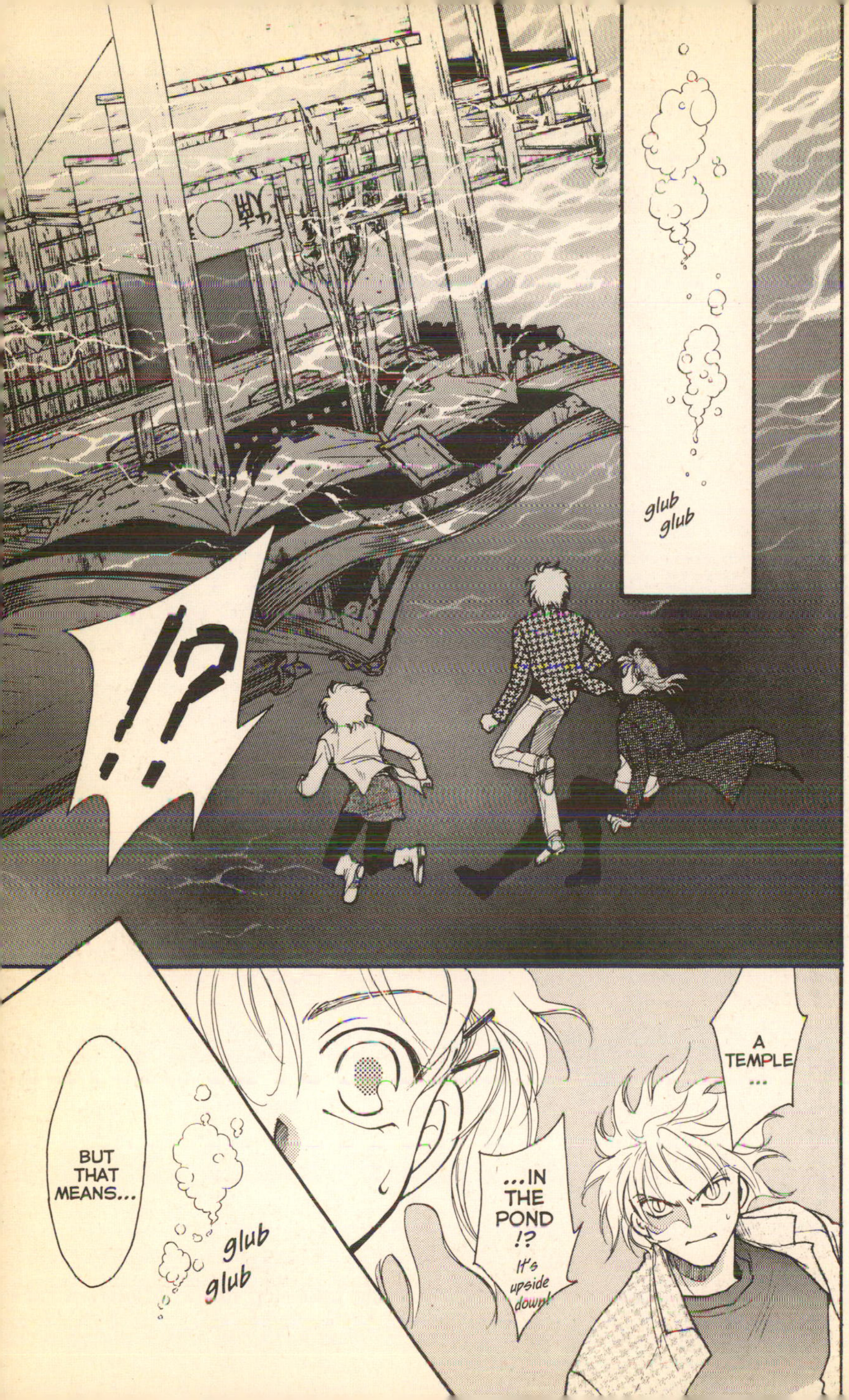
glub glub
!?
A TEMPLE ...
...IN THE POND !?
It's upside down!
BUT THAT MEANS...
glub glub

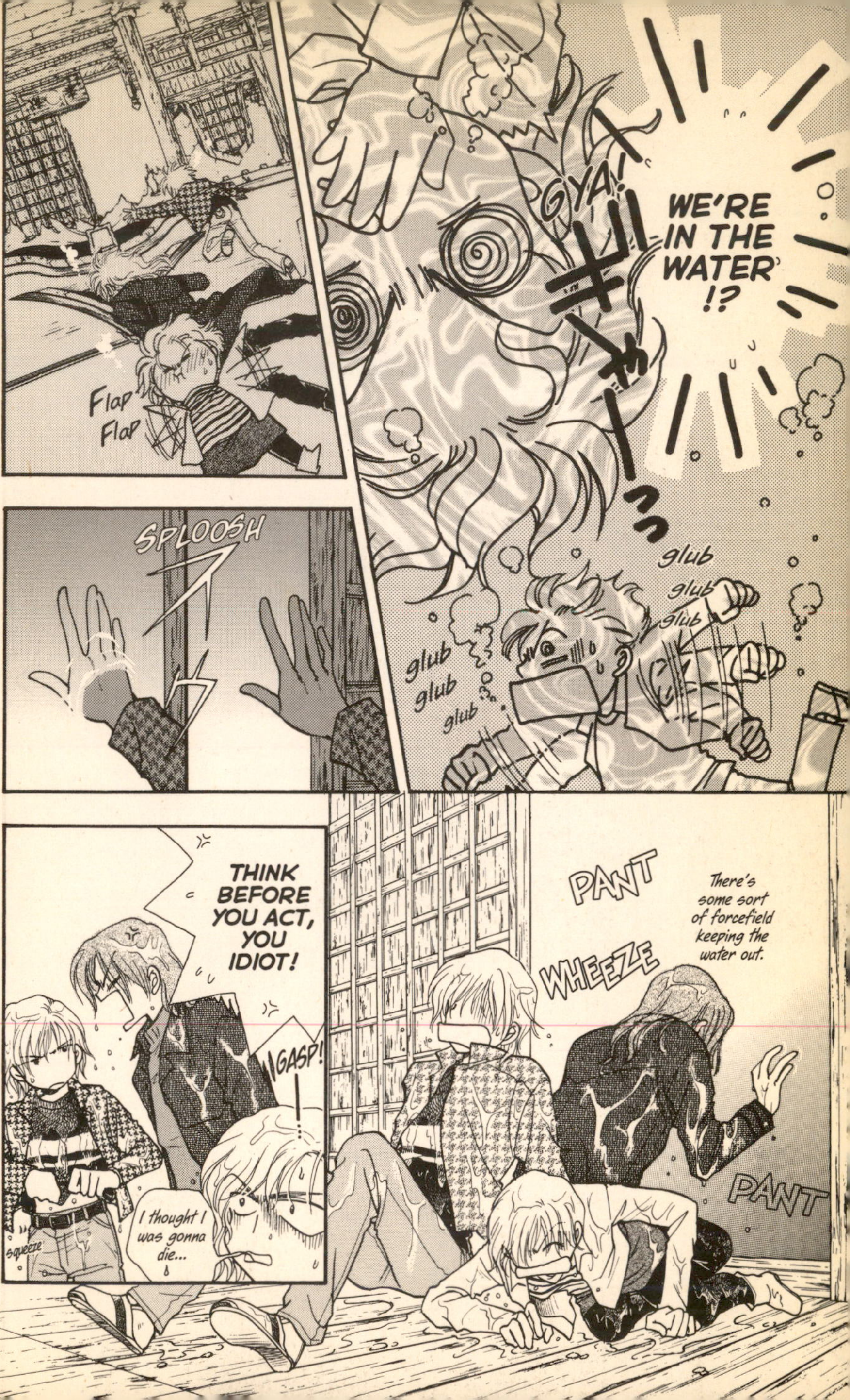
GYA!
WE'RE IN THE WATER !?
glub glub glub
glub glub glub
Flap Flap
SPLOOSH
PANT
There's some sort of forcefield keeping the water out.
WHEEZE
PANT
THINK BEFORE YOU ACT, YOU IDIOT!
GASP!
I thought I was gonna die...
squeeze

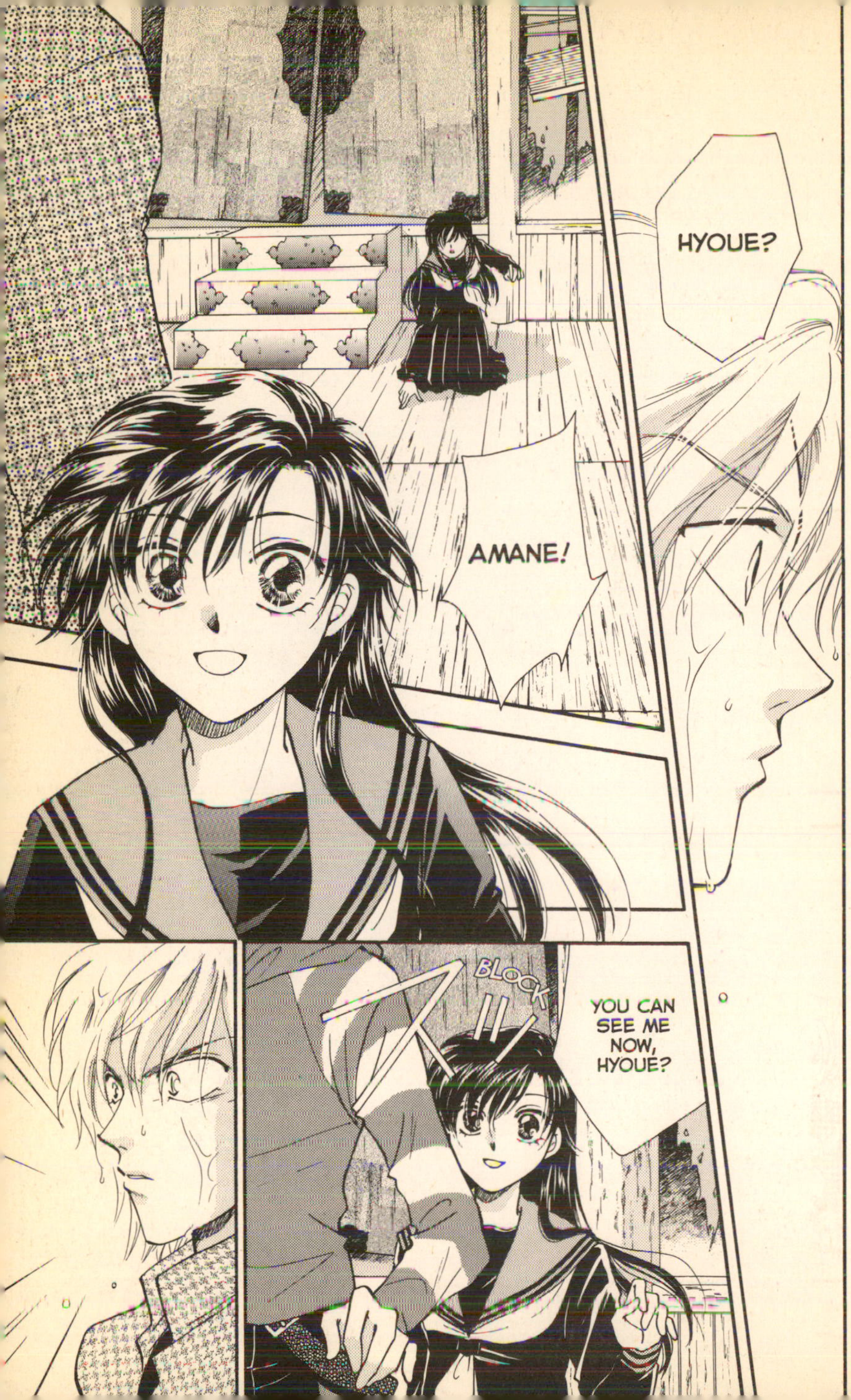
HYOUE?
AMANE!
BLOCK
YOU CAN SEE ME NOW, HYOUE?

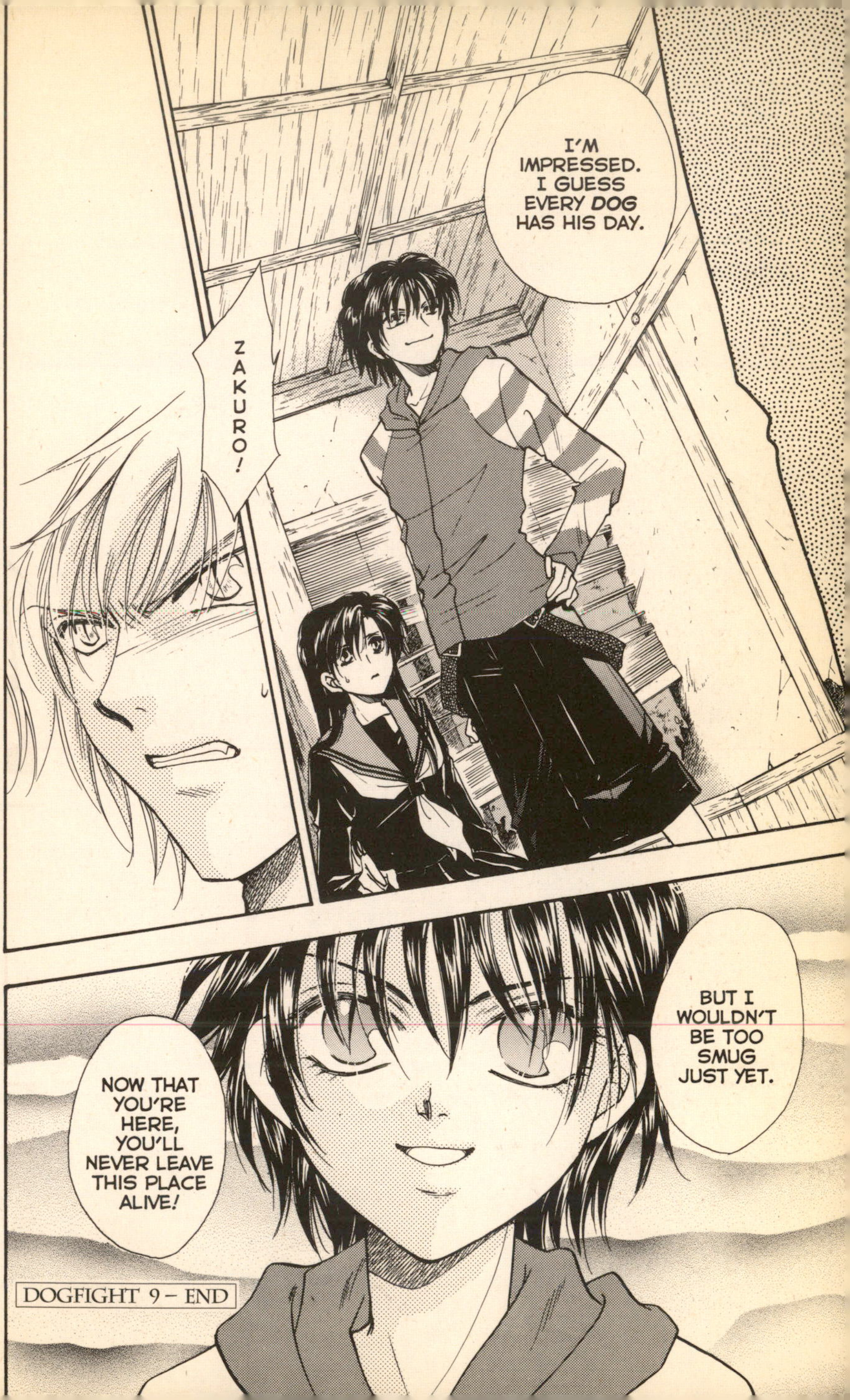

I'M IMPRESSED. I GUESS EVERY *DOG* HAS HIS DAY.
ZAKURO!
BUT I WOULDN'T BE TOO SMUG JUST YET.
NOW THAT YOU'RE HERE, YOU'LL NEVER LEAVE THIS PLACE ALIVE!
DOGFIGHT 9 – END

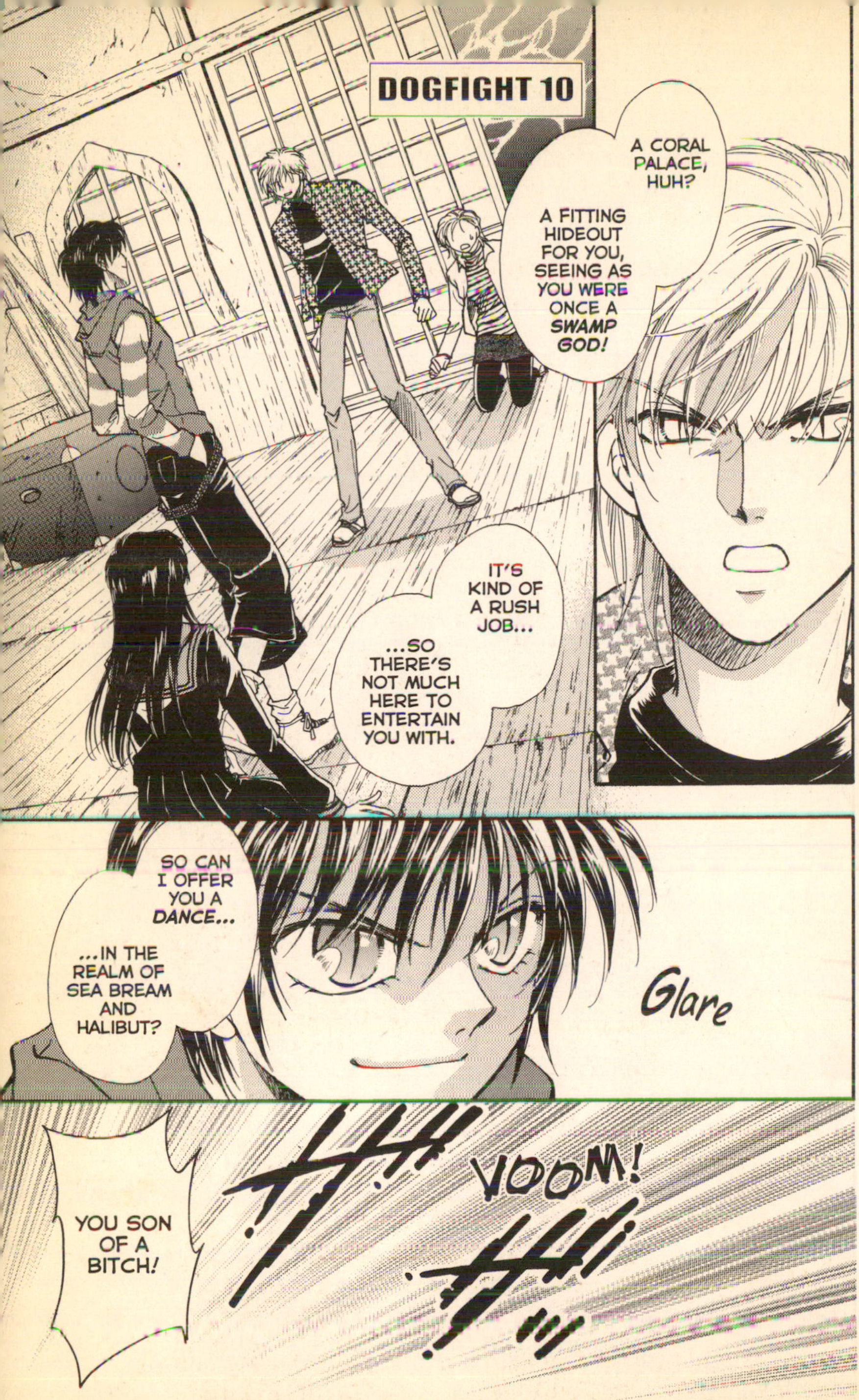
DOGFIGHT 10
A CORAL PALACE, HUH?
A FITTING HIDEOUT FOR YOU, SEEING AS YOU WERE ONCE A *SWAMP GOD!*
IT'S KIND OF A RUSH JOB...
...SO THERE'S NOT MUCH HERE TO ENTERTAIN YOU WITH.
Glare
SO CAN I OFFER YOU A *DANCE...*
...IN THE REALM OF SEA BREAM AND HALIBUT?
VOOM!
YOU SON OF A BITCH!

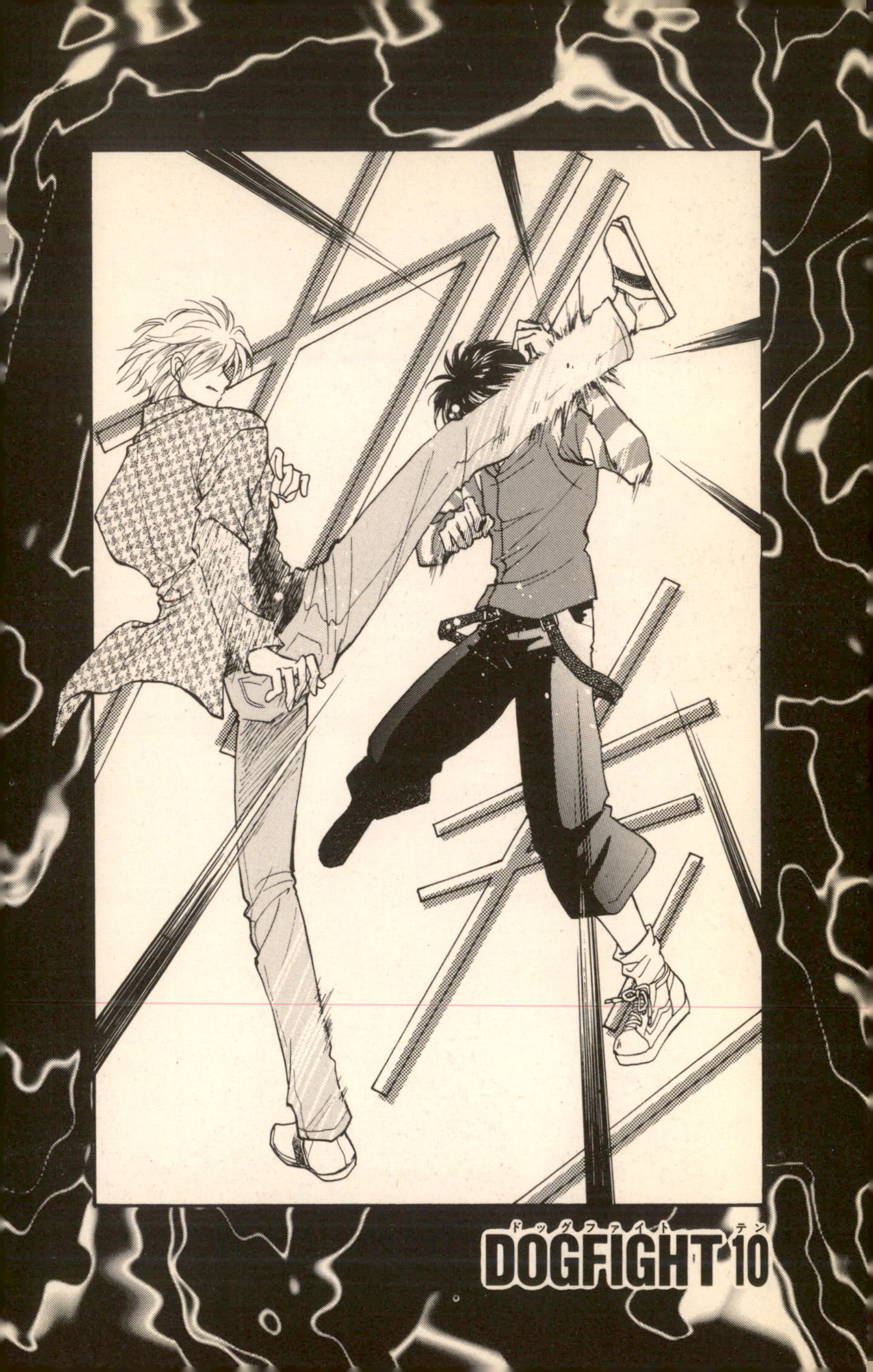
ドッグファイト テン
DOGFIGHT 10

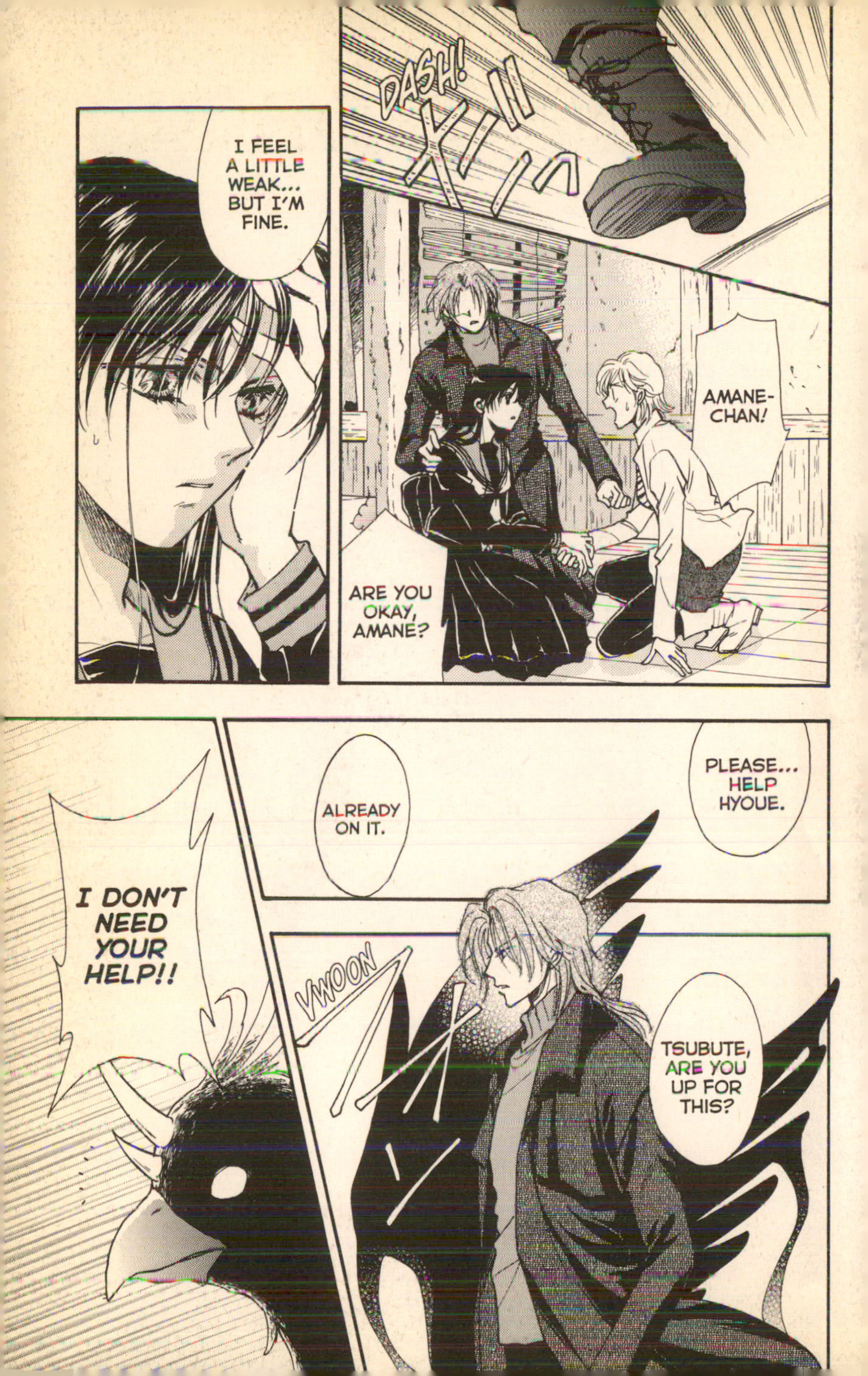
DASH!
AMANE-CHAN!
ARE YOU OKAY, AMANE?
I FEEL A LITTLE WEAK... BUT I'M FINE.
PLEASE... HELP HYOUE.
ALREADY ON IT.
TSUBUTE, ARE YOU UP FOR THIS?
VWOON
I DON'T NEED YOUR HELP!!

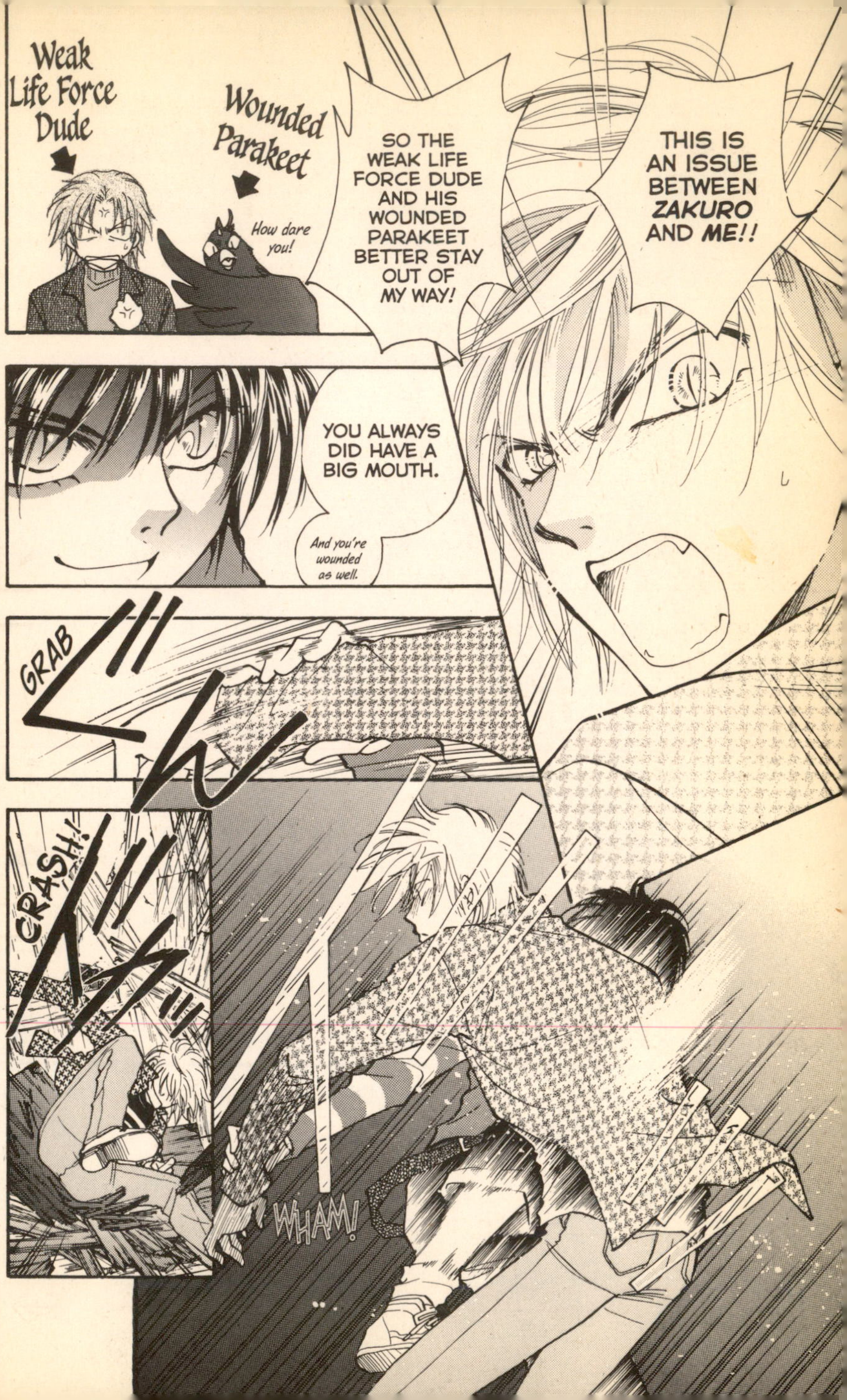
THIS IS AN ISSUE BETWEEN ZAKURO AND ME!!
SO THE WEAK LIFE FORCE DUDE AND HIS WOUNDED PARAKEET BETTER STAY OUT OF MY WAY!
Wounded Parakeet
Weak Life Force Dude
How dare you!
YOU ALWAYS DID HAVE A BIG MOUTH.
And you're wounded as well.
GRAB
CRASH!
WHAM!

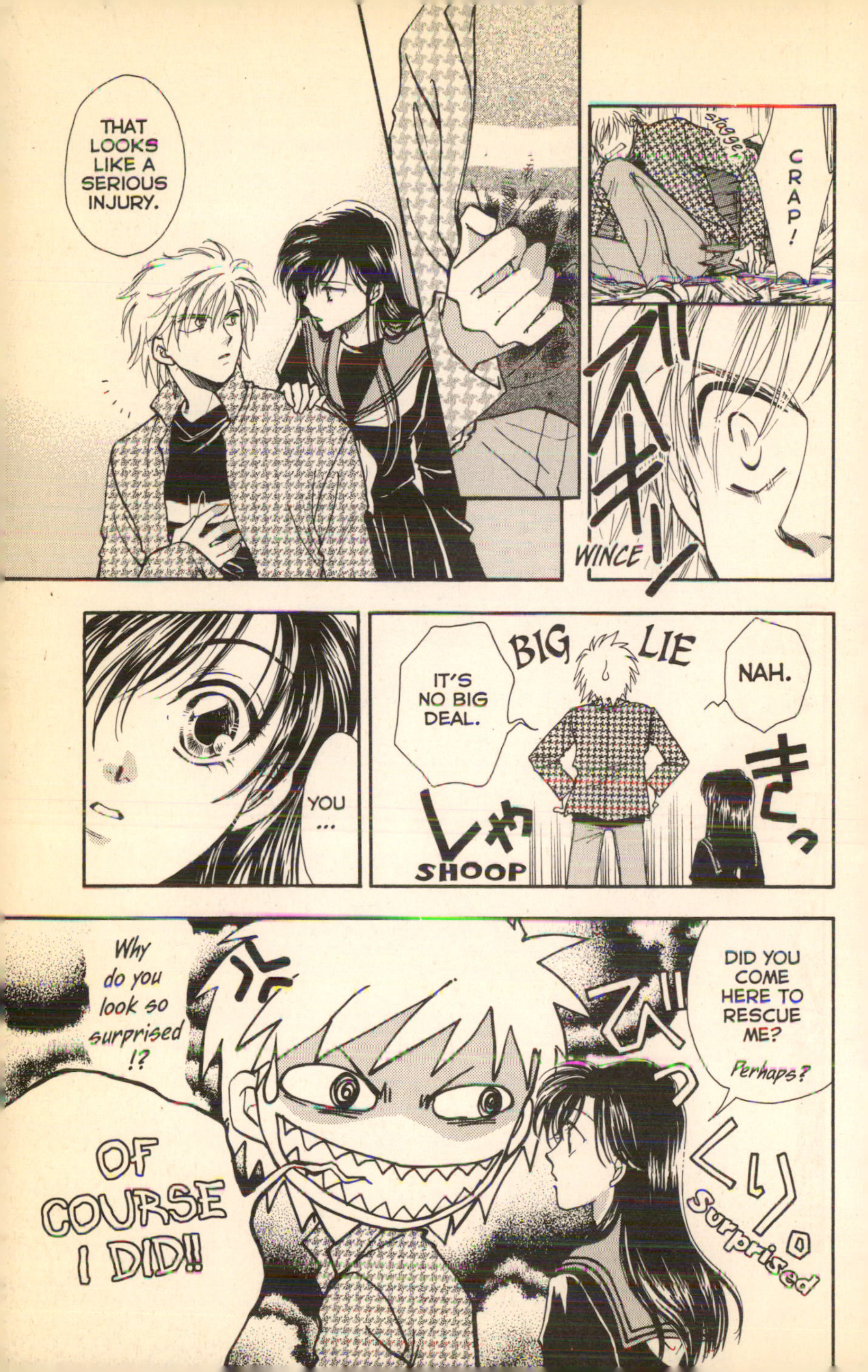
stagger
CRAP!
ズキ
WINCE
THAT LOOKS LIKE A SERIOUS INJURY.
NAH.
きっ
BIG LIE
IT'S NO BIG DEAL.
しゃ
SHOOP
YOU ...
DID YOU COME HERE TO RESCUE ME?
Perhaps?
Surprised
Why do you look so surprised!?
OF COURSE I DID!!

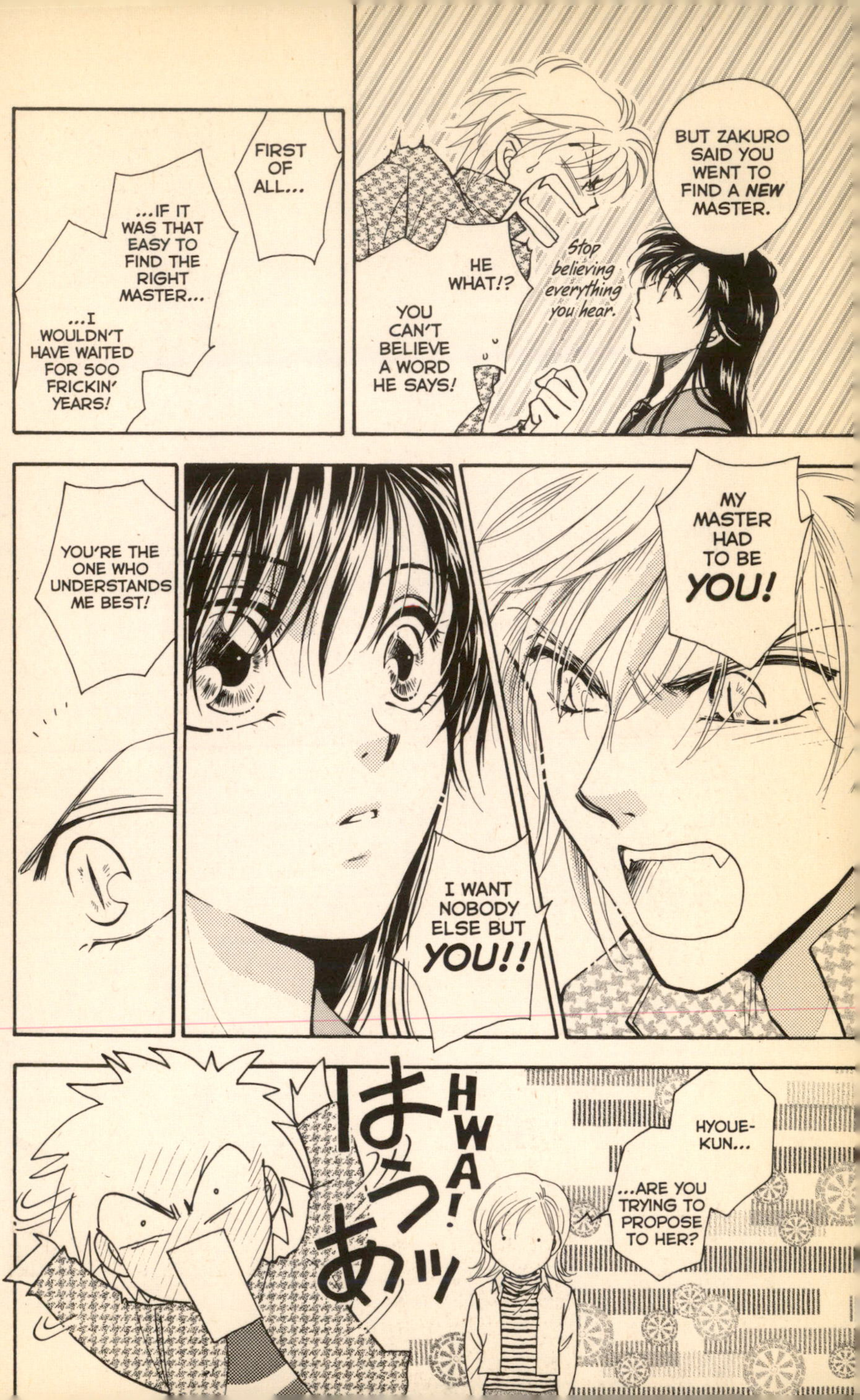
BUT ZAKURO SAID YOU WENT TO FIND A NEW MASTER.
Stop believing everything you hear.
HE WHAT!?
YOU CAN'T BELIEVE A WORD HE SAYS!
FIRST OF ALL...
...IF IT WAS THAT EASY TO FIND THE RIGHT MASTER...
...I WOULDN'T HAVE WAITED FOR 500 FRICKIN' YEARS!
MY MASTER HAD TO BE YOU!
I WANT NOBODY ELSE BUT YOU!!
YOU'RE THE ONE WHO UNDERSTANDS ME BEST!
HYOUE-KUN...
...ARE YOU TRYING TO PROPOSE TO HER?
はうあッ
HWA!

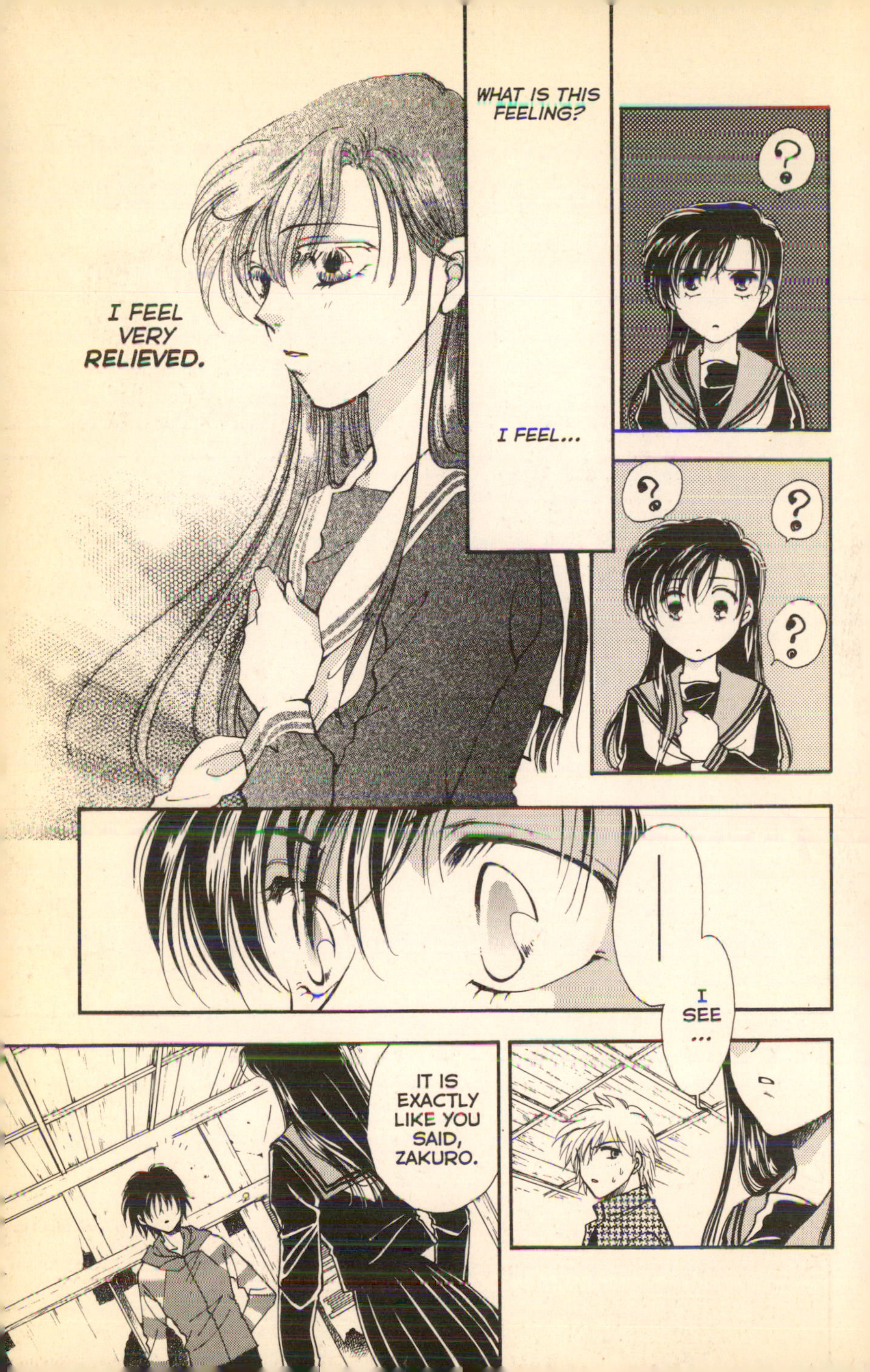

?
?
?
?
WHAT IS THIS FEELING?
I FEEL...
I FEEL VERY RELIEVED.
I SEE...
IT IS EXACTLY LIKE YOU SAID, ZAKURO.

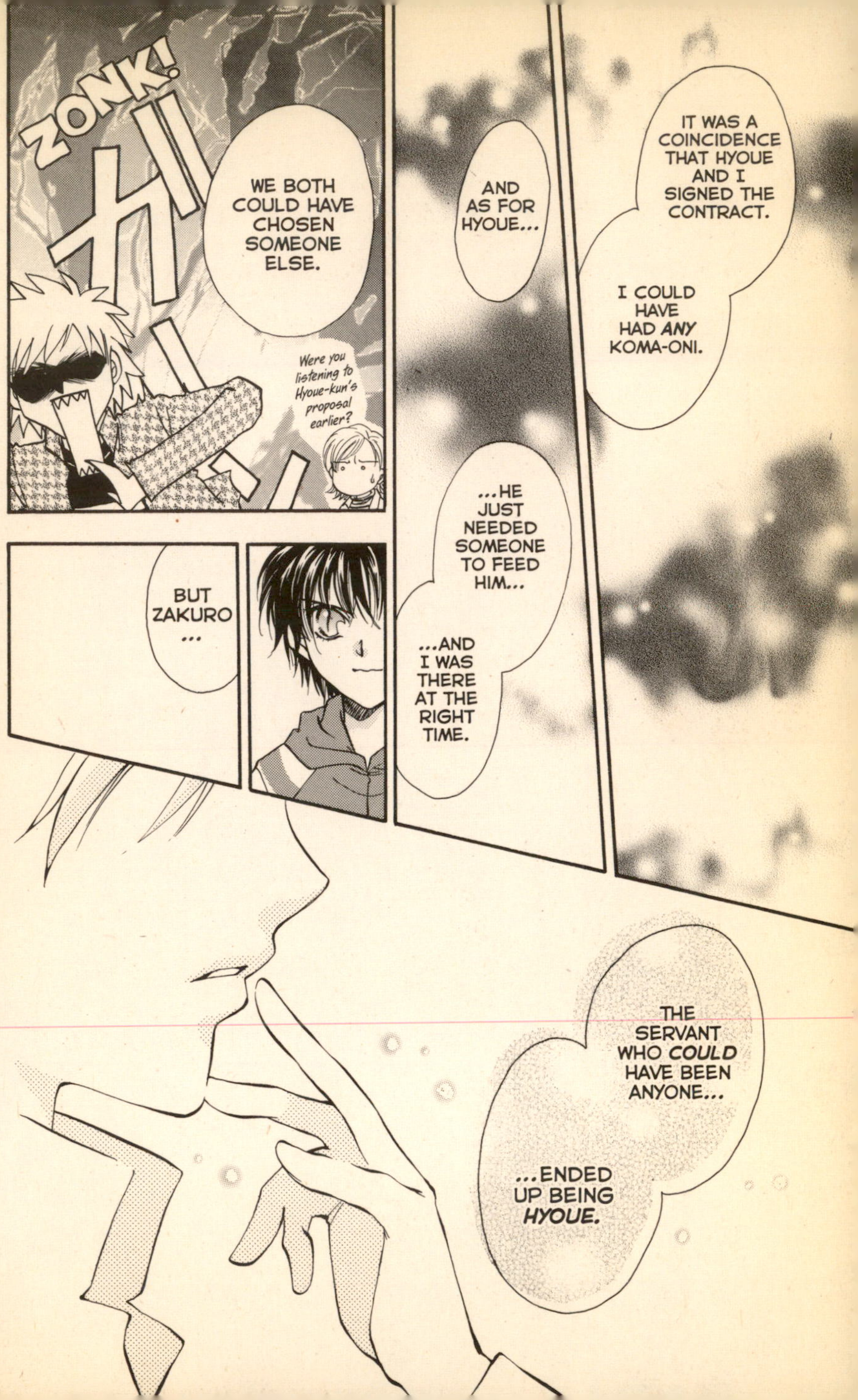
IT WAS A COINCIDENCE THAT HYOUE AND I SIGNED THE CONTRACT.
I COULD HAVE HAD *ANY* KOMA-ONI.
AND AS FOR HYOUE...
...HE JUST NEEDED SOMEONE TO FEED HIM...
...AND I WAS THERE AT THE RIGHT TIME.
WE BOTH COULD HAVE CHOSEN SOMEONE ELSE.
ZONK!
Were you listening to Hyoue-kun's proposal earlier?
BUT ZAKURO...
THE SERVANT WHO *COULD* HAVE BEEN ANYONE...
...ENDED UP BEING ***HYOUE.***

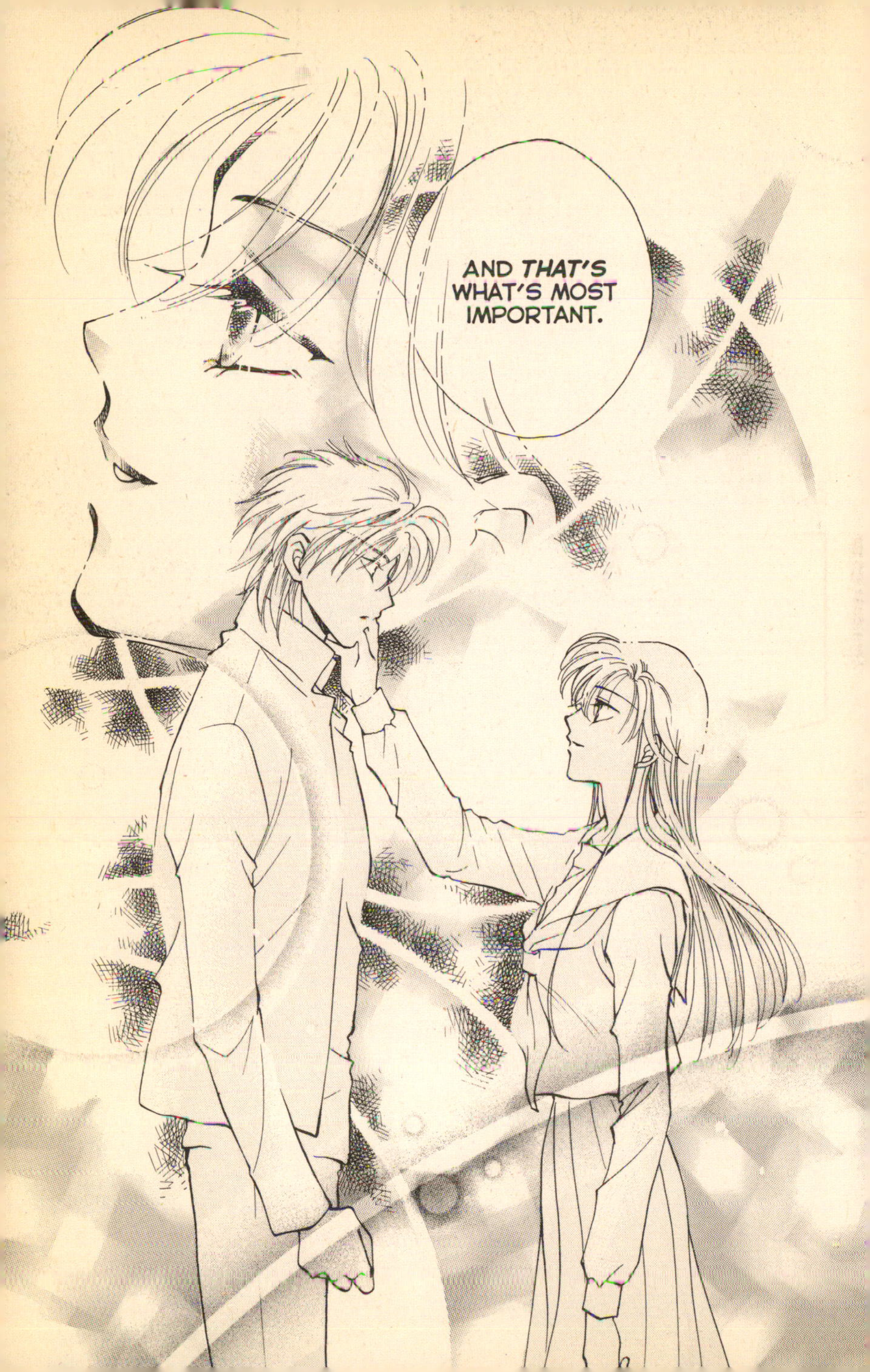
AND *THAT'S* WHAT'S MOST IMPORTANT.

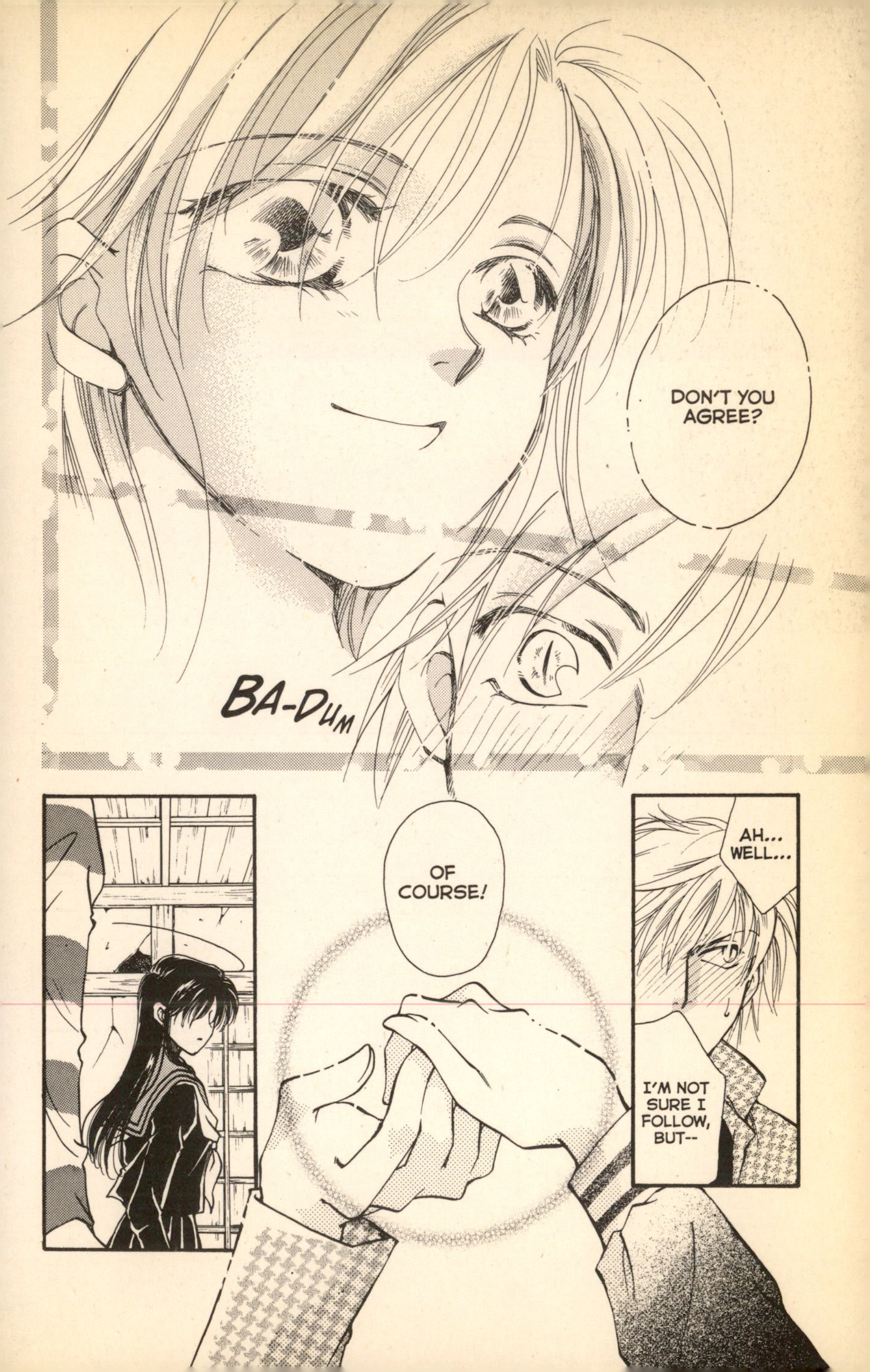
DON'T YOU AGREE?
BA-DUM
AH... WELL...
I'M NOT SURE I FOLLOW, BUT--
OF COURSE!

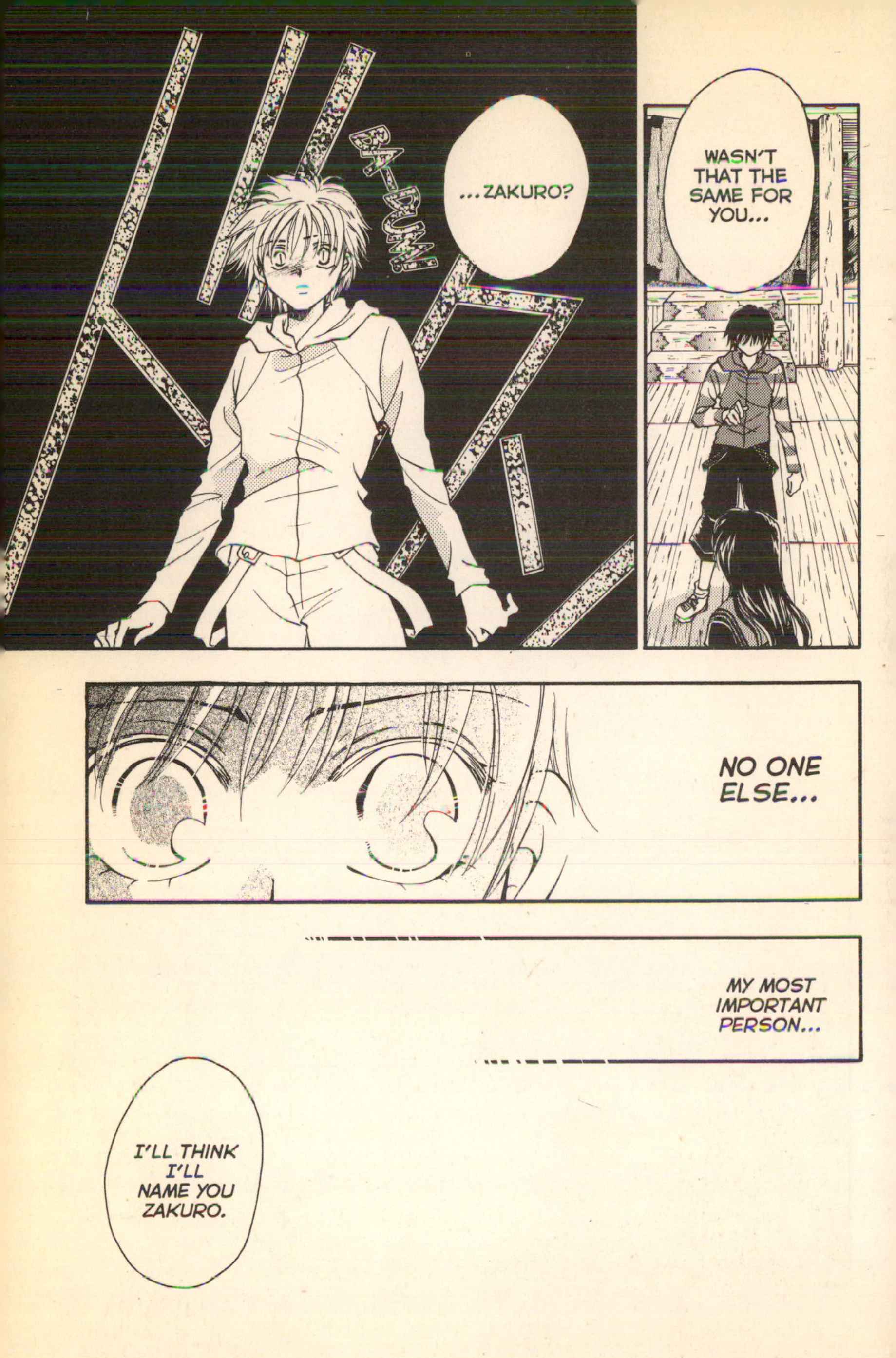
WASN'T THAT THE SAME FOR YOU...
BA-DUM!
...ZAKURO?
NO ONE ELSE...
MY MOST IMPORTANT PERSON...
I'LL THINK I'LL NAME YOU ZAKURO.

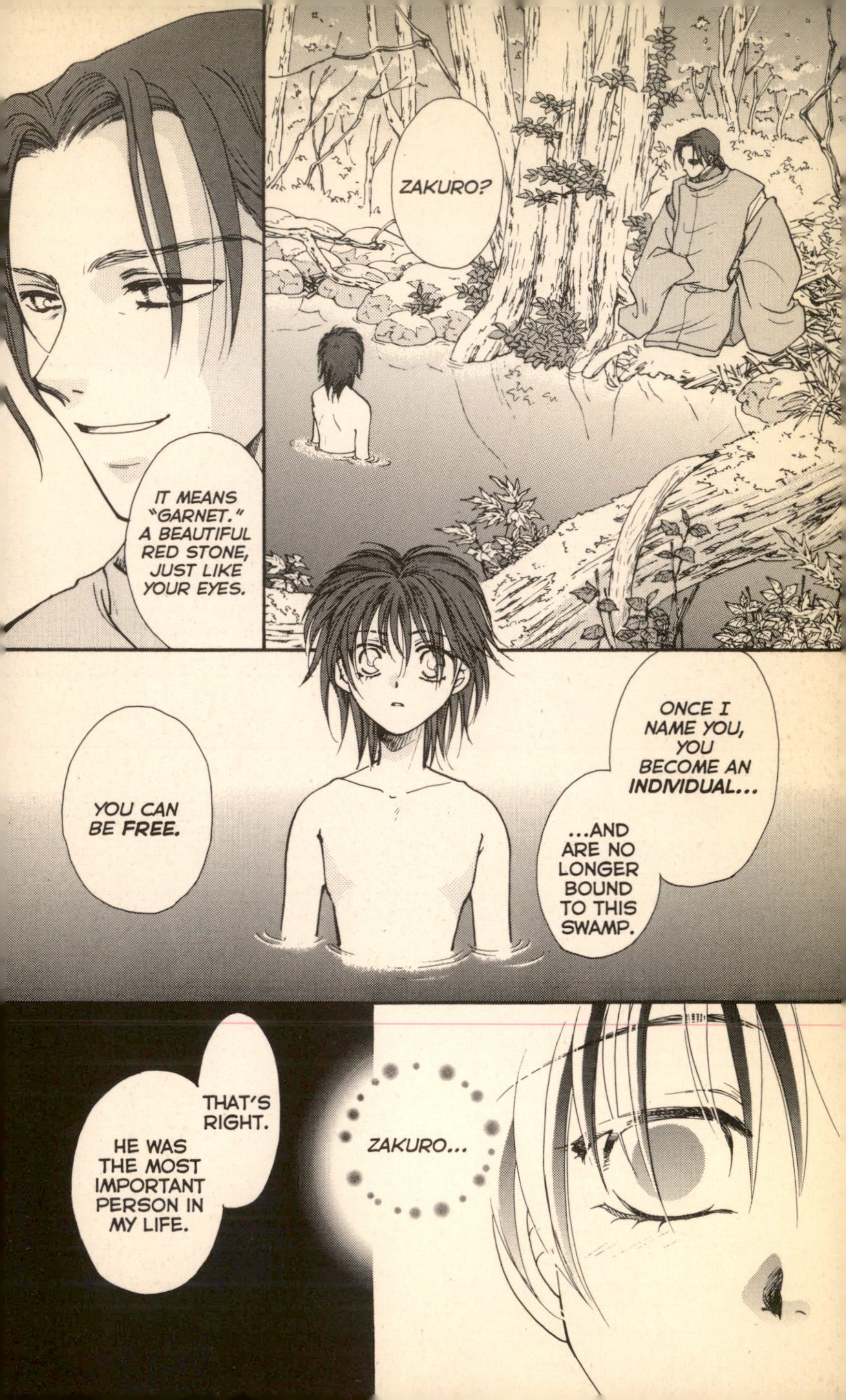
ZAKURO?
IT MEANS "GARNET." A BEAUTIFUL RED STONE, JUST LIKE YOUR EYES.
ONCE I NAME YOU, YOU BECOME AN **INDIVIDUAL**...
...AND ARE NO LONGER BOUND TO THIS SWAMP.
YOU CAN BE **FREE.**
ZAKURO...
THAT'S RIGHT.
HE WAS THE MOST IMPORTANT PERSON IN MY LIFE.

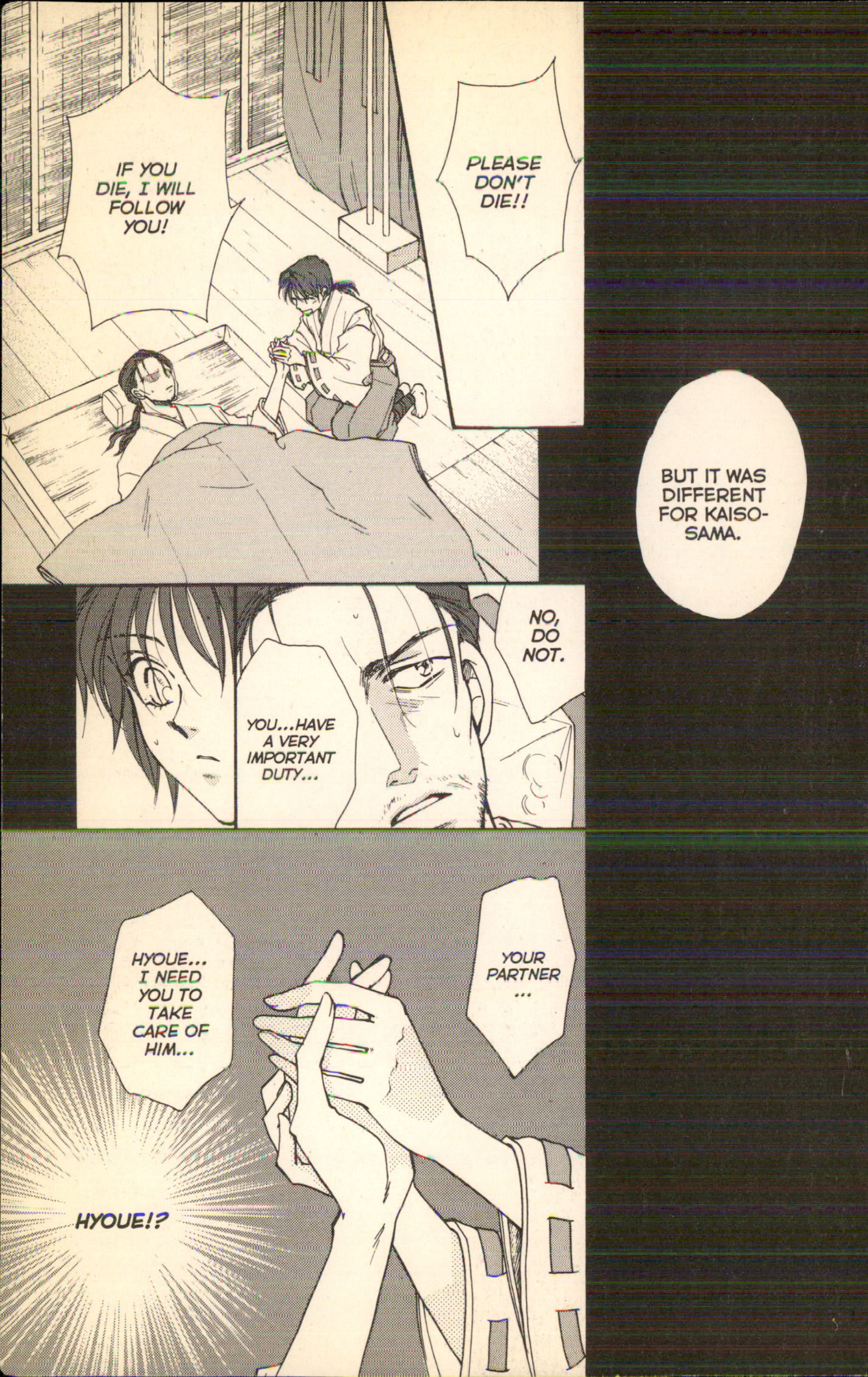
PLEASE DON'T DIE!!
IF YOU DIE, I WILL FOLLOW YOU!
BUT IT WAS DIFFERENT FOR KAISO-SAMA.
NO, DO NOT.
YOU...HAVE A VERY IMPORTANT DUTY...
YOUR PARTNER ...
HYOUE... I NEED YOU TO TAKE CARE OF HIM...
HYOUE!?

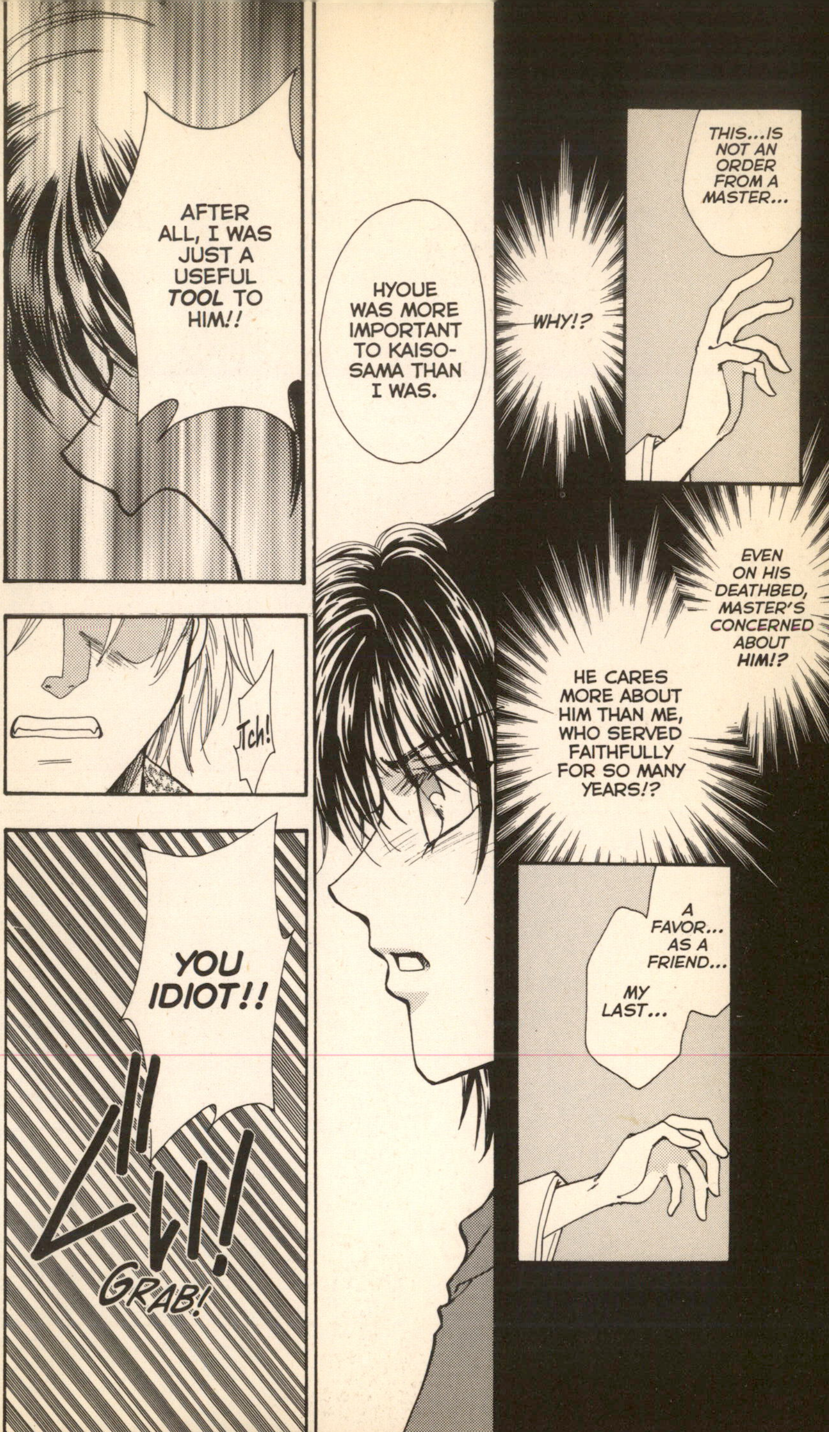

THIS...IS NOT AN ORDER FROM A MASTER...
WHY!?
HYOUE WAS MORE IMPORTANT TO KAISO-SAMA THAN I WAS.
EVEN ON HIS DEATHBED, MASTER'S CONCERNED ABOUT *HIM!?*
HE CARES MORE ABOUT HIM THAN ME, WHO SERVED FAITHFULLY FOR SO MANY YEARS!?
A FAVOR... AS A FRIEND...
MY LAST...
AFTER ALL, I WAS JUST A USEFUL *TOOL* TO HIM!!
Tch!
YOU IDIOT!!
GRAB!

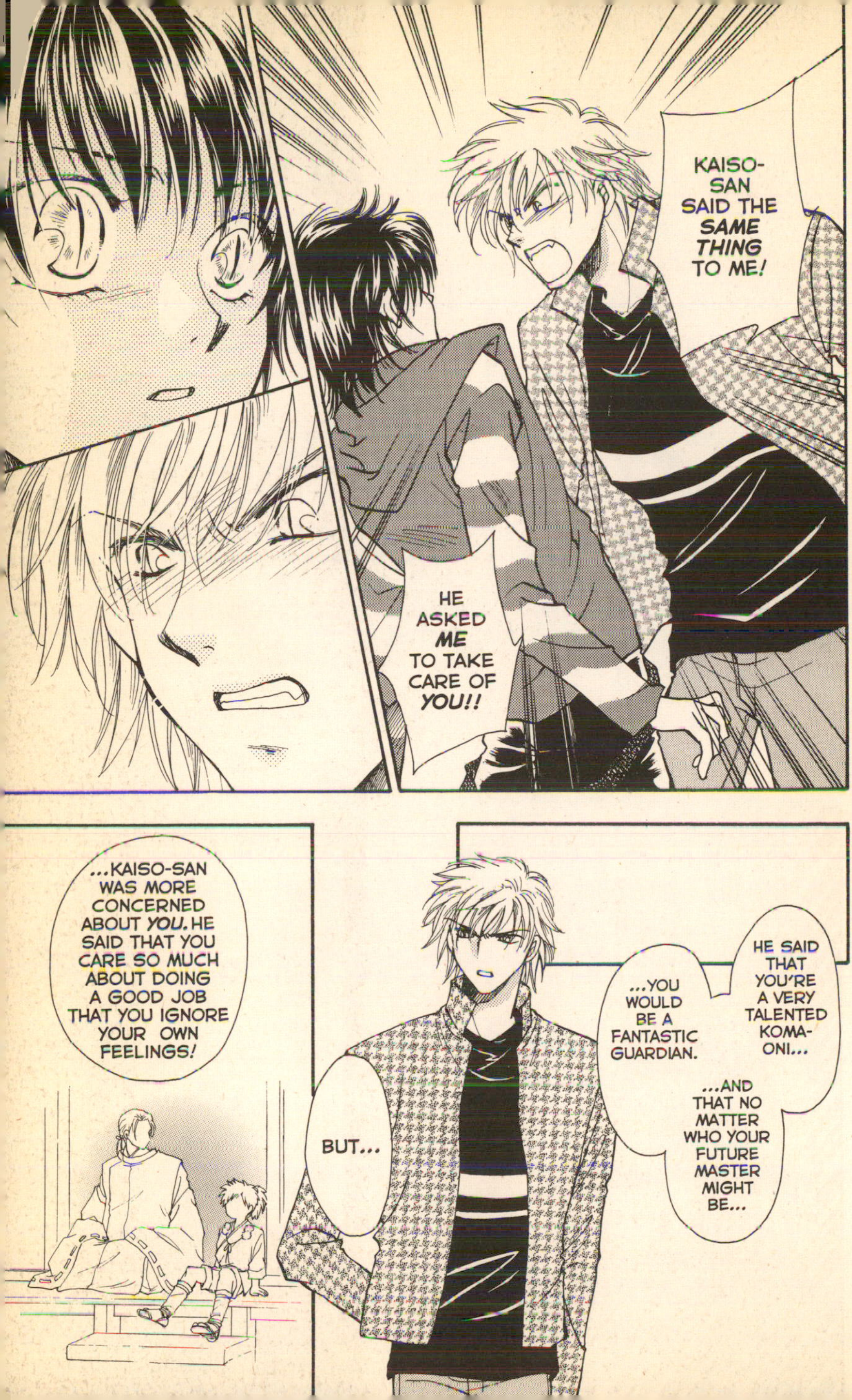
KAISO-SAN SAID THE SAME THING TO ME!
HE ASKED ME TO TAKE CARE OF YOU!!
HE SAID THAT YOU'RE A VERY TALENTED KOMA-ONI...
...YOU WOULD BE A FANTASTIC GUARDIAN.
...AND THAT NO MATTER WHO YOUR FUTURE MASTER MIGHT BE...
BUT...
...KAISO-SAN WAS MORE CONCERNED ABOUT YOU. HE SAID THAT YOU CARE SO MUCH ABOUT DOING A GOOD JOB THAT YOU IGNORE YOUR OWN FEELINGS!

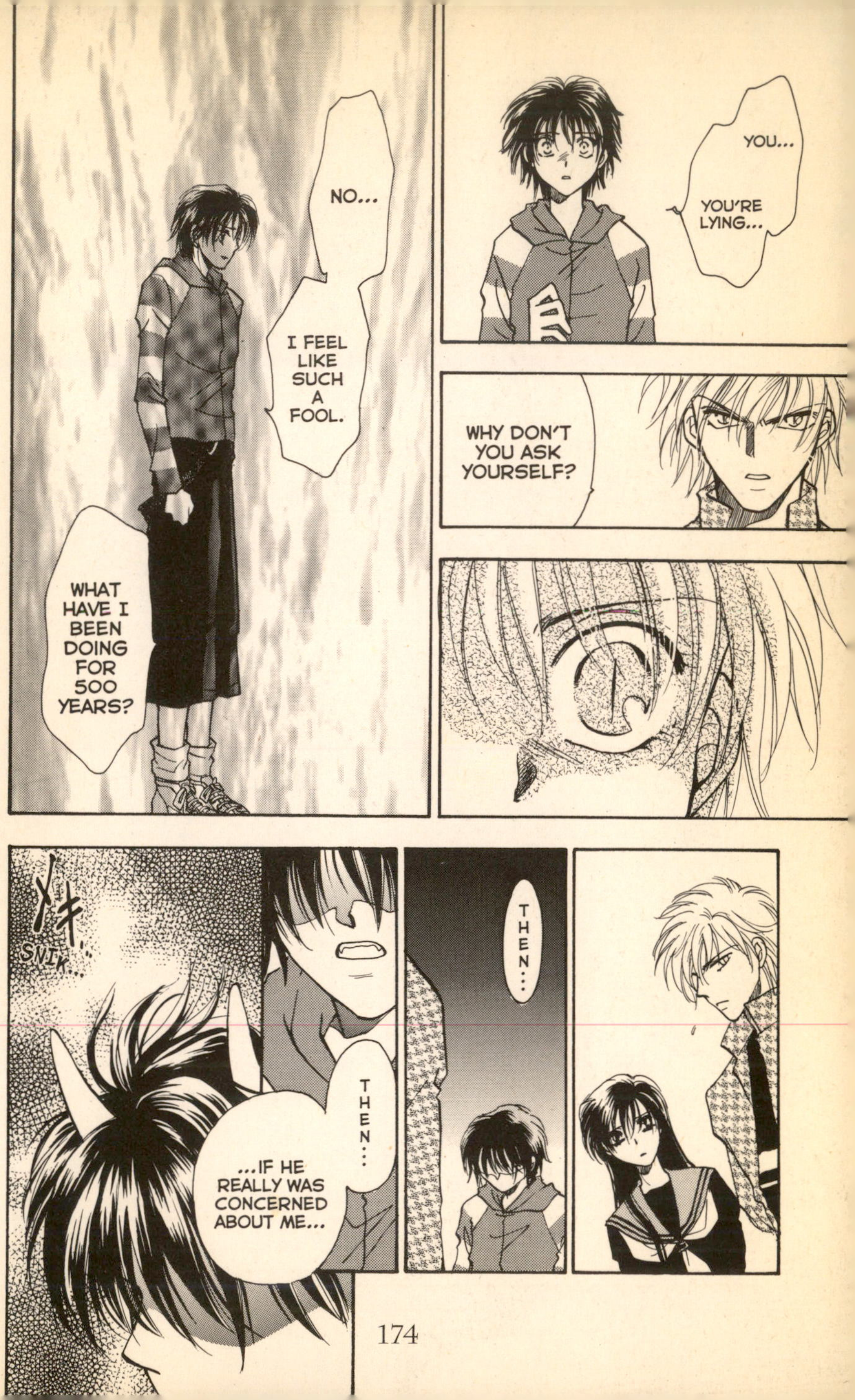
YOU...
YOU'RE LYING...
WHY DON'T YOU ASK YOURSELF?
NO...
I FEEL LIKE SUCH A FOOL.
WHAT HAVE I BEEN DOING FOR 500 YEARS?
THEN...
メキ
SNIK...
THEN...
...IF HE REALLY WAS CONCERNED ABOUT ME...

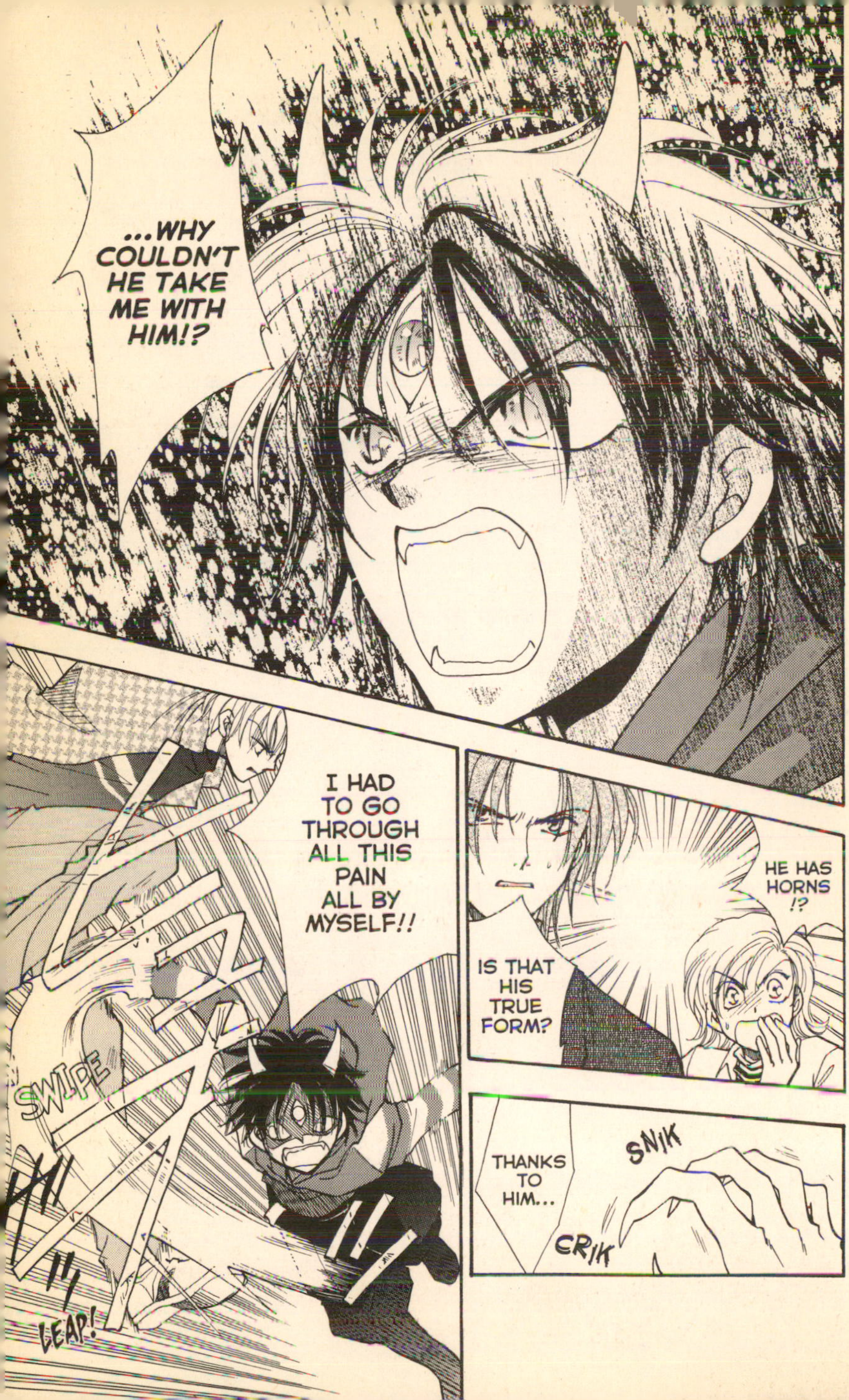
...WHY COULDN'T HE TAKE ME WITH HIM!?
HE HAS HORNS !?
IS THAT HIS TRUE FORM?
THANKS TO HIM...
SNIK
CRIK
I HAD TO GO THROUGH ALL THIS PAIN ALL BY MYSELF!!
SWIPE
LEAP!

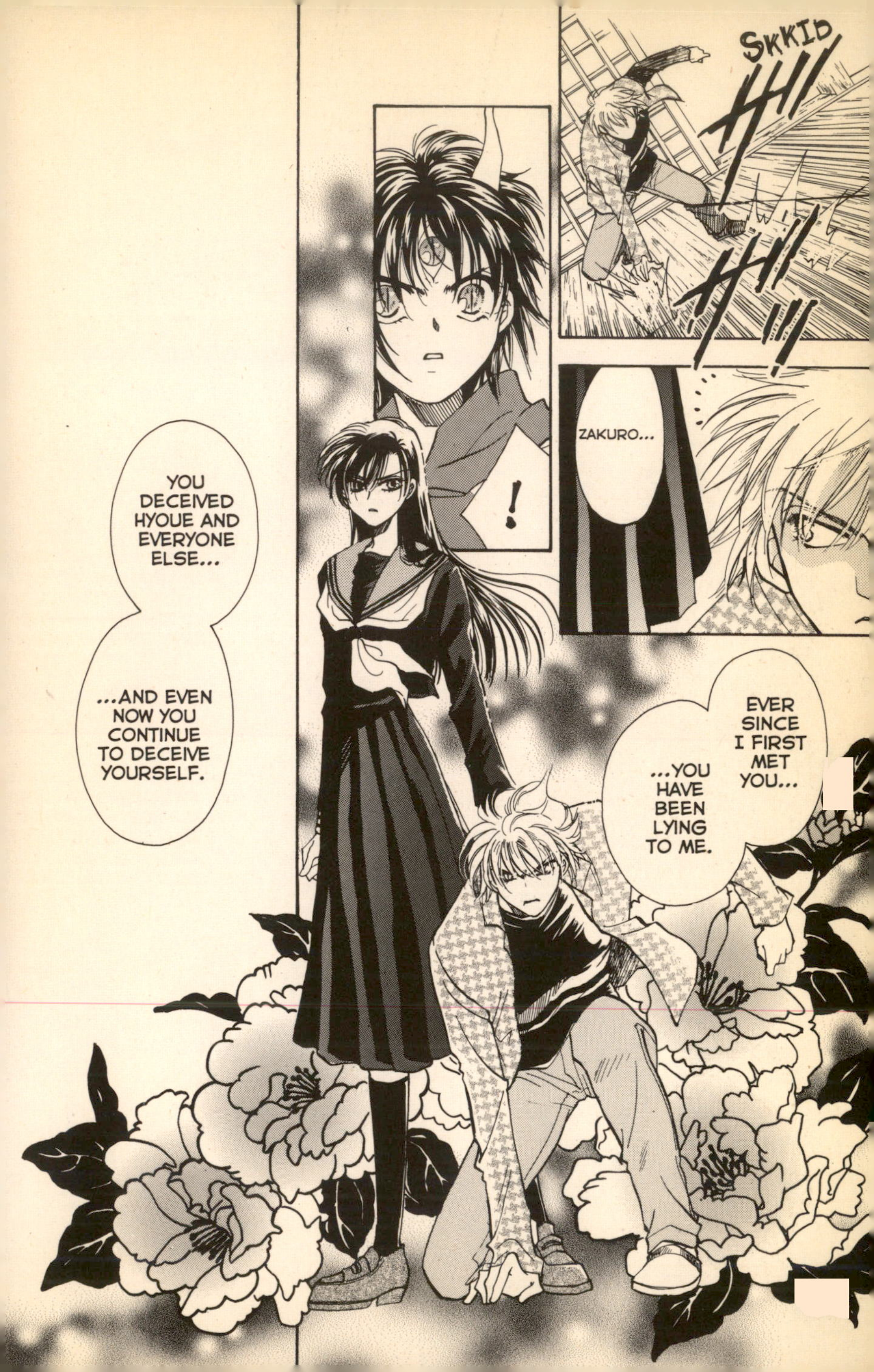
SKKID
ZAKURO...
!
EVER SINCE I FIRST MET YOU...
...YOU HAVE BEEN LYING TO ME.
YOU DECEIVED HYOUE AND EVERYONE ELSE...
...AND EVEN NOW YOU CONTINUE TO DECEIVE YOURSELF.

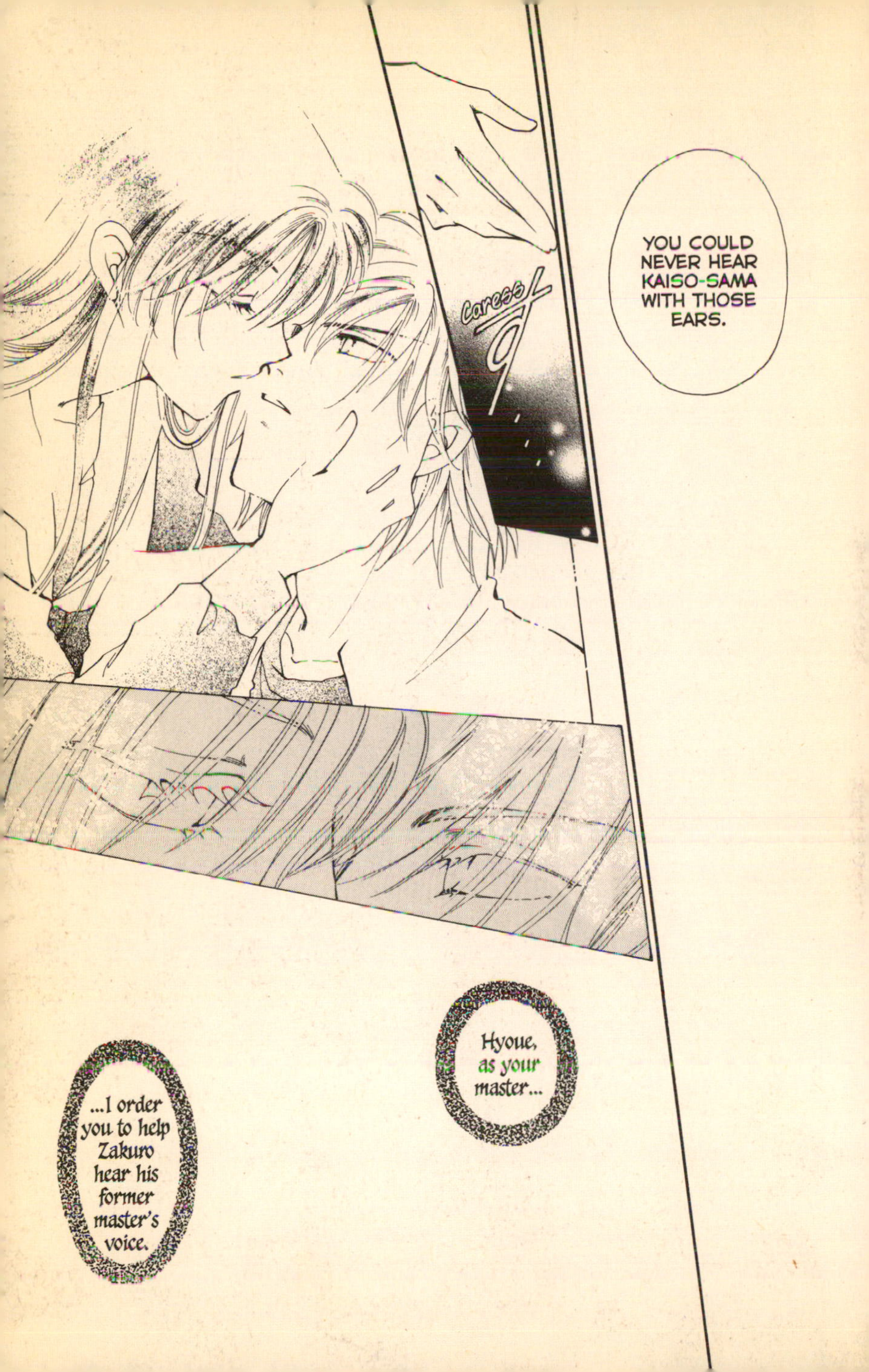
YOU COULD NEVER HEAR KAISO-SAMA WITH THOSE EARS.
caress
Hyoue, as your master...
...I order you to help Zakuro hear his former master's voice.

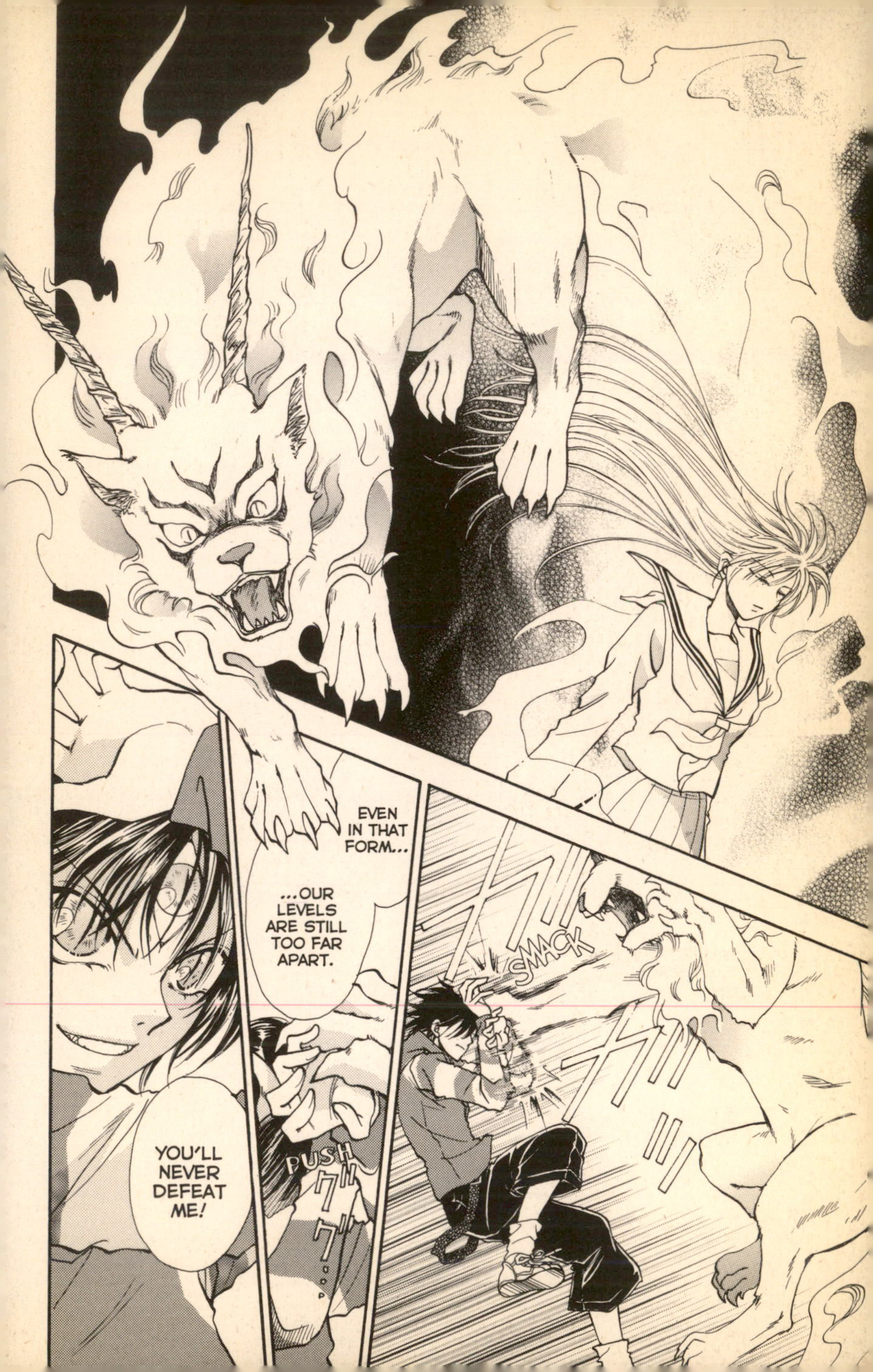
SMACK
EVEN IN THAT FORM...
...OUR LEVELS ARE STILL TOO FAR APART.
PUSH
YOU'LL NEVER DEFEAT ME!

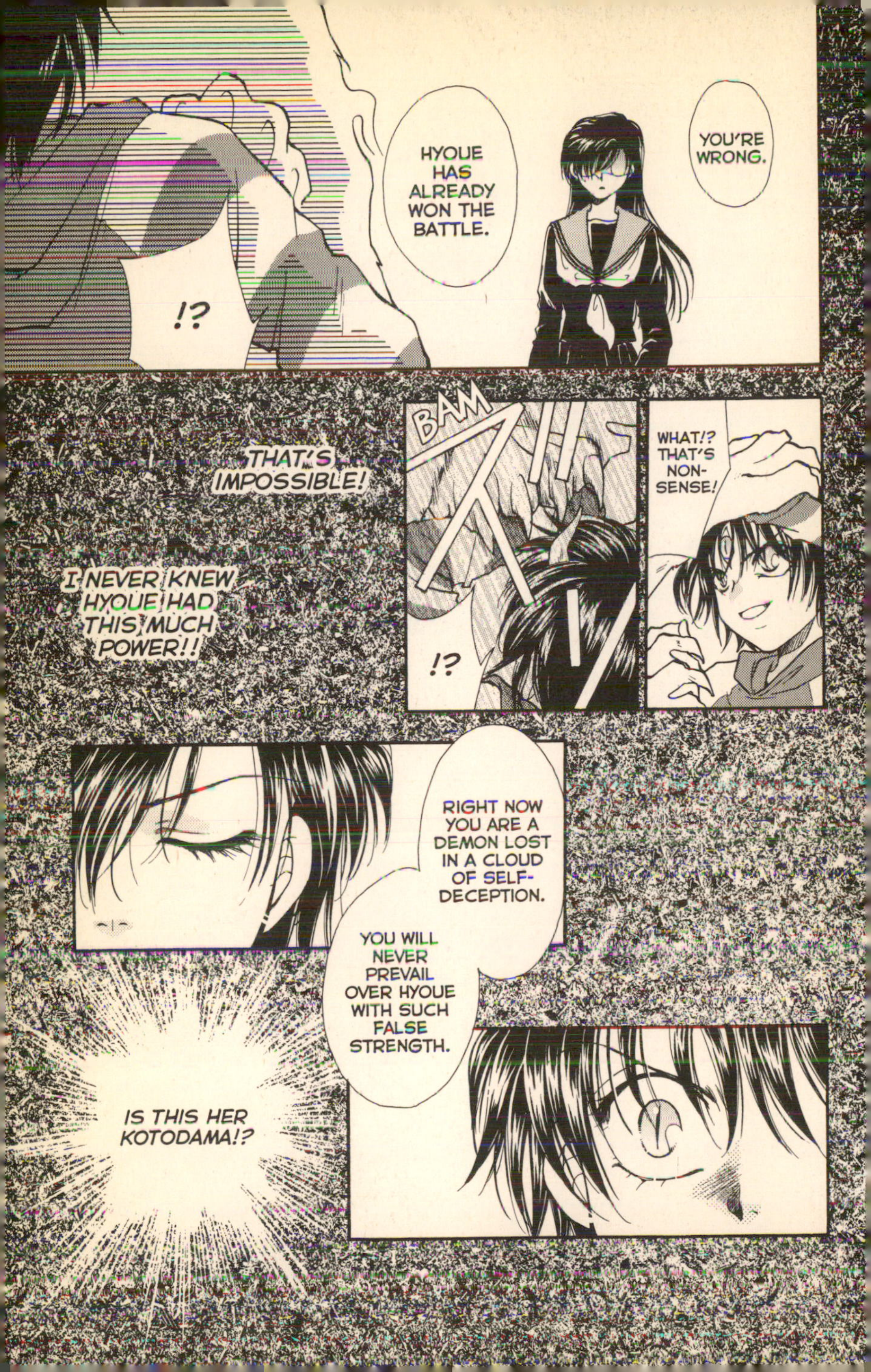
YOU'RE WRONG.
HYOUE HAS ALREADY WON THE BATTLE.
!?
WHAT!? THAT'S NON-SENSE!
BAM
!?
THAT'S IMPOSSIBLE!
I NEVER KNEW HYOUE HAD THIS MUCH POWER!!
RIGHT NOW YOU ARE A DEMON LOST IN A CLOUD OF SELF-DECEPTION.
YOU WILL NEVER PREVAIL OVER HYOUE WITH SUCH FALSE STRENGTH.
IS THIS HER KOTODAMA!?

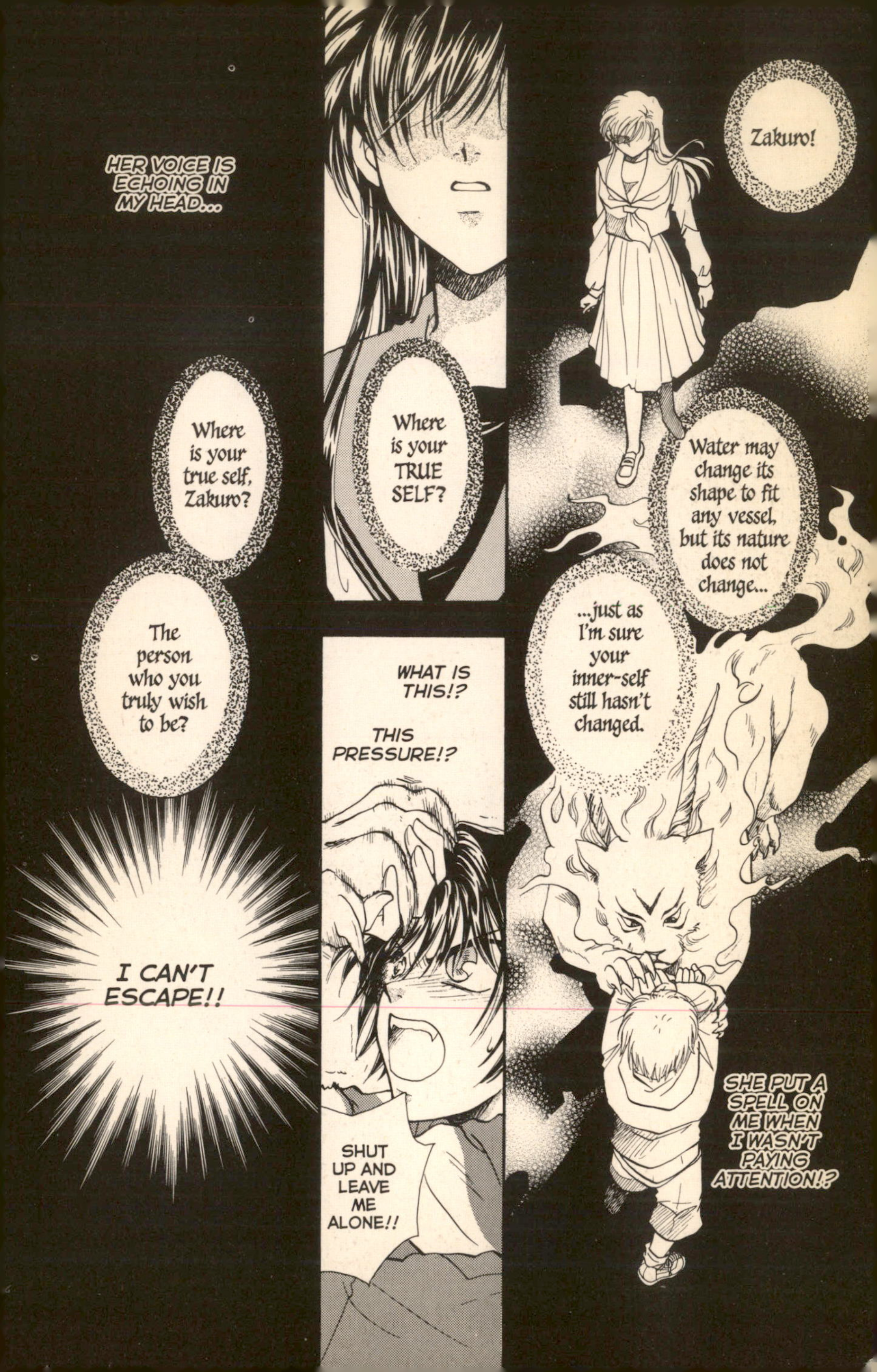
Zakuro!
Water may change its shape to fit any vessel, but its nature does not change...
...just as I'm sure your inner-self still hasn't changed.
SHE PUT A SPELL ON ME WHEN I WASN'T PAYING ATTENTION!?
Where is your TRUE SELF?
WHAT IS THIS!?
THIS PRESSURE!?
SHUT UP AND LEAVE ME ALONE!!
HER VOICE IS ECHOING IN MY HEAD...
Where is your true self, Zakuro?
The person who you truly wish to be?
I CAN'T ESCAPE!!

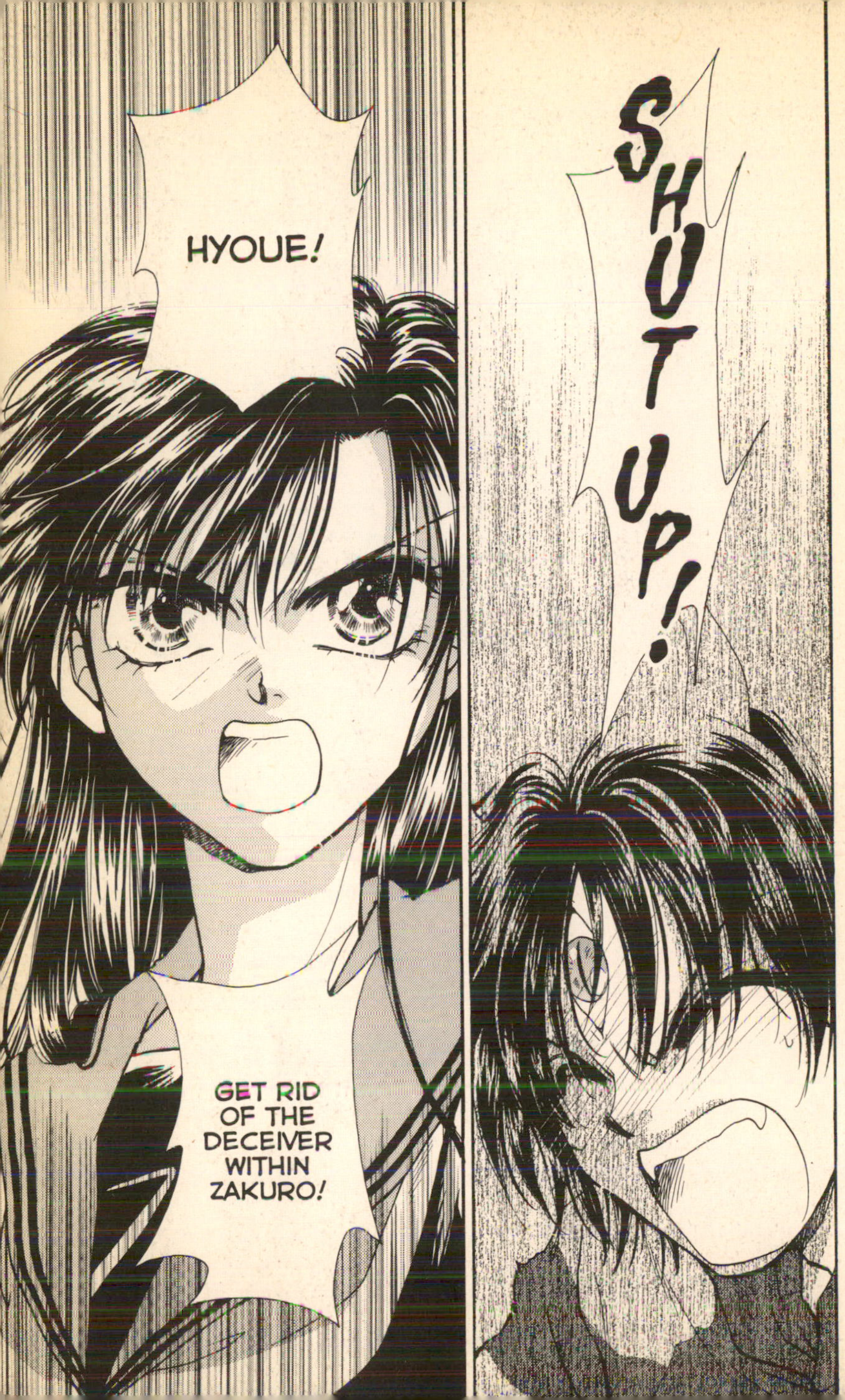
SHUT UP!!
HYOUE!
GET RID OF THE DECEIVER WITHIN ZAKURO!

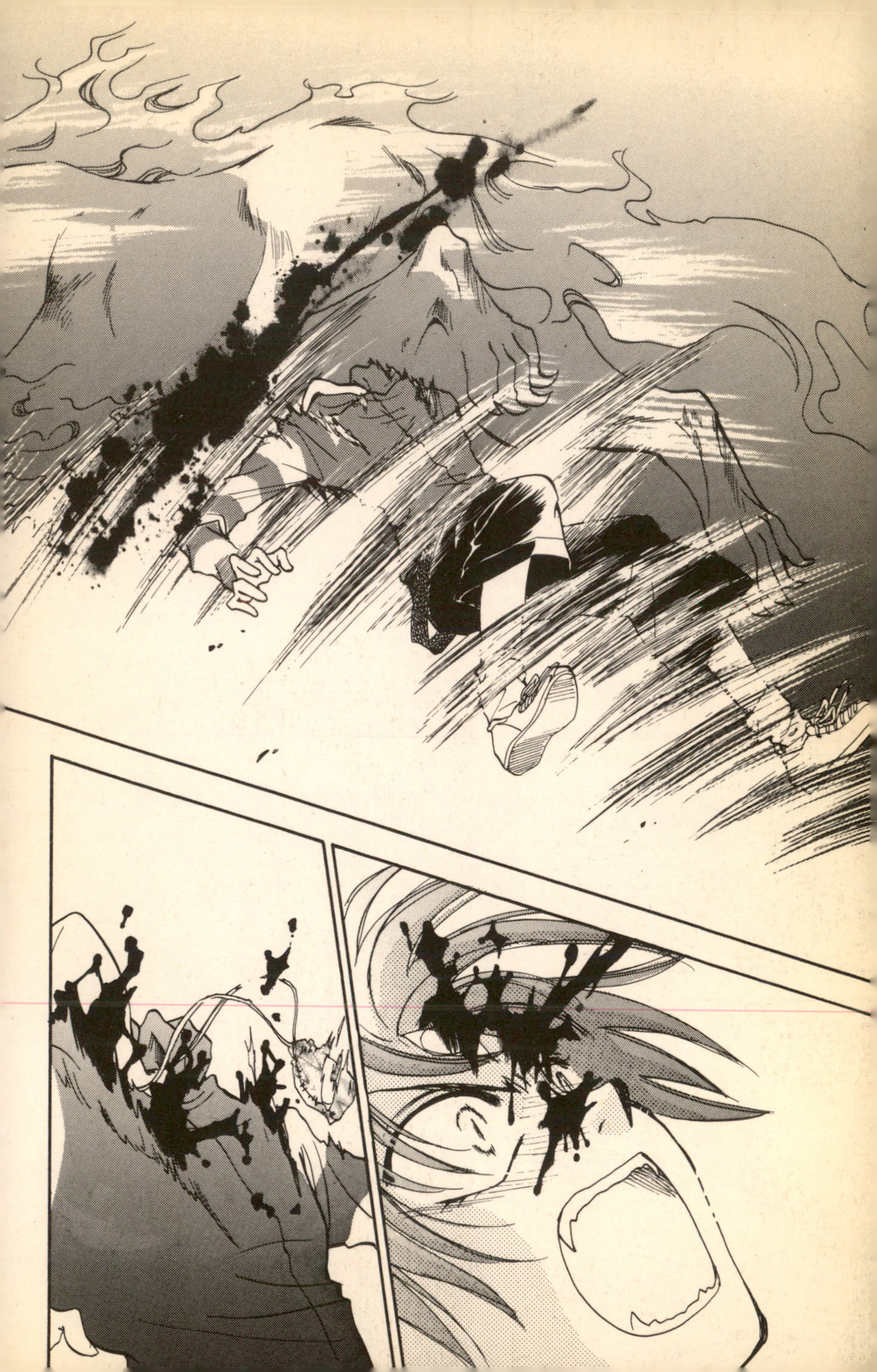

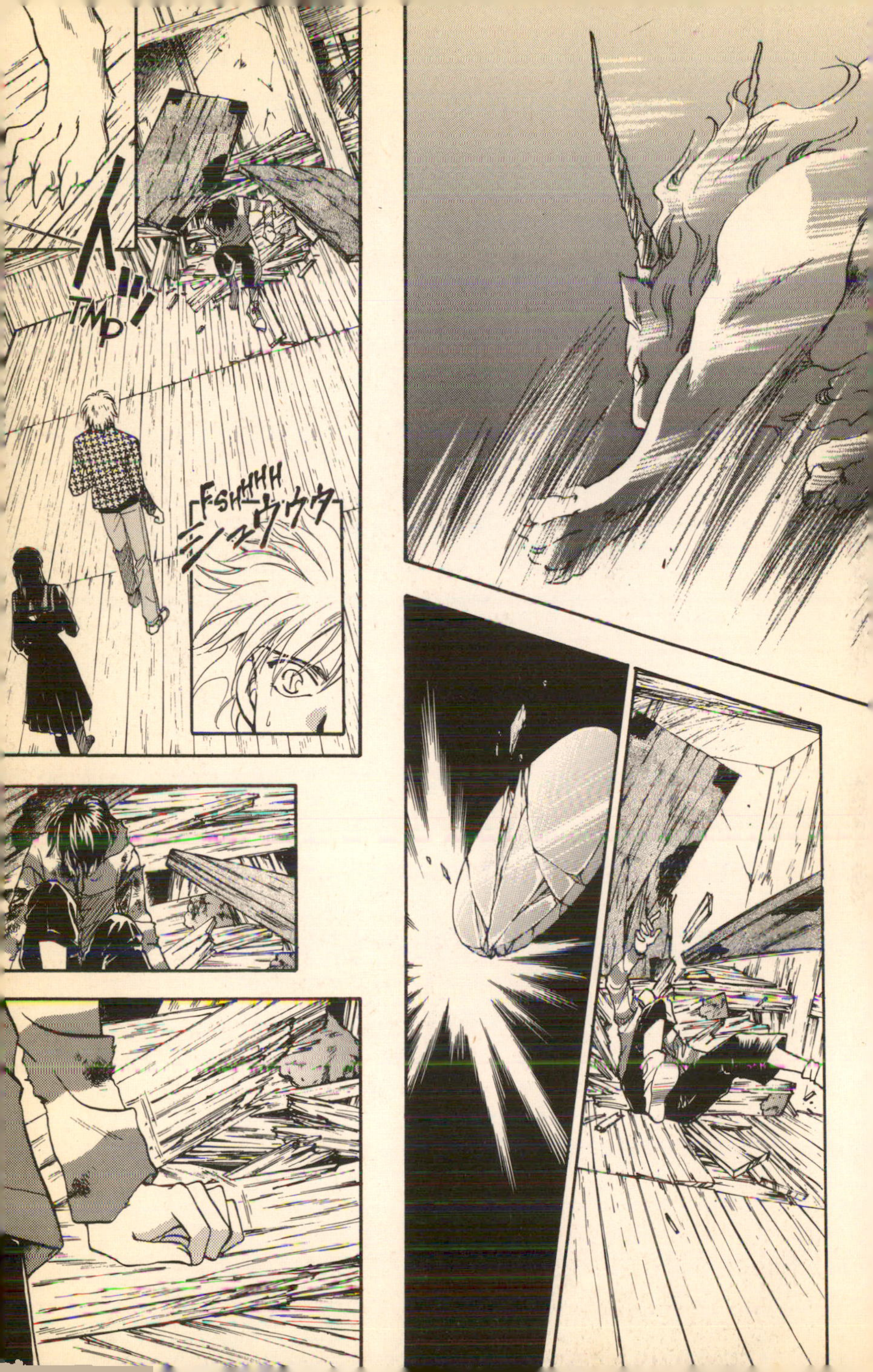
FSHHHH
シュウウウ
TMP

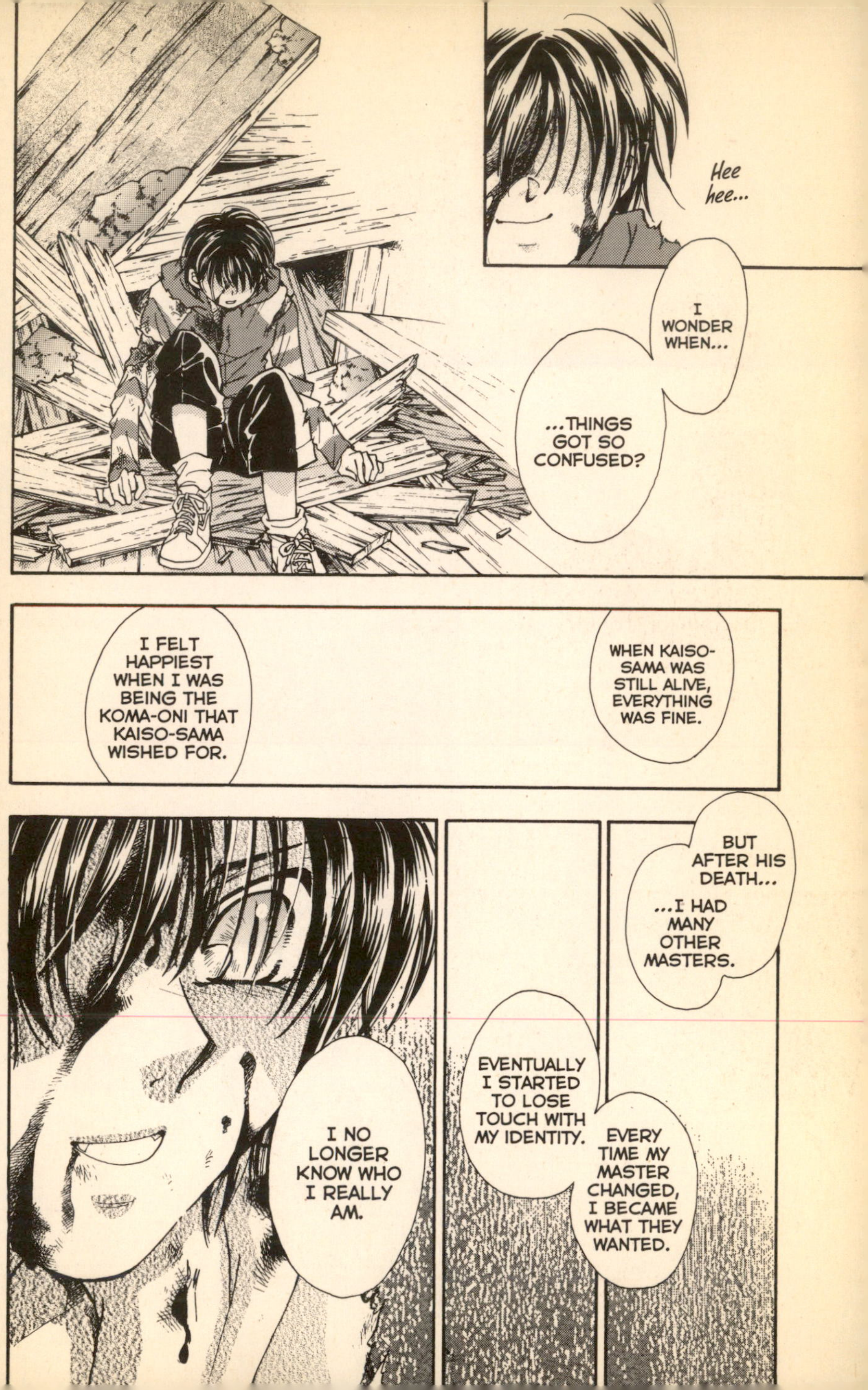
Hee hee...
I WONDER WHEN...
...THINGS GOT SO CONFUSED?
WHEN KAISO-SAMA WAS STILL ALIVE, EVERYTHING WAS FINE.
I FELT HAPPIEST WHEN I WAS BEING THE KOMA-ONI THAT KAISO-SAMA WISHED FOR.
BUT AFTER HIS DEATH...
...I HAD MANY OTHER MASTERS.
EVERY TIME MY MASTER CHANGED, I BECAME WHAT THEY WANTED.
EVENTUALLY I STARTED TO LOSE TOUCH WITH MY IDENTITY.
I NO LONGER KNOW WHO I REALLY AM.

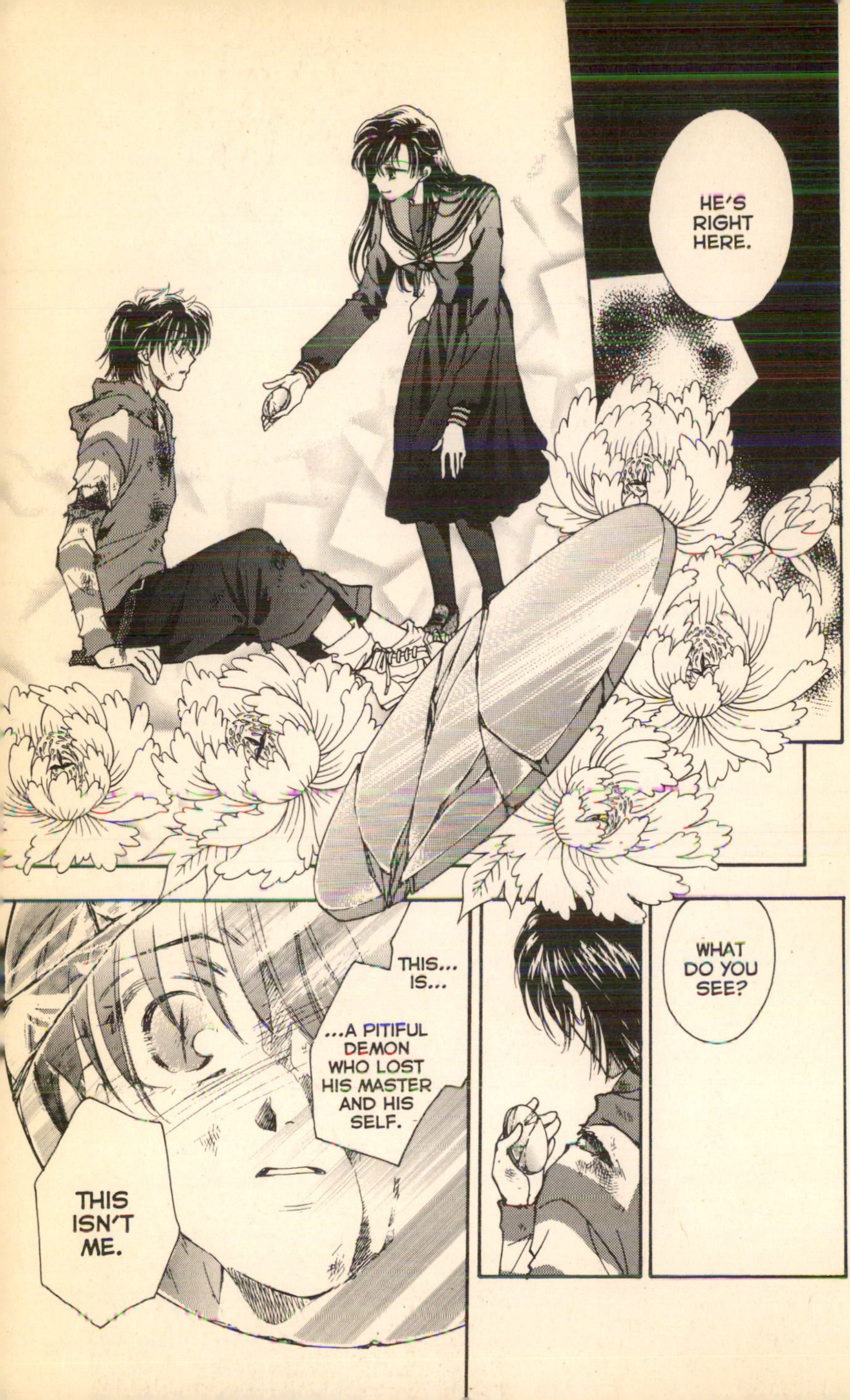
HE'S RIGHT HERE.
WHAT DO YOU SEE?
THIS... IS...
...A PITIFUL DEMON WHO LOST HIS MASTER AND HIS SELF.
THIS ISN'T ME.

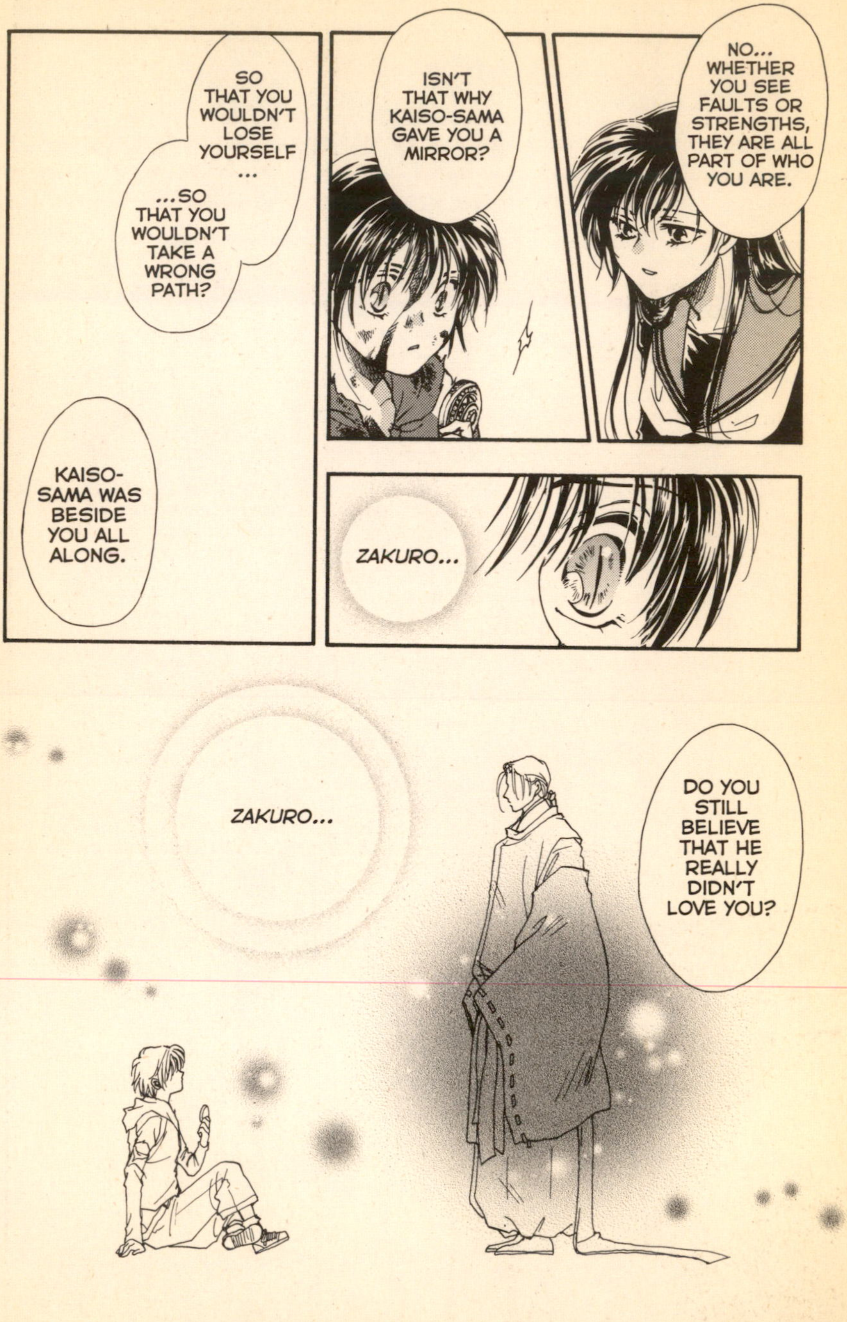

NO... WHETHER YOU SEE FAULTS OR STRENGTHS, THEY ARE ALL PART OF WHO YOU ARE.
ISN'T THAT WHY KAISO-SAMA GAVE YOU A MIRROR?
ZAKURO...
SO THAT YOU WOULDN'T LOSE YOURSELF ...
...SO THAT YOU WOULDN'T TAKE A WRONG PATH?
KAISO-SAMA WAS BESIDE YOU ALL ALONG.
DO YOU STILL BELIEVE THAT HE REALLY DIDN'T LOVE YOU?
ZAKURO...

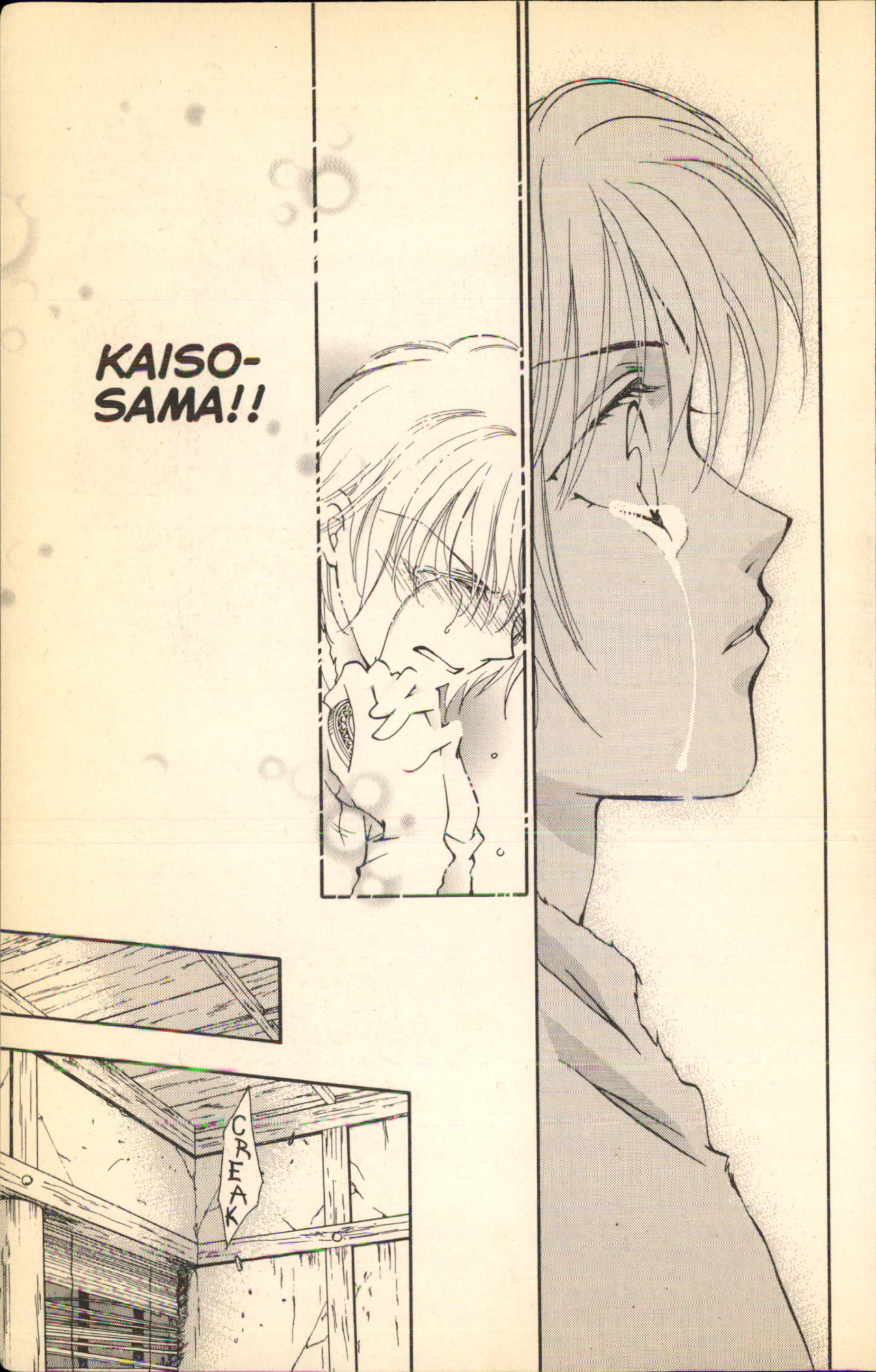
KAISO-SAMA!!
CREAK

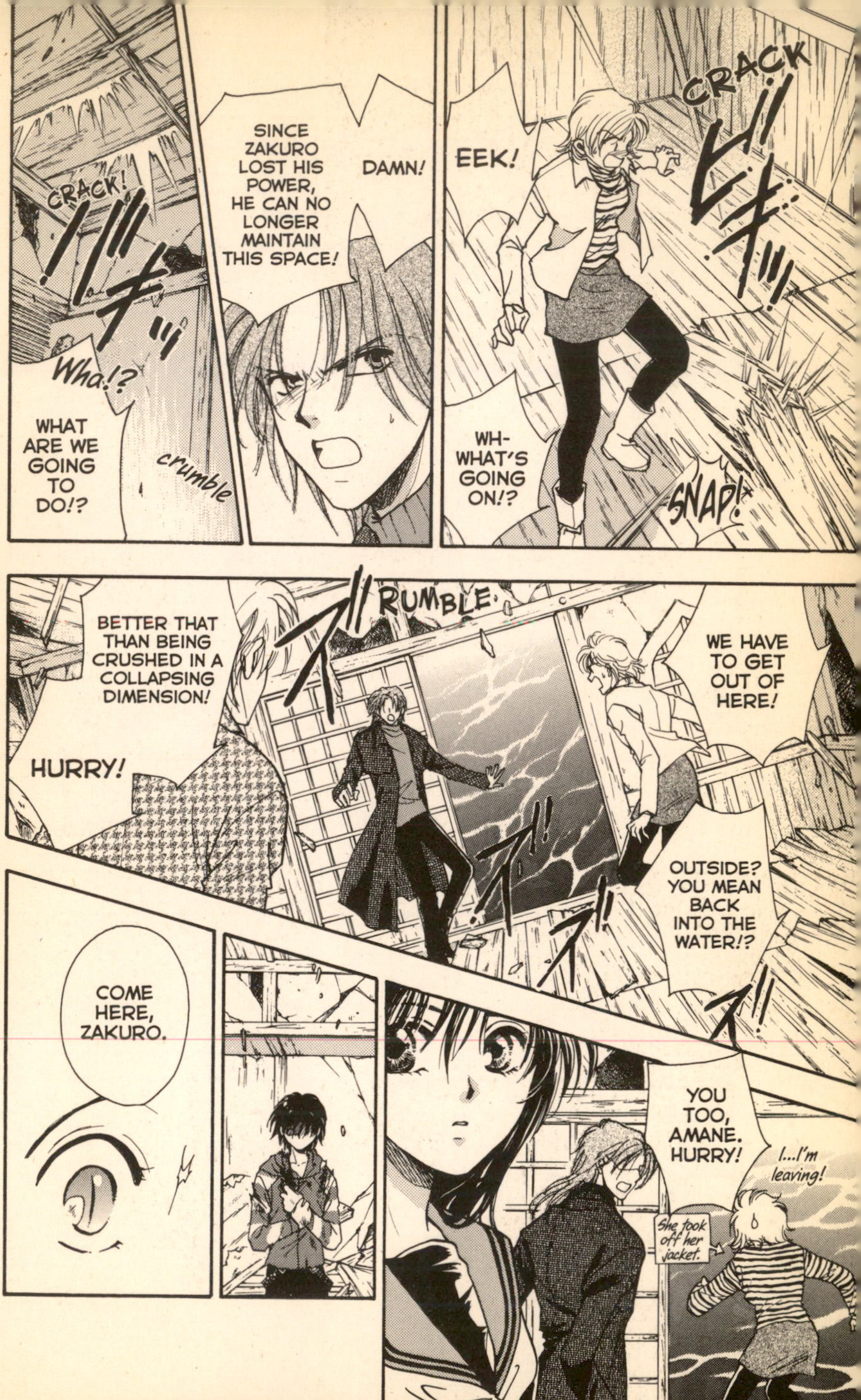
CRACK
EEK!
WH-WHAT'S GOING ON!?
SNAP!
DAMN!
SINCE ZAKURO LOST HIS POWER, HE CAN NO LONGER MAINTAIN THIS SPACE!
CRACK!
Wha!?
WHAT ARE WE GOING TO DO!?
crumble
RUMBLE
WE HAVE TO GET OUT OF HERE!
OUTSIDE? YOU MEAN BACK INTO THE WATER!?
BETTER THAT THAN BEING CRUSHED IN A COLLAPSING DIMENSION!
HURRY!
YOU TOO, AMANE. HURRY!
I...I'm leaving!
She took off her jacket.
COME HERE, ZAKURO.

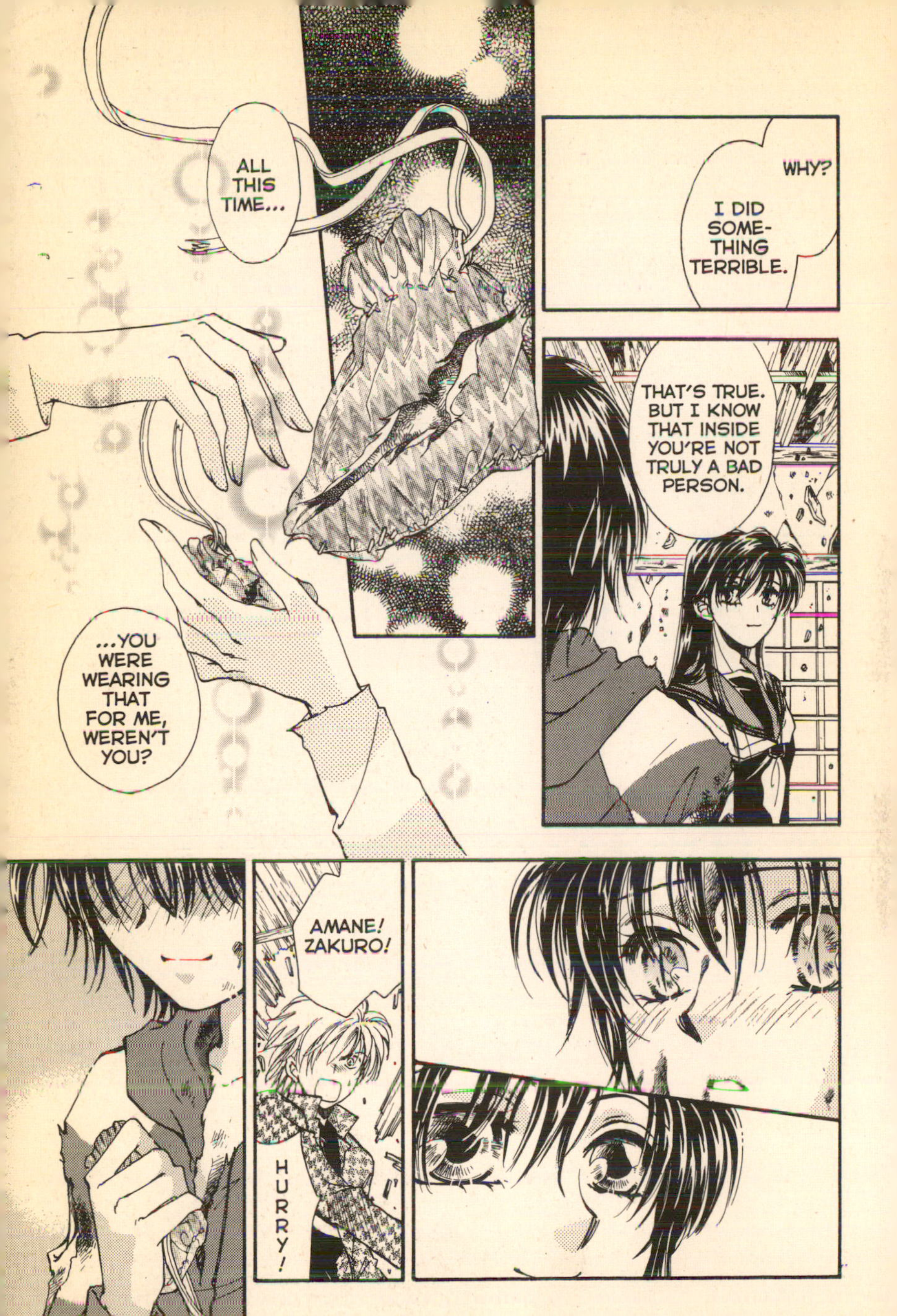
WHY?
I DID SOMETHING TERRIBLE.
THAT'S TRUE. BUT I KNOW THAT INSIDE YOU'RE NOT TRULY A BAD PERSON.
ALL THIS TIME...
...YOU WERE WEARING THAT FOR ME, WEREN'T YOU?
AMANE! ZAKURO!
HURRY!

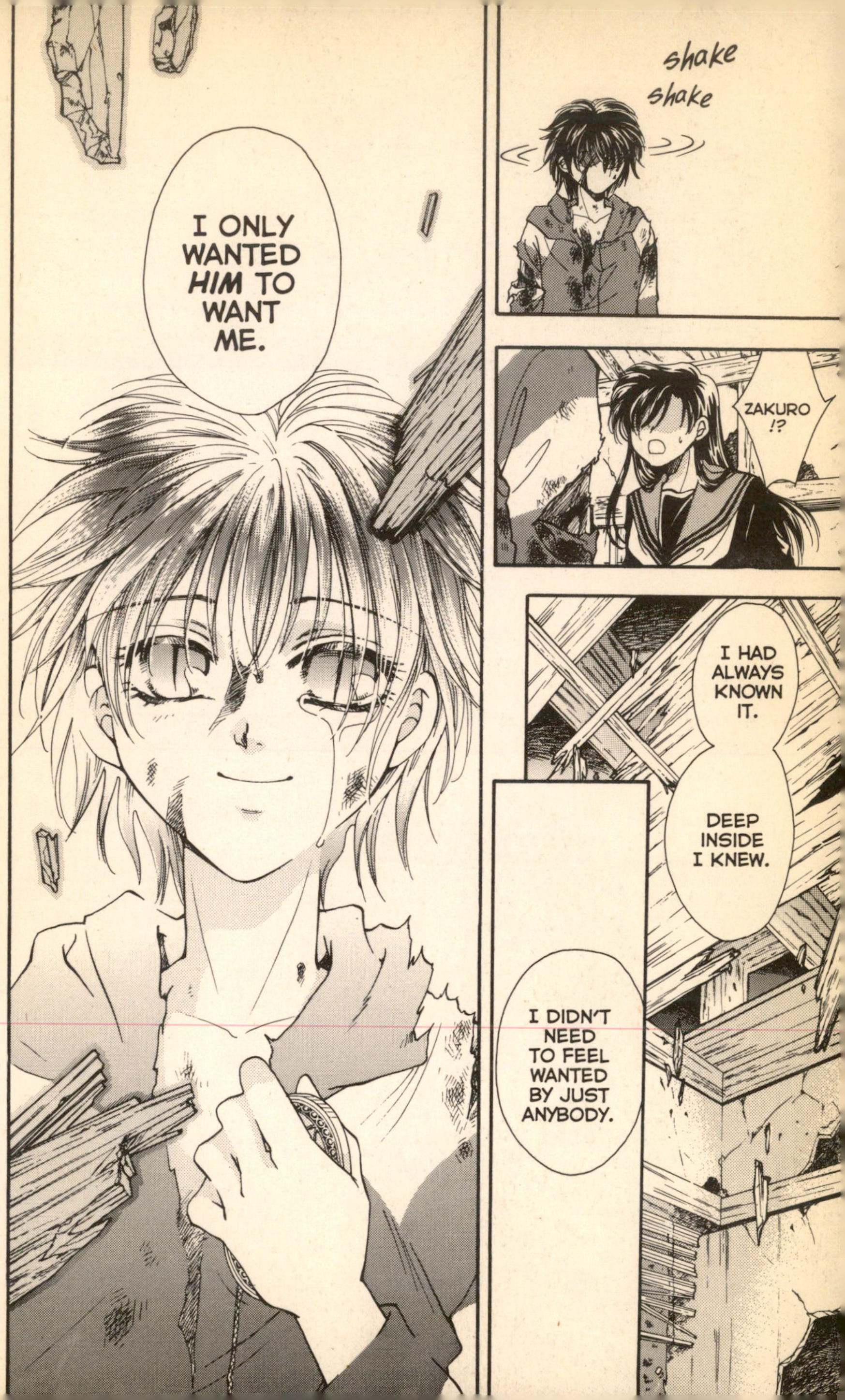
shake
shake
ZAKURO !?
I HAD ALWAYS KNOWN IT.
DEEP INSIDE I KNEW.
I DIDN'T NEED TO FEEL WANTED BY JUST ANYBODY.
I ONLY WANTED *HIM* TO WANT ME.

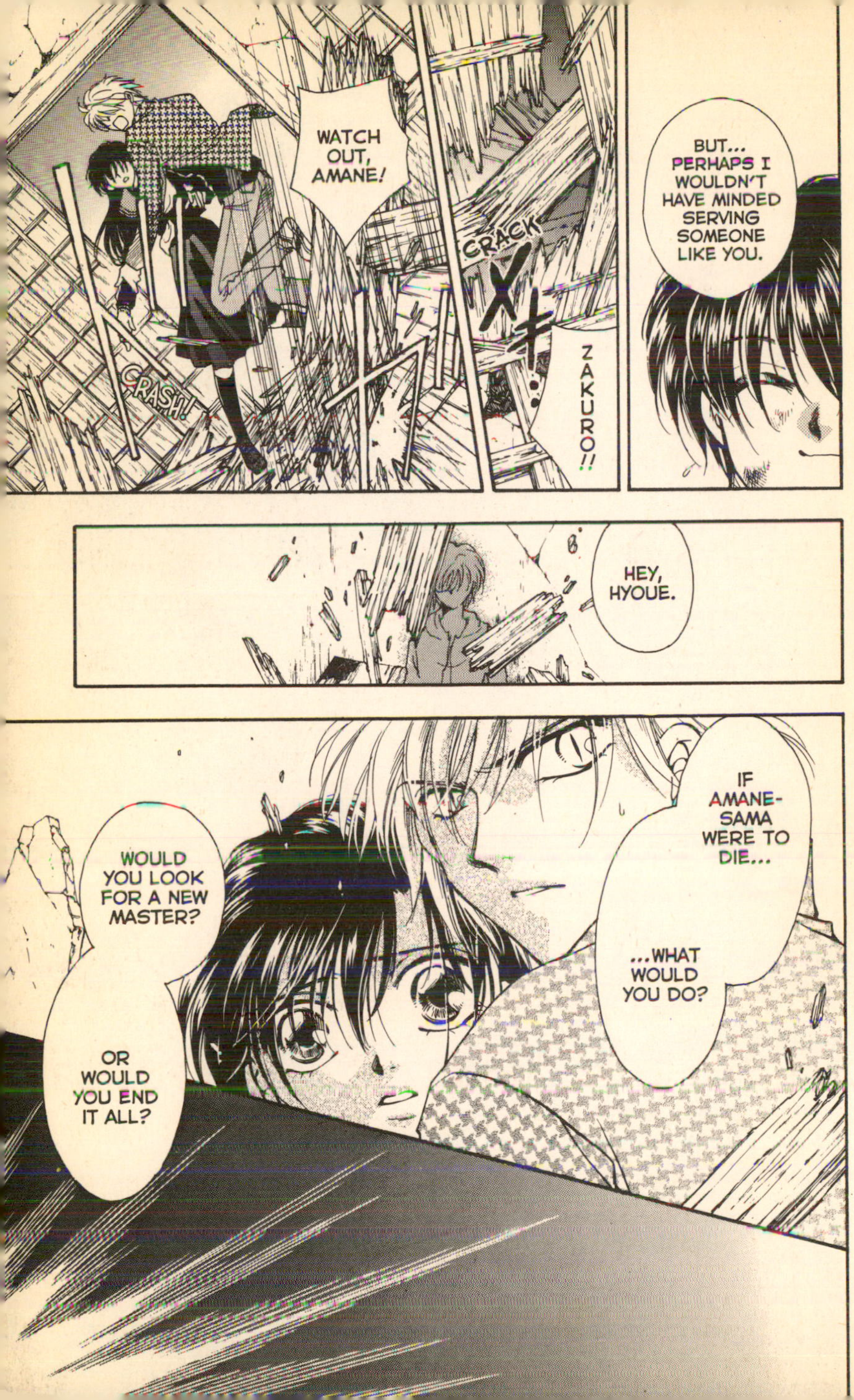
BUT... PERHAPS I WOULDN'T HAVE MINDED SERVING SOMEONE LIKE YOU.
ZAKURO!!
CRACK
WATCH OUT, AMANE!
CRASH!
HEY, HYOUE.
IF AMANE-SAMA WERE TO DIE...
...WHAT WOULD YOU DO?
WOULD YOU LOOK FOR A NEW MASTER?
OR WOULD YOU END IT ALL?

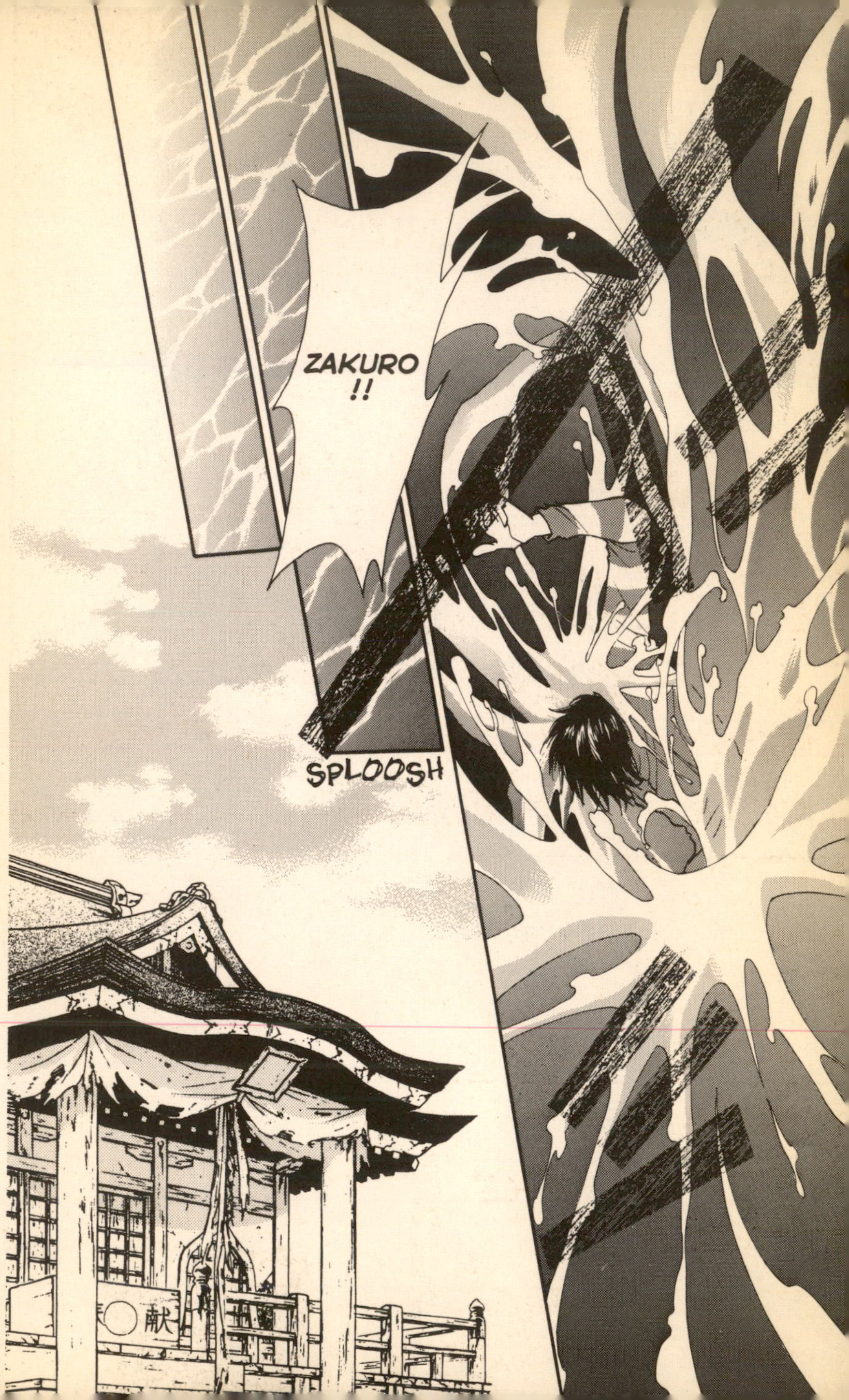
ZAKURO !!
SPLOOSH
献

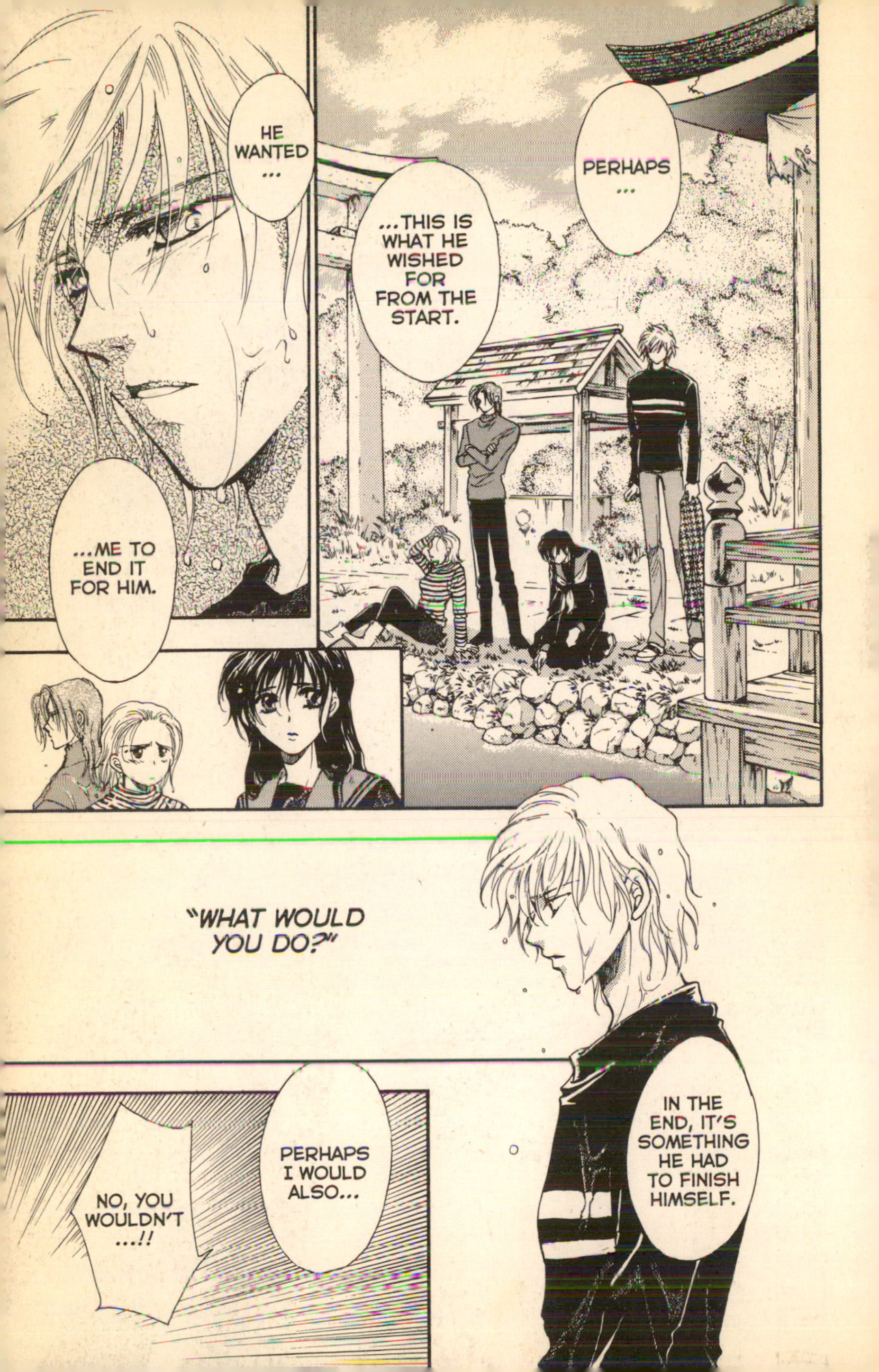
PERHAPS ...
...THIS IS WHAT HE WISHED FOR FROM THE START.
HE WANTED ...
...ME TO END IT FOR HIM.
"WHAT WOULD YOU DO?"
IN THE END, IT'S SOMETHING HE HAD TO FINISH HIMSELF.
PERHAPS I WOULD ALSO...
NO, YOU WOULDN'T ...!!

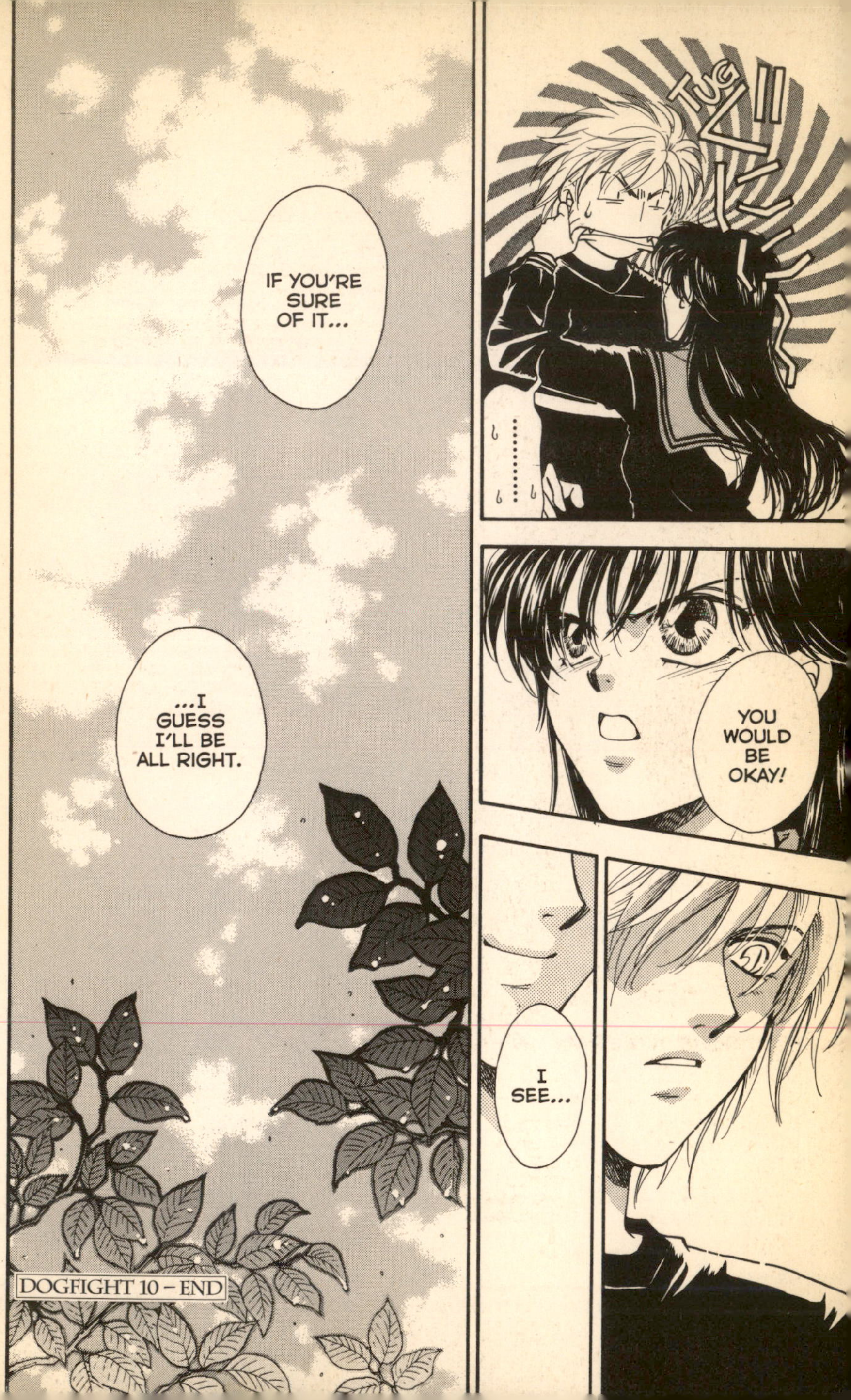
TUG!!
YOU WOULD BE OKAY!
I SEE...
IF YOU'RE SURE OF IT...
...I GUESS I'LL BE ALL RIGHT.
DOGFIGHT 10 – END

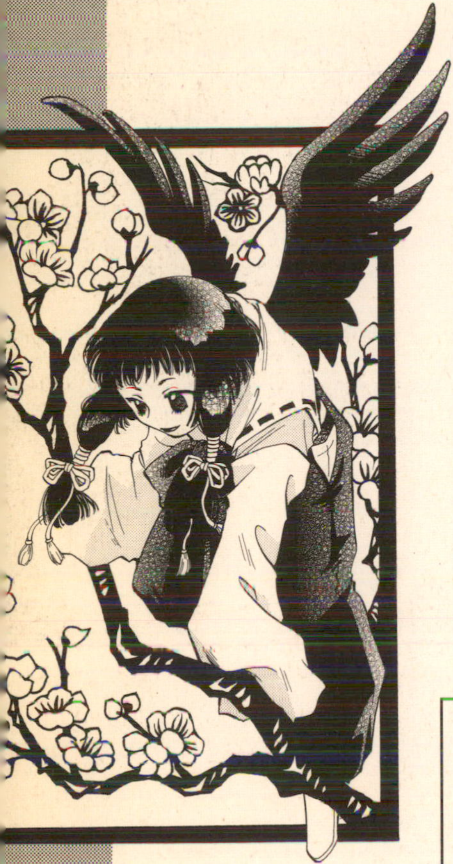

THANK YOU FOR SUPPORTING ME FOR A SECOND VOLUME. ♡ ORIGINALLY THIS WAS GOING TO BE A ONE-OFF (ONE THAT STARTED QUITE SUDDENLY!) AND IN VOLUME 1 I REALLY WASN'T SURE WHERE I WOULD TAKE THE SERIES. THEREFORE EVERY EPISODE I WAS KIND OF WORKING IN THE DARK. BUT AS I CONTINUE TO WRITE, MY IDEA HAS EXPANDED, AND I NOW HAVE MANY CHARACTERS AND EPISODES THAT I'D LIKE TO ADD ON TO THE STORY. IN THIS VOLUME I WONDER IF YOU COULD SEE THAT...? HOW DID YOU LIKE IT? :LAUGH:

AS I STILL HAVE MUCH TO LEARN ABOUT CREATING MANGA, I'M UNCERTAIN HOW MUCH LONGER THE SERIES WILL GO, BUT IF THINGS WORK OUT, THERE ARE MANY STORIES I WOULD LIKE TO TELL YOU!

THERE HAVE BEEN MANY DEPRESSING EVENTS IN THE NEWS LATELY BUT THERE ARE ALSO HAPPY AND WONDERFUL THINGS IN LIFE. I HOPE THAT THIS MANGA WILL BE ONE OF THE HAPPY THINGS IN YOUR LIFE. I WILL CONTINUE TO WORK HARDER SO THIS SERIES WILL BECOME PART OF YOUR HAPPINESS! PLEASE CONTINUE TO SHOW YOUR SUPPORT FOR HER MAJESTY'S DOG. (AND MY OTHER TITLES, AS WELL :LAUGH:)

WELL, I HOPE TO SEE YOU AGAIN SOON.

♡ Mick

SPECIAL THANKS ——

TAKUMI.A
YUKAKO.T
EMU.K
RIU.A
AO.S
AKIRA.K
SHIORI.A
HARUMI.M
HUURI.T
HITOYO.S
Y.IWAHASHI
R.YOKOYAMA

—— & MY FAMILY

Are you caught under Amane's spell? Does Hyoue have you on a leash? Well now's your chance to share the love with other HMD fans. Go! Comi is now accepting fan art for future volumes of *Her Majesty's Dog*! Send your fan art and letters to:

Go! Media Entertainment
5737 Kanan Rd. #591
Agoura Hills CA 91301

HER MAJESTY'S DOG 2 – END

TRANSLATOR'S NOTES

Pg. 8 – *Nengajou* and *Shochu-Mimai*
Nengajou are greeting cards sent to friends, family and coworkers in celebration of the New Year. *Shochu-mimai*, are summer greeting cards. Traditionally they are sent to inquire after a person's health in a hot summer season. For both Nengajou and shochu-mimai, the post office issues post cards with lottery numbers on the back.

Pg. 9 – *Takoyaki* and *Isobeyaki*
Takoyaki are grilled balls of pancake batter with bits of octopus meat inside. They are typically served with with mayonnaise, teriyaki sauce and benito shavings (dried fish flakes). Takoyaki are a regional specialty of the Kansai region, but they are readily available as a street food in cities throughout Japan. *Isobeyaki* is rice cake, grilled and dipped in soy sauce and wrapped with seaweed.

Pg. 41 – *Ateko*
"*Ateru*" is Japanese for the verb "to hit." Ateko is made up with the word, *Ateru* + ko (for a girl's name). Takako says it sounds phony because it sounds like a term for a female car accident victim.

Pg. 50 – *Kaiso*
Kaiso means the founder of a religious sect or an originator of an establishment. This Kaiso-sama's real name was Keiji Kamori but people called him by his title, Kaiso + sama (honorific) = Kaiso-sama.

Pg. 112 – *Satori*
Satori means spiritual enlightenment or awakening. The term is often used in Zen Buddhism.

Pg. 154 – Coral Palace
Coral Palace is a reference to the Japanese folk tale of "Urashima Taro." Taro is a fisherman who one day rescues a sea turtle which was beaten up by kids in the neighborhood. To reward the fisherman, the turtle takes Taro to an undersea palace, and so the tale begins. In panel 3, Zakuro mentions dancing amongst sea bream and halibut. This imagery of the fish dance also comes from the Urashima Taro tale.

IN VOLUME 3 OF

HER MAJESTY'S DOG

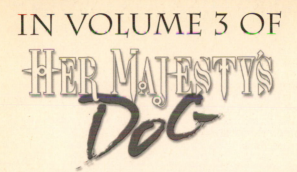

A powerful demon is at large at school, tearing up classrooms for seemingly no reason. It looks like the work of a Koma-oni, but if that's the case, who's controlling it? Meanwhile, there's a new guy at school and he's got his eyes on Amane. It is purely for romantic reasons that Mitsumine has been following Amane, or does he know more than he lets on about her manatsukai powers?

HER MAJESTY'S
DOG
3
Story & Art by
MICK TAKEUCHI

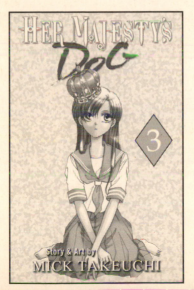

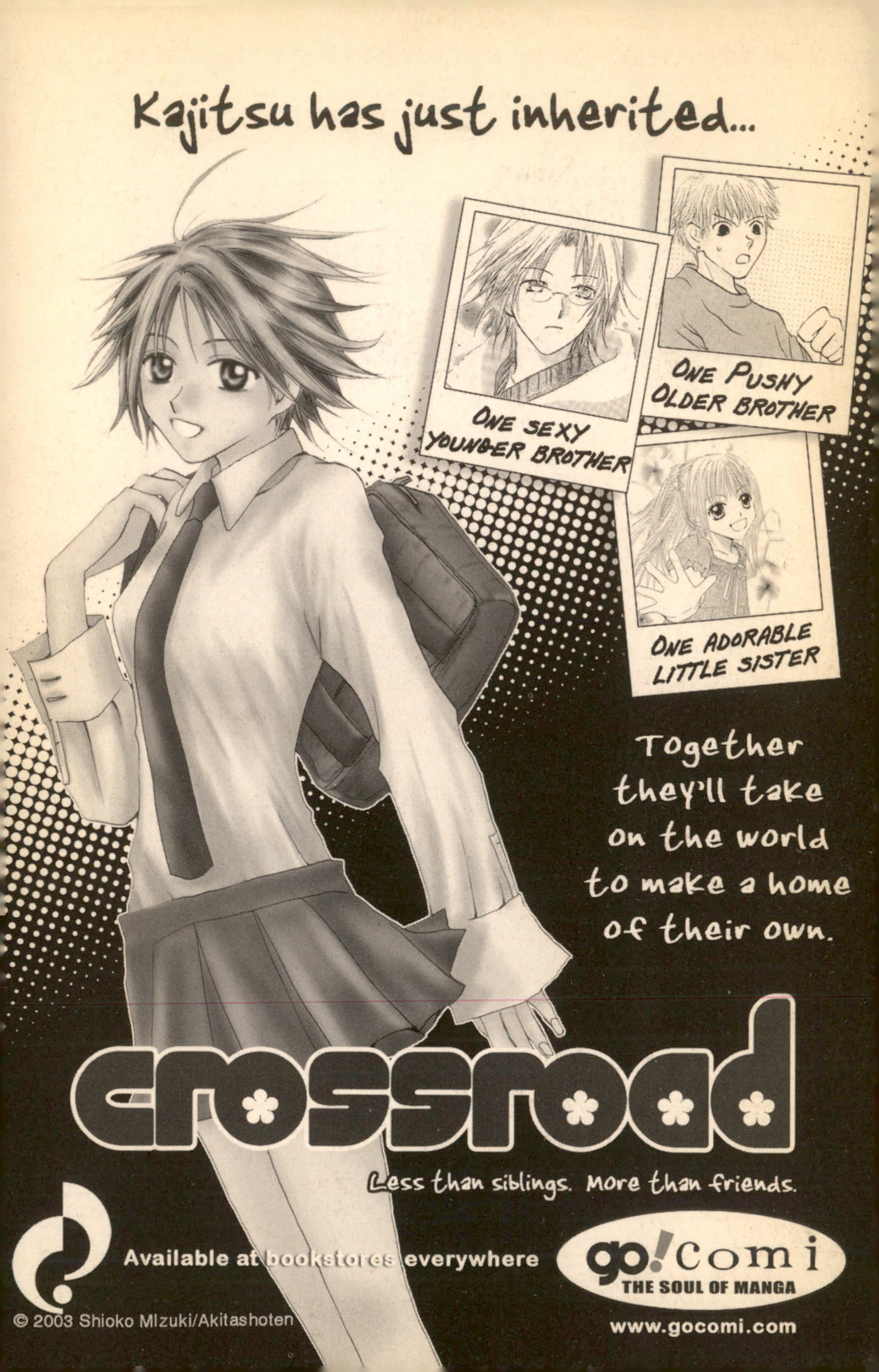
Kajitsu has just inherited...
One sexy younger brother
One pushy older brother
One adorable little sister
Together they'll take on the world to make a home of their own.
crossroad
Less than siblings. More than friends.
Available at bookstores everywhere
go!comi
THE SOUL OF MANGA
www.gocomi.com
© 2003 Shioko MIzuki/Akitashoten

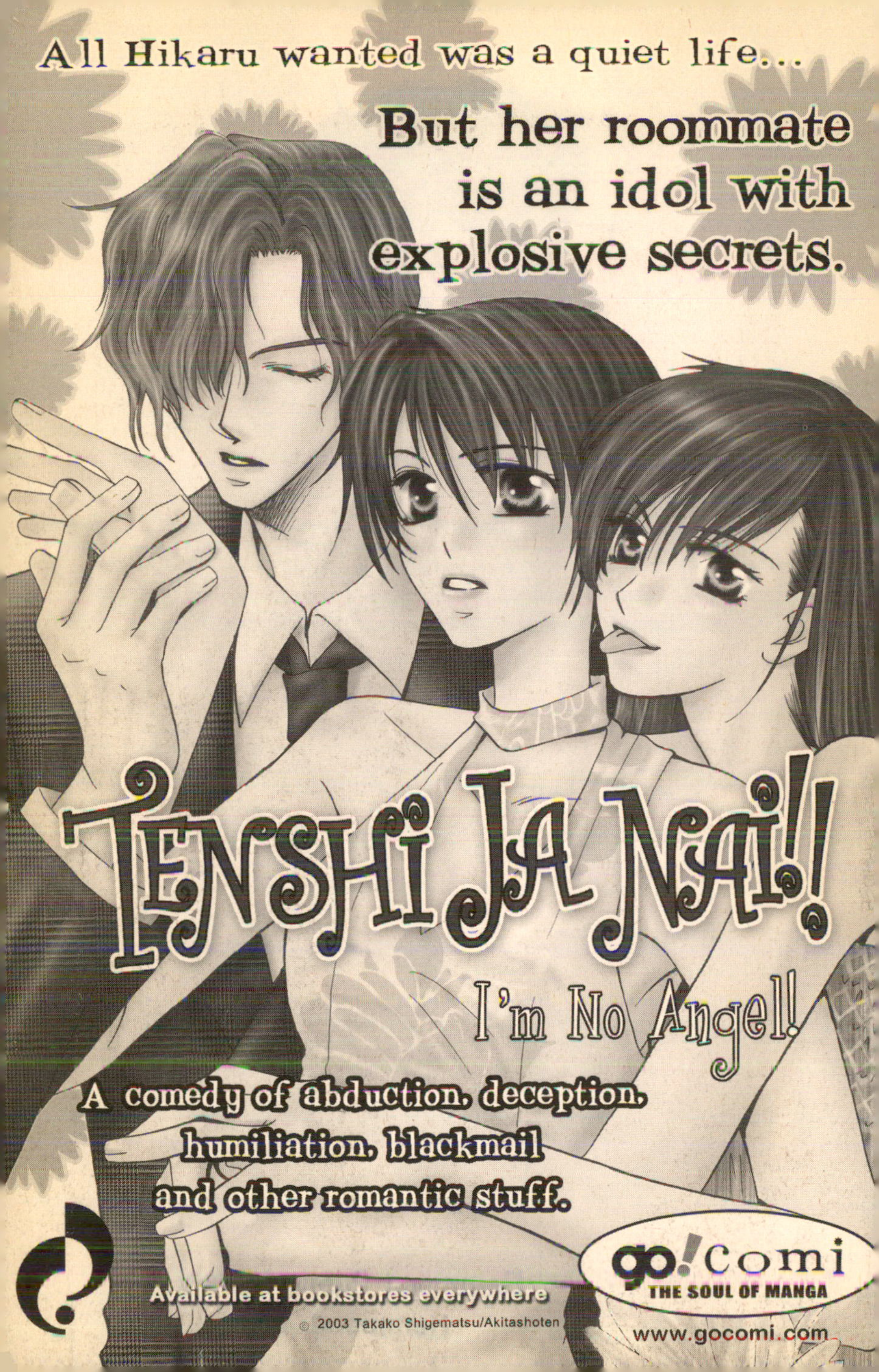

All Hikaru wanted was a quiet life...
But her roommate is an idol with explosive secrets.
TENSHI JA NAI!!
I'm No Angel!
A comedy of abduction, deception, humiliation, blackmail and other romantic stuff.
go!comi
THE SOUL OF MANGA
Available at bookstores everywhere
© 2003 Takako Shigematsu/Akitashoten
www.gocomi.com

MICK TAKEUCHI

"Sometimes while working on inking and cleaning up my artwork, I get so focused that I forget to breath. I literally make myself faint from lack of oxygen. I would be in danger if I didn't have oxygen mask on stand-by next to my desk. (laugh)"

ABOUT THE MANGA-KA

Mick Takeuchi has been creating manga since 1994. Her early works include *Miharu Shinjou Jewelry File, A Wise Man Sleeps,* and *Ayakashi Hime Kurenai.* In October 2000, she began *Her Majesty's Dog* (*Jo-ousama no Inu*), her longest and most popular work. It started out as a part-time project, with quarterly chapters, but was so popular that since 2002, it's been running monthly and has become her sole project. When she's not busy working, she enjoys wandering around the city. Her birthday is July 4th. *Her Majesty's Dog* is her first book to be translated into English.